Nicholas Bell

Exciting
Holiness

'The celebration of the Holy Spirit
at work in many different ways
in the lives of Christian men and women
down the ages,
whose examples excite us to holiness,
is a sign of the great cloud of witnesses
with which we are surrounded.'

From the essay
Daily Prayer in the Life of the Church
in
Celebrating Common Prayer
(which first appeared in **The Daily Office SSF** 1981)

Exciting Holiness

Collects & Readings
for the Festivals & Lesser Festivals

of the Calendar
of the Church of England

authorized for use
from
Advent Sunday, 1997

CANTERBURY
PRESS

Norwich

Published by **Canterbury Press Norwich**
a publishing imprint of Hymns Ancient & Modern Limited,
a registered charity,
St Mary's Works, St Mary's Plain, Norwich, Norfolk, NR3 3BH

First published, September 1997
Reprinted 1997 (twice), 1998,
September 1999 (with revisions)
February 2001

Edited by Brother Tristam SSF

A catalogue record for this book is available
from the British Library.

ISBN 1-85311-174-0

Printed and bound in Great Britain by The Bath Press, Bath

Contents

Introduction

When, in 1935, Bishop Walter Frere first produced his *Collects, Epistles and Gospels for the Lesser Feasts According to the Calendar set out in 1928*, he was providing, for the first time in one book, collects and readings for use on 'Black Letter' saints' days in the Church of England. This tradition has been maintained by the excellent book compiled by Martin Draper and George Timms, *Cloud of Witnesses*, produced to complement the publication of *The Alternative Service Book 1980*, and by many others throughout the Anglican Communion.

When the Church of England Liturgical Commission began its work in 1993 on re-drafting a Calendar, it appointed a Committee of its members consisting of Revd Canon Michael Perham as chair, Revd Canon Jane Sinclair, Revd Canon John Sweet and Brother Tristam SSF. They used as a starting point the Calendar in *Celebrating Common Prayer*, only recently published in 1992. After the various revision processes of the General Synod, the final report entitled *Calendar, Lectionary & Collects 2000*, published as GS1161a, was finally authorised at the November 1996 session, to have authority from Advent 1997, without time limit.

As a result, Michael Perham assisted Cassell Publishing in producing a book for use on Sundays, using what is called the *Temporale* section of the Report. Using the *Sanctorale* in the Report, this Editor was given the task of producing a book for use on saints' days, to be published by Canterbury Press Norwich. Other publishers, including Church House Publishing and SPCK, have produced material for use with the new Calendar.

The aim of all these publications is to make available to the Church the wherewithal to use the new material provided in *Calendar, Lectionary & Collects 2000*. In particular, the Sunday lectionary provision will help the Church of England to come closer in worship to its sisters and brothers in the rest of the Anglican Communion and in other Communions throughout the world.

This book's subtitle adequately sums up its contents and purpose.

Tristam SSF

Notes

CALENDAR

Festivals are not usually displaced. Festivals falling on a Sunday may be kept on that day or transferred to the Monday or another suitable weekday. However, Festivals are not celebrated on a Sunday if they fall in Advent, Lent or Eastertide.

Lesser Festivals are celebrated at the level appropriate to the particular church. The collect, readings and post-communion prayer may supersede the weekly collect, the daily eucharistic lectionary and the weekly post-communion prayer.

When a Lesser Festival falls on a Principal Feast or Holy Day, or on a Festival, its celebration is normally omitted that year unless, for sufficient reason, it is transferred to the nearest available day.

The Minister may be selective as to which Lesser Festivals are celebrated and may choose to observe some as Commemorations.

Commemorations are usually made by a mention in prayers of intercession and thanksgiving. The short hagiography provided may be used at any service at any appropriate point.

A Commemoration may be observed as a Lesser Festival where the day has a special significance. However, care needs to be taken so as not to lose the spirit of the season, especially in Advent and Lent, by too many celebrations that detract from its character.

Festivals, Lesser Festivals and Commemorations may be celebrated on any weekday close to the actual date, should pastoral reasons so require it.

In the text of **The Calendar** (pages 5 to 16), Principal Feasts are printed in **BOLD UPPER CASE**, Festivals are printed in **bold lower case**, Lesser Festivals are printed in ordinary roman typeface and Commemorations are printed in *italics*.

SCRIPTURE

Three readings and a Psalm have been chosen for each *sanctorale* Principal Feast, Festival and Lesser Festival. Two readings are normally the requirement for Lesser Festivals, but a three-readings provision is made for those places where they are celebrated locally as Festivals, such as on a feast of title or of patronage.

As three Scripture readings are provided, there has been no attempt to give an Old Testament alternative where there is a reading from the Apocrypha.

The order of readings is: Old Testament, Psalm, New Testament, Gospel; when only two readings are used, the Psalm, if used, should be said between the two readings.

Where there is a reading from the Book of the Acts as well as an Old Testament reading and an Epistle, the Acts reading may replace the Old Testament reading or the Epistle; the Acts reading is particularly appropriate on feasts of the Apostles, when provided, and should always be one of the readings if only two are being used.

The form of words used to announce the beginning and the end of the Scripture readings is in accord with the latest proposals from the General Synod Revision Committee.

RESPONSORIAL PSALM

The **Canticle** which joins the Old Testament reading to the New Testament Reading is almost always from the Book of the Psalms, often called the prayer book of Jesus. St Augustine said that to sing is to pray twice, and this has to be true with the Psalms. However, their meaning and nuance can be just as easily expressed by a good reader, and the important thing is to hear and understand why the particular Psalm has been chosen for the particular celebration.

The **Response** itself almost always can be said or sung either as one line – by omitting the words in square [ ] brackets – or as two lines. This is to facilitate particular musical or spoken settings; there is no right or wrong option at this point. If other words are already set as a Response, those arranging the worship should feel free to use them at will.

The Calendar

JANUARY

1	**The Naming & Circumcision of Jesus**
2	Basil the Great & Gregory of Nazianzus,
	Bishops, Teachers of the Faith, 379 & 389
2	*Seraphim, Monk of Sarov, Spiritual Guide, 1833*
2	*Vedanayagam Samuel Azariah, Bishop in South India,*
	Evangelist, 1945
6	**THE EPIPHANY**
10	*William Laud, Archbishop of Canterbury, 1645*
11	*Mary Slessor, Missionary in West Africa, 1915*
12	Aelred of Hexham, Abbot of Rievaulx, 1167
12	*Benedict Biscop, Abbot of Wearmouth, Scholar, 689*
13	Hilary, Bishop of Poitiers, Teacher of the Faith, 367
13	*Kentigern (Mungo), Missionary Bishop in Strathclyde*
	& Cumbria, 603
13	*George Fox, Founder of the Society of Friends (the Quakers), 1691*
17	Antony of Egypt, Hermit, Abbot, 356
17	*Charles Gore, Bishop, Founder of the Community*
	of the Resurrection, 1932
18-25	*Week of Prayer for Christian Unity*
19	Wulfstan, Bishop of Worcester, 1095
20	*Richard Rolle of Hampole, Spiritual Writer, 1349*
21	Agnes, Child-Martyr at Rome, 304
22	*Vincent of Saragossa, Deacon, first Martyr of Spain, 304*
24	Francis de Sales, Bishop of Geneva, Teacher of the Faith, 1622
25	**The Conversion of Paul**
26	Timothy & Titus, Companions of Paul
28	Thomas Aquinas, Priest, Philosopher,
	Teacher of the Faith, 1274
30	Charles, King & Martyr, 1649
31	*John Bosco, Priest, Founder of the Salesian Teaching Order, 1888*

FEBRUARY

1 *Brigid, Abbess of Kildare, c.525*
2 **THE PRESENTATION OF CHRIST IN THE TEMPLE**
   (CANDLEMAS)
3 Anskar, Archbishop of Hamburg,
   Missionary in Denmark & Sweden, 865
4 *Gilbert of Sempringham, Founder of the Gilbertine Order, 1189*
6 *The Martyrs of Japan, 1597*
10 *Scholastica, sister of Benedict, Abbess of Plombariola, c.543*
14 Cyril & Methodius, Missionaries to the Slavs, 869 & 885
14 *Valentine, Martyr at Rome, c.269*
15 *Sigfrid, Bishop, Apostle of Sweden, 1045*
15 *Thomas Bray, Priest, Founder of the SPCK and the SPG, 1730*
17 Janani Luwum, Archbishop of Uganda, Martyr, 1977
23 Polycarp, Bishop of Smyrna, Martyr, c.155
27 George Herbert, Priest, Poet, 1633

ALTERNATIVE DATE

Matthias may be celebrated on 24 February instead of 14 May.

MARCH

1	David, Bishop of Menevia, Patron of Wales, c.601
2	Chad, Bishop of Lichfield, Missionary, 672
7	Perpetua, Felicity & their Companions,
	Martyrs at Carthage, 203
8	Edward King, Bishop of Lincoln, 1910
8	*Felix, Bishop, Apostle to the East Angles, 647*
8	*Geoffrey Studdert Kennedy, Priest, Poet, 1929*
17	Patrick, Bishop, Missionary, Patron of Ireland, c.460
18	*Cyril, Bishop of Jerusalem, Teacher of the Faith, 386*
19	**Joseph of Nazareth**
20	Cuthbert, Bishop of Lindisfarne, Missionary, 687
21	Thomas Cranmer, Archbishop of Canterbury,
	Reformation Martyr, 1556
24	*Walter Hilton of Thurgarton, Augustinian Canon, Mystic, 1396*
24	*Oscar Romero, Archbishop of San Salvador, Martyr, 1980*
25	**THE ANNUNCIATION OF OUR LORD**
	TO THE BLESSED VIRGIN MARY
26	*Harriet Monsell , Founder of the Community*
	of St John the Baptist, Clewer, 1883
31	*John Donne, Priest, Poet, 1631*

ALTERNATIVE DATES

Chad may be celebrated with Cedd on 26 October instead of 2 March.
Cuthbert may be celebrated on 4 September instead of 20 March.

APRIL

1	*Frederick Denison Maurice, Priest, Teacher of the Faith, 1872*
9	*Dietrich Bonhoeffer, Lutheran Pastor, Martyr, 1945*
10	William Law, Priest, Spiritual Writer, 1761
10	*William of Ockham, Friar, Philosopher, Teacher of the Faith, 1347*
11	*George Augustus Selwyn, first Bishop of New Zealand, 1878*
16	*Isabella Gilmore, Deaconess, 1923*
19	Alphege, Archbishop of Canterbury, Martyr, 1012
21	Anselm, Abbot of Le Bec, Archbishop of Canterbury, Teacher of the Faith, 1109
23	**George, Martyr, Patron of England**, c.304
24	*Mellitus, Bishop of London, first Bishop at St Paul's, 624*
25	**Mark the Evangelist**
27	*Christina Rossetti, Poet, 1894*
28	*Peter Chanel, Missionary in the South Pacific, Martyr, 1841*
29	Catherine of Siena, Teacher of the Faith, 1380
30	*Pandita Mary Ramabai, Translator of the Scriptures, 1922*

MAY

1	**Philip & James, Apostles**
2	Athanasius, Bishop of Alexandria, Teacher of the Faith, 373
4	English Saints & Martyrs of the Reformation Era
8	Julian of Norwich, Spiritual Writer, c.1417
14	**Matthias the Apostle**
16	*Caroline Chisholm, Social Reformer, 1877*
19	Dunstan, Archbishop of Canterbury, Restorer of Monastic Life, 988
20	Alcuin of York, Deacon, Abbot of Tours, 804
21	*Helena, Protector of the Holy Places, 330*
24	John & Charles Wesley, Evangelists, Hymn Writers, 1791 & 1788
25	The Venerable Bede, Monk at Jarrow, Scholar, Historian, 735
25	*Aldhelm, Bishop of Sherborne, 709*
26	Augustine, first Archbishop of Canterbury, 605
26	*John Calvin, Reformer 1564*
26	*Philip Neri, Founder of the Oratorians, Spiritual Guide, 1595*
28	*Lanfranc, Prior of Le Bec, Archbishop of Canterbury, Scholar, 1089*
30	Josephine Butler, Social Reformer, 1906
30	*Joan of Arc, Visionary, 1431*
30	*Apolo Kivebulaya, Priest, Evangelist in Central Africa, 1933*
31	**The Visit of the Blessèd Virgin Mary to Elizabeth**

ALTERNATIVE DATES

The Visitation of Mary to Elizabeth may be celebrated on 2 July instead of 31 May.
Matthias may be celebrated on 24 February instead of 14 May.

JUNE

1   Justin, Martyr at Rome, c.165
3   *The Martyrs of Uganda, 1886 & 1978*
4   *Petroc, Abbot of Padstow, 6th century*
5   Boniface (Wynfrith) of Crediton, Bishop,
        Apostle of Germany, Martyr, 754
6   *Ini Kopuria, Founder of the Melanesian Brotherhood, 1945*
8   Thomas Ken, Bishop of Bath & Wells, Non-Juror,
        Hymn Writer, 1711
9   Columba, Abbot of Iona, Missionary, 597
9   *Ephrem of Syria, Deacon, Hymn Writer, Teacher of the Faith, 373*
11   **Barnabas the Apostle**
14   *Richard Baxter, Puritan Divine, 1691*
15   *Evelyn Underhill, Spiritual Writer, 1941*
16   Richard, Bishop of Chichester, 1253
16   *Joseph Butler, Bishop of Durham, Philosopher, 1752*
17   *Samuel & Henrietta Barnett, Social Reformers, 1913 & 1936*
18   *Bernard Mizeki, Apostle of the MaShona, Martyr, 1896*
19   *Sundar Singh of India, Sadhu (holy man), Evangelist,*
        Teacher of the Faith, 1929
22   Alban, first Martyr of Britain, c.250
23   Etheldreda, Abbess of Ely, c.678
24   **The Birth of John the Baptist**
27   *Cyril, Bishop of Alexandria, Teacher of the Faith, 444*
28   Irenæus, Bishop of Lyons, Teacher of the Faith, c.200
29   **Peter & Paul, Apostles**

Peter the Apostle may be celebrated alone, without Paul, on 29 June.

JULY

1	*John & Henry Venn, Priests, Evangelical Divines, 1813 & 1873*
3	**Thomas the Apostle**
6	*Thomas More, Scholar, & John Fisher, Bishop of Rochester, Reformation Martyrs, 1535*
11	Benedict of Nursia, Abbot of Monte Cassino, Father of Western Monasticism, c.550
14	John Keble, Priest, Tractarian, Poet, 1866
15	Swithun, Bishop of Winchester, c.862
15	*Bonaventure, Friar, Bishop, Teacher of the Faith, 1274*
16	*Osmund, Bishop of Salisbury, 1099*
18	*Elizabeth Ferard, first Deaconess of the Church of England, Founder of the Community of St Andrew, 1883*
19	Gregory, Bishop of Nyssa, & his sister Macrina, Deaconess, Teachers of the Faith, 394 & 379
20	*Margaret of Antioch, Martyr, 4th Century*
20	*Bartolomé de las Casas, Apostle to the Indies, 1566*
22	**Mary Magdalene**
23	*Bridget of Sweden, Abbess of Vadstena, 1373*
25	**James the Apostle**
26	Anne & Joachim, Parents of the Blessèd Virgin Mary
27	*Brooke Foss Westcott, Bishop of Durham, Teacher of the Faith, 1901*
29	Mary, Martha & Lazarus, Companions of our Lord
30	William Wilberforce, Social Reformer, 1833
31	*Ignatius of Loyola, Founder of the Society of Jesus, 1556*

ALTERNATIVE DATES

The Visitation of Mary to Elizabeth may be celebrated on 2 July instead of 31 May.
Thomas the Apostle may be celebrated on 21 December instead of 3 July.
Thomas Becket may be celebrated on 7 July instead of 29 December.

August

4	*Jean-Baptist Vianney, Curé d'Ars, Spiritual Guide, 1859*
5	Oswald, King of Northumbria, Martyr, 642
6	**The Transfiguration of our Lord**
7	*John Mason Neale, Priest, Hymn Writer, 1866*
8	Dominic, Priest, Founder of the Order of Preachers, 1221
9	Mary Sumner, Founder of the Mothers' Union, 1921
10	Laurence, Deacon at Rome, Martyr, 258
11	Clare of Assisi, Founder of the Minoresses (Poor Clares), 1253
11	*John Henry Newman, Priest, Tractarian, 1890*
13	Jeremy Taylor, Bishop of Down & Connor, Teacher of the Faith, 1667
13	*Florence Nightingale, Nurse, Social Reformer, 1910*
13	*Octavia Hill, Social Reformer, 1912*
14	*Maximilian Kolbe, Friar, Martyr, 1941*
15	**The Blessèd Virgin Mary**
20	Bernard, Abbot of Clairvaux, Teacher of the Faith, 1153
20	*William & Catherine Booth, Founders of the Salvation Army, 1912 & 1890*
24	**Bartholomew the Apostle**
27	Monica, mother of Augustine of Hippo, 387
28	Augustine, Bishop of Hippo, Teacher of the Faith, 430
29	The Beheading of John the Baptist
30	John Bunyan, Spiritual Writer, 1688
31	Aidan, Bishop of Lindisfarne, Missionary, 651

Alternative Date

The Festival of the Blessèd Virgin Mary may be celebrated on 8 September instead of 15 August.

SEPTEMBER

1	*Giles of Provence, Hermit, c.710*
2	*The Martyrs of Papua New Guinea, 1901 & 1942*
3	Gregory the Great, Bishop of Rome, Teacher of the Faith, 604
4	*Birinus, Bishop of Dorchester (Oxon), Apostle of Wessex, 650*
6	*Allen Gardiner, Missionary, Founder of the South American Missionary Society, 1851*
8	The Birth of the Blessèd Virgin Mary
9	*Charles Fuge Lowder, Priest, 1880*
13	John Chrysostom, Bishop of Constantinople, Teacher of the Faith, 407
14	**Holy Cross Day**
15	Cyprian, Bishop of Carthage, Martyr, 258
16	Ninian, Bishop of Galloway, Apostle of the Picts, c.432
16	*Edward Bouverie Pusey, Priest, Tractarian, 1882*
17	Hildegard, Abbess of Bingen, Visionary, 1179
19	*Theodore of Tarsus, Archbishop of Canterbury, 690*
20	John Coleridge Patteson, First Bishop of Melanesia, & his Companions, Martyrs, 1871
21	**Matthew, Apostle & Evangelist**
25	Lancelot Andrewes, Bishop of Winchester, Spiritual Writer, 1626
25	*Sergei of Radonezh, Russian Monastic Reformer, Teacher of the Faith, 1392*
26	*Wilson Carlile, Founder of the Church Army, 1942*
27	Vincent de Paul, Founder of the Congregation of the Mission (Lazarists), 1660
29	**Michael & All Angels**
30	*Jerome, Translator of the Scriptures, Teacher of the Faith, 420*

ALTERNATIVE DATES

The Festival of the Blessèd Virgin Mary may be celebrated on 8 September instead of 15 August.
Cuthbert may be celebrated on 4 September instead of 20 March.

OCTOBER

1	*Remigius, Bishop of Rheims, Apostle of the Franks, 533*
1	*Anthony Ashley Cooper, Earl of Shaftesbury,*
	Social Reformer, 1885
4	Francis of Assisi, Friar, Deacon,
	Founder of the Friars Minor, 1226
6	William Tyndale, Translator of the Scriptures,
	Reformation Martyr, 1536
9	*Denys, Bishop of Paris, & his Companions, Martyrs, c.250*
9	*Robert Grosseteste, Bishop of Lincoln, Philosopher, Scientist, 1253*
10	Paulinus, Bishop of York, Missionary, 644
10	*Thomas Traherne, Poet, Spiritual Writer, 1674*
11	*Ethelburga, Abbess of Barking, 675*
11	*James the Deacon, companion of Paulinus, 7th century*
12	Wilfrid of Ripon, Bishop, Missionary, 709
12	*Elizabeth Fry, Prison Reformer, 1845*
12	*Edith Cavell, Nurse, 1915*
13	Edward the Confessor, King of England, 1066
15	Teresa of Avila, Teacher of the Faith, 1582
16	*Nicholas Ridley, Bishop of London, & Hugh Latimer,*
	Bishop of Worcester, Reformation Martyrs, 1555
17	Ignatius, Bishop of Antioch, Martyr, c.107
18	**Luke the Evangelist**
19	Henry Martyn, Translator of the Scriptures,
	Missionary in India & Persia, 1812
19	*Frideswide, Abbess of Oxford, 727*
25	*Crispin & Crispinian, Martyrs at Rome, c.287*
26	Alfred the Great, King of the West Saxons, Scholar, 899
26	*Cedd, Abbot of Lastingham, Bishop of the East Saxons, 664*
28	**Simon & Jude, Apostles**
29	James Hannington, Bishop of Eastern Equatorial Africa,
	Martyr in Uganda, 1885
31	*Martin Luther, Reformer, 1546*

ALTERNATIVE DATE

Chad may be celebrated with Cedd on 26 October instead of 2 March.

NOVEMBER

1	**ALL SAINTS' DAY**
2	Commemoration of the Faithful Departed (All Souls' Day)
3	Richard Hooker, Priest, Anglican Apologist, Teacher of the Faith, 1600
3	*Martin de Porres, Friar, 1639*
6	*Leonard, Hermit, 6th century*
6	*William Temple, Archbishop of Canterbury,* *Teacher of the Faith, 1944*
7	Willibrord of York, Bishop, Apostle of Frisia, 739
8	The Saints & Martyrs of England
9	*Margery Kempe, Mystic, c.1440*
10	Leo the Great, Bishop of Rome, Teacher of the Faith, 461
11	Martin, Bishop of Tours, c.397
13	Charles Simeon, Priest, Evangelical Divine, 1836
14	*Samuel Seabury, First Anglican Bishop in North America, 1796*
16	Margaret, Queen of Scotland, Philanthropist, Reformer of the Church, 1093
16	*Edmund of Abingdon, Archbishop of Canterbury, 1240*
17	Hugh, Bishop of Lincoln, 1200
18	Elizabeth of Hungary, Princess of Thuringia, Philanthropist, 1231
19	Hilda, Abbess of Whitby, 680
19	*Mechtild, Béguine of Magdeburg, Mystic, 1280*
20	Edmund, King of the East Angles, Martyr, 870
20	*Priscilla Lydia Sellon, a Restorer of the Religious Life* *in the Church of England, 1876*
22	*Cecilia, Martyr at Rome, c.230*
23	Clement, Bishop of Rome, Martyr, c.100
25	*Catherine of Alexandria, Martyr, 4th century*
25	*Isaac Watts, Hymn Writer, 1748*
29	*Day of Intercession & Thanksgiving* *for the Missionary Work of the Church*
30	**Andrew the Apostle**

DECEMBER

1   *Charles de Foucauld, Hermit in the Sahara, 1916*
3   *Francis Xavier, Missionary, Apostle of the Indies, 1552*
4   *John of Damascus, Monk, Teacher of the Faith, c.749*
4   *Nicholas Ferrar, Deacon,*
         Founder of the Little Gidding Community, 1637
6   Nicholas, Bishop of Myra, c.326
7   Ambrose, Bishop of Milan, Teacher of the Faith, 397
8   Conception of the Blessèd Virgin Mary
13   Lucy, Martyr at Syracuse, 304
13   *Samuel Johnson, Moralist, 1784*
14   John of the Cross, Poet, Teacher of the Faith, 1591
17   *O Sapientia*
17   *Eglantine Jebb, Social Reformer,*
         Founder of 'Save The Children', 1928
24   Christmas Eve
25   **CHRISTMAS DAY**
26   **Stephen, Deacon, First Martyr**
27   **John, Apostle & Evangelist**
28   **The Holy Innocents**
29   Thomas Becket, Archbishop of Canterbury, Martyr, 1170
31   *John Wyclif, Reformer, 1384*

ALTERNATIVE DATES

Thomas the Apostle may be celebrated on 21 December instead of 3 July.
Thomas Becket may be celebrated on 7 July instead of 29 December.

The Proper of the Saints

JANUARY

The Naming & Circumcision of Jesus
1 January – Festival – White

The celebration of this scriptural festival marks three events: first-ly, the naming of the infant; secondly, the sign of the covenant between God and Abraham 'and his children for ever', thus Christ's keeping of the Law; and thirdly, traditionally the first shedding of the Christ's blood. The most significant of these in the gospels is the name itself, which means 'Yahweh saves' and so is linked to the question asked by Moses of God: "What is your name?" "I am who I am," was the reply, thus the significance of Jesus' words: "Before Abraham was, I am." This feast has been observed in the church since at least the sixth century.

Collect
Almighty God,
whose blessèd Son was circumcised
in obedience to the law for our sake
and given the Name that is above every name:
give us grace faithfully to bear his Name,
to worship him in the freedom of the Spirit,
and to proclaim him as the Saviour of the world;
who is alive and reigns with you,
in the unity of the Holy Spirit,
one God, now and for ever.

A reading from the book Numbers.

The Lord spoke to Moses, saying: Speak to Aaron and his off-spring, saying, 'Thus you shall bless the Israelites: You shall say to them, "The Lord bless you and keep you; the Lord make his face to shine upon you, and be gracious to you; the Lord lift up his countenance upon you, and give you peace." So they shall put my name on the Israelites, and I will bless them.'

This is the word of the Lord.   *Numbers 6. 22-27*

Responsorial Psalm

**R   O Lord our governor,
    how exalted is your name in all the world!**

Out of the mouths of infants and children
your majesty is praised above the heavens.
You have set up a stronghold against your adversaries,
to quell the enemy and the avenger. **R**

When I consider your heavens, the work of your fingers,
the moon and the stars you have set in their courses;
what are mortals, that you should be mindful of them?;
mere human beings, that you should seek them out?
You have made them little lower than the angels;
you adorn them with glory and honour. **R**

You give them mastery over the works of your hands;
and put all things under their feet,
all sheep and oxen, even the wild beasts of the field,
the birds of the air, the fish of the sea,
and whatsoever walks in the paths of the sea. **R**   *Psalm 8*

A reading from the Letter of Paul to the Galatians.

When the fullness of time had come, God sent his Son, born of a
woman, born under the law, in order to redeem those who were
under the law, so that we might receive adoption as children.
And because you are children, God has sent the Spirit of his Son
into our hearts, crying, "Abba! Father!" So you are no longer a
slave but a child, and if a child then also an heir, through God.

This is the word of the Lord.   *Galatians 4. 4-7*

Hear the gospel of our Lord Jesus Christ according to Luke.

When the angels had left them and gone into heaven, the shepherds said to one another, "Let us go now to Bethlehem and see
this thing that has taken place, which the Lord has made known
to us." So they went with haste and found Mary and Joseph, and
the child lying in the manger. When they saw this, they made
known what had been told them about this child; and all who
heard it were amazed at what the shepherds told them. But Mary
treasured all these words and pondered them in her heart. The

shepherds returned, glorifying and praising God for all they had heard and seen, as it had been told them. After eight days had passed, it was time to circumcise the child; and he was called Jesus, the name given by the angel before he was conceived in the womb.

This is the gospel of the Lord. *Luke 2. 15-21*

Post Communion
Eternal God,
whose incarnate Son was given the name of Saviour:
grant that we who have shared
  in this sacrament of our salvation
may live out our years in the power
  of the name above all other names,
Jesus Christ our Lord.

Basil the Great, Bishop of Caesarea
& Gregory of Nazianzus, Bishop of Constantinople
2 January – Lesser Festival – Teachers of the Faith – White

Gregory and Basil were two friends bound together by their desire to promote and defend the divinity of Christ as proclaimed in the Nicene Creed. This was against the seemingly overwhelming pressure from both Church and State for the establishment of Arianism, which denied Christ's divinity and thus the whole Christian doctrine of the Trinity. Basil was renowned for being headstrong and forceful, in comparison to his friend Gregory, who would rather spend his days in prayer and living the simple, ascetic life. Gregory's brilliance in oratory and theological debate meant that a hidden life was virtually impossible and Basil drew him into the forefront of the controversy. Their joint persuasive eloquence convinced the first Council of Constantinople, meeting in 381, that their teaching was the truly orthodox one and the Council ratified the text of the Nicene Creed in the form it is used in the East to this day. Basil died in 379 and Gregory ten years later.

Collect
Lord God,
whose servants Basil and Gregory
proclaimed the mystery of your Word made flesh,
to build up your Church in wisdom and strength:
grant that we may rejoice in his presence among us,
and so be brought with them to know
the power of your unending love;
through Jesus Christ your Son our Lord,
who is alive and reigns with you,
in the unity of the Holy Spirit,
one God, now and for ever.

A reading from the Wisdom of Solomon.

May God grant me to speak with judgement, and to have thoughts worthy of what I have received; for he is the guide even of wisdom and the corrector of the wise. For both we and our words are in his hand, as are all understanding and skill in crafts. For it is he who gave me unerring knowledge of what exists, to know the structure of the world and the activity of the elements; the beginning and end and middle of times, the alternations of the solstices and the changes of the seasons, the cycles of the year and the constellations of the stars, the natures of animals and the tempers of wild animals, the powers of spirits and the thoughts of human beings, the varieties of plants and the virtues of roots; I learned both what is secret and what is manifest, for wisdom, the fashioner of all things, taught me.

This is the word of the Lord.   *Wisdom 7. 15-22a*

Responsorial Psalm

**R   You say, O Lord, 'Seek my face';
     [Your face only will I seek].**

The Lord is my light and my salvation; whom then shall I fear?
The Lord is the strength of my life; of whom shall I be afraid?
When evildoers came upon me to eat up my flesh,
it was they, my foes and adversaries, who stumbled and fell. **R**

Though an army should encamp against me,
yet my heart shall not be afraid;
and though war should rise up against me,
yet will I put my trust in God. **R**

One thing have I asked of the Lord, one thing I seek:
that I may dwell in the house of the Lord all the days of my life,
to behold the fair beauty of the Lord
and to seek him in his temple. **R**

You speak in my heart and say, "Seek my face."
Your face, Lord, will I seek.
Hide not your face from me,
nor turn away your servant in displeasure.
You have been my helper, cast me not away;
do not forsake me, O God of my salvation. **R**   *From Psalm 27*

A reading from the Second Letter of Paul to Timothy.

In the presence of God and of Christ Jesus, who is to judge the living and the dead, and in view of his appearing and his kingdom, I solemnly urge you: proclaim the message; be persistent whether the time is favourable or unfavourable; convince, rebuke, and encourage, with the utmost patience in teaching. For the time is coming when people will not put up with sound doctrine, but having itching ears, they will accumulate for themselves teachers to suit their own desires, and will turn away from listening to the truth and wander away to myths. As for you, always be sober, endure suffering, do the work of an evangelist, carry out your ministry fully.

 As for me, I am already being poured out as a libation, and the time of my departure has come. I have fought the good fight, I have finished the race, I have kept the faith. From now on there is reserved for me the crown of righteousness, which the Lord, the righteous judge, will give me on that day, and not only to me but also to all who have longed for his appearing.

This is the word of the Lord.   *2 Timothy 4. 1-8*

Hear the gospel of our Lord Jesus Christ according to Matthew.

Jesus said to the crowds: "You are the salt of the earth; but if salt has lost its taste, how can its saltiness be restored? It is no longer good for anything, but is thrown out and trampled under foot.

"You are the light of the world. A city built on a hill cannot be hid. No one after lighting a lamp puts it under the bushel basket, but on the lampstand, and it gives light to all in the house. In the same way, let your light shine before others, so that they may see your good works and give glory to your Father in heaven.

"Do not think that I have come to abolish the law or the prophets; I have come not to abolish but to fulfil. For truly I tell you, until heaven and earth pass away, not one letter, not one stroke of a letter, will pass from the law until all is accomplished. Therefore, whoever breaks one of the least of these commandments, and teaches others to do the same, will be called least in the kingdom of heaven; but whoever does them and teaches them will be called great in the kingdom of heaven."

This is the gospel of the Lord.   *Matthew 5. 13-19*

Post Communion
God of truth,
whose Wisdom set her table
and invited us to eat the bread and drink the wine
  of the kingdom:
help us to lay aside all foolishness
and to live and walk in the way of insight,
that we may come with your servants Basil and Gregory
  to the eternal feast of heaven;
through Jesus Christ our Lord.

Seraphim, Monk of Sarov, Spiritual Guide
2 January – Commemoration
If celebrated as a Lesser Festival, Common of Religious, page 494

Born in 1759 at Kursk in Russia, Seraphim entered the Monastery of our Lady at Sarov near Moscow when he was twenty years old.

He lived as a Solitary for over thirty years but his gifts as a staretz, or spiritual guide, became more widely-known until he found himself sharing his gift of healing spirit, soul and body with the thousands who made the pilgrimage to his monastery. The 'Jesus Prayer' formed the heart of his own devotional life and he stressed the need for all Christians to have an unceasing communion with the person of Jesus. He died on this day in 1833 and is revered in the Russian Orthodox Church as 'an ikon of Orthodox Spirituality.'

Vedanayagam Samuel Azariah, Bishop in South India
2 January – Commemoration
If celebrated as a Lesser Festival, Common of Bishops, page 483

Samuel Azariah was born in 1874 in a small village in South India, his father, Thomas Vedanayagam being a simple village priest and his mother Ellen having a deep love and understanding of the Scriptures. Samuel became a YMCA evangelist whilst still only nineteen, and secretary of the organisation throughout South India a few years later. He saw that, for the Church in India to grow and attract ordinary Indians to the Christian faith, it had to have an indigenous leadership and reduce the strong western influences and almost totally white leadership that pervaded it. He was ordained priest at the age of thirty-five and bishop just three years later, his work moving from primary evangelism to forwarding his desire for more Indian clergy and the need to raise their educational standards. He was an avid ecumenist and was one of the first to see the importance to mission of a united Church. He died on 1 January 1945, just two years before the creation of a united Church of South India.

The Epiphany
6 January – Principal Feast – Gold or White

The subtitle in the *Book of Common Prayer* of this, one of the principal feasts of the Church, is 'The Manifestation of Christ to the Gentiles'. This emphasises that, from the moment of the

Incarnation, the good news of Jesus Christ is for all: Jew and Gentile, the wise and the simple, male and female. Nothing in the Greek text of the gospels indicates that the Magi were all male and even the number three and making them Kings is a much later, non-scriptural tradition. The date chosen to celebrate this feast goes back to the placing of the feast of the Nativity of Christ in the winter solstice: the north European pre-Christian tradition of celebrating the birth of Sun on 25 December differed from the Mediterranean and eastern tradition of having 6 January as the Solstice. As often happens, the two dates merged into a beginning and an end of the same celebration. The western church adopted 'the twelve days of Christmas' climaxing on the eve of Epiphany, or 'Twelfth Night'. The implication by the fifth century was that this was the night on which the Magi arrived. The complications of dating became even more confused with the changing in the West from the Julian to the Gregorian Calendar, the eastern church refusing to play any part in such a radical change. So this day remains the chief day of celebrating the Incarnation in Orthodox Churches.

Collect
O God,
who by the leading of a star
manifested your only Son to the peoples of the earth:
mercifully grant that we,
who know you now by faith,
may at last behold your glory face to face;
through Jesus Christ your Son our Lord,
who is alive and reigns with you,
in the unity of the Holy Spirit,
one God, now and for ever.

A reading from the prophecy of Isaiah.

Arise, shine; for your light has come, and the glory of the Lord has risen upon you. For darkness shall cover the earth, and thick darkness the peoples; but the Lord will arise upon you, and his glory will appear over you. Nations shall come to your light, and kings to the brightness of your dawn.

Lift up your eyes and look around; they all gather together, they come to you; your sons shall come from far away, and your daughters shall be carried on their nurses' arms. Then you shall see and be radiant; your heart shall thrill and rejoice, because the abundance of the sea shall be brought to you, the wealth of the nations shall come to you. A multitude of camels shall cover you, the young camels of Midian and Ephah; all those from Sheba shall come. They shall bring gold and frankincense, and shall proclaim the praise of the Lord.

This is the word of the Lord.   *Isaiah 60. 1-6*

Responsorial Psalm

**R   [May your name remain for ever, for]
      All the nations shall call you blessèd, O God.**

Give the king your justice, O God,
and your righteousness to the king's son,
that he may rule your people righteously
and the poor with justice. **R**

He shall defend the needy among the people;
he shall rescue the poor and crush the oppressor;
he shall live as long as the sun and moon endure,
from one generation to another. **R**

The kings of Tarshish and of the isles shall pay tribute,
the kings of Arabia and Saba offer gifts.
All kings shall bow down before him,
all the nations do him service. **R**

Long may he live,
may there be given to him gold from Arabia;
prayer be made for him always,
may they bless him all the day long. **R**   *From Psalm 72*

A reading from the Letter of Paul to the Ephesians.

This is the reason that I Paul am a prisoner for Christ Jesus for the sake of you Gentiles – for surely you have already heard of the commission of God's grace that was given me for you, and how the mystery was made known to me by revelation, as I wrote above in a few words, a reading of which will enable you to perceive my understanding of the mystery of Christ. In former generations this mystery was not made known to humankind, as it has now been revealed to his holy apostles and prophets by the Spirit: that is, the Gentiles have become fellow heirs, members of the same body, and sharers in the promise in Christ Jesus through the gospel.

Of this gospel I have become a servant according to the gift of God's grace that was given me by the working of his power. Although I am the very least of all the saints, this grace was given to me to bring to the Gentiles the news of the boundless riches of Christ, and to make everyone see what is the plan of the mystery hidden for ages in God who created all things; so that through the church the wisdom of God in its rich variety might now be made known to the rulers and authorities in the heavenly places. This was in accordance with the eternal purpose that he has carried out in Christ Jesus our Lord, in whom we have access to God in boldness and confidence through faith in him.

This is the word of the Lord.   *Ephesians 3. 1-12*

Hear the gospel of our Lord Jesus Christ according to Matthew.

In the time of King Herod, after Jesus was born in Bethlehem of Judea, wise men from the East came to Jerusalem, asking, "Where is the child who has been born king of the Jews? For we observed his star at its rising, and have come to pay him homage." When King Herod heard this, he was frightened, and all Jerusalem with him; and calling together all the chief priests and scribes of the people, he inquired of them where the Messiah was to be born. They told him, "In Bethlehem of Judea; for so it has been written by the prophet: 'And you, Bethlehem, in the land of Judah, are by no means least among the rulers of Judah; for from you shall come a ruler who is to shepherd my people Israel.' "

Then Herod secretly called for the wise men and learned from them the exact time when the star had appeared. Then he sent them to Bethlehem, saying, "Go and search diligently for the child; and when you have found him, bring me word so that I may also go and pay him homage." When they had heard the king, they set out; and there, ahead of them, went the star that they had seen at its rising, until it stopped over the place where the child was. When they saw that the star had stopped, they were overwhelmed with joy. On entering the house, they saw the child with Mary his mother; and they knelt down and paid him homage. Then, opening their treasure chests, they offered him gifts of gold, frankincense, and myrrh. And having been warned in a dream not to return to Herod, they left for their own country by another road.

This is the gospel of the Lord.   *Matthew 2. 1-12*

Post Communion
Lord God,
the bright splendour whom the nations seek:
may we who with the Magi
  have been drawn by your light
discern the glory of your presence in your Son,
the Word made flesh, Jesus Christ our Lord.

William Laud, Archbishop of Canterbury
10 January – Commemoration
If celebrated as a Lesser Festival, Common of Martyrs, page 464

William Laud was appointed Archbishop of Canterbury by his friend and ecclesiastical ally, King Charles, in 1633. The aim of both Archbishop and Monarch was to counter the reforming Puritan movement, which emphasised personal and ecclesial austerity as a means of sustaining conversion. Laud was a High Churchman who felt that the majesty of God should be reflected in the liturgy of the church and rigorously set about ensuring that its ministers should practise what he preached. His relentless approach left no room for variance of practice – but neither did the Puritans – and the latter had the upper hand in Parliament and eventually impeached him in 1640 and imprisoned him in the Tower of London. His friend the King did not – or could not – come to his assistance and he was beheaded on this day in 1645.

Mary Slessor, Missionary in West Africa
11 January – *Commemoration*
If celebrated as a Lesser Festival, Common of Missionaries, page 503

Mary Slessor was born into a working-class, Presbyterian family in Aberdeen in 1848. As a child in Dundee, she was enthralled by stories of missions in Africa. For years, she read diligently as she worked in the mills, and eventually, in 1875, she was accepted as a teacher for the mission in Calabar, Nigeria. Her fluency in the local language, physical resilience and lack of pretension endeared her to those to whom she ministered. She adopted unwanted children, particularly twins who would otherwise, according to local superstition, have been put to death. She was influential in organising trade and in settling disputes, contributing much to the development of the Okoyong people with whom she later settled. She died, still in Africa, on this day in 1915.

Aelred of Hexham
Abbot of Rievaulx, 1167
12 January – *Lesser Festival* – *Religious* – *White*

Aelred was born at Hexham in 1109. His father was a priest and he entered the Cistercian Order at Rievaulx in about 1133, after spending some years in the court of King David of Scotland. He became Abbot of Revesby in 1143 and returned to Rievaulx four years later to become abbot and to spend the remainder of his life. He was profoundly influential through his spiritual writings, which he began at the request of Bernard of Clairvaux, the two having a similar approach to the spiritual life. Because of this, Aelred was often called "The Bernard of the North". He died on this day at Rievaulx in 1167.

Collect
Almighty God,
who endowed Aelred the abbot
with the gift of Christian friendship
and the wisdom to lead others in the way of holiness:
grant to your people that same spirit of mutual affection,

so that, in loving one another,
we may know the love of Christ
and rejoice in the eternal possession
   of your supreme goodness;
through Jesus Christ your Son our Lord,
who is alive and reigns with you,
in the unity of the Holy Spirit,
one God, now and for ever.

A reading from the book Ecclesiasticus.

Whoever fears the Lord will do this, and whoever holds to the law
will obtain wisdom. She will come to meet him like a mother, and
like a young bride she will welcome him. She will feed him with
the bread of learning, and give him the water of wisdom to drink.
He will lean on her and not fall, and he will rely on her and not be
put to shame. She will exalt him above his neighbours, and will
open his mouth in the midst of the assembly. He will find gladness and a crown of rejoicing, and will inherit an everlasting
name.

This is the word of the Lord.   *Ecclesiasticus 15. 1-6*

Responsorial Psalm

R   Lord, may we drink of the water of wisdom
     [and be fed with the bread of life].

O Lord, I am not proud;
I have no haughty looks.
I do not occupy myself with great matters
or with things that are too hard for me. **R**

But I still my soul and make it quiet,
like a child upon its mother's breast;
my soul is quieted within me. **R**

O Israel, wait upon the Lord,
from this time forth for evermore. **R**   *Psalm 131*

A reading from the Letter of Paul to the Philippians.

Whatever gains I had, these I have come to regard as loss because of Christ. More than that, I regard everything as loss because of the surpassing value of knowing Christ Jesus my Lord. For his sake I have suffered the loss of all things, and I regard them as rubbish, in order that I may gain Christ and be found in him, not having a righteousness of my own that comes from the law, but one that comes through faith in Christ, the righteousness from God based on faith. I want to know Christ and the power of his resurrection and the sharing of his sufferings by becoming like him in his death, if somehow I may attain the resurrection from the dead.

Not that I have already obtained this or have already reached the goal; but I press on to make it my own, because Christ Jesus has made me his own. Beloved, I do not consider that I have made it my own; but this one thing I do: forgetting what lies behind and straining forward to what lies ahead, I press on toward the goal for the prize of the heavenly call of God in Christ Jesus.

This is the word of the Lord.   *Philippians 3. 7-14*

Hear the gospel of our Lord Jesus Christ according to Luke.

Jesus said to his disciples, "Do not be afraid, little flock, for it is your Father's good pleasure to give you the kingdom. Sell your possessions, and give alms. Make purses for yourselves that do not wear out, an unfailing treasure in heaven, where no thief comes near and no moth destroys. For where your treasure is, there your heart will be also.

"Be dressed for action and have your lamps lit; be like those who are waiting for their master to return from the wedding banquet, so that they may open the door for him as soon as he comes and knocks. Blessèd are those servants whom the master finds alert when he comes; truly I tell you, he will fasten his belt and have them sit down to eat, and he will come and serve them."

This is the gospel of the Lord.   *Luke 12. 32-37*

Post Communion
Merciful God,
who gave such grace to your servant Aelred
that he served you with singleness of heart
and loved you above all things:

help us, whose communion with you
  has been renewed in this sacrament,
to forsake all that holds us back from following Christ
and to grow into his likeness from glory to glory;
through Jesus Christ our Lord.

Benedict Biscop, Abbot of Wearmouth
12 January – Commemoration
If celebrated as a Lesser Festival, Common of Religious, page 494

Born a Northumbrian nobleman in 628, Benedict Biscop served at
the court of King Oswiu of Northumbria until he joined Wilfrid of
York on his pilgrimage to Rome to the tombs of the apostles. He
made a second trip accompanied by the King's son and on his way
home was clothed a monk at the Benedictine house of Lérins. It
was on his third trip to Rome that he met and returned to England
with Theodore, the newly-appointed Archbishop of Canterbury,
who made him Abbot of St Augustine's in 669. Five years later, he
was permitted to make his own foundation at Wearmouth, which
he had built in the Roman style and endowed with a huge library.
He encouraged the development of the Uncial script which also
acted as a vehicle for the propagation of the Roman Rite. His own
scholarship, and that promoted through the religious houses he
founded, played a large part in the acceptance of the primacy of
Roman over Celtic practice throughout northern England.
Benedict Biscop died on this day in 689.

Hilary, Bishop of Poitiers
13 January – Lesser Festival – Teacher of the Faith – White

Hilary was born at Poitiers in about the year 315; his family,
though pagan, gave him an excellent education and he was proficient in Latin and Greek. After extensive personal study, he tells
us that he was baptised at the age of thirty. He was elected bishop of the city in the year 350 and immediately became caught up
in the Arian controversy, himself asserting that mortals of this
world were created to practise moral virtues thus reflecting the

one in whose image they are made, the eternal and creative first cause, God, and that Jesus Christ, the incarnate Son of God, is of one substance with the Father. His learning and oratory led to his title of "Athanasius of the West". He was known as a gentle, kind friend to all, even though his writings seemed severe at times. He died in the year 367.

Collect
Everlasting God,
whose servant Hilary
steadfastly confessed your Son Jesus Christ
  to be both human and divine:
grant us his gentle courtesy
to bring to all the message of redemption
  in the incarnate Christ,
who is alive and reigns with you,
in the unity of the Holy Spirit,
one God, now and for ever.

A reading from the prophecy of Isaiah.

Listen, and hear my voice; Pay attention, and hear my speech. Do those who plough for sowing plough continually? Do they continually open and harrow their ground? When they have levelled its surface, do they not scatter dill, sow cummin, and plant wheat in rows and barley in its proper place, and spelt as the border? For they are well instructed; their God teaches them. Dill is not threshed with a threshing sledge, nor is a cart wheel rolled over cummin; but dill is beaten out with a stick, and cummin with a rod. Grain is crushed for bread, but one does not thresh it forever; one drives the cart wheel and horses over it, but does not pulverise it. This also comes from the Lord of hosts; he is wonderful in counsel, and excellent in wisdom.

This is the word of the Lord.   *Isaiah 28. 23-29*

Responsorial Psalm
**R   Send us your light and truth, O God,
       [that they may lead us back to you].**

Give judgement for me, O God,
and defend my cause against an ungodly people;
deliver me from the deceitful and wicked
for you are the God of my strength. **R**

Send out your light and your truth, that they may lead me,
and bring me to your holy hill and to your dwelling;
that I may go to the altar of God, to the God of my joy and gladness;
and on the harp I will give thanks to you, O God my God. **R**

Why are you so full of heaviness, O my soul?
and why are you so disquieted within me?
Put your trust in God, for I will yet give thanks to him,
who is the help of my countenance, and my God. **R**

From Psalm 43

A reading from the First Letter of John.

Children, it is the last hour! As you have heard that antichrist is coming, so now many antichrists have come. From this we know that it is the last hour. They went out from us, but they did not belong to us; for if they had belonged to us, they would have remained with us. But by going out they made it plain that none of them belongs to us. But you have been anointed by the Holy One, and all of you have knowledge.

I write to you, not because you do not know the truth, but because you know it, and you know that no lie comes from the truth. Who is the liar but the one who denies that Jesus is the Christ? This is the antichrist, the one who denies the Father and the Son. No one who denies the Son has the Father; everyone who confesses the Son has the Father also. Let what you heard from the beginning abide in you. If what you heard from the beginning abides in you, then you will abide in the Son and in the Father. And this is what he has promised us, eternal life.

This is the word of the Lord. *1 John 2. 18-25*

Hear the gospel of our Lord Jesus Christ according to John.

The Pharisees said to Jesus, "Who are you?" Jesus said to them, "Why do I speak to you at all? I have much to say about you and much to condemn; but the one who sent me is true, and I declare to the world what I have heard from him." They did not understand that he was speaking to them about the Father. So Jesus said, "When you have lifted up the Son of Man, then you will realise that I am he, and that I do nothing on my own, but I speak these things as the Father instructed me. And the one who sent me is with me; he has not left me alone, for I always do what is pleasing to him." As he was saying these things, many believed in him.

Then Jesus said to the Jews who had believed in him, "If you continue in my word, you are truly my disciples; and you will know the truth, and the truth will make you free."

This is the gospel of the Lord.   *John 8. 25-32*

Post Communion
God of truth,
whose Wisdom set her table
and invited us to eat the bread and drink the wine
 of the kingdom:
help us to lay aside all foolishness
and to live and walk in the way of insight,
that we may come with your servant Hilary
 to the eternal feast of heaven;
through Jesus Christ our Lord.

Kentigern, Bishop in Strathclyde & Cumbria
13 January – Commemoration
If celebrated as a Lesser Festival, Common of Missionaries, page 503

Kentigern, also known affectionately as Mungo, which means 'darling', is reputed to have been the grandson of a British prince in southern Scotland and to have attended a monastic school at Culross. The story goes that he became a missionary to the Britons living in Strathclyde and was elected their bishop. Following the persecution of Christians, he fled to Wales, but eventually returned to Strathclyde where he continued his work of evangelism. He died in the year 603 and his tomb is in St Mungo's Cathedral in Glasgow.

George Fox, Founder of the Society of Friends
13 January – Commemoration
If celebrated as a Lesser Festival, Common of any Saint, page 513

George Fox was born at Fenny Drayton in Leicestershire in 1624, the son of a weaver, and was himself apprenticed to a shoe-maker. He became something of a wayfarer from 1643 for about three years, loosening all ties with his family and friends. The 'Inner Light of the Living Christ' became his watchword in 1646 and he began to preach that the truth could only be found through the Inner Voice speaking directly to each soul. His society of 'The Friends of Truth' was formed at about this time, clearly a protest against the authoritarianism of the Presbyterian system, and many believers joined. Because of welcoming God into the soul often whilst in a state of trance, which caused much body movement, Gervase Bennet nicknamed them the Quakers in 1650; although meant as a term of abuse, it quickly became a name they themselves adopted. Fox spent several spells in gaol because of his determination to preach where he would and what he willed; he also made many missionary journeys around England, on the continent and to North America and the West Indies. He had a charismatic personality combined with excellent organisational abilities, which proved a solid foundation for ensuring the continuance of his beliefs and practices. He died on this day in 1691.

Antony of Egypt, Hermit, Abbot
17 January – Lesser Festival – Religious – White

Born in about the year 251, Antony heard the gospel message, "If you would be perfect, go, sell your possessions, and give the money to the poor, and you will have treasure in heaven; then come, follow me." He was twenty years old and rich, following the death of his parents, but he did as the gospel instructed and went to live in the desert, living an austere life of manual work, charity and prayer. His many spiritual struggles left him both wise and sensible and he became a spiritual guide for many who flocked to him. His simple rule of personal discipline and prayer was taken up and spread throughout Christendom. He died peacefully in the desert in the year 356, asking that he be buried secretly, so that his person might be hidden in death as in life.

Collect
Most gracious God,
who called your servant Antony to sell all that he had
and to serve you in the solitude of the desert:
by his example may we learn to deny ourselves
and to love you before all things;
through Jesus Christ your Son our Lord,
who is alive and reigns with you,
in the unity of the Holy Spirit,
one God, now and for ever.

A reading from the First Book of the Kings.

The word of the Lord came to Elijah, saying, "Go from here and turn eastward, and hide yourself by the Wadi Cherith, which is east of the Jordan. You shall drink from the wadi, and I have commanded the ravens to feed you there." So he went and did according to the word of the Lord; he went and lived by the Wadi Cherith, which is east of the Jordan. The ravens brought him bread and meat in the morning, and bread and meat in the evening; and he drank from the wadi.

This is the word of the Lord.   *1 Kings 17. 2-6*

Responsorial Psalm

**R   You call upon me, Lord, and I will answer you;
      [protect me, for you know my name].**

Because you have made the Lord your refuge
and the Most High your habitation,
there shall no evil happen to you,
neither shall any plague come near your dwelling. **R**

For he shall give his angels charge over you,
to keep you in all your ways.
They shall bear you in their hands,
lest you dash your foot against a stone. **R**

You shall tread upon the lion and adder;
you shall trample the young lion and the serpent under your feet.
Because he is bound to me in love, therefore will I deliver him;
I will protect him, because he knows my name. **R**

He shall call upon me and I will answer him;
I am with him in trouble, I will rescue him and bring him to honour.
With long life will I satisfy him,
and show him my salvation. **R**   *From Psalm 91*

A reading from the Letter of Paul to the Philippians.

Whatever gains I had, these I have come to regard as loss because
of Christ. More than that, I regard everything as loss because of
the surpassing value of knowing Christ Jesus my Lord. For his
sake I have suffered the loss of all things, and I regard them as rubbish, in order that I may gain Christ and be found in him, not having a righteousness of my own that comes from the law, but one
that comes through faith in Christ, the righteousness from God
based on faith. I want to know Christ and the power of his resurrection and the sharing of his sufferings by becoming like him in
his death, if somehow I may attain the resurrection from the dead.

Not that I have already obtained this or have already reached the
goal; but I press on to make it my own, because Christ Jesus has
made me his own. Beloved, I do not consider that I have made it
my own; but this one thing I do: forgetting what lies behind and
straining forward to what lies ahead, I press on toward the goal for
the prize of the heavenly call of God in Christ Jesus.

This is the word of the Lord.   *Philippians 3. 7-14*

Hear the gospel of our Lord Jesus Christ according to Matthew.

Someone came to Jesus and said, "Teacher, what good deed must
I do to have eternal life?" And he said to him, "Why do you ask
me about what is good? There is only one who is good. If you
wish to enter into life, keep the commandments." He said to him,
"Which ones?" And Jesus said, "You shall not murder; You shall
not commit adultery; You shall not steal; You shall not bear false
witness; Honour your father and mother; also, You shall love your
neighbour as yourself." The young man said to him, "I have kept

all these; what do I still lack?" Jesus said to him, "If you wish to be perfect, go, sell your possessions, and give the money to the poor, and you will have treasure in heaven; then come, follow me." When the young man heard this word, he went away grieving, for he had many possessions.

Then Jesus said to his disciples, "Truly I tell you, it will be hard for a rich person to enter the kingdom of heaven. Again I tell you, it is easier for a camel to go through the eye of a needle than for someone who is rich to enter the kingdom of God." When the disciples heard this, they were greatly astounded and said, "Then who can be saved?" But Jesus looked at them and said, "For mortals it is impossible, but for God all things are possible."

This is the gospel of the Lord.   *Matthew 19. 16-26*

Post Communion
Merciful God,
who gave such grace to your servant Antony
that he served you with singleness of heart
and loved you above all things:
help us, whose communion with you
  has been renewed in this sacrament,
to forsake all that holds us back from following Christ
and to grow into his likeness from glory to glory;
through Jesus Christ our Lord.

Charles Gore, Bishop & Founder
17 January – Commemoration
If celebrated as a Lesser Festival, Common of Religious, page 494

Born in 1835, Gore became one of the most influential of Anglican theologians. He helped reconcile the Church to some aspects of biblical criticism and scientific discovery, yet was Catholic in his interpretation of the faith and sacraments. He was also concerned to bring Catholic principles to bear on social problems. As an Oxford don and then as a Canon of Westminster, he was renowned for his preaching. In the 1890s, he was the founder – and first leader – of the Community of the Resurrection, which in later years settled at Mirfield in Yorkshire. From 1902, he was successively bishop of Worcester, Birmingham and Oxford. He was much mourned at his death on this day in 1932.

Wulfstan, Bishop of Worcester
19 January – Lesser Festival – Bishop – White

Born in about the year 1009, Wulfstan's first twenty-five years after his ordination was spent in the monastery at Worcester. Against his will, he was elected Bishop of Worcester in 1062 but went on to prove an able administrator and pastor. He carefully and gently nurtured both church and state through the transition from Saxon to Norman rule. He died at Worcester on this day in the year 1095.

Collect
Lord God,
who raised up Wulfstan to be a bishop among your people
  and a leader of your Church:
help us, after his example,
  to live simply,
  to work diligently
  and to make your kingdom known;
through Jesus Christ your Son our Lord,
who is alive and reigns with you,
in the unity of the Holy Spirit,
one God, now and for ever.

A reading from the First Book of Samuel.

The Lord said to Samuel, "How long will you grieve over Saul? I have rejected him from being king over Israel. Fill your horn with oil and set out; I will send you to Jesse the Bethlehemite, for I have provided for myself a king among his sons." When they came, he looked on Eliab and thought, "Surely the Lord's anointed is now before the Lord." But the Lord said to Samuel, "Do not look on his appearance or on the height of his stature, because I have rejected him; for the Lord does not see as mortals see; they look on the outward appearance, but the Lord looks on the heart." Then Jesse called Abinadab, and made him pass before Samuel. He said, "Neither has the Lord chosen this one." Then Jesse made

Shammah pass by. And he said, "Neither has the Lord chosen this one." Jesse made seven of his sons pass before Samuel, and Samuel said to Jesse, "The Lord has not chosen any of these."

Samuel said to Jesse, "Are all your sons here?" And he said, "There remains yet the youngest, but he is keeping the sheep." And Samuel said to Jesse, "Send and bring him; for we will not sit down until he comes here." He sent and brought him in. Now he was ruddy, and had beautiful eyes, and was handsome. The Lord said, "Rise and anoint him; for this is the one." Then Samuel took the horn of oil, and anointed him in the presence of his brothers; and the spirit of the Lord came mightily upon David from that day forward. Samuel then set out and went to Ramah.

This is the word of the Lord. *1 Samuel 16. 1, 6-13*

Responsorial Psalm

**R   God will rule over the nations,
[for he is at your right hand for ever].**

The Lord said to my lord, "Sit at my right hand,
until I make your enemies your footstool."
The Lord will send the sceptre of your power out of Zion,
saying, "Rule over your enemies round about you. **R**

"Princely state has been yours from the day of your birth,
in the beauty of holiness have I begotten you,
like dew from the womb of the morning." **R**

The Lord has sworn and he will not recant:
"You are a priest for ever after the order of Melchizedek."
The Lord who is at your right hand
will smite kings in the day of his wrath;
he will rule over the nations. **R**   *From Psalm 110*

A reading from the First Letter of Paul to the Corinthians.

Think of us in this way, as servants of Christ and stewards of God's mysteries. Moreover, it is required of stewards that they be found trustworthy. But with me it is a very small thing that I should be judged by you or by any human court. I do not even judge myself. I am not aware of anything against myself, but I am not thereby acquitted. It is the Lord who judges me. Therefore do not pronounce judgement before the time, before the Lord comes, who will bring to light the things now hidden in darkness and will disclose the purposes of the heart. Then each one will receive commendation from God.

This is the word of the Lord.   *1 Corinthians 4. 1-5*

Hear the gospel of our Lord Jesus Christ according to Matthew.

Jesus said to his disciples, "Keep awake therefore, for you do not know on what day your Lord is coming. But understand this: if the owner of the house had known in what part of the night the thief was coming, he would have stayed awake and would not have let his house be broken into. Therefore you also must be ready, for the Son of Man is coming at an unexpected hour.

"Who then is the faithful and wise servant, whom his master has put in charge of his household, to give the other servants their allowance of food at the proper time? Blessèd is that servant whom his master will find at work when he arrives."

This is the gospel of the Lord.   *Matthew 24. 42-46*

Post Communion
God, shepherd of your people,
whose servant Wulfstan revealed the loving service of Christ
  in his ministry as a pastor of your people:
by this eucharist in which we share
awaken within us the love of Christ
and keep us faithful to our Christian calling;
through him who laid down his life for us,
but is alive and reigns with you, now and for ever.

Richard Rolle of Hampole
20 January – Commemoration
If celebrated as a Lesser Festival, Common of Spiritual Writers, page 473

Richard Rolle was born in about the year 1300 in Thornton in Yorkshire, where he first began to live the hermit life at the age of eighteen, after breaking off his education at the University of

Oxford. After moving his hermitage to several other sites, he finally settled close to the Cistercian nuns at Hampole, where he undertook much of his prolific writing on mysticism and asceticism. He wrote in Latin but also produced many texts directly in English and even in the Northumbrian dialect. His writings were widely influential and he was venerated for at least three hundred years after his death on this day in the year 1349.

Agnes, Child-Martyr at Rome
21 January – Lesser Festival – Martyr – Red

The reason Agnes is one of the most well-known and widely-venerated of the early Roman martyrs is perhaps because of the expression of mature resilience and sheer bravery in a thirteen-year-old girl. Agnes is reputed to have refused an arranged marriage because of her total dedication to Christ and stated that she preferred even death of the body to the death of her consecrated virginity. The growing veneration for the state of consecrated virginity at this time, combined with the last, major Roman persecution under the emperor Diocletian, climaxing in the shedding of an innocent virgin-child's blood willingly for Christ, placed her at the forefront of veneration almost from the moment the persecution ended. She is believed to have died in the year 304 and her feast has ever since been celebrated on this day.

Collect
Eternal God, Shepherd of your sheep,
whose child Agnes was strengthened to bear witness
  in her living and her dying
to the true love of her Redeemer:
grant us the power to understand, with all your saints,
what is the breadth and length and height and depth
and to know the love that surpasses knowledge,
even Jesus Christ your Son our Lord,
who is alive and reigns with you,
in the unity of the Holy Spirit,
one God, now and for ever.

A reading from the book Ecclesiasticus.

I give you thanks, O Lord and King, and praise you, O God my Saviour. I give thanks to your name, for you have been my protector and helper and have delivered me from destruction and from the trap laid by a slanderous tongue, from lips that fabricate lies. In the face of my adversaries you have been my helper and delivered me, in the greatness of your mercy and of your name, from grinding teeth about to devour me, from the hand of those seeking my life, from the many troubles I endured.

This is the word of the Lord.   *Ecclesiasticus 51. 1-3*

Responsorial Psalm

**R   Your name, O God, will be ever remembered
       [from one generation to another].**

Hear, O daughter; consider and listen closely;
forget your people and your family's house.
The king will have pleasure in your beauty;
he is your master; therefore do him honour. **R**

The people of Tyre are here with a gift;
the rich among the people seek your favour.
All glorious is the princess as she enters;
her gown is cloth-of-gold. **R**

In embroidered apparel she is brought to the king;
after her the bridesmaids follow in procession.
With joy and gladness they are brought,
and enter into the palace of the king. **R**   *From Psalm 45*

A reading from the Revelation to John.

One of the elders addressed me, saying, "Who are these, robed in white, and where have they come from?" I said to him, "Sir, you are the one that knows." Then he said to me, "These are they who have come out of the great ordeal; they have washed their robes and made them white in the blood of the Lamb.

"For this reason they are before the throne of God, and worship him day and night within his temple, and the one who is seated on the throne will shelter them.

"They will hunger no more, and thirst no more; the sun will not strike them, nor any scorching heat; for the Lamb at the centre of the throne will be their shepherd, and he will guide them to springs of the water of life, and God will wipe away every tear from their eyes."

This is the word of the Lord.   *Revelation 7. 13-17*

Hear the gospel of our Lord Jesus Christ according to Matthew.

The disciples came to Jesus and asked, "Who is the greatest in the kingdom of heaven?" He called a child, whom he put among them, and said, "Truly I tell you, unless you change and become like children, you will never enter the kingdom of heaven. Whoever becomes humble like this child is the greatest in the kingdom of heaven. Whoever welcomes one such child in my name welcomes me. If any of you put a stumbling block before one of these little ones who believe in me, it would be better for you if a great millstone were fastened around your neck and you were drowned in the depth of the sea. Woe to the world because of stumbling blocks! Occasions for stumbling are bound to come, but woe to the one by whom the stumbling block comes!"

This is the gospel of the Lord.   *Matthew 18. 1-7*

Post Communion
God,
who gave us this holy meal
in which we have celebrated the glory of the cross
and the victory of your martyr Agnes:
by our communion with Christ
in his saving death and resurrection,
give us with all your saints the courage to conquer evil
and so to share the fruit of the tree of life;
through Jesus Christ our Lord.

Vincent of Saragossa, Deacon, first Martyr of Spain
22 January – Commemoration
If celebrated as a Lesser Festival, Common of Martyrs, page 464

Vincent was born in Saragossa in Aragon in the latter part of the third century and was ordained to the diaconate by Valerian, his bishop in that city. When the Diocletian persecutions began, both men were brought before the Roman governor but, because Valerian stammered badly, he relied on Vincent to speak for them both. Vincent spoke eloquently for both his bishop and his church, proclaiming the good news of Jesus Christ and condemning paganism. He so angered the governor that he was immediately condemned to a painful death, reputedly on the gridiron. Thus he lived and gave his life in the tradition of Stephen, the first martyr and also a deacon; he died in the year 304 and his feast has been celebrated on this day since the persecutions ended in 312.

Francis de Sales, Bishop of Geneva
24 January – Lesser Festival – Teacher of the Faith – White

Francis de Sales was born in 1567 in the castle at Sales in Savoy. He was educated in Paris and Padua, first as a legal advocate and then as a priest. His preaching against Calvinism begin in 1593 to win back the Chablais to Roman Catholicism. In 1599, he was appointed Bishop-Coadjutor of Geneva and moved to Annecy from where he administered the diocese when he became the diocesan in 1602. It was not until 1799 that Roman Catholic worship was officially permitted in Geneva again. In his preaching and writings, particularly his book *Introduction to the Devout Life*, Francis concentrated in putting prayer and meditation within the reach of all Christians. He died at Lyons on 28 December 1622 and his body was translated to Annecy on this day in 1623.

Collect
Holy God,
who called your bishop Francis de Sales
to bring many to Christ through his devout life
and to renew your Church with patience and understanding:
grant that we may, by word and example,
reflect your gentleness and love to all we meet;
through Jesus Christ our Saviour,
who is alive and reigns with you,
in the unity of the Holy Spirit,
one God, now and for ever.

A reading from the Book of Proverbs.

Happy are those who find wisdom, and those who get understanding, for her income is better than silver, and her revenue better than gold. She is more precious than jewels, and nothing you desire can compare with her. Long life is in her right hand; in her left hand are riches and honour. Her ways are ways of pleasantness, and all her paths are peace. She is a tree of life to those who lay hold of her; those who hold her fast are called happy.

This is the word of the Lord. *Proverbs 3. 13-18*

Responsorial Psalm

R **The heavens declare your glory, O God,**
[and the firmament shows forth your handiwork].

The law of the Lord is perfect
and revives the soul;
the testimony of the Lord is sure
and gives wisdom to the innocent. **R**

The statutes of the Lord are just
and rejoice the heart;
the commandment of the Lord is clear
and gives light to the eyes. **R**

The fear of the Lord is clean
and endures for ever;
the judgements of the Lord are true
and righteous altogether. **R**

More to be desired are they than gold,
more than much fine gold,
sweeter far than honey,
than honey in the comb. **R** *From Psalm 19*

A reading from the First Letter of Paul to the Corinthians.

When I came to you, brothers and sisters, I did not come proclaiming the mystery of God to you in lofty words or wisdom. For I decided to know nothing among you except Jesus Christ, and him crucified. And I came to you in weakness and in fear and in much trembling. My speech and my proclamation were not with plausible words of wisdom, but with a demonstration of the Spirit and of power, so that your faith might rest not on human wisdom but on the power of God.

Yet among the mature we do speak wisdom, though it is not a wisdom of this age or of the rulers of this age, who are doomed to perish. But we speak God's wisdom, secret and hidden, which God decreed before the ages for our glory. None of the rulers of this age understood this; for if they had, they would not have crucified the Lord of glory. But, as it is written, "What no eye has seen, nor ear heard, nor the human heart conceived, what God has prepared for those who love him" – these things God has revealed to us through the Spirit; for the Spirit searches everything, even the depths of God.

This is the word of the Lord.   *1 Corinthians 2. 1-10*

Hear the gospel of our Lord Jesus Christ according to John.

Jesus said to Nicodemus, "Indeed, God did not send the Son into the world to condemn the world, but in order that the world might be saved through him. Those who believe in him are not condemned; but those who do not believe are condemned already, because they have not believed in the name of the only Son of God. And this is the judgement, that the light has come into the world, and people loved darkness rather than light because their deeds were evil. For all who do evil hate the light and do not come to the light, so that their deeds may not be exposed. But those who do what is true come to the light, so that it may be clearly seen that their deeds have been done in God."

This is the gospel of the Lord.   *John 3. 17-21*

Post Communion
God of truth,
whose Wisdom set her table
and invited us to eat the bread and drink the wine
  of the kingdom:
help us to lay aside all foolishness
and to live and walk in the way of insight,
that we may come with your servant Francis de Sales
  to the eternal feast of heaven;
through Jesus Christ our Lord.

The Conversion of Paul
25 January – Festival – Apostle – White

The conversion of the anti-Christian zealot, Saul, to the apostle of Christ, Paul, is clearly related in the reading from the Acts of the Apostles, but it has to be remembered that this was a beginning: Saul took some time to become Paul and some time to begin to understand that his call to preach – to Jew and to Gentile – the saving power of Jesus, the Son of God, was something that was a whole life's journey for him. Paul says in his Letter to the Church in Galatia, "God set me apart before I was born and called me through his grace . . . Three years after (the Damascus Road conversion), I went up to Jerusalem." The preparation for this moment of his conversion was his whole life. This feast has been celebrated in the Church since the sixth century but became universal in the twelfth century.

Collect
Almighty God,
who caused the light of the gospel
to shine throughout the world
through the preaching of your servant Saint Paul:
grant that we who celebrate his wonderful conversion
may follow him in bearing witness to your truth;
through Jesus Christ your Son our Lord,
who is alive and reigns with you,
in the unity of the Holy Spirit,
one God, now and for ever.

Jeremiah 1. 4-10	*or*	Acts 9. 1-22
Psalm 67		Psalm 67
Acts 9. 1-22		Galatians 1. 11-16*a*
Matthew 19. 27-30		Matthew 19. 27-30

A reading from the prophecy of Jeremiah.

The word of the Lord came to me saying, "Before I formed you in the womb I knew you, and before you were born I consecrated you; I appointed you a prophet to the nations."

Then I said, "Ah, Lord God! Truly I do not know how to speak, for

I am only a boy." But the Lord said to me, "Do not say, 'I am only a boy'; for you shall go to all to whom I send you, and you shall speak whatever I command you. Do not be afraid of them, for I am with you to deliver you, says the Lord."

Then the Lord put out his hand and touched my mouth; and the Lord said to me, "Now I have put my words in your mouth. See, today I appoint you over nations and over kingdoms, to pluck up and to pull down, to destroy and to overthrow, to build and to plant."

This is the word of the Lord.   *Jeremiah 1. 4-10*

Responsorial Psalm

**R   Let the peoples praise you, O God,
        [let all the peoples praise you].**

God, be merciful to us and bless us,
show us the light of your countenance and come to us.
Let your ways be known upon earth,
your saving health among all nations. **R**

Let the nations be glad and sing for joy,
for you judge the peoples with equity
and guide all the nations upon earth. **R**

The earth has brought forth her increase;
may God, our own God, give us his blessing.
May God give us his blessing,
and may all the ends of the earth stand in awe of him. **R** *Psalm 67*

A reading from the Acts of the Apostles.

Saul, still breathing threats and murder against the disciples of the Lord, went to the high priest and asked him for letters to the synagogues at Damascus, so that if he found any who belonged to the Way, men or women, he might bring them bound to Jerusalem. Now as he was going along and approaching Damascus, suddenly a light from heaven flashed around him. He fell to the ground and heard a voice saying to him, "Saul, Saul, why do you persecute me?" He asked, "Who are you, Lord?" The reply came, "I am Jesus, whom you are persecuting. But get up and enter the city, and you will be told what you are to do." The men who were travelling with him stood speechless because they heard the voice but saw no one. Saul got up from the ground, and though his eyes were open, he could see nothing; so they led him by the hand and brought him into Damascus. For three days he was without sight, and neither ate nor drank.

Now there was a disciple in Damascus named Ananias. The Lord said to him in a vision, "Ananias." He answered, "Here I am, Lord." The Lord said to him, "Get up and go to the street called Straight, and at the house of Judas look for a man of Tarsus named Saul. At this moment he is praying, and he has seen in a vision a man named Ananias come in and lay his hands on him so that he might regain his sight." But Ananias answered, "Lord, I have heard from many about this man, how much evil he has done to your saints in Jerusalem; and here he has authority from the chief priests to bind all who invoke your name." But the Lord said to him, "Go, for he is an instrument whom I have chosen to bring my name before Gentiles and kings and before the people of Israel; I myself will show him how much he must suffer for the sake of my name."

So Ananias went and entered the house. He laid his hands on Saul and said, "Brother Saul, the Lord Jesus, who appeared to you on your way here, has sent me so that you may regain your sight and be filled with the Holy Spirit." And immediately something like scales fell from his eyes, and his sight was restored. Then he got up and was baptised, and after taking some food, he regained his strength. For several days he was with the disciples in Damascus, and immediately he began to proclaim Jesus in the synagogues, saying, "He is the Son of God." All who heard him were amazed and said, "Is not this the man who made havoc in Jerusalem among those who invoked this name? And has he not come here for the purpose of bringing them bound before the chief priests?" Saul became increasingly more powerful and confounded the Jews who lived in Damascus by proving that Jesus was the Messiah.

This is the word of the Lord.   *Acts 9. 1-22*

A reading from the Letter of Paul to the Galatians.

For I want you to know, brothers and sisters, that the gospel that was proclaimed by me is not of human origin; for I did not receive it from a human source, nor was I taught it, but I received it through a revelation of Jesus Christ. You have heard, no doubt, of my earlier life in Judaism. I was violently persecuting the church of God and was trying to destroy it. I advanced in Judaism beyond many among my people of the same age, for I was far more zealous for the traditions of my ancestors. But God, who had set me apart before I was born and called me through his grace, was pleased to reveal his Son to me, so that I might proclaim him among the Gentiles.

This is the word of the Lord.   *Galatians 1. 11-16a*

Hear the gospel of our Lord Jesus Christ according to Matthew.

Then Peter said in reply, "Look, we have left everything and followed you. What then will we have?" Jesus said to them, "Truly I tell you, at the renewal of all things, when the Son of Man is seated on the throne of his glory, you who have followed me will also sit on twelve thrones, judging the twelve tribes of Israel. And everyone who has left houses or brothers or sisters or father or mother or children or fields, for my name's sake, will receive a hundredfold, and will inherit eternal life. But many who are first will be last, and the last will be first."

This is the gospel of the Lord.   *Matthew 19. 27-30*

Post Communion
Almighty God,
who on the day of Pentecost
sent your Holy Spirit to the apostles
with the wind from heaven and in tongues of flame,
filling them with joy and boldness to preach the gospel:
by the power of the same Spirit
strengthen us to witness to your truth
and to draw everyone to the fire of your love;
through Jesus Christ our Lord.

Timothy & Titus, Companions of Paul
26 January – Lesser Festival – Bishops – White

On the day following the Conversion of St Paul, the Church remembers his two companions, 'partners and fellow-workers in

God's service'. Timothy, we are told, had a Jewish mother and a Greek father, whilst Titus was wholly Greek. It was because of Titus that Paul stood out against compulsory circumcision but, to avoid suspicion from other Jews, Timothy was circumcised. They are honoured in the Church for their devotion and faithfulness to the gospel.

Collect
Heavenly Father,
who sent your apostle Paul to preach the gospel,
and gave him Timothy and Titus
  to be his companions in faith:
grant that our fellowship in the Holy Spirit
may bear witness to the name of Jesus,
who is alive and reigns with you,
in the unity of the Holy Spirit,
one God, now and for ever.

A reading from the prophecy of Isaiah.

The spirit of the Lord God is upon me, because the Lord has anointed me; he has sent me to bring good news to the oppressed, to bind up the brokenhearted, to proclaim liberty to the captives, and release to the prisoners; to proclaim the year of the Lord's favour, and the day of vengeance of our God; to comfort all who mourn; to provide for those who mourn in Zion – to give them a garland instead of ashes, the oil of gladness instead of mourning, the mantle of praise instead of a faint spirit. They will be called oaks of righteousness, the planting of the Lord, to display his glory.

This is the word of the Lord.   *Isaiah 61. 1-3a*

Responsorial Psalm

**R   God's faithfulness endures from age to age,
[and his mercy is everlasting].**

Be joyful in the Lord, all you lands;
serve the Lord with gladness
and come before his presence with a song. **R**

Know this: that the Lord himself is God;
he himself has made us and we are his;
we are his people and the sheep of his pasture. **R**

Enter his gates with thanksgiving;
go into his courts with praise;
give thanks to him and call upon his name. **R**   *Psalm 100*

A reading from the Second Letter of Paul to Timothy.

You then, my child, be strong in the grace that is in Christ Jesus;
and what you have heard from me through many witnesses
entrust to faithful people who will be able to teach others as well.
Share in suffering like a good soldier of Christ Jesus. No one serving in the army gets entangled in everyday affairs; the soldier's
aim is to please the enlisting officer. And in the case of an athlete,
no one is crowned without competing according to the rules. It is
the farmer who does the work who ought to have the first share of
the crops. Think over what I say, for the Lord will give you understanding in all things.

Remember Jesus Christ, raised from the dead, a descendant of
David – that is my gospel.

This is the word of the Lord.   *2 Timothy 2. 1-8*

Or:

A reading from the Letter of Paul to Titus.

Paul, a servant of God and an apostle of Jesus Christ, for the sake
of the faith of God's elect and the knowledge of the truth that is in
accordance with godliness, in the hope of eternal life that God,
who never lies, promised before the ages began – in due time he
revealed his word through the proclamation with which I have
been entrusted by the command of God our Saviour:

To Titus, my loyal child in the faith we share: Grace and peace
from God the Father and Christ Jesus our Saviour. I left you
behind in Crete for this reason, so that you should put in order
what remained to be done, and should appoint elders in every
town, as I directed you.

This is the word of the Lord.   *Titus 1. 1-5*

Hear the gospel of our Lord Jesus Christ according to Luke.

After this the Lord Jesus appointed seventy other disciples and sent them on ahead of him in pairs to every town and place where he himself intended to go. He said to them, "The harvest is plentiful, but the labourers are few; therefore ask the Lord of the harvest to send out labourers into his harvest. Go on your way. See, I am sending you out like lambs into the midst of wolves. Carry no purse, no bag, no sandals; and greet no one on the road. Whatever house you enter, first say, 'Peace to this house!' And if anyone is there who shares in peace, your peace will rest on that person; but if not, it will return to you. Remain in the same house, eating and drinking whatever they provide, for the labourer deserves to be paid. Do not move about from house to house. Whenever you enter a town and its people welcome you, eat what is set before you; cure the sick who are there, and say to them, 'The kingdom of God has come near to you.' "

This is the gospel of the Lord.   *Luke 10. 1-9*

Post Communion
Holy Father,
who gathered us here around the table of your Son
to share this meal with the whole household of God:
in that new world where you reveal
  the fullness of your peace,
gather people of every race and language
to share with Timothy and Titus and all your saints
in the eternal banquet of Jesus Christ our Lord.

Thomas Aquinas, Dominican Friar
28 January – Lesser Festival – Teacher of the Faith – White

Thomas Aquinas has been described as the greatest thinker and teacher of the mediæval church. Born at Rocca Secca, near Aquino, in Italy, Thomas was educated first by the Benedictines at Monte Cassino and then at the University of Naples. Against his family's wishes, he joined the mendicant Dominican Order of Preachers. His profound, theological wisdom and capacity to impart this, as well in homilies as in hymns, along with his gentleness of spirit in dealing with all, earned him the title "the angelic doctor". He died on 7 March 1274, en route to the Council of Lyons, and his feast has been celebrated on this day since 1970.

Collect
Eternal God,
who enriched your Church with the learning and holiness
 of your servant Thomas Aquinas:
give to all who seek you
a humble mind and a pure heart
that they may know your Son Jesus Christ
as the Way, the Truth and the Life;
who is alive and reigns with you,
in the unity of the Holy Spirit,
one God, now and for ever.

A reading from the Book of Wisdom.

Therefore I prayed, and understanding was given me; I called on God, and the spirit of wisdom came to me. I preferred her to sceptres and thrones, and I accounted wealth as nothing in comparison with her. Neither did I liken to her any priceless gem, because all gold is but a little sand in her sight, and silver will be accounted as clay before her. I loved her more than health and beauty, and I chose to have her rather than light, because her radiance never ceases.

All good things came to me along with her and in her hands uncounted wealth. I rejoiced in them all, because wisdom leads them; but I did not know that she was their mother. I learned without guile and I impart without grudging. I do not hide her wealth, for it is an unfailing treasure for mortals; those who get it obtain friendship with God, commended for the gifts that come from instruction. May God grant me to speak with judgement, and to have thoughts worthy of what I have received; for he is the guide even of wisdom and the corrector of the wise. For both we and our words are in his hand, as are all understanding and skill in crafts.

This is the word of the Lord.   *Wisdom 7. 7-10, 15-16*

Responsorial Psalm

**R Let the words of my mouth, O Lord,
be acceptable in your sight.**

The heavens declare the glory of God,
and the firmament shows his handiwork.
One day tells its tale to another,
and one night imparts knowledge to another. **R**

Although they have no words or language,
and their voices are not heard,
their sound has gone out into all lands,
and their message to the ends of the world. **R**

Above all, keep your servant from presumptuous sins;
let them not get dominion over me;
then shall I be whole and sound,
and innocent of a great offence. **R**   *From Psalm 19*

A reading from the First Letter of Paul to the Corinthians.

As it is written, "What no eye has seen, nor ear heard, nor the
human heart conceived, what God has prepared for those who
love him" – these things God has revealed to us through the Spirit;
for the Spirit searches everything, even the depths of God. For
what human being knows what is truly human except the human
spirit that is within? So also no one comprehends what is truly
God's except the Spirit of God. Now we have received not the
spirit of the world, but the Spirit that is from God, so that we may
understand the gifts bestowed on us by God. And we speak of
these things in words not taught by human wisdom but taught by
the Spirit, interpreting spiritual things to those who are spiritual.

 Those who are unspiritual do not receive the gifts of God's Spirit,
for they are foolishness to them, and they are unable to understand them because they are spiritually discerned. Those who are
spiritual discern all things, and they are themselves subject to no
one else's scrutiny.

 "For who has known the mind of the Lord so as to instruct him?"
But we have the mind of Christ.

This is the word of the Lord.   *1 Corinthians 2. 9-16*

Hear the gospel of our Lord Jesus Christ according to John.

Jesus said to his disciples, "I still have many things to say to you, but you cannot bear them now. When the Spirit of truth comes, he will guide you into all the truth; for he will not speak on his own, but will speak whatever he hears, and he will declare to you the things that are to come. He will glorify me, because he will take what is mine and declare it to you. All that the Father has is mine. For this reason I said that he will take what is mine and declare it to you."

This is the gospel of the Lord. *John 16. 12-15*

Post Communion
God of truth,
whose Wisdom set her table
and invited us to eat the bread and drink the wine
 of the kingdom:
help us to lay aside all foolishness
and to live and walk in the way of insight,
that we may come with your servant Thomas Aquinas
 to the eternal feast of heaven;
through Jesus Christ our Lord.

Charles Stuart, King of England
30 January – Lesser Festival – Martyr – Red

Born in 1600, the second son of James the First, Charles became heir apparent when he was twelve years old on the death of his brother. He succeeded to the throne in 1625, where he came up against the increasing power of an antagonistic Parliament. Combined with the religious puritanism which was prevalent, this made Charles staunch in his resistance of the power of either force in the land. He frequently dismissed sittings of Parliament and tried to enforce high-church Anglican practice on all, throughout both kingdoms of England and Scotland. Opposition resulted in civil war. After Charles' imprisonment and trial, he was put to death on this day in 1649. Although some see him as a victim of his own pride, his faith and willingness to suffer and die for what he believed in are not in doubt.

Collect

King of kings and Lord of lords,
whose faithful servant Charles
prayed for those who persecuted him
and died in the living hope of your eternal kingdom:
grant us by your grace so to follow his example
that we may love and bless our enemies,
through the intercession of your Son, our Lord Jesus Christ,
who is alive and reigns with you,
in the unity of the Holy Spirit,
one God, now and for ever.

A reading from the book Ecclesiasticus.

Woe to timid hearts and to slack hands, and to the sinner who walks a double path! Woe to the fainthearted who have no trust! Therefore they will have no shelter. Woe to you who have lost your nerve! What will you do when the Lord's reckoning comes? Those who fear the Lord do not disobey his words, and those who love him keep his ways. Those who fear the Lord seek to please him, and those who love him are filled with his law. Those who fear the Lord prepare their hearts, and humble themselves before him. Let us fall into the hands of the Lord, but not into the hands of mortals; for equal to his majesty is his mercy, and equal to his name are his works.

This is the word of the Lord. *Ecclesiasticus 2. 12-17*

Responsorial Psalm

**R   O Lord, give victory to the king
[and answer us when we call].**

May the Lord answer you in the day of trouble,
the name of the God of Jacob defend you;
send you help from his holy place
and strengthen you out of Zion. **R**

May God remember all your offerings
and accept your burnt sacrifice;
grant you your heart's desire
and prosper all your plans. **R**

Now I know that the Lord gives victory to his anointed;
he will answer him out of his holy heaven,
with the victorious strength of his right hand. **R**

Some put their trust in chariots and some in horses,
but we will call upon the name of the Lord our God.
They collapse and fall down,
but we will arise and stand upright. **R**   *From Psalm 20*

A reading from the First Letter of Paul to Timothy.

Fight the good fight of the faith; take hold of the eternal life, to
which you were called and for which you made the good confession in the presence of many witnesses. In the presence of God,
who gives life to all things, and of Christ Jesus, who in his testimony before Pontius Pilate made the good confession, I charge
you to keep the commandment without spot or blame until the
manifestation of our Lord Jesus Christ, which he will bring about
at the right time – he who is the blessèd and only Sovereign, the
King of kings and Lord of lords. It is he alone who has immortality and dwells in unapproachable light, whom no one has ever
seen or can see; to him be honour and eternal dominion. Amen.
This is the word of the Lord.   *1 Timothy 6. 12-16*

Hear the gospel of our Lord Jesus Christ according to Matthew.

Jesus called his disciples to him and said, "You know that the
rulers of the Gentiles lord it over them, and their great ones are
tyrants over them. It will not be so among you; but whoever wishes to be great among you must be your servant, and whoever
wishes to be first among you must be your servant; just as the Son
of Man came not to be served but to serve, and to give his life a
ransom for many."

This is the gospel of the Lord.   *Matthew 20. 25-28*

Post Communion
God our Redeemer,
whose Church was strengthened
 by the blood of your servant Charles:
so bind us, in life and death, to Christ's sacrifice
that our lives, broken and offered with his,
may carry his death and proclaim his resurrection in the world;
through Jesus Christ our Lord.

John Bosco, Priest, Founder of the Salesians
31 January – *Commemoration*
If celebrated as a Lesser Festival, Common of Pastors, page 483

Born in 1815 to a peasant family, John Bosco spent most of his life in the Turin area of Italy. He had a particular call to help young men and pioneered new educational methods, for example, in rejecting corporal punishment. His work with homeless youth received the admiration even of anticlerical politicians and his promotion of vocational training, including evening classes and industrial schools, became a pattern for others to follow. To extend the work, he founded in 1859 a religious community, the Pious Society of St Francis de Sales, usually known as the Salesians. It grew rapidly and was well-established in several countries by the time of his death on this day in 1888.

FEBRUARY

Brigid, Abbess of Kildare
1 February – Commemoration
If celebrated as a Lesser Festival, Common of Religious, page 494

Brigid (also known as Bride) was born in the latter part of the fifth century, of humble origin just five miles from Kildare. She was to become first a nun in the monastery there and then its Abbess. She is believed to have been baptised by St Patrick and the stories of her portray a woman of great compassion. She is even said to have been consecrated a bishop by Bishop Ibor, because of her resemblance to the Virgin Mary, but this may have been put abroad to support the claim of the primacy of the Abbey of Kildare. By her prayers and miracles, she is reputed to have strongly influenced the formation of the Church throughout Ireland, where she is, with St Patrick, the patron saint. She died in about the year 525.

The Presentation of Christ in the Temple (Candlemas)
2 February – Principal Feast – Gold or White

This day marks the completion of forty days since the birth of Jesus, when Mary and Joseph took the child to the Temple in Jerusalem. The requirement in Levitical law was for Mary to be 'cleansed', the completion of her purification following the birth of a male child. Until that day, she could touch no holy thing nor enter the sanctuary. Yet on seeing the holy family, Simeon praised God and acclaimed the infant as 'the light to enlighten the nations' and the prophet Anna gave thanks and proclaimed him her Redeemer. The image of Christ as the Light has led to the celebration of light countering darkness, with candles often taking a central place in the observance.

Almighty and ever-living God,
clothed in majesty,
whose beloved Son
  was this day presented in the Temple,
in substance of our flesh:
grant that we may be presented to you
with pure and clean hearts,
by your Son Jesus Christ our Lord,
who is alive and reigns with you,
in the unity of the Holy Spirit,
one God, now and for ever.

A reading from the prophecy of Malachi.

See, I am sending my messenger to prepare the way before me,
and the Lord whom you seek will suddenly come to his temple.
The messenger of the covenant in whom you delight – indeed, he
is coming, says the Lord of hosts. But who can endure the day of
his coming, and who can stand when he appears?

For he is like a refiner's fire and like fullers' soap; he will sit as a
refiner and purifier of silver, and he will purify the descendants of
Levi and refine them like gold and silver, until they present offerings to the Lord in righteousness. Then the offering of Judah and
Jerusalem will be pleasing to the Lord as in the days of old and as
in former years. Then I will draw near to you for judgement; I will
be swift to bear witness against the sorcerers, against the adulterers, against those who swear falsely, against those who oppress
the hired workers in their wages, the widow and the orphan,
against those who thrust aside the alien, and do not fear me, says
the Lord of hosts.

This is the word of the Lord.   *Malachi 3. 1-5*

Responsorial Psalm

**R The Lord whom you seek
     will suddenly come to his temple.**

Lift up your heads, O gates;
lift them high, O everlasting doors;
and the King of glory shall come in. **R**

Who is this King of glory?
"The Lord, strong and mighty,
the Lord, mighty in battle." **R**

Lift up your heads, O gates;
lift them high, O everlasting doors;
and the King of glory shall come in. **R**

Who is he, this King of glory?
"The Lord of hosts,
he is the King of glory." **R**   *From Psalm 24*

A reading from the Letter to the Hebrews.

Since, therefore, the children share flesh and blood, Jesus himself
likewise shared the same things, so that through death he might
destroy the one who has the power of death, that is, the devil, and
free those who all their lives were held in slavery by the fear of
death. For it is clear that he did not come to help angels, but the
descendants of Abraham. Therefore he had to become like his
brothers and sisters in every respect, so that he might be a merciful and faithful high priest in the service of God, to make a sacrifice of atonement for the sins of the people. Because he himself
was tested by what he suffered, he is able to help those who are
being tested.

This is the word of the Lord.   *Hebrews 2. 14-18*

Hear the gospel of our Lord Jesus Christ according to Luke.

When the time came for their purification according to the law of
Moses, Mary and Joseph brought Jesus up to Jerusalem to present
him to the Lord (as it is written in the law of the Lord, "Every firstborn male shall be designated as holy to the Lord"), and they
offered a sacrifice according to what is stated in the law of the
Lord, "a pair of turtledoves or two young pigeons."

Now there was a man in Jerusalem whose name was Simeon; this
man was righteous and devout, looking forward to the consolation of Israel, and the Holy Spirit rested on him. It had been
revealed to him by the Holy Spirit that he would not see death
before he had seen the Lord's Messiah. Guided by the Spirit,
Simeon came into the temple; and when the parents brought in

the child Jesus, to do for him what was customary under the law, Simeon took him in his arms and praised God, saying, "Master, now you are dismissing your servant in peace, according to your word; for my eyes have seen your salvation, which you have prepared in the presence of all peoples, a light for revelation to the Gentiles and for glory to your people Israel."

The child's father and mother were amazed at what was being said about him. Then Simeon blessed them and said to his mother Mary, "This child is destined for the falling and the rising of many in Israel, and to be a sign that will be opposed so that the inner thoughts of many will be revealed – and a sword will pierce your own soul too."

There was also a prophet, Anna the daughter of Phanuel, of the tribe of Asher. She was of a great age, having lived with her husband seven years after her marriage, then as a widow to the age of eighty-four. She never left the temple but worshipped there with fasting and prayer night and day. At that moment she came, and began to praise God and to speak about the child to all who were looking for the redemption of Jerusalem.

When they had finished everything required by the law of the Lord, they returned to Galilee, to their own town of Nazareth. The child grew and became strong, filled with wisdom; and the favour of God was upon him.

This is the gospel of the Lord.   *Luke 2. 22-40*

Post Communion
Lord, you fulfilled the hope of Simeon and Anna,
who lived to welcome the Messiah:
may we, who have received these gifts beyond words,
prepare to meet Christ Jesus when he comes
 to bring us to eternal life;
for he is alive and reigns, now and for ever.

Anskar, Apostle of the North
3 February – Lesser Festival – Missionary – White

A native of Picardy, Anskar was a monk of Corbie near Amiens who, after the conversion of the King of Denmark to Christianity, went to Schleswig and attempted to start a Christian school there. He was expelled by the locals but went on to Sweden, where he is reputed to have built the first Christian church. In 832 he was consecrated Bishop of Hamburg and sixteen years later became Archbishop of Bremen. He returned to Denmark to convert the King of Jutland. He preached widely throughout Scandinavia and was much-loved for his work with the poor and in mitigating the slave trade. He is the patron saint of Denmark. He died in the year 865.

Collect
God of grace and might,
who sent your servant Anskar
to spread the gospel to the Nordic peoples:
raise up, we pray, in our generation
  messengers of your good news
  and heralds of your kingdom
that the world may come to know
  the immeasurable riches of our Saviour Jesus Christ,
who is alive and reigns with you,
in the unity of the Holy Spirit,
one God, now and for ever.

A reading from the prophecy of Isaiah.

How beautiful upon the mountains are the feet of the messenger who announces peace, who brings good news, who announces salvation, who says to Zion, "Your God reigns." Listen! Your sentinels lift up their voices, together they sing for joy; for in plain sight they see the return of the Lord to Zion. Break forth together into singing, you ruins of Jerusalem; for the Lord has comforted his people, he has redeemed Jerusalem. The Lord has bared his holy arm before the eyes of all the nations; and all the ends of the earth shall see the salvation of our God.

This is the word of the Lord.   *Isaiah 52. 7-10*

Responsorial Psalm

**R Break forth together into singing God's praises,
[for the Lord has comforted his people].**

You are to be praised, O God, in Zion;
to you shall vows be performed in Jerusalem.
To you that hear prayer shall all flesh come,
because of their transgressions. **R**

Happy are they whom you choose
and draw to your courts to dwell there!
they will be satisfied by the beauty of your house,
by the holiness of your temple. **R**

Awesome things will you show us in your righteousness,
O God of our salvation,
O Hope of all the ends of the earth
and of the seas that are far away. **R**   *From Psalm 65*

A reading from the Letter of Paul to the Romans.

The scripture says, "No one who believes in him will be put to
shame." For there is no distinction between Jew and Greek; the
same Lord is Lord of all and is generous to all who call on him.
For, "everyone who calls on the name of the Lord shall be saved."
But how are they to call on one in whom they have not believed?
And how are they to believe in one of whom they have never
heard? And how are they to hear without someone to proclaim
him? And how are they to proclaim him unless they are sent? As
it is written, "How beautiful are the feet of those who bring good
news!"

This is the word of the Lord.   *Romans 10. 11-15*

Hear the gospel of our Lord Jesus Christ according to Mark.

Jesus called the twelve and began to send them out two by two,
and gave them authority over the unclean spirits. He ordered
them to take nothing for their journey except a staff; no bread, no
bag, no money in their belts; but to wear sandals and not to put on
two tunics. He said to them, "Wherever you enter a house, stay
there until you leave the place. If any place will not welcome you

and they refuse to hear you, as you leave, shake off the dust that is on your feet as a testimony against them." So they went out and proclaimed that all should repent. They cast out many demons, and anointed with oil many who were sick and cured them.

This is the gospel of the Lord. *Mark 6. 7-13*

Post Communion
Holy Father,
who gathered us here around the table of your Son
to share this meal with the whole household of God:
in that new world where you reveal
  the fullness of your peace,
gather people of every race and language
to share with your servant Anskar and all your saints
in the eternal banquet of Jesus Christ our Lord.

Gilbert of Sempringham
4 February – Commemoration
If celebrated as a Lesser Festival, Common of Religious, page 494

Born in 1083 in Sempringham, the son of the squire, Gilbert became the parish priest in 1131. He encouraged the vocation of seven women of the town and formed them into a company of lay sisters. A group of lay brothers also came into being and they all kept the Benedictine Rule. Gilbert was unsuccessful in his bid to obtain pastoral guidance from Cîteaux for the incipient communities and they came under the ambit of Augustinian canons, Gilbert himself becoming the Master. At Gilbert's death in 1189, aged 106, there were nine double monasteries in England and four of male canons only. It was the only purely English monastic foundation before the Dissolution of the Monasteries in the sixteenth century.

The Martyrs of Japan
6 February – Commemoration
If celebrated as a Lesser Festival, Common of Martyrs, page 464

Almost fifty years after Francis Xavier had arrived in Japan as its first Christian apostle, the presence of several thousand baptised Christians in the land became a subject of suspicion to the ruler Hideyoshi, who soon began a period of persecution. Twenty-six men and women, Religious and lay, were first mutilated then crucified near Nagasaki in 1597, the most famous of whom was Paul Miki. After their martyrdom, their blooded- clothes were kept and held in reverence by their fellow Christians. The period of persecution continued for another thirty-five years, many new witness-martyrs being added to their number.

Scholastica, Abbess of Plombariola
10 February – *Commemoration*
If celebrated as a Lesser Festival, Common of Religious, page 494

Scholastica is a more shadowy figure than her famous brother, St Benedict. She too was born at Nursia, central Italy, around the year 480. At an early age she chose to consecrate herself to God, but probably continued to live at home. Only after Benedict moved to Monte Cassino did she settle at Plombariola nearby, joining or maybe founding a nunnery under his direction. As abbess she sought to follow his Rule, and met him each year at a house near his monastery where they would praise God together and discuss spiritual matters. She died in about the year 543. Benedict had a vision of her soul rising up to heaven and, collecting her body, he had her buried in the tomb prepared for himself. Scholastica soon became a figure for veneration by all nuns who followed Benedict's Rule.

Cyril & Methodius
14 February – *Lesser Festival* – *Missionaries* – *White*

Cyril and his older brother Methodius were born in Thessalonica, both developing in their youth the ability to speak several languages, including Slavonic, a language not yet written down, at least in an alphabet understood by others. Cyril created the Slavonic alphabet and set about translating the Scriptures and other liturgical texts into the language. They established the church in Moravia, but in so doing entered into the controversy between indigenous and centralised religious practices and worship. Cyril died on this day in the year 869, whilst the brothers were in Rome, there to obtain papal approval for their evangelistic work. Methodius returned to Moravia as archbishop, where he completed the translation of the Bible and continued the missionary work. He died in the year 885. Today they are revered in both Christian East and West and, as such, are seen as patron saints of ecumenism between these two great branches of Christendom.

Collect
Lord of all,
who gave to your servants Cyril and Methodius
the gift of tongues to proclaim the gospel to the Slavs:
make your whole Church one as you are one
that all Christians may honour one another,
and east and west acknowledge
  one Lord, one faith, one baptism,
and you, the God and Father of all;
through Jesus Christ your Son our Lord,
who is alive and reigns with you,
in the unity of the Holy Spirit,
one God, now and for ever.

A reading from the prophecy of Isaiah.

Listen to me, O coastlands, pay attention, you peoples from far away! The Lord called me before I was born, while I was in my mother's womb he named me. He made my mouth like a sharp sword, in the shadow of his hand he hid me; he made me a polished arrow, in his quiver he hid me away. And he said to me, "You are my servant, Israel, in whom I will be glorified." But I said, "I have laboured in vain, I have spent my strength for nothing and vanity; yet surely my cause is with the Lord, and my reward with my God." And now the Lord says, who formed me in the womb to be his servant, to bring Jacob back to him, and that Israel might be gathered to him, for I am honoured in the sight of the Lord, and my God has become my strength – he says, "It is too light a thing that you should be my servant to raise up the tribes

of Jacob and to restore the survivors of Israel; I will give you as a
light to the nations, that my salvation may reach to the end of the
earth."

This is the word of the Lord. *Isaiah 49. 1-6*

Responsorial Psalm

R Lift up your heads, O gates,
    and the King of glory shall come in.

The earth is the Lord's and all that is in it,
the world and all who dwell therein.
For it is he who founded it upon the seas
and made it firm upon the rivers of the deep. **R**

"Who can ascend the hill of the Lord?
and who can stand in his holy place?"
"Those who have clean hands and a pure heart,
who have not pledged themselves to falsehood,
nor sworn by what is a fraud. **R**

"They shall receive a blessing from the Lord
and a just reward from the God of their salvation."
Such is the generation of those who seek him,
of those who seek your face, O God of Jacob. **R** *Psalm 24*

A reading from the Letter of Paul to the Romans.

The scripture says, "No one who believes in the Lord will be put
to shame." For there is no distinction between Jew and Greek; the
same Lord is Lord of all and is generous to all who call on him.
For, "Everyone who calls on the name of the Lord shall be saved."
But how are they to call on one in whom they have not believed?
And how are they to believe in one of whom they have never
heard? And how are they to hear without someone to proclaim
him? And how are they to proclaim him unless they are sent? As
it is written, "How beautiful are the feet of those who bring good
news!"

This is the word of the Lord. *Romans 10. 11-15*

Hear the gospel of our Lord Jesus Christ according to Luke.

Jesus called the twelve together and gave them power and authority over all demons and to cure diseases, and he sent them out to proclaim the kingdom of God and to heal. He said to them, "Take nothing for your journey, no staff, nor bag, nor bread, nor money – not even an extra tunic. Whatever house you enter, stay there, and leave from there. Wherever they do not welcome you, as you are leaving that town shake the dust off your feet as a testimony against them." They departed and went through the villages, bringing the good news and curing diseases everywhere.

This is the gospel of the Lord.   *Luke 9. 1-6*

Post Communion
Holy Father,
who gathered us here around the table of your Son
to share this meal with the whole household of God:
in that new world where you reveal
  the fullness of your peace,
gather people of every race and language
to share with Cyril and Methodius and all your saints
in the eternal banquet of Jesus Christ our Lord.

Valentine, Martyr at Rome, c.269
14 February – Commemoration
If celebrated as a Lesser Festival, Common of Martyrs, page 464

Valentine was a priest or a bishop of Terni who was martyred at Rome under the Emperor Claudius. The connection of this celebration with lovers seems to be either as the traditional day in mediæval belief when birds mated, or more likely as being linked with the pagan Lupercalia festival in Rome, which occurred on the Ides of February. For Christians, the day marks an acknowledgement of an all-loving God who blesses those who love one another, as Jesus implored his own disciples so to do.

Sigfrid, Bishop, Apostle of Sweden
15 February – Commemoration
If celebrated as a Lesser Festival, Common of Missionaries, page 503

Sigfrid was most probably an Englishman sent by King Ethelred to assist in the evangelisation of Norway and Sweden in the eleventh century. He took with him two fellow missionaries, all three of whom were eventually consecrated bishops. Sigfrid was made Bishop of Vaxjo (pronounced Vek-sha) in Sweden, though his missionary journeys also took him into Denmark. He died in Vaxjo in 1045, much revered throughout Scandinavia.

Thomas Bray, Priest
15 February – Commemoration
If celebrated as a Lesser Festival, Common of Pastors, page 483

Born at Marton in Shropshire in 1656, Thomas Bray was educated at Oxford and subsequently ordained. He was chosen by the Bishop of London to assist with the work of organising the church in Maryland in the USA but, during an extended delay in his setting out, he managed to organise a system of free libraries, initially for use in America but later instituted in England. This led to his founding the Society for the Promotion of Christian Knowledge (SPCK) in 1698. On his return to Europe in 1699, he also founded The Society for the Propagation of the Gospel (SPG). He died on this day in the year 1730.

Janani Luwum, Archbishop of Uganda
17 February – Lesser Festival – Martyr – Red

Janani Luwum was born in 1922 at Acholi in Uganda. His childhood and youth were spent as a goatherd but he quickly showed an ability to learn and absorb knowledge when given the opportunity. Soon after he became a teacher, he was converted to Christianity and was eventually ordained in 1956, becoming Bishop of Northern Uganda in 1969 and Archbishop of Uganda in 1974. Idi Amin had come to power in Uganda in 1971 as the result of a military coup and his undemocratic and harsh rule was the subject of much criticism by the Church and others. After receiving a letter from the bishops protesting at the virtual institution of state murder, Janani and two of Amin's own government ministers were stated as having been found dead following a car accident. It emerged quickly that they had in fact died on the implicit instructions of the President. Janani's enthusiasm for the good news of Jesus, combined with his willingness to sacrifice even his own life for what he believed in, led him to his martyrdom on this day in 1977.

Collect
God of truth,
whose servant Janani Luwum walked in the light,
and in his death defied the powers of darkness:
free us from fear of those who kill the body,
that we too may walk as children of light,
through him who overcame darkness
  by the power of the cross,
Jesus Christ your Son our Lord,
who is alive and reigns with you,
in the unity of the Holy Spirit,
one God, now and for ever.

A reading from the book Ecclesiasticus.

Watch for the opportune time, and beware of evil, and do not be ashamed to be yourself. For there is a shame that leads to sin, and there is a shame that is glory and favour. Do not show partiality, to your own harm, or deference, to your downfall. Do not refrain from speaking at the proper moment, and do not hide your wisdom. For wisdom becomes known through speech, and education through the words of the tongue. Never speak against the truth, but be ashamed of your ignorance. Do not be ashamed to confess your sins, and do not try to stop the current of a river. Do not subject yourself to a fool, or show partiality to a ruler. Fight to the death for truth, and the Lord God will fight for you.

This is the word of the Lord.   *Ecclesiasticus 4. 20-28*

Responsorial Psalm

**R Let your loving-kindness come to me, O Lord,
     [and your salvation, according to your promise].**

Do not take the word of truth out of my mouth,
for my hope is in your judgements.
I shall continue to keep your law;
I shall keep it for ever and ever. **R**

I will walk at liberty,
because I study your commandments.
I will tell of your decrees before kings
and will not be ashamed. **R**

I delight in your commandments,
which I have always loved.
I will lift up my hands to your commandments,
and I will meditate on your statutes. **R**   *From Psalm 119*

A reading from the Second Letter of Paul to Timothy.

In the presence of God and of Christ Jesus, who is to judge the living and the dead, and in view of his appearing and his kingdom, I solemnly urge you: proclaim the message; be persistent whether the time is favourable or unfavourable; convince, rebuke, and encourage, with the utmost patience in teaching. For the time is coming when people will not put up with sound doctrine, but having itching ears, they will accumulate for themselves teachers to suit their own desires, and will turn away from listening to the truth and wander away to myths. As for you, always be sober, endure suffering, do the work of an evangelist, carry out your ministry fully.

As for me, I am already being poured out as a libation, and the time of my departure has come. I have fought the good fight, I have finished the race, I have kept the faith. From now on there is reserved for me the crown of righteousness, which the Lord, the righteous judge, will give me on that day, and not only to me but also to all who have longed for his appearing.

This is the word of the Lord.   *2 Timothy 4. 1-8*

Hear the gospel of our Lord Jesus Christ according to John.

Jesus said: "Very truly, I tell you, unless a grain of wheat falls into the earth and dies, it remains just a single grain; but if it dies, it bears much fruit. Those who love their life lose it, and those who hate their life in this world will keep it for eternal life. Whoever serves me must follow me, and where I am, there will my servant be also. Whoever serves me, the Father will honour.

"Now my soul is troubled. And what should I say – 'Father, save me from this hour'? No, it is for this reason that I have come to this hour. Father, glorify your name." Then a voice came from heaven, "I have glorified it, and I will glorify it again." The crowd standing there heard it and said that it was thunder. Others said, "An angel has spoken to him." Jesus answered, "This voice has come for your sake, not for mine. Now is the judgement of this world; now the ruler of this world will be driven out. And I, when I am lifted up from the earth, will draw all people to myself."

This is the gospel of the Lord. *John 12. 24-32*

Post Communion
God our Redeemer,
whose Church was strengthened
  by the blood of your martyr Janani Luwum:
so bind us, in life and death, to Christ's sacrifice
that our lives, broken and offered with his,
may carry his death and proclaim his resurrection in the world;
through Jesus Christ our Lord.

Polycarp, Bishop of Smyrna
23 February – Lesser Festival – Martyr – Red

Honoured as one of the first Christian martyrs, Polycarp had been Bishop of Smyrna on the Adriatic coast of Asia Minor for over forty years when the persecution of Christians began. He was arrested and given the option to renounce his faith and so save his life. His response was: "I have been Christ's servant for eighty-six years and he has done me no harm. Can I now blaspheme my King and my Saviour?" He was immediately burnt at the stake. His remains were gathered together and buried outside the city; thus began the practice of celebrating the eucharist over his burial place on the anniversary of his death, a practice which also grew over the martyrs' tombs in the Roman catacombs. Polycarp died in the year 155.

Collect
Almighty God,
who gave to your servant Polycarp
boldness to confess the name of our Saviour Jesus Christ
  before the rulers of this world
and courage to die for his faith:
grant that we also may be ready
to give an answer for the faith that is in us
and to suffer gladly for the sake of our Lord Jesus Christ,
who is alive and reigns with you,
in the unity of the Holy Spirit,
one God, now and for ever.

A reading from the Wisdom of Solomon.

The righteous live forever, and their reward is with the Lord; the Most High takes care of them. Therefore they will receive a glorious crown and a beautiful diadem from the hand of the Lord, because with his right hand he will cover them, and with his arm he will shield them. The Lord will take his zeal as his whole armour, and will arm all creation to repel his enemies; he will put on righteousness as a breastplate, and wear impartial justice as a helmet; he will take holiness as an invincible shield, and sharpen stern wrath for a sword, and creation will join with him to fight against his frenzied foes.

This is the word of the Lord.   *Wisdom 5. 15-20*

Responsorial Psalm

**R I will bless the Lord at all times;
   [his praise shall ever be in my mouth].**

I will glory in the Lord;
let the humble hear and rejoice.
Proclaim with me the greatness of the Lord;
let us exalt his name together. **R**

I sought the Lord and he answered me
and delivered me out of all my terror.
Look upon him and be radiant,
and let not your faces be ashamed. **R**

I called in my affliction and the Lord heard me
and saved me from all my troubles.
The angel of the Lord encompasses those who fear him,
and he will deliver them. **R**

Taste and see that the Lord is good;
happy are they who trust in him!
Fear the Lord, you that are his saints,
for those who fear him lack nothing. **R**   *From Psalm 34*

A reading from the Revelation to John.

One like the Son of Man said to me, "To the angel of the church in
Smyrna write: These are the words of the first and the last, who
was dead and came to life: 'I know your affliction and your poverty, even though you are rich. I know the slander on the part of
those who say that they are Jews and are not, but are a synagogue
of Satan. Do not fear what you are about to suffer. Beware, the
devil is about to throw some of you into prison so that you may be
tested, and for ten days you will have affliction. Be faithful until
death, and I will give you the crown of life. Let anyone who has
an ear listen to what the Spirit is saying to the churches. Whoever
conquers will not be harmed by the second death.'"

This is the word of the Lord.   *Revelation 2. 8-11*

Hear the gospel of our Lord Jesus Christ according to John.

Jesus said to his disciples, "I am the true vine, and my Father is the
vinegrower. He removes every branch in me that bears no fruit.
Every branch that bears fruit he prunes to make it bear more fruit.
You have already been cleansed by the word that I have spoken to
you. Abide in me as I abide in you. Just as the branch cannot bear
fruit by itself unless it abides in the vine, neither can you unless
you abide in me. I am the vine, you are the branches. Those who
abide in me and I in them bear much fruit, because apart from me
you can do nothing. Whoever does not abide in me is thrown

away like a branch and withers; such branches are gathered, thrown into the fire, and burned. If you abide in me, and my words abide in you, ask for whatever you wish, and it will be done for you. My Father is glorified by this, that you bear much fruit and become my disciples."

This is the gospel of the Lord.   *John 15. 1-8*

Post Communion
God our Redeemer,
whose Church was strengthened
  by the blood of your martyr Polycarp:
so bind us, in life and death, to Christ's sacrifice
that our lives, broken and offered with his,
may carry his death and proclaim his resurrection in the world;
through Jesus Christ our Lord.

George Herbert, Priest
27 February – Lesser Festival – Pastor – White

Born in 1593 into the aristocratic Pembroke family, George Herbert went up to Cambridge in 1614, eventually becoming a fellow of Trinity College. At the age of twenty-five, he became Public Orator in the University and then a Member of Parliament, apparently destined for a life at court. To everyone's surprise, he decided to be ordained and, after spending a time with his friend Nicholas Ferrar at Little Gidding, he was made deacon in 1626. He married in 1629, was priested in 1630 and given the care of souls of the parish of Bemerton, near Salisbury, where he spent the rest of his short life. He wrote prolifically, his hymns still being popular throughout the English-speaking world. His treatise, *The Country Parson,* on the priestly life, and his poetry, especially *The Temple,* earned Herbert a leading place in English literature. He never neglected the care of the souls of Bemerton, however, and encouraged attendance at the weekday recitation of the daily office, calling to mind the words of his hymn, 'Seven whole days, not one in seven, I will praise thee'. He died on this day in 1633.

King of glory, King of peace,
who called your servant George Herbert
from the pursuit of worldly honours
to be a priest in the temple of his God and King:
grant us also the grace to offer ourselves
with singleness of heart in humble obedience to your service;
through Jesus Christ your Son our Lord,
who is alive and reigns with you,
in the unity of the Holy Spirit,
one God, now and for ever.

A reading from the prophecy of Malachi.

The Lord said, "My covenant with Levi was a covenant of life and
well-being, which I gave him; this called for reverence, and he
revered me and stood in awe of my name. True instruction was in
his mouth, and no wrong was found on his lips. He walked with
me in integrity and uprightness, and he turned many from iniquity. For the lips of a priest should guard knowledge, and people
should seek instruction from his mouth, for he is the messenger of
the Lord of hosts."

This is the word of the Lord. *Malachi 2. 5-7*

Responsorial Psalm

R The Lord our God the Almighty reigns.
[Let us rejoice and exult and give him the glory].

Happy are they who have not walked in the counsel of the wicked.
Their delight is in the law of the Lord,
and they meditate on his law day and night. **R**

They are like trees planted by streams of water,
bearing fruit in due season,
with leaves that do not wither;
everything they do shall prosper. **R** *From Psalm 1*

A reading from the Revelation to John.

From the throne came a voice saying, "Praise our God, all you his
servants, and all who fear him, small and great." Then I heard

what seemed to be the voice of a great multitude, like the sound of many waters and like the sound of mighty thunderpeals, crying out, "Alleluia! For the Lord our God the Almighty reigns. Let us rejoice and exult and give him the glory, for the marriage of the Lamb has come, and his bride has made herself ready; to her it has been granted to be clothed with fine linen, bright and pure" – for the fine linen is the righteous deeds of the saints.

And the angel said to me, "Write this: Blessèd are those who are invited to the marriage supper of the Lamb." And he said to me, "These are true words of God."

This is the word of the Lord.   *Revelation 19. 5-9*

Hear the gospel of our Lord Jesus Christ according to Matthew.

At that time Jesus said, "I thank you, Father, Lord of heaven and earth, because you have hidden these things from the wise and the intelligent and have revealed them to infants; yes, Father, for such was your gracious will. All things have been handed over to me by my Father; and no one knows the Son except the Father, and no one knows the Father except the Son and anyone to whom the Son chooses to reveal him.

"Come to me, all you that are weary and are carrying heavy burdens, and I will give you rest. Take my yoke upon you, and learn from me; for I am gentle and humble in heart, and you will find rest for your souls. For my yoke is easy, and my burden is light."

This is the gospel of the Lord.   *Matthew 11. 25-30*

Post Communion
God, shepherd of your people,
whose servant George Herbert
  revealed the loving service of Christ
  in his ministry as a pastor of your people:
by this eucharist in which we share
awaken within us the love of Christ
and keep us faithful to our Christian calling;
through him who laid down his life for us,
but is alive and reigns with you,
now and for ever.

MARCH

David, Patron Saint of Wales
1 March – Lesser Festival – Bishop – White

David, or Dewi, was a monk and a bishop in the sixth century. He was reputed to be an exemplar of the ascetic, spiritual life but was also highly regarded for his kindness and compassion to others, particularly the poor and the sick. He is believed to have founded the monastery at Menevia, now St David's, and also at least a dozen other monasteries. He is said to have based his Rule for his monasteries on that of the Egyptian desert monks, with a strong emphasis on hard work, abstinence from alcohol and a refraining from unnecessary speech. He died in about the year 601 and has been regarded as the patron saint of Wales since at least the twelfth century.

Collect
Almighty God,
who called your servant David
  to be a faithful and wise steward of your mysteries
  for the people of Wales:
in your mercy, grant that,
  following his purity of life and zeal for the gospel of Christ,
we may with him receive the crown of everlasting life;
through Jesus Christ your Son our Lord,
who is alive and reigns with you,
in the unity of the Holy Spirit,
one God, now and for ever.

A reading from the book Ecclesiasticus.

Whoever fears the Lord will do this, and whoever holds to the law will obtain wisdom. She will come to meet him like a mother, and like a young bride she will welcome him. She will feed him with the bread of learning, and give him the water of wisdom to drink. He will lean on her and not fall, and he will rely on her and not be put to shame. She will exalt him above his neighbours, and will open his mouth in the midst of the assembly. He will find gladness and a crown of rejoicing, and will inherit an everlasting name.

This is the word of the Lord. *Ecclesiasticus 15. 1-6*

Responsorial Psalm

**R Before I formed you in the womb, I knew you, says the Lord;
[before you were born, I consecrated you].**

Protect me, O God, for I take refuge in you;
I have said to the Lord, "You are my Lord, my good above all other."
All my delight is upon the godly that are in the land,
upon those who are noble among the people. **R**

O Lord, you are my portion and my cup;
it is you who uphold my lot.
My boundaries enclose a pleasant land;
indeed, I have a goodly heritage. **R**

I will bless the Lord who gives me counsel;
my heart teaches me, night after night.
I have set the Lord always before me;
because he is at my right hand I shall not fall. **R**   *From Psalm 16*

A reading from the First Letter of Paul to the Thessalonians.

Though we had already suffered and been shamefully mistreated
at Philippi, as you know, we had courage in our God to declare to
you the gospel of God in spite of great opposition. For our appeal
does not spring from deceit or impure motives or trickery, but just
as we have been approved by God to be entrusted with the message of the gospel, even so we speak, not to please mortals, but to
please God who tests our hearts. As you know and as God is our
witness, we never came with words of flattery or with a pretext for
greed; nor did we seek praise from mortals, whether from you or
from others, though we might have made demands as apostles of
Christ. But we were gentle among you, like a nurse tenderly caring for her own children. So deeply do we care for you that we are
determined to share with you not only the gospel of God but also
our own selves, because you have become very dear to us.

You remember our labour and toil, brothers and sisters; we
worked night and day, so that we might not burden any of you
while we proclaimed to you the gospel of God. You are witnesses,

and God also, how pure, upright, and blameless our conduct was toward you believers. As you know, we dealt with each one of you like a father with his children, urging and encouraging you and pleading that you lead a life worthy of God, who calls you into his own kingdom and glory.

This is the word of the Lord.   *1 Thessalonians 2. 2-12*

Hear the gospel of our Lord Jesus Christ according to Matthew.

Then Jesus told his disciples, "If any want to become my followers, let them deny themselves and take up their cross and follow me. For those who want to save their life will lose it, and those who lose their life for my sake will find it. For what will it profit them if they gain the whole world but forfeit their life? Or what will they give in return for their life?

"For the Son of Man is to come with his angels in the glory of his Father, and then he will repay everyone for what has been done."

This is the gospel of the Lord.   *Matthew 16. 24-27*

Post Communion
God, shepherd of your people,
whose servant David revealed the loving service of Christ
 in his ministry as a pastor of your people:
by this eucharist in which we share
awaken within us the love of Christ
and keep us faithful to our Christian calling;
through him who laid down his life for us,
but is alive and reigns with you, now and for ever.

Chad, Bishop of Lichfield
2 March – Lesser Festival – Bishop – White

Chad was born in Northumbria, the youngest of four sons, all of whom became both priests and monks. They entered the monastery on the isle of Lindisfarne and were taught by St Aidan. Chad's brother Cedd had founded the abbey at Lastingham and, on his brother's death, Chad was elected abbot. During the confusion in ecclesiastical discipline between the Celtic-oriented,

Anglo-Saxon hierarchy and the pressure from Rome for conformity, Chad became Bishop of York for a time. He graciously stepped back with the arrival in Britain of Theodore, who doubted the validity of indigenous consecrations. This was eventually rectified and Chad became Bishop of Mercia, a huge diocese the centre of which he moved from Repton to Lichfield. Chad travelled extensively and became much loved for his wisdom and gentleness in otherwise difficult situations. The plague was prevalent at this time and Chad died on this day in the year 672.

Collect

Almighty God,
from the first fruits of the English nation
  who turned to Christ,
you called your servant Chad
to be an evangelist and bishop of his own people:
give us grace so to follow his peaceable nature,
  humble spirit and prayerful life,
that we may truly commend to others
the faith which we ourselves profess;
through Jesus Christ your Son our Lord,
who is alive and reigns with you,
in the unity of the Holy Spirit,
one God, now and for ever.

A reading from the book Ecclesiasticus.

My child, perform your tasks with humility; then you will be loved by those whom God accepts. The greater you are, the more you must humble yourself; so you will find favour in the sight of the Lord. For great is the might of the Lord; but by the humble he is glorified. Neither seek what is too difficult for you, nor investigate what is beyond your power. Reflect upon what you have been commanded, for what is hidden is not your concern. Do not meddle in matters that are beyond you, for more than you can understand has been shown you. For their conceit has led many astray, and wrong opinion has impaired their judgement.

This is the word of the Lord.   *Ecclesiasticus 3. 17-24*

Responsorial Psalm

**R Great is the might of the Lord;
    [by the humble he is glorified].**

How dear to me is your dwelling,
O Lord of hosts!
My soul has a desire and longing for the courts of the Lord;
my heart and my flesh rejoice in the living God. **R**

The sparrow has found her a house
and the swallow a nest where she may lay her young;
by the side of your altars, O Lord of hosts,
my King and my God. **R**

Happy are they who dwell in your house;
they will always be praising you.
Happy are the people whose strength is in you,
whose hearts are set on the pilgrims' way. **R**

Those who go through the desolate valley
will find it a place of springs,
for the early rains have covered it with pools of water.
They will climb from height to height
and the God of gods will reveal himself in Zion. **R**   *Psalm 84*

A reading from the First Letter of Paul to Timothy.

Pursue righteousness, godliness, faith, love, endurance, gentleness; fight the good fight of the faith; take hold of the eternal life, to which you were called and for which you made the good confession in the presence of many witnesses.

In the presence of God, who gives life to all things, and of Christ Jesus, who in his testimony before Pontius Pilate made the good confession, I charge you to keep the commandment without spot or blame until the manifestation of our Lord Jesus Christ, which he will bring about at the right time – he who is the blessèd and only Sovereign, the King of kings and Lord of lords. It is he alone who has immortality and dwells in unapproachable light, whom no one has ever seen or can see; to him be honour and eternal dominion. Amen.

This is the word of the Lord.   *1 Timothy 6. 11b-16*

Hear the gospel of our Lord Jesus Christ according to Luke.

When Jesus noticed how the guests chose the places of honour, he told them a parable. "When you are invited by someone to a wedding banquet, do not sit down at the place of honour, in case someone more distinguished than you has been invited by your host; and the host who invited both of you may come and say to you, 'Give this person your place,' and then in disgrace you would start to take the lowest place. But when you are invited, go and sit down at the lowest place, so that when your host comes, he may say to you, 'Friend, move up higher'; then you will be honoured in the presence of all who sit at the table with you. For all who exalt themselves will be humbled, and those who humble themselves will be exalted."

This is the gospel of the Lord. *Luke 14. 7-11*

Post Communion
Holy Father,
who gathered us here around the table of your Son
to share this meal with the whole household of God:
in that new world where you reveal
  the fullness of your peace,
gather people of every race and language
to share with your servant Chad and all your saints
in the eternal banquet of Jesus Christ our Lord.

Perpetua, Felicity & their Companions
7 March – Lesser Festival – Martyrs – Red

The moving, contemporary account of these early third-century, African martyrs proved to be of great significance in the life of the early Church. Vibia Perpetua was a young, married noblewoman of Carthage and Felicity was her personal slave. Saturas was possibly a priest and there were two other men, Saturninus and Revocatus, the latter also a slave. Felicity was pregnant. It seems most of them were catechumens when arrested and only baptised later in prison. They were condemned as Christians by the Roman authorities and dispatched to the public arena, there to be mauled by wild animals. They all survived and were then taken to be executed by the sword. Before this, they all exchanged the Kiss of Peace and affirmed their faith in Christ, the Son of God. The contemporary account was much circulated secretly throughout the Christian congregations and proved both to give renown to their courage and to give encouragement to their fellow Christians in the face of adversity. They were martyred for their faith on this day in the year 203.

Collect
Holy God,
who gave great courage to Perpetua, Felicity
    and their companions:
grant that we may be worthy to climb the ladder of sacrifice
and be received into the garden of peace;
through Jesus Christ your Son our Lord,
who is alive and reigns with you,
in the unity of the Holy Spirit,
one God, now and for ever.

A reading from the Song of Songs.

Set me as a seal upon your heart, as a seal upon your arm; for love is strong as death, passion fierce as the grave. Its flashes are flashes of fire, a raging flame. Many waters cannot quench love, neither can the floods drown it. If one offered for love all the wealth of his house, it would be utterly scorned.

This is the word of the Lord.   *Song of Songs 8. 6-7*

Responsorial Psalm
**R   Many waters cannot quench God's love,
      [neither can the floods drown it].**

Save me, O God, by your name;
in your might, defend my cause.
Hear my prayer, O God;
give ear to the words of my mouth. **R**

For the arrogant have risen up against me,
and the ruthless have sought my life,
those who have no regard for God. **R**

Behold, God is my helper;
it is the Lord who sustains my life.
I will offer you a freewill sacrifice
and praise your name, O Lord, for it is good. **R**   *Psalm 54*

A reading from the Revelation to John.

Then I heard a loud voice in heaven, proclaiming, "Now have
come the salvation and the power and the kingdom of our God
and the authority of his Messiah, for the accuser of our comrades
has been thrown down, who accuses them day and night before
our God. But they have conquered him by the blood of the Lamb
and by the word of their testimony, for they did not cling to life
even in the face of death. Rejoice then, you heavens and those
who dwell therein!"

This is the word of the Lord.   *Revelation 12. 10-12a*

Hear the gospel of our Lord Jesus Christ according to Matthew.

Jesus said to his disciples, "They will hand you over to be tortured
and will put you to death, and you will be hated by all nations
because of my name. Then many will fall away, and they will
betray one another and hate one another. And many false
prophets will arise and lead many astray. And because of the
increase of lawlessness, the love of many will grow cold. But the
one who endures to the end will be saved.

This is the gospel of the Lord.   *Matthew 24. 9-13*

Post Communion
God,
who gave us this holy meal
in which we have celebrated the glory of the cross
and the victory of your martyrs Perpetua and Felicity:
by our communion with Christ
in his saving death and resurrection,
give us with all your saints the courage to conquer evil
and so to share the fruit of the tree of life;
through Jesus Christ our Lord.

Edward King, Bishop of Lincoln
8 March – Lesser Festival – Bishop – White

Born in London in 1829, Edward King, both as a priest and then as a bishop, was revered for the holiness of his life and the wisdom of his counsel. He was chaplain, then principal, of Cuddesdon Theological College, followed by a dozen years as a professor of theology in Oxford, during which time he exercised a great influence on a generation of ordinands. In 1885, he was consecrated bishop of the diocese of Lincoln, a position he held until his death. His advocacy of Catholic principles in ritual as well as theology involved him in controversy, but his significant gift to the Church was his example as a pastoral and caring bishop to both clergy and laity.

Collect
God of peace,
who gave such grace to your servant Edward King
that whomever he met he drew to Christ:
fill us, we pray, with tender sympathy and joyful faith,
that we also may win others
  to know the love that passes knowledge;
through him who is the shepherd and guardian of our souls,
Jesus Christ your Son our Lord,
who is alive and reigns with you,
in the unity of the Holy Spirit,
one God, now and for ever.

A reading from the prophecy of Ezekiel.

Thus says the Lord God: I myself will search for my sheep, and will seek them out. As shepherds seek out their flocks when they are among their scattered sheep, so I will seek out my sheep. I will rescue them from all the places to which they have been scattered on a day of clouds and thick darkness. I will bring them out from the peoples and gather them from the countries, and will bring them into their own land; and I will feed them on the mountains of Israel, by the watercourses, and in all the inhabited parts of the land. I will feed them with good pasture, and the mountain heights of Israel shall be their pasture; there they shall lie down in good grazing land, and they shall feed on rich pasture on the mountains of Israel.

I myself will be the shepherd of my sheep, and I will make them lie down, says the Lord God. I will seek the lost, and I will bring back the strayed, and I will bind up the injured, and I will strengthen the weak, but the fat and the strong I will destroy. I will feed them with justice.

This is the word of the Lord. *Ezekiel 34. 11-16*

Responsorial Psalm

**R I myself will search for my sheep, says the Lord,
    [and I will seek them out].**

I will give thanks to the Lord with my whole heart,
in the assembly of the upright, in the congregation.
Great are the deeds of the Lord!
they are studied by all who delight in them. **R**

His work is full of majesty and splendour
and his righteousness endures for ever.
He makes his marvellous works to be remembered;
the Lord is gracious and full of compassion. **R**

God sent redemption to his people;
he commanded his covenant for ever;
holy and awesome is his name. **R**

The fear of the Lord is the beginning of wisdom;
those who act accordingly have a good understanding;
his praise endures for ever. **R** *From Psalm 111*

A reading from the Letter to the Hebrews.

Let mutual love continue. Do not neglect to show hospitality to strangers, for by doing that some have entertained angels without knowing it. Remember those who are in prison, as though you were in prison with them; those who are being tortured, as though you yourselves were being tortured. Let marriage be held in honour by all, and let the marriage bed be kept undefiled; for God will judge fornicators and adulterers. Keep your lives free from the love of money, and be content with what you have; for he has said, "I will never leave you or forsake you." So we can say with confidence, "The Lord is my helper; I will not be afraid. What can anyone do to me?"

Remember your leaders, those who spoke the word of God to you; consider the outcome of their way of life, and imitate their faith. Jesus Christ is the same yesterday and today and forever.

This is the word of the Lord.   *Hebrews 13. 1-8*

Hear the gospel of our Lord Jesus Christ according to Matthew.

Jesus said, "Blessèd are those who are persecuted for righteousness' sake, for theirs is the kingdom of heaven. Blessèd are you when people revile you and persecute you and utter all kinds of evil against you falsely on my account. Rejoice and be glad, for your reward is great in heaven, for in the same way they persecuted the prophets who were before you."

This is the gospel of the Lord.   *Matthew 5. 10-12*

Post Communion
God, shepherd of your people,
whose servant Edward King revealed the loving service of Christ
 in his ministry as a pastor of your people:
by this eucharist in which we share
awaken within us the love of Christ
and keep us faithful to our Christian calling;
through him who laid down his life for us,
but is alive and reigns with you, now and for ever.

Felix, Apostle to the East Angles
8 March – Commemoration
If celebrated as a Lesser Festival, Common of Missionaries, page 503

Born in Burgundy at the beginning of the seventh century, Felix reputedly converted the exiled King Sigebert of the East Angles and, after the King's return to Britain, was consecrated bishop and then persuaded by the King to follow him to effect the conversion of his subjects. He was commissioned by Honorius, Archbishop of Canterbury, to this work and made Dunwich the centre of his new See. He established schools and monasteries and ministered in his diocese for seventeen years. He died in the year 647.

Geoffrey Studdert Kennedy, Priest, Poet
8 March – Commemoration
If observed as a Lesser Festival, Common of Pastors, page 483

Born in 1883, Studdert Kennedy was a young vicar in Worcester who became an army chaplain during the First World War. His warm personality soon earned the respect of soldiers, who nicknamed him 'Woodbine Willie' after the brand of cigarettes he shared with them. After the First World War, he became a writer and regular preacher, drawing large crowds, who were attracted by his combination of traditional sacramental theology with more unconventional theological views. He worked tirelessly for the Christian Industrial Fellowship, but his frail health gave way and he died (still a young man) on this day in 1929.

Patrick, Patron Saint of Ireland
17 March – Lesser Festival – Missionary – White

Patrick was born in Celtic Cornwall around the year 390 and was captured by Irish raiders when he was sixteen years old and taken to Ireland as a slave. After six years, he escaped and seems to have gone to the Continent. He eventually found his way back to his own family, where his previously-nominal Christian faith grew and matured. He returned to Gaul and was there trained as a priest and much influenced by the form of monasticism evolving under Martin of Tours. When he was in his early forties, he returned to Ireland as a bishop, and made his base at Armagh, which became the centre of his See. He evangelised the people of the land by walking all over the island, gently bringing men and women to a knowledge of Christ. Although he faced fierce opposition and possible persecution, he continued his missionary journeys. Despite being unsuccessful in his attempts to establish the diocesan system he had experienced in Gaul, his monastic foundations proved to be the infrastructure required to maintain the faith after his death, which occurred on this day in the year 460.

Collect
Almighty God,
who in your providence chose your servant Patrick
to be the apostle of the Irish people:
keep alive in us the fire of the faith he kindled
and strengthen us in our pilgrimage
  towards the light of everlasting life;
through Jesus Christ your Son our Lord,
who is alive and reigns with you,
in the unity of the Holy Spirit,
one God, now and for ever.

A reading from the prophecy of Isaiah.

Listen to me, you that pursue righteousness, you that seek the Lord. Look to the rock from which you were hewn, and to the quarry from which you were dug. Look to Abraham your father and to Sarah who bore you; for he was but one when I called him, but I blessed him and made him many. For the Lord will comfort Zion; he will comfort all her waste places, and will make her wilderness like Eden, her desert like the garden of the Lord; joy and gladness will be found in her, thanksgiving and the voice of song.

Listen to me, my people, and give heed to me, my nation; for a teaching will go out from me, and my justice for a light to the peoples. I will bring near my deliverance swiftly, my salvation has gone out and my arms will rule the peoples; the coastlands wait for me, and for my arm they hope. Lift up your eyes to the heavens, and look at the earth beneath; for the heavens will vanish like smoke, the earth will wear out like a garment, and those who live on it will die like gnats; but my salvation will be forever, and my deliverance will never be ended.

Listen to me, you who know righteousness, you people who have my teaching in your hearts; do not fear the reproach of others, and do not be dismayed when they revile you. For the moth will eat them up like a garment, and the worm will eat them like wool; but my deliverance will be forever, and my salvation to all generations.

Awake, awake, put on strength, O arm of the Lord! Awake, as in days of old, the generations of long ago! Was it not you who cut Rahab in pieces, who pierced the dragon? Was it not you who dried up the sea, the waters of the great deep; who made the depths of the sea a way for the redeemed to cross over? So the ransomed of the Lord shall return, and come to Zion with singing; everlasting joy shall be upon their heads; they shall obtain joy and gladness, and sorrow and sighing shall flee away.

This is the word of the Lord.   *Isaiah 51. 1-11*

Responsorial Psalm

**R   Declare God's glory among the nations
     [and his wonders among all peoples].**

Sing to the Lord a new song;
sing to the Lord, all the whole earth.
Sing to the Lord and bless his name;
proclaim the good news of his salvation from day to day. **R**

Declare his glory among the nations
and his wonders among all peoples,
for great is the Lord and greatly to be praised;
he is more to be feared than all gods. **R**

Worship the Lord in the beauty of holiness;
let the whole earth tremble before him.
Let the heavens rejoice and let the earth be glad;
let the sea thunder and all that is in it;
let the field be joyful and all that is therein. **R**   *From Psalm 96*

A reading from the Revelation to John.

The angel showed me the river of the water of life, bright as crystal, flowing from the throne of God and of the Lamb through the middle of the street of the city. On either side of the river is the tree of life with its twelve kinds of fruit, producing its fruit each month; and the leaves of the tree are for the healing of the nations. Nothing accursed will be found there any more. But the throne of

God and of the Lamb will be in it, and his servants will worship him; they will see his face, and his name will be on their foreheads. And there will be no more night; they need no light of lamp or sun, for the Lord God will be their light, and they will reign forever and ever.

This is the word of the Lord.   *Revelation 22. 1-5*

Hear the gospel of our Lord Jesus Christ according to Matthew.

Jesus said to his disciples, "See, I am sending you out like sheep into the midst of wolves; so be wise as serpents and innocent as doves. Beware of them, for they will hand you over to councils and flog you in their synagogues; and you will be dragged before governors and kings because of me, as a testimony to them and the Gentiles. When they hand you over, do not worry about how you are to speak or what you are to say; for what you are to say will be given to you at that time; for it is not you who speak, but the Spirit of your Father speaking through you.

Brother will betray brother to death, and a father his child, and children will rise against parents and have them put to death; and you will be hated by all because of my name. But the one who endures to the end will be saved. When they persecute you in one town, flee to the next; for truly I tell you, you will not have gone through all the towns of Israel before the Son of Man comes."

This is the gospel of the Lord.   *Matthew 10. 16-23*

Post Communion
Holy Father,
who gathered us here around the table of your Son
to share this meal with the whole household of God:
in that new world where you reveal
  the fullness of your peace,
gather people of every race and language
to share with your servant Patrick and all your saints
in the eternal banquet of Jesus Christ our Lord.

Cyril, Bishop of Jerusalem
18 March – Commemoration
If celebrated as a Lesser Festival, Common of Teachers, page 473

Born in about the year 315, probably in Caesarea, Cyril became Bishop of Jerusalem when he was about thirty-four years old. There he nurtured both the resident Christian population and the many pilgrims, following the end of the era of persecution, who were beginning to make their way from all over Christendom to the places associated with Christ. Cyril taught the faith in line with the orthodoxy of the Council of Nicaea and the credal statement that became associated with it. Though he found difficulty with the word in that creed which described Jesus as being 'of one substance with the Father', nevertheless he took the side of the Nicene Party against the Arians, who denied the divinity of Christ. His teaching through his *Catechetical Lectures*, intended for those preparing for baptism, show him to be a man profoundly orthodox and sound, and his liturgical innovations to celebrate the observance of Holy Week and Easter are the foundation of Christian practices to this day. He died in the year 386.

Joseph of Nazareth
19 March – Festival – White

In the gospel of Matthew, Joseph is depicted as a good man, a working carpenter, who trusted in God. He received God's messenger who shared with him God's will for him and for Mary, to whom he was engaged to be married. Luke's gospel describes how Joseph took the new-born child as if he were his own. He was with Mary when, on the fortieth day after the birth, Jesus was presented in the Temple, 'where every first-born male is designated as holy to the Lord'. The adoption of Jesus by Joseph also established Jesus in the descent of David, to accord with the prophecy that Israel's deliverer would be of the House and lineage of David.

God our Father,
who from the family of your servant David
raised up Joseph the carpenter
to be the guardian of your incarnate Son
and husband of the Blessèd Virgin Mary:
give us grace to follow him
in faithful obedience to your commands;
through Jesus Christ your Son our Lord,
who is alive and reigns with you,
in the unity of the Holy Spirit,
one God, now and for ever.

A reading from the Second Book of Samuel

The word of the Lord came to Nathan: Go and tell my servant
David: Thus says the Lord: Are you the one to build me a house to
live in? I have not lived in a house since the day I brought up the
people of Israel from Egypt to this day, but I have been moving
about in a tent and a tabernacle. Wherever I have moved about
among all the people of Israel, did I ever speak a word with any of
the tribal leaders of Israel, whom I commanded to shepherd my
people Israel, saying, "Why have you not built me a house of
cedar?" Now therefore thus you shall say to my servant David:
Thus says the Lord of hosts: I took you from the pasture, from following the sheep to be prince over my people Israel; and I have
been with you wherever you went, and have cut off all your enemies from before you; and I will make for you a great name, like
the name of the great ones of the earth. And I will appoint a place
for my people Israel and will plant them, so that they may live in
their own place, and be disturbed no more; and evildoers shall
afflict them no more, as formerly, from the time that I appointed
judges over my people Israel; and I will give you rest from all your
enemies.

Moreover the Lord declares to you that the Lord will make you a
house. When your days are fulfilled and you lie down with your
ancestors, I will raise up your offspring after you, who shall come
forth from your body, and I will establish his kingdom. He shall
build a house for my name, and I will establish the throne of his

kingdom forever. I will be a father to him, and he shall be a son to me. When he commits iniquity, I will punish him with a rod such as mortals use, with blows inflicted by human beings. But I will not take my steadfast love from him, as I took it from Saul, whom I put away from before you. Your house and your kingdom shall be made sure forever before me; your throne shall be established forever.

This is the word of the Lord. *2 Samuel 7. 4-16*

Responsorial Psalm

**R I will be a father to him, says God,
    [and he shall be to me a son].**

God said: I will make him my first-born
and higher than the kings of the earth.
I will keep my love for him for ever,
and my covenant will stand firm for him. **R**

I will not break my covenant,
nor change what has gone out of my lips.
Once for all I have sworn by my holiness:
I will not lie to David. **R**

His line shall endure for ever
and his throne as the sun before me;
it shall stand fast for evermore like the moon,
the abiding witness in the sky. **R** *From Psalm 89*

A reading from the Letter of Paul to the Romans.

For the promise that he would inherit the world did not come to Abraham or to his descendants through the law but through the righteousness of faith. If it is the adherents of the law who are to be the heirs, faith is null and the promise is void. For the law brings wrath; but where there is no law, neither is there violation.

For this reason it depends on faith, in order that the promise may rest on grace and be guaranteed to all his descendants, not only to the adherents of the law but also to those who share the faith of Abraham (for he is the father of all of us, as it is written, "I have made you the father of many nations") – in the presence of the God in whom he believed, who gives life to the dead and calls into existence the things that do not exist. Hoping against hope, he believed that he would become "the father of many nations," according to what was said, "So numerous shall your descendants be."

This is the word of the Lord. *Romans 4. 13-18*

Hear the gospel of our Lord Jesus Christ according to Matthew.

Now the birth of Jesus the Messiah took place in this way. When his mother Mary had been engaged to Joseph, but before they lived together, she was found to be with child from the Holy Spirit. Her husband Joseph, being a righteous man and unwilling to expose her to public disgrace, planned to dismiss her quietly. But just when he had resolved to do this, an angel of the Lord appeared to him in a dream and said, "Joseph, son of David, do not be afraid to take Mary as your wife, for the child conceived in her is from the Holy Spirit. She will bear a son, and you are to name him Jesus, for he will save his people from their sins."

All this took place to fulfil what had been spoken by the Lord through the prophet: "Look, the virgin shall conceive and bear a son, and they shall name him Emmanuel," which means, "God is with us." When Joseph awoke from sleep, he did as the angel of the Lord commanded him; he took her as his wife, but had no marital relations with her until she had borne a son; and he named him Jesus.

This is the gospel of the Lord. *Matthew 1. 18-25*

Post Communion
Heavenly Father,
whose Son grew in wisdom and stature
in the home of Joseph the carpenter of Nazareth
and on the wood of the cross perfected the work
   of the world's salvation:
help us, strengthened by this sacrament of his passion,
to count the wisdom of the world as foolishness,
and to walk with him in simplicity and trust;
through Jesus Christ our Lord.

Cuthbert, Bishop of Lindisfarne
20 March – Lesser Festival – Missionary – White

Cuthbert was probably born in the Scottish lowlands around the year 640. At the age of eight a prophetic remark from a playmate turned his mind to sober and godly thoughts, and his upbringing as a shepherd gave him ample time for prayer. One night he saw in the sky a dazzling light and angels carrying a soul up to heaven, and resolved to dedicate his life to God. Some years later Cuthbert came to Melrose Abbey asking to be admitted as a monk. It was from here that he began his missionary work, which he continued from Lindisfarne when he became abbot there. Consecrated bishop in 685 he remained an indefatigable traveller and preacher, walking all over his diocese, and spending time as a hermit on Farne Island in between. After only a year however, he felt his end coming and resigned his office, dying on Farne in the company of a few of his monks.

Collect
Almighty God,
who called your servant Cuthbert from following the flock
to follow your Son and to be a shepherd of your people:
in your mercy, grant that we, following his example,
may bring those who are lost home to your fold;
through Jesus Christ your Son our Lord,
who is alive and reigns with you,
in the unity of the Holy Spirit,
one God, now and for ever.

A reading from the prophecy of Ezekiel.

Thus says the Lord God: I myself will search for my sheep, and will seek them out. As shepherds seek out their flocks when they are among their scattered sheep, so I will seek out my sheep. I will rescue them from all the places to which they have been scattered on a day of clouds and thick darkness. I will bring them out from the peoples and gather them from the countries, and will bring them into their own land; and I will feed them on the mountains of Israel, by the watercourses, and in all the inhabited parts of the land. I will feed them with good pasture, and the mountain heights of Israel shall be their pasture; there they shall lie down in good grazing land, and they shall feed on rich pasture on the mountains of Israel. I myself will be the shepherd of my sheep, and I will make them lie down, says the Lord God. I will seek the lost, and I will bring back the strayed, and I will bind up the injured, and I will strengthen the weak, but the fat and the strong I will destroy. I will feed them with justice.

This is the word of the Lord. *Ezekiel 34. 11-16*

Responsorial Psalm

R I myself will search for my sheep, says the Lord, [and I will seek them out].

The Lord is my shepherd;
I shall not be in want.
He makes me lie down in green pastures
and leads me beside still waters. **R**

The Lord revives my soul
and guides me along right pathways
for his own name's sake. **R**

Though I walk through the valley of the shadow of death,
I shall fear no evil;
for you are with me;
your rod and your staff, they comfort me. **R**

You spread a table before me
in the presence of those who trouble me;
you have anointed my head with oil,
and my cup is running over. **R**

Surely your goodness and mercy shall follow me
all the days of my life,
and I will dwell in your house,
the house of the Lord for ever. **R** *Psalm 23*

A reading from the Second Letter of Paul to the Corinthians.

As we work together with him, we urge you also not to accept the grace of God in vain. For he says, "At an acceptable time I have listened to you, and on a day of salvation I have helped you." See, now is the acceptable time; see, now is the day of salvation!

We are putting no obstacle in anyone's way, so that no fault may be found with our ministry, but as servants of God we have commended ourselves in every way: through great endurance, in afflictions, hardships, calamities, beatings, imprisonments, riots, labours, sleepless nights, hunger; by purity, knowledge, patience, kindness, holiness of spirit, genuine love, truthful speech, and the power of God; with the weapons of righteousness for the right hand and for the left; in honour and dishonour, in ill repute and good repute. We are treated as impostors, and yet are true; as unknown, and yet are well known; as dying, and see – we are alive; as punished, and yet not killed; as sorrowful, yet always rejoicing; as poor, yet making many rich; as having nothing, and yet possessing everything.

This is the word of the Lord.   *2 Corinthians 6. 1-10*

Hear the gospel of our Lord Jesus Christ according to Matthew.

Jesus said to his disciples: What do you think? If a shepherd has a hundred sheep, and one of them has gone astray, does he not leave the ninety-nine on the mountains and go in search of the one that went astray? And if he finds it, truly I tell you, he rejoices over it more than over the ninety-nine that never went astray. So it is not the will of your Father in heaven that one of these little ones should be lost.

This is the gospel of the Lord.   *Matthew 18. 12-14*

Post Communion
Holy Father,
who gathered us here around the table of your Son
to share this meal with the whole household of God:
in that new world where you reveal
  the fullness of your peace,
gather people of every race and language
to share with your servant Cuthbert and all your saints
in the eternal banquet of Jesus Christ our Lord.

Thomas Cranmer, Archbishop of Canterbury
21 March – Lesser Festival – Martyr – Red

Born in Aslockton in Nottinghamshire in 1489, Thomas Cranmer, from an unspectacular Cambridge academic career, was recruited for diplomatic service in 1527. Two years later he joined the team working to annul Henry VIII's marriage to Catherine of Aragon. He was made Archbishop of Canterbury in 1533 and duly pronounced the Aragon marriage annulled. By now a convinced Church reformer, he married in 1532 while clerical marriage was still illegal in England. He worked closely with Thomas Cromwell to further reformation, but survived Henry's final, unpredictable years to become a chief architect of Edwardian religious change, constructing two editions of *The Book of Common Prayer*, in 1549 and 1552, the Ordinal in 1550 and the original version of the later Thirty-Nine Articles.

Cranmer acquiesced in the unsuccessful attempt to make Lady Jane Grey Queen of England. Queen Mary's regime convicted him of treason in 1553 and of heresy in 1554. Demoralised by imprisonment, he signed six recantations, but was still condemned to the stake at Oxford. Struggling with his conscience, he made a final, bold statement of Protestant faith. Perhaps too fair-minded and cautious to be a ready-made hero in Reformation disputes, he was an impressively learnèd scholar, and his genius for formal prose has left a lasting mark on Anglican liturgy. He was burnt at the stake on this day in the year 1556.

Collect

Father of all mercies,
who through the work of your servant Thomas Cranmer
  renewed the worship of your Church
and through his death
  revealed your strength in human weakness:
by your grace strengthen us to worship you in spirit and in truth
and so to come to the joys of your everlasting kingdom;
through Jesus Christ our Mediator and Advocate,
who is alive and reigns with you,
in the unity of the Holy Spirit,
one God, now and for ever.

A reading from the prophecy of Isaiah.

Thus says the Lord, he who created you, O Jacob, he who formed you, O Israel: Do not fear, for I have redeemed you; I have called you by name, you are mine. When you pass through the waters, I will be with you; and through the rivers, they shall not overwhelm you; when you walk through fire you shall not be burned, and the flame shall not consume you. For I am the Lord your God, the Holy One of Israel, your Saviour.

This is the word of the Lord. *Isaiah 43. 1-3a*

Responsorial Psalm

**R Do not fear, for I have redeemed you, says your God;
[I have called you by name, you are mine].**

Let my cry come before you, O Lord;
give me understanding, according to your word.
Let my supplication come before you;
deliver me, according to your promise. **R**

My lips shall pour forth your praise,
when you teach me your statutes.
My tongue shall sing of your promise,
for all your commandments are righteous. **R**

Let your hand be ready to help me,
for I have chosen your commandments.
I long for your salvation, O Lord,
and your law is my delight. **R**

Let me live and I will praise you, let your judgements help me.
I have gone astray like a sheep that is lost;
search for your servant,
for I do not forget your commandments. **R**   *From Psalm 119*

A reading from the Second Letter of Paul to Timothy.

Remember Jesus Christ, raised from the dead, a descendant of David – that is my gospel, for which I suffer hardship, even to the point of being chained like a criminal. But the word of God is not chained. Therefore I endure everything for the sake of the elect, so that they may also obtain the salvation that is in Christ Jesus, with eternal glory. The saying is sure: If we have died with him, we will also live with him; if we endure, we will also reign with him; if we deny him, he will also deny us; if we are faithless, he remains faithful – for he cannot deny himself.

Remind them of this, and warn them before God that they are to avoid wrangling over words, which does no good but only ruins those who are listening. Do your best to present yourself to God as one approved by him, a worker who has no need to be ashamed, rightly explaining the word of truth.

This is the word of the Lord.   *2 Timothy 2. 8-15*

Hear the gospel of our Lord Jesus Christ according to John.

Jesus said, "I am the good shepherd. The good shepherd lays down his life for the sheep. The hired hand, who is not the shepherd and does not own the sheep, sees the wolf coming and leaves the sheep and runs away – and the wolf snatches them and scatters them. The hired hand runs away because a hired hand does not care for the sheep. I am the good shepherd. I know my own and my own know me, just as the Father knows me and I know the Father. And I lay down my life for the sheep.

This is the gospel of the Lord.   *John 10. 11-15*

Post Communion
God our Redeemer,
whose Church was strengthened
  by the blood of your martyr Thomas Cranmer:
so bind us, in life and death, to Christ's sacrifice
that our lives, broken and offered with his,
may carry his death and proclaim his resurrection in the world;
through Jesus Christ our Lord.

Walter Hilton of Thurgarton, Mystic
24 March – Commemoration
If observed as a Lesser Festival, Common of Religious, page 494

Born in 1343, Walter Hilton studied Canon Law at Cambridge but after a period as a hermit, he joined the community of Augustinian

Canons at Thurgarton in Nottinghamshire in about 1386. Highly regarded in his lifetime as a spiritual guide, he wrote in both Latin and English and translated several Latin devotional works. Controversy with 'enthusiasts' and with the Lollard movement gave a sharper definition to his exposition of the aims, methods and disciplines of traditional spirituality. Amongst his major works, *Ladder of Perfection (Book Two)* declares that contemplation, understood in a profoundly Trinitarian context as awareness of grace and sensitivity to the Spirit, may and should be sought by all serious Christians. He died on this day in the year 1396.

Oscar Romero, Archbishop of San Salvador
24 March – Commemoration
If observed as a Lesser Festival, Common of Martyrs, page 464

Oscar Arnulfo Romero y Galdamez was born in a small village in El Salvador in 1917. Ordained priest, he was known as a quiet and unassuming pastor. By 1977, amidst the political and social turmoil suffered by his country, he was therefore seen as a neutral choice to be its Archbishop. Courageously, however, he began to speak out against violence and his homilies supported the demands of the poor for economic and social justice. He refused to be silenced and continued to preach even under threat of assassination. On this day in 1980, whilst presiding at Mass, Archbishop Romero was assassinated by a gunman. He has since been widely regarded as a martyr for the faith.

The Annunciation of our Lord to the Blessèd Virgin Mary
25 March – Principal Feast – White or Gold

The story of the announcement of the coming of God made flesh in the person of his Son, Jesus the Christ, the Anointed One, is heard in today's proclamation of the good news from the gospel of Luke. The feast marks the conception of Christ in the womb of Mary and has been celebrated in the Church at least since the late fourth century. The perfect humanity and the complete divinity of Jesus is affirmed, following the controversies around those orthodox assertions, which themselves led to the acknowledgement of Mary as Theotokos, God-bearer, which in the West became translated as Mother of God. The celebration thus took on strong associations with the person of Mary, and became known in England as Lady Day. In recent years, the Church has reaffirmed the day as a Feast of our Lord, on which his virgin-mother still has a unique place of honour and veneration.

Collect
We beseech you, O Lord,
pour your grace into our hearts,
that as we have known the incarnation
  of your Son Jesus Christ
by the message of an angel,
so by his cross and passion
we may be brought to the glory of his resurrection;
through Jesus Christ your Son our Lord,
who is alive and reigns with you,
in the unity of the Holy Spirit,
one God, now and for ever.

A reading from the prophecy of Isaiah.

The Lord spoke to Ahaz, saying: Ask a sign of the Lord your God; let it be deep as Sheol or high as heaven. But Ahaz said, I will not ask, and I will not put the Lord to the test. Then Isaiah said: "Hear then, O house of David! Is it too little for you to weary mortals, that you weary my God also? Therefore the Lord himself will give you a sign. Look, the young woman is with child and shall bear a son, and shall name him Immanuel."

This is the word of the Lord.   *Isaiah 7. 10-14a*

Responsorial Psalm

**R   We have come to do your will, O God,
    [for it is by your will that we are sanctified].**

Great things are they that you have done, O Lord my God;
how great your wonders and your plans for us,
there is none who can be compared with you. **R**

O that I could make them known and tell them
but they are more than I can count.
In sacrifice and offering you take no pleasure;
you have given me ears to hear you. **R**

Burnt-offering and sin-offering you have not required,
and so I said: Behold, I come.
In the roll of the book it is written concerning me:
"I love to do your will, O my God;
your law is deep in my heart." **R**

I proclaimed righteousness in the great congregation;
behold, I did not restrain my lips;
and that, O Lord, you know. **R**   *From Psalm 40*

A reading from the Letter to the Hebrews.

It is impossible for the blood of bulls and goats to take away sins.
Consequently, when Christ came into the world, he said,
"Sacrifices and offerings you have not desired, but a body you
have prepared for me; in burnt offerings and sin offerings you
have taken no pleasure. Then I said, 'See, God, I have come to do
your will, O God' (in the scroll of the book it is written of me)."
When he said, "You have neither desired nor taken pleasure in
sacrifices and offerings and burnt offerings and sin offerings"
(these are offered according to the law), then he added, "See, I
have come to do your will." He abolishes the first in order to
establish the second. And it is by God's will that we have been
sanctified through the offering of the body of Jesus Christ once for
all.

This is the word of the Lord.   *Hebrews 10. 4-10*

Hear the gospel of our Lord Jesus Christ according to Luke.

In the sixth month the angel Gabriel was sent by God to a town in Galilee called Nazareth, to a virgin engaged to a man whose name was Joseph, of the house of David. The virgin's name was Mary. And he came to her and said, "Greetings, favoured one! The Lord is with you." But she was much perplexed by his words and pondered what sort of greeting this might be. The angel said to her, "Do not be afraid, Mary, for you have found favour with God. And now, you will conceive in your womb and bear a son, and you will name him Jesus. He will be great, and will be called the Son of the Most High, and the Lord God will give to him the throne of his ancestor David. He will reign over the house of Jacob forever, and of his kingdom there will be no end."

Mary said to the angel, "How can this be, since I am a virgin?" The angel said to her, "The Holy Spirit will come upon you, and the power of the Most High will overshadow you; therefore the child to be born will be holy; he will be called Son of God. And now, your relative Elizabeth in her old age has also conceived a son; and this is the sixth month for her who was said to be barren. For nothing will be impossible with God." Then Mary said, "Here am I, the servant of the Lord; let it be with me according to your word." Then the angel departed from her.

This is the gospel of the Lord.   *Luke 1. 26-38*

Post Communion
God Most High,
whose handmaid bore the Word made flesh:
we thank you that in this sacrament of our redemption
you visit us with your Holy Spirit
and overshadow us by your power;
strengthen us to walk with Mary the joyful path of obedience
and so to bring forth the fruits of holiness;
through Jesus Christ our Lord.

Harriet Monsell of Clewer
26 March – Commemoration
If celebrated as a Lesser Festival, Common of Religious, page 494

Of Irish parentage, Harriet Monsell (née O'Brien) was born in 1811. After the death of her clergyman husband, she went to work in a penitentiary at Clewer near Windsor. Here, under the guidance of the local Vicar, T T Carter, she was professed as a Religious in 1852 and became the first Superior of the Community of St John the Baptist. Under her care, the community grew rapidly and undertook a range of social work in a variety of locations, with foundations in India and America by the 1880s. The sisters cared for orphans, ran schools and hospitals, and opened mission houses in parishes. In 1875 Mother Harriet retired as Superior through ill-health, moving to a small hermitage in Folkestone, where she died on Easter Day 1883.

John Donne, Priest & Poet
31 March – Commemoration
If celebrated as a Lesser Festival, Common of Spiritual Writers, page 473

John Donne was born in about the year 1571 and brought up as a Roman Catholic. He was a great-great nephew of Thomas More, although this seems to have had little influence on him because, as a youth, he was sceptical about all religion. He went up to Oxford when he was fourteen, studied further at Cambridge and perhaps on the Continent, and eventually discovered his Christian faith in the Church of England. After much heart-searching, he accepted ordination and later the post of Dean of St Paul's Cathedral. Much of his cynicism dissolved and he became a strong advocate for the discerning of Christian vocation, and in particular affirming his own vocation as a priest, loving and loved by the crucified Christ. The people of London flocked to his sermons. He died on this day in the year 1631. His love-poetry – addressed mainly to his wife – and religious poems took on a renewed life in the twentieth century and his place both as a patristic scholar and as a moral theologian are confirmed by his prolific writings and the publication of his sermons.

APRIL

Frederick Denison Maurice
1 April – Commemoration
If celebrated as a Lesser Festival, Common of Teachers, page 473

Born into a Unitarian family in 1805, Frederick Maurice became an Anglican in his twenties and was then ordained. He was one of the founders of the Christian Socialist Movement, in which his particular concern was providing education for working men. As a theologian, Maurice's ideas on Anglican comprehensiveness have remained influential. His best-remembered book, *The Kingdom of Christ*, demonstrated his philosophical approach to theology. His radicalism was revealed in his attack on traditional concepts of hell in *Theological Essays*, which cost him his Professorship at Kings College, London, in 1853. In 1866, however, he was given a chair in Cambridge, which he held until his death on this day in 1872.

Dietrich Bonhoeffer, Lutheran Pastor
9 April – Commemoration
If celebrated as a Lesser Festival, Common of Martyrs, page 464

Dietrich Bonhoeffer was born in 1906 into an academic family. Ordained in the Lutheran Church, his theology was influenced by Karl Barth and he became a lecturer: in Spain, the USA and in 1931 back in Berlin. Opposed to the philosophy of Nazism, he was one of the leaders of the Confessing Church, a movement which broke away from the Nazi-dominated Lutherans in 1934. Banned from teaching, and harassed by Hitler's regime, he bravely returned to Germany at the outbreak of war in 1939, despite being on a lecture tour in the United States at the time. His defiant opposition to the Nazis led to his arrest in 1943. His experiences led him to propose a more radical theology in his later works, which have been influential among post-war theologians. He was murdered by the Nazi police in Flossenburg concentration camp on this day in 1945.

William Law, Priest

10 April – Lesser Festival – Pastor – White

Born at Kings Cliffe in Northamptonshire in 1686, William Law was educated at Emmanuel College Cambridge and, after ordination as a deacon, became a fellow of the College in 1711. When George I came to the throne in 1714, William declined to take the Oath of Allegiance, being a member of the Non-Juror party who believed the anointed but deposed monarch James II and his heirs should occupy the throne. He lost his fellowship but in 1728 he was made a priest and in the same year published *A Serious Call to a Devout and Holy Life*, which much influenced such people as Samuel Johnson and John and Charles Wesley. In it he stresses the moral virtues, a personal prayer life and asceticism. He returned to Kings Cliffe in 1740, where he led a life of devotion and simplicity and caring for the poor. He remained there the rest of his life and died on this day in the year 1761.

Collect
Almighty God,
who called your servant William Law
to a devout and holy life:
grant that by your spirit of love
and through faithfulness in prayer
we may find the way to divine knowledge
and so come to see the hidden things of God;
through Jesus Christ your Son our Lord,
who is alive and reigns with you,
in the unity of the Holy Spirit,
one God, now and for ever.

A reading from the Book of Tobit.

I performed many acts of charity to my kindred, those of my tribe: I would give my food to the hungry and my clothing to the naked; and if I saw the dead body of any of my people thrown out behind the wall of Nineveh, I would bury it. I also buried any whom the king put to death when he came fleeing from Judea in those days of judgement that the king of heaven executed upon him because of his blasphemies. For in his anger he put to death many Israelites; but I would secretly remove the bodies and bury them.

This is the word of the Lord. *Tobit 1. 16b-18a*

Responsorial Psalm

R **The free gift of God is eternal life**
   [for the Lord redeems his people].

Bless the Lord, O my soul,
and all that is within me, bless his holy name.
Bless the Lord, O my soul,
and forget not all his benefits. **R**

He forgives all your sins
and heals all your infirmities;
he redeems your life from the grave
and crowns you with mercy and loving-kindness. **R**

He satisfies you with good things,
and your youth is renewed like an eagle's.
The Lord executes righteousness
and judgement for all who are oppressed. **R**   *From Psalm 103*

A reading from the Letter of Paul to the Romans.

When you were slaves of sin, you were free in regard to righteousness. So what advantage did you then get from the things of which you now are ashamed? The end of those things is death. But now that you have been freed from sin and enslaved to God, the advantage you get is sanctification. The end is eternal life. For the wages of sin is death, but the free gift of God is eternal life in Christ Jesus our Lord.

This is the word of the Lord. *Romans 6. 20-23*

Hear the gospel of our Lord Jesus Christ according to Luke.

Jesus said to the crowds, "No one after lighting a lamp puts it in a cellar, but on the lampstand so that those who enter may see the light. Your eye is the lamp of your body. If your eye is healthy, your whole body is full of light; but if it is not healthy, your body is full of darkness. Therefore consider whether the light in you is not darkness. If then your whole body is full of light, with no part of it in darkness, it will be as full of light as when a lamp gives you light with its rays."

This is the gospel of the Lord.   *Luke 11. 33-36*

Post Communion
God of truth,
whose Wisdom set her table
and invited us to eat the bread and drink the wine
  of the kingdom:
help us to lay aside all foolishness
and to live and walk in the way of insight,
that we may come with your servant William Law
  to the eternal feast of heaven;
through Jesus Christ our Lord.

William of Ockham, Franciscan Friar, Philosopher
10 April – Commemoration
If celebrated as a Lesser Festival, Common of Teachers, page 473

Born at Ockham in Surrey in about the year 1285, William entered the Franciscan Order and, as a friar, he first studied and then taught at Oxford. He writings were ever the subject of close scrutiny, this being a time when heresy was suspected everywhere, it seemed, but he never received any formal condemnation. Later in life, he entered the controversy between the rival popes and had to flee for his life. His much-used principle of economy – often referred to as 'Occam's Razor' – stated that only individual things exist and that they are directly understood by the thinking mind and that this intuitive knowledge is caused naturally. His doctrine of God led him to destroy the thirteenth-century concept of the relationship between theology and philosophy and took the study of the philosophy of religion onto a new level. He died on this day in the year 1347.

George Augustus Selwyn, Bishop of New Zealand
11 April – *Commemoration*
If celebrated as a Lesser Festival, Common of Bishops, page 483

George Augustus Selwyn was born in 1809, educated at Cambridge and ordained as curate of Windsor. In 1841 he was made the first Bishop of New Zealand and remained there for twenty-seven years, during the first years travelling when few roads or bridges existed. In the wars between colonists and Maoris he stood out heroically for Maori rights, at the cost of fierce attacks from both sides and grave personal danger in his efforts to part the warriors, until later he was revered as one of the founders of New Zealand as well as of its Church. He taught himself to navigate and gathered congregations in the Melanesian Islands. His Constitution for the New Zealand Church influenced the churches of the Anglican Communion and he was a chief founder of the Lambeth Conferences of bishops. In 1868 he was persuaded to become the Bishop of Lichfield in England and died there on this day in 1878.

Isabella Gilmore, Deaconess
16 April – *Commemoration*
If celebrated as a Lesser Festival, Common of Pastors, page 483

Born in 1842, Isabella Gilmore, the sister of William Morris, was a nurse at Guy's Hospital in London and in 1886, was asked by Bishop Thorold of Rochester to pioneer deaconess work in his diocese. The bishop overcame her initial reluctance and together they planned for an Order of Deaconesses along the same lines as the ordained ministry. She was made a deaconess in 1887 and a training house developed on North Side, Clapham Common, later to be called Gilmore House in her memory. Isabella herself retired in 1906 and, during her nineteen years of service, she trained head deaconesses for at least seven other dioceses. At her memorial service, Dr Randall Davidson predicted that "Some day, those who know best will be able to trace much of the origin and root of the revival of the Deaconess Order to the life, work, example and words of Isabella Gilmore." She died on this day in 1923.

Alphege, Archbishop of Canterbury
19 April – Lesser Festival – Martyr – Red

Alphege became a monk at Deerhurst near Gloucester and with-drew in later life to be a hermit in Somerset. The Archbishop of Canterbury, Dunstan, drew him back to be Abbot of Bath and, in 984, Bishop of Winchester. In 1005 he was made Archbishop of Canterbury, where his austere life and lavish almsgiving made him a revered and much-loved man. In the year 1011, the Danes overran south-east England, taking Alphege prisoner. They put the enormous ransom of £3000 on his head, but Alphege refused to pay it and forbade anyone from doing so, knowing that it would impoverish the ordinary people even more. He was brutally murdered by his captors at Greenwich on this day in the year 1012.

Collect
Merciful God,
who raised up your servant Alphege
to be a pastor of your people
and gave him grace to suffer for justice and true religion:
grant that we who celebrate his martyrdom
may know the power of the risen Christ in our hearts
and share his peace in lives offered to your service;
through Jesus Christ your Son our Lord,
who is alive and reigns with you,
in the unity of the Holy Spirit,
one God, now and for ever.

A reading from the prophecy of Isaiah.

Thus says the Lord, he who created you, O Jacob, he who formed you, O Israel: Do not fear, for I have redeemed you; I have called you by name, you are mine. When you pass through the waters, I will be with you; and through the rivers, they shall not over-whelm you; when you walk through fire you shall not be burned, and the flame shall not consume you. For I am the Lord your God, the Holy One of Israel, your Saviour. I give Egypt as your ransom, Ethiopia and Seba in exchange for you. Because you are precious in my sight, and honoured, and I love you, I give people in return for you, nations in exchange for your life. Do not fear, for I am with you; I will bring your offspring from the east, and from the west I will gather you; I will say to the north, "Give them up," and to the south, "Do not withhold; bring my sons from far away and my daughters from the end of the earth – everyone who is called by my name, whom I created for my glory, whom I formed and made."

This is the word of the Lord.   *Isaiah 43. 1-7*

Responsorial Psalm

**R   Into your hands, O Lord,
      I commend my spirit.**

You, O Lord, are a shield about me;
you are my glory, the one who lifts up my head.
I call aloud upon the Lord
and he answers me from his holy hill. **R**

I lie down and go to sleep;
I wake again, because the Lord sustains me.
Deliverance belongs to the Lord.
Your blessing be upon your people! **R**   *From Psalm 3*

A reading from the Letter to the Hebrews.

Every high priest chosen from among mortals is put in charge of things pertaining to God on their behalf, to offer gifts and sacrifices for sins. He is able to deal gently with the ignorant and wayward, since he himself is subject to weakness; and because of this he must offer sacrifice for his own sins as well as for those of the people. And one does not presume to take this honour, but takes it only when called by God, just as Aaron was.

This is the word of the Lord.   *Hebrews 5. 1-4*

ear the gospel of our Lord Jesus Christ according to Matthew.

Jesus told his disciples, "If any want to become my followers, let them deny themselves and take up their cross and follow me. For those who want to save their life will lose it, and those who lose their life for my sake will find it. For what will it profit them if they gain the whole world but forfeit their life? Or what will they give in return for their life?"

This is the gospel of the Lord.   *Matthew 16. 24-26*

God, who gave us this holy meal
in which we have celebrated the glory of the cross
and the victory of your martyr Alphege:
by our communion with Christ
in his saving death and resurrection,
give us with all your saints the courage to conquer evil
and so to share the fruit of the tree of life;
through Jesus Christ our Lord.

Anselm, Archbishop of Canterbury
21 April – Lesser Festival – Teacher of the Faith – White

Anselm was born in Aosta, northern Italy, in 1033. As a young man, he left home and travelled north, visiting many monasteries and other centres of learning. One such visit was to the abbey of Bec, where he met Lanfranc who advised him to embrace monastic life. Anselm had a powerful and original mind and, during his 34 years at Bec (as monk, prior and finally abbot), he taught many others and wrote theological, philosophical and devotional works. When Lanfranc died Anselm was made Archbishop of Canterbury and had to subordinate his scholarly work to the needs of the diocese and nation. Twice he endured exile for championing the rights of the Church against the authority of the king but, despite his stubbornness, intellectual rigour, and personal austerity, he was admired by the Norman nobility as well as loved by his monks. He died in 1109.

Collect
Eternal God,
who gave great gifts to your servant Anselm
  as a pastor and teacher:
grant that we, like him, may desire you with our whole heart
and, so desiring, may seek you
and, seeking, may find you;
through Jesus Christ your Son our Lord,
who is alive and reigns with you, in the unity of the Holy Spirit,
one God, now and for ever.

A reading from the Book of Wisdom.

For who can learn the counsel of God? Or who can discern what the Lord wills? For the reasoning of mortals is worthless, and our designs are likely to fail; for a perishable body weighs down the soul, and this earthy tent burdens the thoughtful mind. We can hardly guess at what is on earth, and what is at hand we find with labour; but who has traced out what is in the heavens? Who has learned your counsel, unless you have given wisdom and sent your holy spirit from on high? And thus the paths of those on earth were set right, and people were taught what pleases you, and were saved by wisdom.

This is the word of the Lord.   *Wisdom 9. 13-18*

Responsorial Psalm

**R   You have given us wisdom and understanding, O Lord,
      [and sent your Holy Spirit from on high].**

In you, O Lord, have I taken refuge;
let me never be ashamed.
In your righteousness, deliver me and set me free;
incline your ear to me and save me. **R**

For you are my hope, O Lord God,
I have been sustained by you ever since I was born;
from my mother's womb you have been my strength;
my praise shall be always of you. **R**

I have become a portent to many;
but you are my refuge and my strength.
Let my mouth be full of your praise
and your glory all the day long. **R**   *From Psalm 71*

A reading from the Letter of Paul to the Romans.

God proves his love for us in that while we still were sinners Christ died for us. Much more surely then, now that we have been justified by his blood, will we be saved through him from the wrath of God. For if while we were enemies, we were reconciled to God through the death of his Son, much more surely, having been reconciled, will we be saved by his life. But more than that, we even boast in God through our Lord Jesus Christ, through whom we have now received reconciliation.

This is the word of the Lord. *Romans 5. 8-11*

Hear the gospel of our Lord Jesus Christ according to Luke.

In the hearing of all the people Jesus said to the disciples, "When you hear of wars and insurrections, do not be terrified; for these things must take place first, but the end will not follow immediately. Nation will rise against nation, and kingdom against kingdom; there will be great earthquakes, and in various places famines and plagues; and there will be dreadful portents and great signs from heaven.

"But before all this occurs, they will arrest you and persecute you; they will hand you over to synagogues and prisons, and you will be brought before kings and governors because of my name. This will give you an opportunity to testify. So make up your minds not to prepare your defence in advance; for I will give you words and a wisdom that none of your opponents will be able to withstand or contradict."

This is the gospel of the Lord. *Luke 21. 9-15*

Post Communion
God of truth,
whose Wisdom set her table
and invited us to eat the bread and drink the wine
  of the kingdom:
help us to lay aside all foolishness
and to live and walk in the way of insight,
that we may come with your servant Anselm
  to the eternal feast of heaven;
through Jesus Christ our Lord.

George, Patron Saint of England
23 April – Festival – Martyr – Red

St George was probably a soldier living in Palestine at the beginning of the fourth century. He was martyred at Lydda in about the year 304, the beginning of the Diocletian persecution, and became known throughout the East as 'The Great Martyr'. There were churches in England dedicated to St George before the Norman conquest. The story of his slaying the dragon is probably due to his being mistaken in iconography for St Michael, himself usually depicted wearing armour; or it may again be a mistaken identity representing Perseus's slaying of the sea monster, a myth also associated with the area of Lydda. George replaced Edward the Confessor as Patron Saint of England following the Crusades, when returning soldiers brought back with them a renewed cult of St George. Edward III made St George patron of the Order of the Garter, which seems finally to have confirmed his position.

Collect
God of hosts,
who so kindled the flame of love
in the heart of your servant George
that he bore witness to the risen Lord
by his life and by his death:
give us the same faith and power of love
that we who rejoice in his triumphs
may come to share with him the fullness of the resurrection;
through Jesus Christ your Son our Lord,
who is alive and reigns with you,
in the unity of the Holy Spirit,
one God, now and for ever.

A reading from the First Book of the Maccabees.

Hananiah, Azariah, and Mishael believed and were saved from the flame. Daniel, because of his innocence, was delivered from the mouth of the lions. And so observe, from generation to generation, that none of those who put their trust in him will lack strength. Do not fear the words of sinners, for their splendour will turn into dung and worms. Today they will be exalted, but tomorrow they will not be found, because they will have returned to the dust, and their plans will have perished. My children, be courageous and grow strong in the law, for by it you will gain honour.

This is the word of the Lord.   *1 Maccabees 2. 59-64*

Or:

A reading from the Revelation to John.

War broke out in heaven; Michael and his angels fought against the dragon. The dragon and his angels fought back, but they were defeated, and there was no longer any place for them in heaven. The great dragon was thrown down, that ancient serpent, who is called the Devil and Satan, the deceiver of the whole world – he was thrown down to the earth, and his angels were thrown down with him.

Then I heard a loud voice in heaven, proclaiming, "Now have come the salvation and the power and the kingdom of our God and the authority of his Messiah, for the accuser of our comrades has been thrown down, who accuses them day and night before our God. But they have conquered him by the blood of the Lamb and by the word of their testimony, for they did not cling to life even in the face of death. Rejoice then, you heavens and those who dwell therein! But woe to the earth and the sea, for the devil has come down to you with great wrath, because he knows that his time is short!"

This is the word of the Lord.   *Revelation 12. 7-12*

Responsorial Psalm

**R Rejoice then, you heavens
[and those who dwell therein].**

When the Lord restored the fortunes of Zion,
then were we like those who dream.
Then was our mouth filled with laughter,
and our tongue with shouts of joy. **R**

Then they said among the nations:
"The Lord has done great things for them."
The Lord has done great things for us,
and we are glad indeed. **R**

Restore our fortunes, O Lord,
like the watercourses of the Negev.
Those who sowed with tears
will reap with songs of joy. **R**   *From Psalm 126*

A reading from the Second Letter of Paul to Timothy.

Share in suffering like a good soldier of Christ Jesus. No one serving in the army gets entangled in everyday affairs; the soldier's aim is to please the enlisting officer. And in the case of an athlete, no one is crowned without competing according to the rules. It is the farmer who does the work who ought to have the first share of the crops. Think over what I say, for the Lord will give you understanding in all things.

Remember Jesus Christ, raised from the dead, a descendant of David – that is my gospel, for which I suffer hardship, even to the point of being chained like a criminal. But the word of God is not chained. Therefore I endure everything for the sake of the elect, so that they may also obtain the salvation that is in Christ Jesus, with eternal glory. The saying is sure: If we have died with him, we will also live with him; if we endure, we will also reign with him; if we deny him, he will also deny us; if we are faithless, he remains faithful – for he cannot deny himself.

This is the word of the Lord.   *2 Timothy 2. 3-13*

Hear the gospel of our Lord Jesus Christ according to John.

Jesus said to his disciples: "If the world hates you, be aware that it hated me before it hated you. If you belonged to the world, the world would love you as its own. Because you do not belong to the world, but I have chosen you out of the world – therefore the world hates you. Remember the word that I said to you, 'Servants are not greater than their master.' If they persecuted me, they will persecute you; if they kept my word, they will keep yours also. But they will do all these things to you on account of my name, because they do not know him who sent me."
This is the gospel of the Lord.   *John 15. 18-21*

Post Communion
God, who gave us this holy meal
in which we have celebrated the glory of the cross
and the victory of your martyr George:
by our communion with Christ
in his saving death and resurrection,
give us with all your saints the courage to conquer evil
and so to share the fruit of the tree of life;
through Jesus Christ our Lord.

Mellitus, first Bishop at St Paul's, Archbishop of Canterbury
24 April – Commemoration
If celebrated as a Lesser Festival, Common of Bishops, page 483

Mellitus was a Roman abbot and sent to England by Pope Gregory the Great to undergird the work of Augustine, who consecrated him Bishop of the East Saxons with his see at London and his first church that of St Paul. After some local setbacks and having to reside in northern France, he and his fellow bishops were recalled to England, but Mellitus was unable to return to London. He was made archbishop in the year 619 and died on this day in the year 624. He was buried close to Augustine in the Church of Ss Peter & Paul in Canterbury.

Mark the Evangelist
25 April – Festival – Evangelist – Red

John Mark was a Jew and, according to Paul's letter to the Colossians, was cousin to Barnabas. He accompanied Barnabas and Paul on their first missionary journey. Afterwards, he went to Cyprus with Barnabas and to Rome with first Paul and then Peter. Mark's gospel is generally regarded as the earliest and was most likely written whilst he was in Rome. It was probably based as much on Peter's preaching of the good news as on Mark's own memory. Mark's gospel has a sharpness and an immediacy about it and he does not spare the apostles in noting their weaknesses and lack of understanding that Jesus the Christ would suffer for the world's redemption. Sharing in the glory of the resurrection means sharing in the giving of self, both in body and spirit, even to death; sharing the gospel was, for all, in essence both excessively generous and ultimately sacrificial.

Collect
Almighty God,
who enlightened your holy Church
through the inspired witness
  of your evangelist Saint Mark:
grant that we, being firmly grounded
  in the truth of the gospel,
may be faithful to its teaching both in word and deed;
through Jesus Christ your Son our Lord,
who is alive and reigns with you,
in the unity of the Holy Spirit,
one God, now and for ever.

A reading from the Book of Proverbs.

The mind of the righteous ponders how to answer, but the mouth of the wicked pours out evil. The Lord is far from the wicked, but he hears the prayer of the righteous. The light of the eyes rejoices the heart, and good news refreshes the body.

This is the word of the Lord.   *Proverbs 15. 28-33*

Or:

A reading from the Acts of the Apostles.

Paul and Barnabas remained in Antioch, and there, with many others, they taught and proclaimed the word of the Lord. After some days Paul said to Barnabas, "Come, let us return and visit the believers in every city where we proclaimed the word of the Lord and see how they are doing." Barnabas wanted to take with them John called Mark. But Paul decided not to take with them one who had deserted them in Pamphylia and had not accompanied them in the work. The disagreement became so sharp that they parted company; Barnabas took Mark with him and sailed away to Cyprus.   But Paul chose Silas and set out, the believers commending him to the grace of the Lord. He went through Syria and Cilicia, strengthening the churches.

This is the word of the Lord. *Acts 15. 35-41*

Responsorial Psalm

**R The light of the eyes rejoices the heart
[and good news refreshes the body].**

How shall the young cleanse their way?
By keeping to your words.
With my whole heart I seek you;
let me not stray from your commandments. **R**

I treasure your promise in my heart,
that I may not sin against you.
Blessèd are you, O Lord;
instruct me in your statutes. **R**

With my lips will I recite
all the judgements of your mouth.
I have taken greater delight in the way of your decrees
than in all manner of riches. **R**

I will meditate on your commandments
and give attention to your ways.
My delight is in your statutes;
I will not forget your word. **R** *From Psalm 119*

A reading from the Letter of Paul to the Ephesians.

Each of us was given grace according to the measure of Christ's gift. Therefore it is said, "When he ascended on high he made captivity itself a captive; he gave gifts to his people." When it says, "He ascended," what does it mean but that he had also descended into the lower parts of the earth? He who descended is the same one who ascended far above all the heavens, so that he might fill all things.

The gifts he gave were that some would be apostles, some prophets, some evangelists, some pastors and teachers, to equip the saints for the work of ministry, for building up the body of Christ, until all of us come to the unity of the faith and of the knowledge of the Son of God, to maturity, to the measure of the full stature of Christ. We must no longer be children, tossed to and fro and blown about by every wind of doctrine, by people's trickery, by their craftiness in deceitful scheming. But speaking the truth in love, we must grow up in every way into him who is the head, into Christ, from whom the whole body, joined and knit together by every ligament with which it is equipped, as each part is working properly, promotes the body's growth in building itself up in love.

This is the word of the Lord. *Ephesians 4. 7-16*

Hear the gospel of our Lord Jesus Christ according to Mark.

Jesus said to Peter, James, John and Andrew: "Beware that no one leads you astray. Many will come in my name and say, 'I am he!' and they will lead many astray. When you hear of wars and rumours of wars, do not be alarmed; this must take place, but the end is still to come. For nation will rise against nation, and kingdom against kingdom; there will be earthquakes in various places; there will be famines. This is but the beginning of the birth pangs.

"As for yourselves, beware; for they will hand you over to councils; and you will be beaten in synagogues; and you will stand before governors and kings because of me, as a testimony to them. And the good news must first be proclaimed to all nations. When they bring you to trial and hand you over, do not worry beforehand about what you are to say; but say whatever is given you at that time, for it is not you who speak, but the Holy Spirit. Brother will betray brother to death, and a father his child, and children will rise against parents and have them put to death; and you will be hated by all because of my name. But the one who endures to the end will be saved."

This is the gospel of the Lord. *Mark 13. 5-13*

Post Communion
Almighty God,
who on the day of Pentecost
sent your Holy Spirit to the disciples
with the wind from heaven and in tongues of flame,
filling them with joy and boldness to preach the gospel:
by the power of the same Spirit
strengthen us to witness to your truth
and to draw everyone to the fire of your love;
through Jesus Christ our Lord.

Christina Rossetti, Poet
27 April – Commemoration
If celebrated as a Lesser Festival, Common of Spiritual Writers, page 473

Christina Rossetti was born in 1830 and was associated with the Pre-Raphaelite Brotherhood, of which her older brother, Dante, was a prominent member. Her elder sister became an Anglican Religious. Christina's own fame rests upon her poetry, which dealt mainly with religious subjects but also the sadness of unrequited or disappointed love. Her first recorded verses, addressed to her mother on the latter's birthday, were written on 27 April 1842. She was the author of the Christmas-tide carol *In the bleak mid-winter*. She died on 29 December 1894.

Peter Chanel, Missionary in the South Pacific
28 April – Commemoration
If celebrated as a Lesser Festival, Common of Martyrs, page 464

Peter Chanel was born at Cras in France in 1803 and, after ordination, joined the Marist missionary congregation in 1831. In 1836 he was sent to the islands of the South Pacific to preach the faith. Peter and his companions brought healing medicines as well as the gospel and were much loved and respected. On the island of Futuna in the Fiji group, where Peter was living, the chief's son asked for baptism, which so infuriated his father that he dispatched a group of warriors with explicit orders to murder Peter. They attacked him with clubs, axes and knives and he died on this day in the year 1841. Within a year, the whole island was Christian and Peter became revered throughout the Pacific Islands and Australasia as its protomartyr.

Catherine of Siena
29 April – Lesser Festival – Teacher of the Faith – White

Catherine Benincasa was born in 1347, the second youngest of twenty-five children. Pious from her earliest years, she overcame family opposition to her vocation and became a Dominican tertiary at the age of eighteen. Nourished by a life of contemplative prayer and mystical experience, she devoted herself to active care for the poor and sick. She became increasingly sought out as an adviser on political as well as religious matters and, in 1376, she journeyed to Avignon as an ambassador to the pope and influenced his decision to return to Rome. She wrote a *Dialogue* on the spiritual life as well as numerous letters of counsel and direction, which stressed her devotion to the Precious Blood of Jesus. She suffered a stroke on 21 April and died eight days later, on this day in the year 1380.

Collect
God of compassion,
who gave your servant Catherine of Siena
a wondrous love of the passion of Christ:
grant that your people
  may be united to him in his majesty
and rejoice for ever in the revelation of his glory;
who is alive and reigns with you,
in the unity of the Holy Spirit,
one God, now and for ever.

A reading from the Book of Proverbs.

Does not wisdom call, and does not understanding raise her voice? Hear, for I will speak noble things, and from my lips will come what is right; for my mouth will utter truth; wickedness is an abomination to my lips. All the words of my mouth are righteous; there is nothing twisted or crooked in them. They are all straight to one who understands and right to those who find knowledge. Take my instruction instead of silver, and knowledge rather than choice gold; for wisdom is better than jewels, and all that you may desire cannot compare with her.

This is the word of the Lord.   *Proverbs 8. 1, 6-11*

Responsorial Psalm

R Wisdom speaks noble things
[and from her lips comes forth truth].

Great things are they that you have done, O Lord my God!
how great your wonders and your plans for us!
there is none who can be compared with you. **R**

O that I could make them known and tell them!
but they are more than I can count.
In sacrifice and offering you take no pleasure. **R**

In the roll of the book it is written concerning me:
"I love to do your will, O my God;
your·law is deep in my heart." **R**

I proclaimed righteousness in the great congregation;
behold, I did not restrain my lips;
and that, O Lord, you know. **R**   *From Psalm 40*

A reading from the Third Letter of John.

Beloved, I pray that all may go well with you and that you may be in good health, just as it is well with your soul. I was overjoyed when some of the friends arrived and testified to your faithfulness to the truth, namely how you walk in the truth. I have no greater joy than this, to hear that my children are walking in the truth. Beloved, you do faithfully whatever you do for the friends, even though they are strangers to you; they have testified to your love before the church. You will do well to send them on in a manner worthy of God; for they began their journey for the sake of Christ, accepting no support from non-believers. Therefore we ought to support such people, so that we may become co-workers with the truth.

This is the word of the Lord.   *3 John 2-8*

Hear the gospel of our Lord Jesus Christ according to John.

Jesus, looking up to heaven, said to the Father: "While I was with those whom you gave me from the world, I protected them in your name that you have given me. I guarded them, and not one of them was lost except the one destined to be lost, so that the scripture might be fulfilled. But now I am coming to you, and I speak these things in the world so that they may have my joy made complete in themselves. I have given them your word, and the world has hated them because they do not belong to the world, just as I do not belong to the world. I am not asking you to take them out of the world, but I ask you to protect them from the evil one. They do not belong to the world, just as I do not belong to the world. Sanctify them in the truth; your word is truth. As you have sent me into the world, so I have sent them into the world. And for their sakes I sanctify myself, so that they also may be sanctified in truth.

"I ask not only on behalf of these, but also on behalf of those who will believe in me through their word, that they may all be one. As you, Father, are in me and I am in you, may they also be in us, so that the world may believe that you have sent me. The glory that you have given me I have given them, so that they may be one, as we are one, I in them and you in me, that they may become completely one, so that the world may know that you have sent me and have loved them even as you have loved me. Father, I desire that those also, whom you have given me, may be with me where I am, to see my glory, which you have given me because you loved me before the foundation of the world.

"Righteous Father, the world does not know you, but I know you; and these know that you have sent me. I made your name known to them, and I will make it known, so that the love with which you have loved me may be in them, and I in them."

This is the gospel of the Lord.   *John 17 12-26*

Post Communion
God of truth,
whose Wisdom set her table
and invited us to eat the bread and drink the wine
  of the kingdom:
help us to lay aside all foolishness
and to live and walk in the way of insight,
that we may come with your servant Catherine
  to the eternal feast of heaven;
through Jesus Christ our Lord.

Pandita Mary Ramabai, Translator of the Scriptures
30 April – Commemoration
If celebrated as a Lesser Festival, Common of any Saint, page 531

Mary Ramabai was born in 1858, the daughter of a Sanscrit scholar who believed in educating women. Converting to Christianity,
she nevertheless remained loyal to many aspects of her Hindu
background, pioneering an Indian vision of the faith. She became
well known as a lecturer on social questions, becoming the first
woman to be awarded the title 'Pandita'. She spent many years
working for the education of women and orphans, founding
schools and homes. Personally, she lived in great simplicity and
was a prominent opponent of the caste system and child marriage.
She died on this day in 1922.

MAY

Philip & James, Apostles
1 May – Festival – Apostles – Red

Philip and James appear in the list of the twelve apostles in the first three gospels but are frequently confused with other early saints who share their names. In John's gospel, Philip has a more prominent rôle, being the third of the apostles to be called by Jesus and then himself bringing his friend Nathanael to the Lord. Philip is the spokesman for the other apostles who are questioning the capacity for feeding the five thousand and, at the Last Supper, enters into a sort of dialogue with Jesus which leads to the Farewell Discourses of our Lord.

James is said to be the son of Alphæus and is often known as 'James the Less' to distinguish him. He may also be the 'James the Younger' who, in Mark's gospel, is a witness at the Crucifixion.

They are celebrated on the same day because the church in Rome, where their relics rest, was dedicated on this day in the year 560.

Collect
Almighty Father,
whom truly to know is eternal life:
teach us to know your Son Jesus Christ
as the way, the truth, and the life;
that we may follow the steps
   of your holy apostles Philip and James,
and walk steadfastly in the way that leads to your glory;
through Jesus Christ your Son our Lord,
who is alive and reigns with you,
in the unity of the Holy Spirit,
one God, now and for ever.

A reading from the prophecy of Isaiah.

Thus said the Lord God, the Holy One of Israel: In returning and rest you shall be saved; in quietness and in trust shall be your strength. But you refused and said, "No! We will flee upon horses" – therefore you shall flee! and, "We will ride upon swift steeds" – therefore your pursuers shall be swift! A thousand shall flee at the threat of one, at the threat of five you shall flee, until you are left like a flagstaff on the top of a mountain, like a signal on a hill. Therefore the Lord waits to be gracious to you; therefore he will rise up to show mercy to you. For the Lord is a God of justice; blessèd are all those who wait for him.

Truly, O people in Zion, inhabitants of Jerusalem, you shall weep no more. He will surely be gracious to you at the sound of your cry; when he hears it, he will answer you. Though the Lord may give you the bread of adversity and the water of affliction, yet your Teacher will not hide himself any more, but your eyes shall see your Teacher. And when you turn to the right or when you turn to the left, your ears shall hear a word behind you, saying, "This is the way; walk in it."

This is the word of the Lord.   *Isaiah 30. 15-21*

Responsorial Psalm

**R   In returning and rest you shall be saved;
     [in quietness and in trust shall be your strength].**

Happy are they whose way is blameless,
who walk in the law of the Lord!
Happy are they who observe your decrees
and seek you with all their hearts. **R**

Happy are they who never do any wrong,
but always walk in your ways.
You laid down your commandments,
that we should fully keep them. **R**

O that my ways were made so direct
that I might keep your statutes!
Then I should not be put to shame,
when I regard all your commandments. **R**

I will thank you with an unfeigned heart,
when I have learned your righteous judgements.
I will keep your statutes;
do not utterly forsake me. **R**   *From Psalm 119*

A reading from the Letter of Paul to the Ephesians.

This is the reason that I, Paul, am a prisoner for Christ Jesus for the sake of you Gentiles – for surely you have already heard of the commission of God's grace that was given me for you, and how the mystery was made known to me by revelation, as I wrote above in a few words, a reading of which will enable you to perceive my understanding of the mystery of Christ. In former generations this mystery was not made known to humankind, as it has now been revealed to his holy apostles and prophets by the Spirit: that is, the Gentiles have become fellow heirs, members of the same body, and sharers in the promise in Christ Jesus through the gospel.

Of this gospel I have become a servant according to the gift of God's grace that was given me by the working of his power. Although I am the very least of all the saints, this grace was given to me to bring to the Gentiles the news of the boundless riches of Christ, and to make everyone see what is the plan of the mystery hidden for ages in God who created all things; so that through the church the wisdom of God in its rich variety might now be made known to the rulers and authorities in the heavenly places.

This is the word of the Lord. *Ephesians 3. 1-10*

Hear the gospel of our Lord Jesus Christ according to John.

Jesus said to his disciples, "Do not let your hearts be troubled. Believe in God, believe also in me. In my Father's house there are many dwelling places. If it were not so, would I have told you that I go to prepare a place for you? And if I go and prepare a place for you, I will come again and will take you to myself, so that where I am, there you may be also. And you know the way to the place where I am going." Thomas said to him, "Lord, we do not know where you are going. How can we know the way?" Jesus said to him, "I am the way, and the truth, and the life. No one comes to the Father except through me. If you know me, you will know my Father also. From now on you do know him and have seen him."

Philip said to him, "Lord, show us the Father, and we will be satisfied." Jesus said to him, "Have I been with you all this time, Philip, and you still do not know me? Whoever has seen me has seen the Father. How can you say, 'Show us the Father'? Do you not believe that I am in the Father and the Father is in me? The words that I say to you I do not speak on my own; but the Father who dwells in me does his works. Believe me that I am in the Father and the Father is in me; but if you do not, then believe me because of the works themselves. Very truly, I tell you, the one who believes in me will also do the works that I do and, in fact, will do greater works than these, because I am going to the Father. I will do whatever you ask in my name, so that the Father may be glorified in the Son. If in my name you ask me for anything, I will do it. "

This is the gospel of the Lord.   *John 14. 1-14*

Post Communion
Lord God, the source of truth and love,
keep us faithful to the apostles' teaching and fellowship,
united in prayer and the breaking of bread,
and one in joy and simplicity of heart,
in Jesus Christ our Lord.

Athanasius, Bishop of Alexandria
2 May – Lesser Festival – Teacher of the Faith – White

Athanasius was born in about the year 296 of Christian parents and educated at the Catechetical school in Alexandria. He was present at the Council of Nicæa as a deacon, accompanying his bishop Alexander, whom he succeeded as Patriarch in the year 328. Athanasius held firmly to the doctrines of the Church as defined by that Council, and became the leader of those opposed to the teachings of Arian, which denied the divinity of Christ. He was deposed from – and restored to – his See several times because of his uncompromising faith. In or out of exile, Athanasius continued to write. Ever the proponent of orthodoxy over heterodoxy, he expounded the need for the Church to teach the true doctrines of the faith rather than watered-down versions of it. He was a strong believer in asceticism as a means of restoring the divine image in humanity and thus a supporter of monasticism, which was in its nascent state at that time. He was a friend of Pachomius and wrote the *Life of Antony* of Egypt, which showed the cenobitic life as holding a balance between things earthly and heavenly. He died on this day in the year 373.

Collect
Everliving God,
whose servant Athanasius testified
  to the mystery of the Word made flesh for our salvation:
help us, with all your saints,
to contend for the truth
and to grow into the likeness of your Son,
Jesus Christ our Lord,
who is alive and reigns with you,
in the unity of the Holy Spirit,
one God, now and for ever.

A reading from the book Ecclesiasticus.

Watch for the opportune time, and beware of evil, and do not be ashamed to be yourself. For there is a shame that leads to sin, and there is a shame that is glory and favour. Do not show partiality, to your own harm, or deference, to your downfall. Do not refrain from speaking at the proper moment, and do not hide your wisdom. For wisdom becomes known through speech, and education through the words of the tongue. Never speak against the truth, but be ashamed of your ignorance. Do not be ashamed to confess your sins, and do not try to stop the current of a river. Do not subject yourself to a fool, or show partiality to a ruler. Fight to the death for truth, and the Lord God will fight for you.

This is the word of the Lord.   *Ecclesiasticus 4. 20-28*

Responsorial Psalm

**R   Acknowledge the servants who bow before you, O Lord,
      [and bless the inheritance of your Son's redeeming].**

Why are the nations in an uproar?
Why do the peoples mutter empty threats?
Why do the kings of the earth rise up in revolt
  and the princes plot together,
against the Lord and against his anointed? **R**

Let me announce the decree of the Lord:
he said to me, "You are my Son, this day have I begotten you.
Ask of me and I will give you the nations for your inheritance
and the ends of the earth for your possession." **R**

And now, you kings, be wise;
be warned, you rulers of the earth.
Submit to the Lord with fear,
and with trembling bow before him; **R**

Lest he be angry and you perish;
for his wrath is quickly kindled.
Happy are they all
who take refuge in him! **R**   *From Psalm 2*

A reading from the Letter of Paul to the Colossians.

May you be made strong with all the strength that comes from his
glorious power, and may you be prepared to endure everything
with patience, while joyfully giving thanks to the Father, who has
enabled you to share in the inheritance of the saints in the light.
He has rescued us from the power of darkness and transferred us
into the kingdom of his beloved Son, in whom we have redemption, the forgiveness of sins.

  He is the image of the invisible God, the firstborn of all creation;
for in him all things in heaven and on earth were created, things
visible and invisible, whether thrones or dominions or rulers or
powers – all things have been created through him and for him.
He himself is before all things, and in him all things hold together.
He is the head of the body, the church; he is the beginning, the
firstborn from the dead, so that he might come to have first place
in everything. For in him all the fullness of God was pleased to
dwell, and through him God was pleased to reconcile to himself all
things, whether on earth or in heaven, by making peace through
the blood of his cross.

This is the word of the Lord.   *Colossians 1. 11-20*

Hear the gospel of our Lord Jesus Christ according to Matthew.

Jesus said to his disciples, "A disciple is not above the teacher, nor
a servant above the master; it is enough for the disciple to be like

the teacher, and the servant like the master. If they have called the master of the house Beelzebul, how much more will they malign those of his household! So have no fear of them; for nothing is covered up that will not be uncovered, and nothing secret that will not become known. What I say to you in the dark, tell in the light; and what you hear whispered, proclaim from the housetops."

This is the gospel of the Lord.   *Matthew 10. 24-27*

Post Communion
God of truth,
whose Wisdom set her table
and invited us to eat the bread and drink the wine
  of the kingdom:
help us to lay aside all foolishness
and to live and walk in the way of insight,
that we may come with your servant Athanasius
  to the eternal feast of heaven;
through Jesus Christ our Lord.

English Saints & Martyrs of the Reformation Era
4 May – Lesser Festival – Of any Saint – White

This day is set aside to remember all who witnessed to their Christian faith during the conflicts in church and state in England, which lasted from the fourteenth to the seventeenth centuries but were at their most intense in the sixteenth century. Though the reform movement was aimed chiefly at the Papacy, many Christian men and women of holiness suffered for their allegiance to what they believed to be the truth of the gospel. As the movement grew in strength, it suffered its own internecine struggles, with one group determined that they were the keepers of truth and that all others were therefore at least in a state of ignorance and at worst heretical. In the twentieth century, ecumenical links drew the churches closer to each other in faith and worship and all now recognise both the good and evil that evolved from the Reformation Era.

Collect

Merciful God,
who, when your Church on earth was torn apart
  by the ravages of sin,
raised up men and women in this land
who witnessed to their faith with courage and constancy:
give to your Church that peace which is your will,
and grant that those who have been divided on earth
  may be reconciled in heaven,
and share together in the vision of your glory;
through Jesus Christ your Son our Lord,
who is alive and reigns with you,
in the unity of the Holy Spirit,
one God, now and for ever.

A reading from the prophecy of Isaiah.

Thus says the Lord, he who created you, O Jacob, he who formed you, O Israel: Do not fear, for I have redeemed you; I have called you by name, you are mine. When you pass through the waters, I will be with you; and through the rivers, they shall not overwhelm you; when you walk through fire you shall not be burned, and the flame shall not consume you. For I am the Lord your God, the Holy One of Israel, your Saviour. I give Egypt as your ransom, Ethiopia and Seba in exchange for you.

Because you are precious in my sight, and honoured, and I love you, I give people in return for you, nations in exchange for your life. Do not fear, for I am with you; I will bring your offspring from the east, and from the west I will gather you; I will say to the north, "Give them up," and to the south, "Do not withhold; bring my sons from far away and my daughters from the end of the earth – everyone who is called by my name, whom I created for my glory, whom I formed and made."

This is the word of the Lord. *Isaiah 43. 1-7*

Responsorial Psalm

R Do not fear, for I have redeemed you, says your Maker;
[I have called you by name, you are mine].

On the holy mountain stands the city he has founded
and the Lord loves the gates of Zion
more than all the dwellings of Jacob. **R**

Glorious things are spoken of you, O city of our God.
Of Zion it shall be said: "Everyone was born in her,
and the Most High himself shall sustain her." **R**

The Lord will record as he enrols the peoples:
"These also were born there."
The singers and the dancers will say:
"All my fresh springs are in you." **R**   *From Psalm 87*

A reading from the Second Letter of Paul to the Corinthians.

We do not proclaim ourselves, we proclaim Jesus Christ as Lord
and ourselves as your servants for Jesus' sake. For it is the God
who said, "Let light shine out of darkness," who has shone in our
hearts to give the light of the knowledge of the glory of God in the
face of Jesus Christ.

  But we have this treasure in clay jars, so that it may be made clear
that this extraordinary power belongs to God and does not come
from us. We are afflicted in every way, but not crushed; perplexed, but not driven to despair; persecuted, but not forsaken;
struck down, but not destroyed; always carrying in the body the
death of Jesus, so that the life of Jesus may also be made visible in
our bodies. For while we live, we are always being given up to
death for Jesus' sake, so that the life of Jesus may be made visible
in our mortal flesh. So death is at work in us, but life in you.

This is the word of the Lord.   *2 Corinthians 4. 5-12*

Hear the gospel of our Lord Jesus Christ according to John.

Among those who went up to worship at the festival were some
Greeks. They came to Philip, who was from Bethsaida in Galilee,
and said to him, "Sir, we wish to see Jesus." Philip went and told
Andrew; then Andrew and Philip went and told Jesus. Jesus

answered them, "The hour has come for the Son of Man to be glorified. Very truly, I tell you, unless a grain of wheat falls into the earth and dies, it remains just a single grain; but if it dies, it bears much fruit. Those who love their life lose it, and those who hate their life in this world will keep it for eternal life. Whoever serves me must follow me, and where I am, there will my servant be also. Whoever serves me, the Father will honour."

This is the gospel of the Lord.   *John 12. 20-26*

Post Communion
God, the source of all holiness
  and giver of all good things:
may we who have shared at this table
  as strangers and pilgrims here on earth
be welcomed with all your saints
  to the heavenly feast on the day of your kingdom;
through Jesus Christ our Lord.

Julian of Norwich
8 May – Lesser Festival – Religious – White

On this day in the year 1373, when she was thirty years old and suffering from what was considered to be a terminal illness, a woman of Norwich, whose own name is unrecorded, experienced a series of sixteen visions, which revealed aspects of the love of God. Following her recovery, she spent the next twenty years of her life pondering their meaning and recorded her conclusions in what became the first book written by a woman in English, *The Revelations of Divine Love*. At an unknown point in her life, she became an anchoress attached to the Church of St Julian in Norwich, and it was by this name of Julian that she came to be known to later generations. She died around the year 1417.

Collect
Most holy God, the ground of our beseeching,
who through your servant Julian
revealed the wonders of your love:

grant that as we are created in your nature
  and restored by your grace,
our wills may be made one with yours,
that we may come to see you face to face
and gaze on you for ever;
through Jesus Christ your Son our Lord,
who is alive and reigns with you,
in the unity of the Holy Spirit,
one God, now and for ever.

A reading from the First Book of the Kings.

Elijah came to a cave, and spent the night there. Then the word of
the Lord came to him, saying, "What are you doing here, Elijah?"
He answered, "I have been very zealous for the Lord, the God of
hosts; for the Israelites have forsaken your covenant, thrown
down your altars, and killed your prophets with the sword.
I alone am left, and they are seeking my life, to take it away." He
said, "Go out and stand on the mountain before the Lord, for the
Lord is about to pass by." Now there was a great wind, so strong
that it was splitting mountains and breaking rocks in pieces before
the Lord, but the Lord was not in the wind; and after the wind an
earthquake, but the Lord was not in the earthquake; and after the
earthquake a fire, but the Lord was not in the fire; and after the fire
a sound of sheer silence. When Elijah heard it, he wrapped his
face in his mantle and went out and stood at the entrance of the
cave.

This is the word of the Lord.   *1 Kings 19. 9-13a*

Responsorial Psalm

R **Stand on the mountain before your God,
    [for the Lord is about to pass by].**

The Lord is my light and my salvation;
whom then shall I fear?
the Lord is the strength of my life;
of whom then shall I be afraid? **R**

Though an army should encamp against me,
yet my heart shall not be afraid;
And though war should rise up against me,
yet will I put my trust in him. **R**

One thing have I asked of the Lord; one thing I seek;
that I may dwell in the house of the Lord all the days of my life;
To behold the fair beauty of the Lord
and to seek him in his temple. **R**

For in the day of trouble
he shall keep me safe in his shelter;
he shall hide me in the secrecy of his dwelling
and set me high upon a rock. **R**   *From Psalm 27*

A reading from the First Letter of Paul to the Corinthians.

Love never ends. But as for prophecies, they will come to an end;
as for tongues, they will cease; as for knowledge, it will come to an
end. For we know only in part, and we prophesy only in part; but
when the complete comes, the partial will come to an end. When
I was a child, I spoke like a child, I thought like a child, I reasoned
like a child; when I became an adult, I put an end to childish ways.
For now we see in a mirror, dimly, but then we will see face to face.
Now I know only in part; then I will know fully, even as I have
been fully known. And now faith, hope, and love abide, these
three; and the greatest of these is love.

This is the word of the Lord.   *1 Corinthians 13. 8-13*

Hear the gospel of our Lord Jesus Christ according to John.

Mary stood weeping outside the tomb. As she wept, she bent over
to look into the tomb; and she saw two angels in white, sitting
where the body of Jesus had been lying, one at the head and the
other at the feet. They said to her, "Woman, why are you weeping?" She said to them, "They have taken away my Lord, and I do
not know where they have laid him." When she had said this, she
turned around and saw Jesus standing there, but she did not
know that it was Jesus. Jesus said to her, "Woman, why are you
weeping? Whom are you looking for?" Supposing him to be the
gardener, she said to him, "Sir, if you have carried him away, tell

me where you have laid him, and I will take him away." Jesus said to her, "Mary!" She turned and said to him in Hebrew, "Rabbouni!" (which means Teacher). Jesus said to her, "Do not hold on to me, because I have not yet ascended to the Father. But go to my brothers and say to them, 'I am ascending to my Father and your Father, to my God and your God.' " Mary Magdalene went and announced to the disciples, "I have seen the Lord"; and she told them that he had said these things to her.

This is the gospel of the Lord. *John 20. 11-18*

Post Communion
Merciful God,
who gave such grace to your servant Julian
that she served you with singleness of heart
and loved you above all things:
help us, whose communion with you
 has been renewed in this sacrament,
to forsake all that holds us back from following Christ
and to grow into his likeness from glory to glory;
through Jesus Christ our Lord.

Matthias the Apostle
14 May – Festival – Apostle – Red

After the betrayal of Jesus by Judas Iscariot, the apostles brought their number back to twelve by choosing Matthias to replace him. He was chosen by lot from amongst the disciples. The author of the Acts of the Apostles sees apostleship differently from Paul's interpretation of the rôle and seems to reflect the understanding of the gospel of Luke. The number had to be restored so that they might "sit on thrones judging the twelve tribes of Israel". It was conditional that they had to have been with Jesus during his earthly ministry and witnesses to the resurrection. The point of being chosen by lot, rather than by some democratic method, indicated the election or choosing by God, rather than by mortals.

Collect
Almighty God,
who in the place of the traitor Judas
chose your faithful servant Matthias
to be of the number of the Twelve:
preserve your Church from false apostles
and, by the ministry of faithful pastors and teachers,
keep us steadfast in your truth;
through Jesus Christ your Son our Lord,
who is alive and reigns with you,
in the unity of the Holy Spirit,
one God, now and for ever.

Isaiah 22. 15-25	*or*	Acts 1. 15-26
Psalm 15		Psalm 15
Acts 1. 15-26		1 Corinthians 4. 1-7
John 15. 9-17		John 15. 9-17

A reading from the prophecy of Isaiah.

Thus says the Lord God of hosts: Come, go to this steward, to Shebna, who is master of the household, and say to him: What right do you have here? Who are your relatives here, that you have cut out a tomb here for yourself, cutting a tomb on the height, and carving a habitation for yourself in the rock? The Lord is about to hurl you away violently, my fellow. He will seize firm hold on you, whirl you round and round, and throw you like a ball into a wide land; there you shall die, and there your splendid chariots shall lie, O you disgrace to your master's house! I will thrust you from your office, and you will be pulled down from your post.

On that day I will call my servant Eliakim son of Hilkiah, and will clothe him with your robe and bind your sash on him. I will commit your authority to his hand, and he shall be a father to the inhabitants of Jerusalem and to the house of Judah. I will place on his shoulder the key of the house of David; he shall open, and no one shall shut; he shall shut, and no one shall open. I will fasten him like a peg in a secure place, and he will become a throne of honour to his ancestral house. And they will hang on him the whole weight of his ancestral house, the offspring and issue, every small vessel, from the cups to all the flagons. On that day, says the Lord of hosts, the peg that was fastened in a secure place will give way; it will be cut down and fall, and the load that was on it will perish, for the Lord has spoken.

This is the word of the Lord.   *Isaiah 22. 15-25*

Responsorial Psalm

R Lord, you know the hearts of all,
   [so let us love one another, as you have loved us].

Lord, who may dwell in your tabernacle?
who may abide upon your holy hill?
Whoever leads a blameless life and does what is right,
who speaks the truth from his heart. **R**

There is no guile upon his tongue; he does no evil to his friend;
he does not heap contempt upon his neighbour.
In his sight the wicked is rejected,
but he honours those who fear the Lord. **R**

He has sworn to do no wrong
and does not take back his word.
Whoever does these things
shall never be overthrown. **R**   *From Psalm 15*

A reading from the Acts of the Apostles.

In those days Peter stood up among the believers (together the crowd numbered about one hundred and twenty persons) and said, "Friends, the scripture had to be fulfilled, which the Holy Spirit through David foretold concerning Judas, who became a guide for those who arrested Jesus – for he was numbered among us and was allotted his share in this ministry." (Now this man acquired a field with the reward of his wickedness; and falling headlong, he burst open in the middle and all his bowels gushed out. This became known to all the residents of Jerusalem, so that the field was called in their language Hakeldama, that is, Field of Blood.) "For it is written in the book of Psalms, 'Let his homestead become desolate, and let there be no one to live in it'; and 'Let another take his position of overseer.' So one of the men who have accompanied us during all the time that the Lord Jesus went in and out among us, beginning from the baptism of John until the day when he was taken up from us – one of these must become a witness with us to his resurrection."

So they proposed two, Joseph called Barsabbas, who was also known as Justus, and Matthias. Then they prayed and said, "Lord, you know everyone's heart. Show us which one of these two you have chosen to take the place in this ministry and apostleship from which Judas turned aside to go to his own place." And they cast lots for them, and the lot fell on Matthias; and he was added to the eleven apostles.

This is the word of the Lord. *Acts 1. 15-26*

A reading from the First Letter of Paul to the Corinthians.

Think of us in this way, as servants of Christ and stewards of God's mysteries. Moreover, it is required of stewards that they be found trustworthy. But with me it is a very small thing that I should be judged by you or by any human court. I do not even judge myself. I am not aware of anything against myself, but I am not thereby acquitted. It is the Lord who judges me. Therefore do not pronounce judgement before the time, before the Lord comes, who will bring to light the things now hidden in darkness and will disclose the purposes of the heart. Then each one will receive commendation from God. I have applied all this to Apollos and myself for your benefit, brothers and sisters, so that you may learn through us the meaning of the saying, "Nothing beyond what is written," so that none of you will be puffed up in favour of one against another. For who sees anything different in you? What do you have that you did not receive? And if you received it, why do you boast as if it were not a gift?

This is the word of the Lord. *1 Corinthians 4. 1-7*

Hear the gospel of our Lord Jesus Christ according to John.

Jesus said to his disciples, "As the Father has loved me, so I have loved you; abide in my love. If you keep my commandments, you will abide in my love, just as I have kept my Father's commandments and abide in his love. I have said these things to you so that my joy may be in you, and that your joy may be complete.

"This is my commandment, that you love one another as I have loved you. No one has greater love than this, to lay down one's life for one's friends. You are my friends if you do what I command you. I do not call you servants any longer, because the servant does not know what the master is doing; but I have called you friends, because I have made known to you everything that I have heard from my Father. You did not choose me but I chose you. And I appointed you to go and bear fruit, fruit that will last, so that the Father will give you whatever you ask him in my name. I am giving you these commands so that you may love one another."

This is the gospel of the Lord.   *John 15. 9-17*

Post Communion
Almighty God,
who on the day of Pentecost
sent your Holy Spirit to the apostles
with the wind from heaven and in tongues of flame,
filling them with joy and boldness to preach the gospel:
by the power of the same Spirit
strengthen us to witness to your truth
and to draw everyone to the fire of your love;
through Jesus Christ our Lord.

Caroline Chisholm, Social Reformer
16 May – Commemoration
If celebrated as a Lesser Festival, Common of any Saint, page 527

Caroline Jones was born in 1808. On her marriage to Archibald Chisholm, she took her husband's Roman Catholic faith. They emigrated to Madras in 1831 where she set up a school for soldiers' daughters. In 1838, the family moved to Australia and, almost immediately, Caroline began to work for the vulnerable immigrants arriving at Sydney. She was especially concerned for the women, who were often lured and bullied into brothels. She set up a free Registry Office to help them obtain legitimate work and a shelter and she campaigned for improved conditions. She returned to Britain in 1846 to press for emigration reform and founded the Family Colonisation Loan Society. Her Christian ministry and action led to the ending of what had virtually been the institutionalisation of the abuse of poor women.

Dunstan, Archbishop of Canterbury
19 May – Lesser Festival – Religious – White

Dunstan was born near Glastonbury around 910 into a noble family. He received a good education and spent time at the court of the King of Wessex. A saintly uncle urged him to enter the monastic life; he delayed, but followed the advice in time, on recovering from an illness. Returning to Glastonbury, Dunstan lived as a monk, devoting his work time to creative pursuits: illuminating, music, and metalwork. In 943 the new king made him abbot, and this launched a great revival of monastic life in England. Starting with Glastonbury, Dunstan restored discipline to several monasteries and promoted study and teaching. Under two later kings, he rose to political and ecclesiastical eminence, being chief minister and Archbishop of Canterbury under King Edgar. This enabled him and his followers to extend his reforms to the whole English Church. In 970 he fell from political favour but continued as archbishop, preaching and teaching. He died in 988.

Collect
Almighty God,
who raised up Dunstan to be a true shepherd of the flock,
a restorer of monastic life
and a faithful counsellor to those in authority:
give to all pastors the same gifts of your Holy Spirit
that they may be true servants of Christ
  and of all his people;
through Jesus Christ your Son our Lord,
who is alive and reigns with you,
in the unity of the Holy Spirit,'
one God, now and for ever.

A reading from the book of the Exodus.

The Lord spoke to Moses: See, I have called by name Bezalel son of Uri son of Hur, of the tribe of Judah: and I have filled him with divine spirit, with ability, intelligence, and knowledge in every kind of craft, to devise artistic designs, to work in gold, silver, and bronze, in cutting stones for setting, and in carving wood, in every kind of craft.

This is the word of the Lord.   *Exodus 31. 1-5*

Responsorial Psalm

**R   Behold God's faithful and wise servant,
      [whom the master has put in charge of his household].**

The king rejoices in your strength, O Lord;
how greatly he exults in your victory!
You have given him his heart's desire;
you have not denied him the request of his lips. **R**

For you meet him with blessings of prosperity,
and set a crown of fine gold upon his head.
He asked you for life and you gave it to him;
length of days, for ever and ever. **R**

His honour is great, because of your victory;
splendour and majesty have you bestowed upon him.
For you will give him everlasting felicity
and will make him glad with the joy of your presence. **R**

For the king puts his trust in the Lord;
because of the loving-kindness of the Most High, he will not fall.
Be exalted, O Lord, in your might;
we will sing and praise your power. **R**   *From Psalm 21*

A reading from the Second Letter of Paul to the Corinthians.

We know that if the earthly tent we live in is destroyed, we have a building from God, a house not made with hands, eternal in the heavens. For in this tent we groan, longing to be clothed with our heavenly dwelling – if indeed, when we have taken it off we will not be found naked. For while we are still in this tent, we groan under our burden, because we wish not to be unclothed but to be further clothed, so that what is mortal may be swallowed up by life. He who has prepared us for this very thing is God, who has given us the Spirit as a guarantee.

So we are always confident; even though we know that while we are at home in the body we are away from the Lord – for we walk by faith, not by sight. Yes, we do have confidence, and we would rather be away from the body and at home with the Lord. So whether we are at home or away, we make it our aim to please him. For all of us must appear before the judgement seat of Christ, so that each may receive recompense for what has been done in the body, whether good or evil.

This is the word of the Lord.   *2 Corinthians 5. 1-10*

Hear the gospel of our Lord Jesus Christ according to Matthew.

Jesus said to his disciples, "Keep awake therefore, for you do not know on what day your Lord is coming. But understand this: if the owner of the house had known in what part of the night the thief was coming, he would have stayed awake and would not have let his house be broken into. Therefore you also must be ready, for the Son of Man is coming at an unexpected hour.

"Who then is the faithful and wise servant, whom his master has put in charge of his household, to give the other servants their allowance of food at the proper time? Blessèd is that servant whom his master will find at work when he arrives."

This is the gospel of the Lord.   *Matthew 24. 42-46*

Post Communion
God, shepherd of your people,
whose servant Dunstan revealed the loving service of Christ
 in his ministry as a pastor of your people:
by this eucharist in which we share
awaken within us the love of Christ
and keep us faithful to our Christian calling;
through him who laid down his life for us,
but is alive and reigns with you,
now and for ever.

Alcuin of York, Abbot of Tours
20 May – Lesser Festival – Teacher of the Faith – White

Alcuin was descended from a noble Northumbrian family. Although the date and place of his birth are not known, he was probably born in the year 735 in or near York. He entered the cathedral school there as a child, continued as a Scholar and became Master.   In 781, he went to Aachen as adviser to Charlemagne on religious and educational matters and as Master of the Palace School, where he established an important library. Although not a monk and in deacon's orders, in 796 he became Abbot of Tours, where he died in the year 804. Alcuin wrote poetry, revised the lectionary, compiled a sacramentary and was involved in other significant liturgical work.

Collect
God of Wisdom, Eternal Light,
who shone in the heart of your servant Alcuin,
revealing to him your power and pity:
scatter the darkness of our ignorance
that, with all our heart and mind and strength,
we may seek your face
and be brought with all your saints
to your holy presence;
through Jesus Christ your Son our Lord,
who is alive and reigns with you,
in the unity of the Holy Spirit,
one God, now and for ever.

A reading from the prophecy of Isaiah.

I will greatly rejoice in the Lord, my whole being shall exult in my God; for he has clothed me with the garments of salvation, he has covered me with the robe of righteousness, as a bridegroom decks himself with a garland, and as a bride adorns herself with her jewels. For as the earth brings forth its shoots, and as a garden causes what is sown in it to spring up, so the Lord God will cause righteousness and praise to spring up before all the nations.

For Zion's sake I will not keep silent, and for Jerusalem's sake I will not rest, until her vindication shines out like the dawn, and her salvation like a burning torch. The nations shall see your vindication, and all the kings your glory; and you shall be called by a new name that the mouth of the Lord will give. You shall be a crown of beauty in the hand of the Lord, and a royal diadem in the hand of your God.

This is the word of the Lord.   *Isaiah 61.10 - 62.3*

Responsorial Psalm

**R   To you, O God, I lift up my eyes,
[to you enthroned in the heavens].**

As the eyes of servants look to the hand of their masters,
and the eyes of a maid to the hand of her mistress,
so our eyes look to the Lord our God,
until he show us his mercy. **R**

Have mercy upon us, O Lord, have mercy,
for we have had more than enough of contempt,
too much of the scorn of the indolent rich,
and of the derision of the proud. **R**   *Psalm 123*

A reading from the Letter of Paul to the Colossians.

As God's chosen ones, holy and beloved, clothe yourselves with compassion, kindness, humility, meekness, and patience. Bear with one another and, if anyone has a complaint against another, forgive each other; just as the Lord has forgiven you, so you also must forgive. Above all, clothe yourselves with love, which binds everything together in perfect harmony. And let the peace of Christ rule in your hearts, to which indeed you were called in the one body. And be thankful. Let the word of Christ dwell in you richly; teach and admonish one another in all wisdom; and with gratitude in your hearts sing psalms, hymns, and spiritual songs to God.

This is the word of the Lord.   *Colossians 3. 12-16*

Hear the gospel of our Lord Jesus Christ according to John.

The Samaritan woman at the well said to Jesus, "Sir, I see that you are a prophet. Our ancestors worshiped on this mountain, but you Jews say that the place where people must worship is in Jerusalem." Jesus said to her, "Woman, believe me, the hour is coming when you will worship the Father neither on this mountain nor in Jerusalem. You worship what you do not know; we worship what we know, for salvation is from the Jews. But the hour is coming, and is now here, when the true worshippers will worship the Father in spirit and truth, for the Father seeks such as these to worship him. God is spirit, and those who worship him must worship in spirit and truth."

This is the gospel of the Lord.   *John 4. 19-24*

Post Communion
Merciful God,
who gave such grace to your servant Alcuin
that he served you with singleness of heart
and loved you above all things:
help us, whose communion with you
  has been renewed in this sacrament,
to forsake all that holds us back from following Christ
and to grow into his likeness from glory to glory;
through Jesus Christ our Lord.

Helena, Protector of the Holy Places
21 May – Commemoration
If celebrated as a Lesser Festival, Common of any Saint, page 523

The Empress Helena only came to power in the Roman Empire when her son Constantine became Emperor, in the year 306. Although she had previously been abandoned by her husband, her son raised her to a position of great honour. As Helena was a Christian she gave her support to their cause and, in the year 326, she made a pilgrimage to the Holy Land. There she provided the wherewithal to found the building of a basilica on the Mount of Olives and another at Bethlehem. According to fourth-century historians, she discovered the cross on which Christ was crucified. In the Eastern Church, she is commemorated on this day, together with her son Constantine.

John & Charles Wesley

24 May – Lesser Festival – Pastors – White

Born at Epworth Rectory in Lincolnshire, John Wesley was the son of an Anglican clergyman and a Puritan mother. He entered Holy Orders and, following a religious experience on this day in 1738, began an itinerant ministry which recognised no parish boundaries. This resulted, after his death, in the development of a world-wide Methodist Church. His spirituality involved an Arminian affirmation of grace, frequent communion and a disciplined corporate search for holiness. His open-air preaching, concern for education and for the poor, liturgical revision, organisation of local societies and training of preachers provided a firm basis for Christian growth and mission in England.

Charles shared with his brother John the building up of early Methodist societies, as they travelled the country. His special concern was that early Methodists should remain loyal to Anglicanism. He married and settled in Bristol, later in London, concentrating his work on the local Christian communities. His thousands of hymns established a resource of lyrical piety which has enabled generations of Christians to re-discover the refining power of God's love. They celebrate God's work of grace from birth to death, the great events of God's work of salvation and the rich themes of eucharistic worship, anticipating the taking up of humanity into the divine life.

John died on 2 March 1791 and Charles on 29 March 1788.

Collect

God of mercy,
who inspired John and Charles Wesley
  with zeal for your gospel:
grant to all people boldness to proclaim your word
and a heart ever to rejoice in singing your praises;
through Jesus Christ your Son our Lord,
who is alive and reigns with you,
in the unity of the Holy Spirit,
one God, now and for ever.

A reading from the prophecy of Ezekiel.

The Lord God said to me: O mortal, stand up on your feet, and I
will speak with you. And when he spoke to me, a spirit entered
into me and set me on my feet; and I heard him speaking to me.
He said to me, Mortal, I am sending you to the people of Israel, to
a nation of rebels who have rebelled against me; they and their
ancestors have transgressed against me to this very day. The
descendants are impudent and stubborn. I am sending you to
them, and you shall say to them, "Thus says the Lord God."
Whether they hear or refuse to hear (for they are a rebellious
house), they shall know that there has been a prophet among
them.

This is the word of the Lord.   *Ezekiel 2. 1-5*

Responsorial Psalm

**R   Sing God's praises among the nations;
[let all the earth come to know the Lord].**

Rejoice in the Lord, you righteous;
it is good for the just to sing praises.
Praise the Lord with the harp;
play to him upon the psaltery and lyre. **R**

Sing for him a new song;
sound a fanfare with all your skill upon the trumpet.
For the word of the Lord is right,
and all his works are sure. **R**

He loves righteousness and justice;
the loving-kindness of the Lord fills the whole earth.
By the word of the Lord were the heavens made,
by the breath of his mouth all the heavenly hosts. **R**

He gathers up the waters of the ocean as in a water-skin
and stores up the depths of the sea.
Let all the earth fear the Lord;
let all who dwell in the world stand in awe of him. **R**

From Psalm 33

A reading from the Letter of Paul to the Ephesians.

Be careful then how you live, not as unwise people but as wise, making the most of the time, because the days are evil. So do not be foolish, but understand what the will of the Lord is. Do not get drunk with wine, for that is debauchery; but be filled with the Spirit, as you sing psalms and hymns and spiritual songs among yourselves, singing and making melody to the Lord in your hearts, giving thanks to God the Father at all times and for everything in the name of our Lord Jesus Christ.

This is the word of the Lord.   *Ephesians 5. 15-20*

Hear the gospel of our Lord Jesus Christ according to Mark.

The apostles gathered around Jesus, and told him all that they had done and taught. He said to them, "Come away to a deserted place all by yourselves and rest a while." For many were coming and going, and they had no leisure even to eat. And they went away in the boat to a deserted place by themselves. Now many saw them going and recognised them, and they hurried there on foot from all the towns and arrived ahead of them. As he went ashore, he saw a great crowd; and he had compassion for them, because they were like sheep without a shepherd; and he began to teach them many things.

This is the gospel of the Lord.   *Mark 6. 30-34*

Post Communion
God, shepherd of your people,
whose servants John and Charles Wesley
revealed the loving service of Christ
  in their ministry as pastors of your people:
by this eucharist in which we share
awaken within us the love of Christ
and keep us faithful to our Christian calling;
through him who laid down his life for us,
but is alive and reigns with you, now and for ever.

The Venerable Bede
25 May – Lesser Festival – Religious – White

Bede was born in Northumbria around the year 670. When he was
seven years old, his family gave him to the monastery of St Peter
and St Paul at Wearmouth. He then moved to Jarrow, where he
lived as a monk for the rest of his life. Although it seems he never
travelled further than York, his monastery – first under Abbot
Benet Biscop and then Abbot Ceolfrith – was a centre of learning,
and Bede studied extensively. He used all the resources available
to write the most complete history of Christian England up to the
year 729, as well as commentaries on books of the Bible. He was
renowned for his monastic fidelity and his love of teaching, and
was fondly remembered by his pupils, including his biographer.
He died peacefully in 735.

Collect
God our Maker,
whose Son Jesus Christ gave to your servant Bede
grace to drink in with joy
  the Word that leads us to know you and to love you:
in your goodness
grant that we also may come at length to you,
the source of all wisdom,
and stand before your face;
through Jesus Christ your Son our Lord,
who is alive and reigns with you, in the unity of the Holy Spirit,
one God, now and for ever.

A reading from the book Ecclesiasticus.

The one who devotes himself to the study of the law seeks out the wisdom of all the ancients, and is concerned with prophecies; he preserves the sayings of the famous and penetrates the subtleties of parables; he seeks out the hidden meanings of proverbs and is at home with the obscurities of parables. He serves among the great and appears before rulers; he travels in foreign lands and learns what is good and evil in the human lot. He sets his heart to rise early to seek the Lord who made him, and to petition the Most High; he opens his mouth in prayer and asks pardon for his sins.

If the great Lord is willing, he will be filled with the spirit of understanding; he will pour forth words of wisdom of his own and give thanks to the Lord in prayer. The Lord will direct his counsel and knowledge, as he meditates on his mysteries. He will show the wisdom of what he has learned, and will glory in the law of the Lord's covenant. Many will praise his understanding; it will never be blotted out. His memory will not disappear, and his name will live through all generations. Nations will speak of his wisdom, and the congregation will proclaim his praise.

This is the word of the Lord.   *Ecclesiasticus 39. 1-10*

Responsorial Psalm

R   Nations will speak of God's wisdom
[and the congregation will proclaim his praise].

Hear my teaching, O my people;
incline your ears to the words of my mouth.
I will open my mouth in a parable;
I will declare the mysteries of ancient times. **R**

That which we have heard and known,
and what our forebears have told us,
we will not hide from their children.
we will recount to generations to come. **R**

He gave his decrees to Jacob
and established a law for Israel,
which he commanded them to teach their children,
that the generations to come might know. **R**

That they in their turn might tell it to their children
and that they might put their trust in God
and not forget the deeds of God,
but keep his commandments. **R**   *From Psalm 78*

A reading from the First Letter of Paul to the Corinthians.

The message about the cross is foolishness to those who are perishing, but to us who are being saved it is the power of God. For it is written, "I will destroy the wisdom of the wise, and the discernment of the discerning I will thwart." Where is the one who is wise? Where is the scribe? Where is the debater of this age? Has not God made foolish the wisdom of the world? For since, in the wisdom of God, the world did not know God through wisdom, God decided, through the foolishness of our proclamation, to save those who believe. For Jews demand signs and Greeks desire wisdom, but we proclaim Christ crucified, a stumbling block to Jews and foolishness to Gentiles, but to those who are the called, both Jews and Greeks, Christ the power of God and the wisdom of God. For God's foolishness is wiser than human wisdom, and God's weakness is stronger than human strength.

This is the word of the Lord.   *1 Corinthians 1. 18-25*

Hear the gospel of our Lord Jesus Christ according to John.

Peter turned and saw the disciple whom Jesus loved following them; he was the one who had reclined next to Jesus at the supper and had said, "Lord, who is it that is going to betray you?" When Peter saw him, he said to Jesus, "Lord, what about him?" Jesus said to him, "If it is my will that he remain until I come, what is that to you? Follow me!" So the rumour spread in the community that this disciple would not die. Yet Jesus did not say to him that he would not die, but, "If it is my will that he remain until I come, what is that to you?" This is the disciple who is testifying to these things and has written them, and we know that his testimony is true. But there are also many other things that Jesus did; if every one of them were written down, I suppose that the world itself could not contain the books that would be written.

This is the gospel of the Lord.   *John 21. 20-25*

Post Communion
Merciful God,
who gave such grace to your servant Bede
that he served you with singleness of heart
and loved you above all things:
help us, whose communion with you
  has been renewed in this sacrament,
to forsake all that holds us back from following Christ
and to grow into his likeness from glory to glory;
through Jesus Christ our Lord.

Aldhelm, Bishop of Sherborne
25 May – *Commemoration*
If celebrated as a Lesser Festival, Common of Bishops, page 483

Born in the year 639, Aldhelm became a monk at Malmesbury, and later was elected its abbot. When the growing Wessex diocese was divided in 705, he became the first Bishop of Sherborne, founding the abbey church. Aldhelm was a great scholar, teacher and singer who, 'by his preaching completed the conquest of Wessex', according to Bede. Tradition has it that he would attract listeners by his singing and then preach the gospel to them. It seems he may have also been responsible for introducing the Rule of St Benedict to the area. He built churches all over Dorset, and the headland – commonly called St Alban's Head – is in reality *Saint Aldhelm's Head*, where there is an ancient chapel. His old English verse, sung to harp accompaniment, was praised by King Alfred. Aldhelm died on this day in the year 709 at Doulting in Somerset, on his way to Malmesbury.

Augustine, Archbishop of Canterbury
26 May – *Lesser Festival* – *Missionary* – *White*

Augustine was prior of the monastery of St Andrew in Rome. In 596, at the instigation of Pope Gregory the Great, he was dispatched as the leader of a group of forty monks to re-evangelise the English Church. Augustine appears not to have been a particularly confident person and, in Gaul, he wanted to turn back, but Pope Gregory's firm resolution held the group to their mission. The monks finally landed in Kent in the summer of 597 where they were well received by King Ethelbert whose wife, Bertha, was a Christian. Once established, Augustine returned temporarily to Gaul to receive ordination as a bishop. Pope Gregory would have preferred London to have become the primatial see, but in the event Canterbury was chosen and thus Augustine became the first archbishop of Canterbury. He died in either 604 or 605.

Collect
Almighty God,
whose servant Augustine was sent as the apostle
 of the English people:
grant that as he laboured in the Spirit
to preach Christ's gospel in this land
so all who hear the good news
may strive to make your truth known in all the world;
through Jesus Christ your Son our Lord,
who is alive and reigns with you,
in the unity of the Holy Spirit,
one God, now and for ever.

A reading from the prophecy of Isaiah.

Thus says the Lord God: I will soon lift up my hand to the nations, and raise my signal to the peoples; and they shall bring your sons in their bosom, and your daughters shall be carried on their shoulders. Kings shall be your foster fathers, and their queens your nursing mothers. With their faces to the ground they shall bow down to you, and lick the dust of your feet. Then you will know that I am the Lord; those who wait for me shall not be put to shame. Can the prey be taken from the mighty, or the captives of a tyrant be rescued? But thus says the Lord: Even the captives of the mighty shall be taken, and the prey of the tyrant be rescued; for I will contend with those who contend with you, and I will save your children.

This is the word of the Lord.   *Isaiah 49. 22-25*

Responsorial Psalm

R I will lift up my hand to the nations, says God,
[and raise my signal to the peoples].

Sing to the Lord a new song,
for he has done marvellous things.
With his right hand and his holy arm
has he won for himself the victory. **R**

The Lord has made known his victory;
in the sight of the nations
all the ends of the earth have seen
the victory of our God. **R**

Shout with joy to the Lord, all you lands;
lift up your voice, rejoice and sing.
Sing to the Lord with the harp,
with the harp and the voice of song. **R**

With trumpets and the sound of the horn
shout with joy before the King, the Lord.
Let the sea make a noise and all that is in it,
the lands and those who dwell therein. **R**   *From Psalm 98*

A reading from the First Letter of Paul to the Thessalonians.

As you know, we had courage in our God to declare to you the
gospel of God in spite of great opposition. For our appeal does not
spring from deceit or impure motives or trickery, but just as we
have been approved by God to be entrusted with the message of
the gospel, even so we speak, not to please mortals, but to please
God who tests our hearts. As you know and as God is our witness,
we never came with words of flattery or with a pretext for greed;
nor did we seek praise from mortals, whether from you or from
others, though we might have made demands as apostles of
Christ. But we were gentle among you, like a nurse tenderly caring for her own children. So deeply do we care for you that we are
determined to share with you not only the gospel of God but also
our own selves, because you have become very dear to us.

This is the word of the Lord.   *1 Thessalonians 2. 2b-8*

Hear the gospel of our Lord Jesus Christ according to Matthew.

Jesus put before his disciples another parable: "The kingdom of heaven is like a mustard seed that someone took and sowed in his field; it is the smallest of all the seeds, but when it has grown it is the greatest of shrubs and becomes a tree, so that the birds of the air come and make nests in its branches."

He told them another parable: "The kingdom of heaven is like yeast that a woman took and mixed in with three measures of flour until all of it was leavened."

This is the gospel of the Lord.   *Matthew 13. 31-33*

Post Communion
God, shepherd of your people,
whose servant Augustine revealed the loving service of Christ
 in his ministry as a pastor of your people:
by this eucharist in which we share
awaken within us the love of Christ
and keep us faithful to our Christian calling;
through him who laid down his life for us,
but is alive and reigns with you, now and for ever.

John Calvin, Reformer
26 May – Commemoration
If celebrated as a Lesser Festival, Common of Pastors, page 483

The French reformer John Calvin was born at Noyon in Picardy in 1509 and, since he was intended for an ecclesiastical career, he received the tonsure and his first benefice at the age of twelve, not untypical at this time. It proved to be the only 'order' he ever received. Two years later he began studying theology at Paris but for some reason changed to law and moved to Orléans where he came under his first Protestant influences. He broke with the Roman Church in 1533, having had a religious experience which he believed commissioned him to purify and restore the Church of Christ. The first edition of his *Institutes* appeared in 1536, being basically a justification of Reformation principles. Calvin accepted a position in Geneva which involved organising the Reformation in that city and, with a few absences, spent most of the the the rest of his life there, becoming the undisputed master of the moral and ecclesial lives of the citizenry. His pre-eminence could be seen in that he wrote to the Protector Somerset in England indicating to him what changes he felt should be made and corresponded similarly with other nations' leaders. During all this, his literary output never wavered. His immense reputation and influence have continued in the churches of the Reform to the present day. He died on this day in 1564.

Philip Neri, Founder of the Oratorians
26 May – Commemoration
If celebrated as a Lesser Festival, Common of Pastors, page 483

Born in 1515 in Florence, Philip Neri went to Rome when he was eighteen, resolved to give his life to God. He studied hard and led a noticeably austere life and, after a time living the life of a virtual hermit in the Roman catacombs, founded a fraternity to assist pilgrims and the sick. He was ordained in 1551 and he joined a company of priests working in San Girolamo Church, where he soon became a popular confessor and spiritual guide. As many regularly came to the oratory in that church, where he held spiritual conferences, other priests were attracted to his teaching and the Congregation of the Oratory was founded. It finally received papal approval in 1575. Philip was such a popular and revered person in the city that he was treated almost like a living saint, even instructing the Pope to grant absolution to the French monarch, Henry IV, to prevent a political catastrophe. This kind and gentle priest gave his life for the service of others and died on this day in the year 1595.

Lanfranc, Prior of Le Bec, Archbishop of Canterbury
28 May – Commemoration
If celebrated as a Lesser Festival, Common of Bishops, page 483

Lanfranc was born in Pavia, Italy, around the year 1005. At the age of thirty-five, he became a monk of Le Bec, in Normandy, where he founded the school which rose rapidly to renown throughout Europe. In 1062 William of Normandy appointed him Abbot of Caen, then in 1070 Archbishop of Canterbury. Lanfranc was a great ecclesiastical statesman, overseeing administrative, judicial and ecclesial reforms with the same energy and rigour that the Conqueror displayed in his new kingdom. Lanfranc did not forget his monastic formation: he wrote Constitutions for Christchurch, Canterbury, based on the customs of Le Bec, and appointed many Norman abbots to implement his vision in the English abbeys. He died in 1089.

Josephine Butler, Social Reformer
30 May – Lesser Festival – Of any Saint – White

Josephine Butler (née Grey) was born in April 1828, and baptised on this day that year, in Northumberland. She married an Anglican priest in 1852. She became incensed by the way contemporary society treated prostitutes, most of whom were forced into such activity through desperate poverty. From 1869, she campaigned for the repeal of the legislation which put all opprobrium onto the women concerned, and the issue became international after she travelled in Europe addressing meetings in 1874-75. Her campaign succeeded with the repeal of the Contagious Diseases Act in 1883. She was a devout Anglican and a woman of prayer, basing her spirituality on that of St Catherine of Siena, whose biography she wrote. She died on 30 December 1906.

Collect
God of compassion and love,
by whose grace your servant Josephine Butler
followed in the way of your Son
in caring for those in need:
help us like her to work with strength
for the restoration of all
to the dignity and freedom of those created in your image;
through Jesus Christ our Saviour,
who is alive and reigns with you,
in the unity of the Holy Spirit,
one God, now and for ever.

A reading from the prophecy of Isaiah.

Is not this the fast that I choose: to loose the bonds of injustice, to undo the thongs of the yoke, to let the oppressed go free, and to break every yoke? Is it not to share your bread with the hungry, and bring the homeless poor into your house; when you see the naked, to cover them, and not to hide yourself from your own kin? Then your light shall break forth like the dawn, and your healing shall spring up quickly; your vindicator shall go before you, the glory of the Lord shall be your rear guard. Then you shall call, and the Lord will answer; you shall cry for help, and he will say, Here I am. If you remove the yoke from among you, the pointing of the finger, the speaking of evil, if you offer your food to the hungry and satisfy the needs of the afflicted, then your light shall rise in the darkness and your gloom be like the noonday. The Lord will guide you continually, and satisfy your needs in parched places, and make your bones strong; and you shall be like a watered garden, like a spring of water, whose waters never fail.

This is the word of the Lord. *Isaiah 58. 6-11*

Responsorial Psalm

R You shall call, and the Lord will answer
[you shall cry, and he will say, "Here am I"].

Help me, Lord, for there is no godly one left;
the faithful have vanished from among us.
Everyone speaks falsely with their neighbour;
with a smooth tongue they speak from a double heart. **R**

O that the Lord would cut off all smooth tongues,
and close the lips that utter proud boasts!
Those who say, "With our tongue will we prevail;
our lips are our own; who is lord over us?" **R**

"Because the needy are oppressed,
and the poor cry out in misery,
I will rise up", says the Lord,
"and give them the help they long for." **R**

The words of the Lord are pure words,
like silver refined from ore and purified seven times in the fire.
O Lord, watch over us
and save us from this generation for ever. **R**   *From Psalm 12*

A reading from the First Letter of John.

Little children, let us love, not in word or speech, but in truth and action. And by this we will know that we are from the truth and will reassure our hearts before him whenever our hearts condemn us; for God is greater than our hearts, and he knows everything. Beloved, if our hearts do not condemn us, we have boldness before God; and we receive from him whatever we ask, because we obey his commandments and do what pleases him.

And this is his commandment, that we should believe in the name of his Son Jesus Christ and love one another, just as he has commanded us.

This is the word of the Lord.   *1 John 3. 18-23*

Hear the gospel of our Lord Jesus Christ according to Matthew.

As Jesus sat at dinner in Matthew's house, many tax collectors and sinners came and were sitting with him and his disciples. When the Pharisees saw this, they said to his disciples, "Why does your teacher eat with tax collectors and sinners?" But when he heard this, he said, "Those who are well have no need of a physician, but those who are sick. Go and learn what this means, 'I desire mercy, not sacrifice.' For I have come to call not the righteous but sinners."

This is the gospel of the Lord.   *Matthew 9. 10-13*

Post Communion
God our Redeemer,
who inspired your servant Josephine Butler
  to witness to your love
and to work for the coming of your kingdom:
may we, who in this sacrament share the bread of heaven,
be fired by your Spirit to proclaim the gospel in our daily living
and never to rest content until your kingdom come,
on earth as it is in heaven;
through Jesus Christ our Lord.

Joan of Arc, Visionary
30 May – Commemoration
If celebrated as a Lesser Festival, Common of any Saint, page 513

Joan of Arc was born at Domrémy in 1412, the daughter of a peasant farmer. She first heard voices of particular saints when she
was fourteen years old, telling her to save France, which was
caught up in the Hundred Years War with England. Though at
first she was dismissed, her credibility increased when some of her
predictions began to come true. She managed to identify the dis-
guised dauphin – later to become Charles VII – whose approval
she gained. She persuaded troops to be set to relieve Orléans and
rode at their head, wearing white armour. They were successful
in battle, which increased the morale of the army and enhanced
the reputation of Joan. When the dauphin was crowned king at
Rheims, she stood at his side. Her voices had warned her that her
life would be short yet she was dangerously naïve in not seeing
the jealousies she provoked. After some failures in battle, she lost
favour and was eventually sold by the Duke of Burgundy to the
English, tried in a court for heresy by the Bishop of Beauvais and
eventually burned at the stake on this day in 1431. Twenty-five
years later, the pope formally declared her innocent. She was
made second patron of France after her canonisation in 1920.

Apolo Kivebulaya, Evangelist in Central Africa
30 May – Commemoration
If celebrated as a Lesser Festival, Common of Missionaries, page 503

Apolo Kivebulaya's first contact with Christian teaching was in
1884 and he was baptised the following year, becoming a teacher
in the Church of Uganda. He went as an evangelist and catechist
to Boga in the Belgian Congo and was ordained priest in 1903. He
built many churches and prepared countless catechumens for baptism. He spent the rest of his life at Boga, training teachers, super-
vising the school and evangelising the people of the forest. After
his death on this day in 1933, the Church Missionary Society sent
British missionaries to carry on his work.

The Visit of the Blessèd Virgin Mary to Elizabeth
31 May – Festival – of the BVM – White

The church today recalls the visit of Elizabeth to her cousin Mary, as recorded in Luke's gospel. The celebration of the feast first occurred at a Franciscan Order General Chapter in 1263 but quickly spread throughout Europe. Since it is a celebration clearly described in the gospel, the churches of the Reformation were less inclined to proscribe it as they were other Marian feasts, particularly as it was the occasion for Mary to sing her great hymn of praise in honour of her Lord and God. Just as Luke sees John the Baptist as the last of the prophets of the old covenant, he uses John's leaping in Elizabeth's womb as the first time John bears witness to Christ as the promised Messiah. Thereby he links the old covenant with the new. He seems to be saying that just as the old covenant clearly points to Jesus, so does its last prophet, yet to be born.

Collect
Almighty God,
by whose grace Elizabeth rejoiced with Mary
and greeted her as the mother of the Lord:
look with favour on your lowly servants
that, with Mary, we may magnify your holy name
and rejoice to acclaim her Son our Saviour,
who is alive and reigns with you,
in the unity of the Holy Spirit,
one God, now and for ever.

A reading from the prophecy of Zephaniah.

Sing aloud, O daughter Zion; shout, O Israel! Rejoice and exult with all your heart, O daughter Jerusalem! The Lord has taken away the judgments against you, he has turned away your enemies. The king of Israel, the Lord, is in your midst; you shall fear disaster no more. On that day it shall be said to Jerusalem: Do not fear, O Zion; do not let your hands grow weak. The Lord, your God, is in your midst, a warrior who gives victory; he will rejoice over you with gladness, he will renew you in his love; he will exult over you with loud singing as on a day of festival. I will remove disaster from you, so that you will not bear reproach for it.

This is the word of the Lord.   *Zephaniah 3. 14-18*

Responsorial Psalm

**R   Sing aloud to God, O daughter Zion!
[rejoice and exult with all your heart, O daughter Jerusalem!]**

Alleluia! Give praise, you servants of the Lord;
praise the name of the Lord.
Let the name of the Lord be blessed,
from this time forth for evermore. **R**

From the rising of the sun to its going down
let the name of the Lord be praised.
The Lord is high above all nations,
and his glory above the heavens. **R**

Who is like the Lord our God, who sits enthroned on high,
but stoops to behold the heavens and the earth?
He takes up the weak out of the dust
and lifts up the poor from the ashes. **R**

He sets them with the princes,
with the princes of his people.
He makes the woman of a childless house
to be a joyful mother of children. Alleluia! **R**   *Psalm 113*

A reading from the Letter of Paul to the Romans.

Let love be genuine; hate what is evil, hold fast to what is good; love one another with mutual affection; outdo one another in showing honour. Do not lag in zeal, be ardent in spirit, serve the Lord. Rejoice in hope, be patient in suffering, persevere in prayer. Contribute to the needs of the saints; extend hospitality to strangers. Bless those who persecute you; bless and do not curse them. Rejoice with those who rejoice, weep with those who weep. Live in harmony with one another; do not be haughty, but associate with the lowly; do not claim to be wiser than you are.

This is the word of the Lord.   *Romans 12. 9-16*

Hear the gospel of our Lord Jesus Christ according to Luke.

In those days Mary set out and went with haste to a Judean town in the hill country, where she entered the house of Zechariah and greeted Elizabeth. When Elizabeth heard Mary's greeting, the child leaped in her womb. And Elizabeth was filled with the Holy Spirit and exclaimed with a loud cry, "Blessèd are you among women, and blessèd is the fruit of your womb. And why has this happened to me, that the mother of my Lord comes to me? For as soon as I heard the sound of your greeting, the child in my womb leaped for joy. And blessèd is she who believed that there would be a fulfilment of what was spoken to her by the Lord."

And Mary said, "My soul magnifies the Lord, and my spirit rejoices in God my Saviour, for he has looked with favour on the lowliness of his servant. Surely, from now on all generations will call me blessèd; for the Mighty One has done great things for me, and holy is his name."

["His mercy is for those who fear him from generation to generation. He has shown strength with his arm; he has scattered the proud in the thoughts of their hearts. He has brought down the powerful from their thrones, and lifted up the lowly; he has filled the hungry with good things, and sent the rich away empty. He has helped his servant Israel, in remembrance of his mercy, according to the promise he made to our ancestors, to Abraham and to his descendants forever."

And Mary remained with her about three months and then returned to her home.]

This is the gospel of the Lord.   *Luke 1. 39-49 [50-56]*

Post Communion
Gracious God,
who gave joy to Elizabeth and Mary
as they recognised the signs of redemption
  at work within them:
help us, who have shared in the joy of this eucharist,
to know the Lord deep within us
and his love shining out in our lives,
that the world may rejoice in your salvation;
through Jesus Christ our Lord.

JUNE

Justin, Martyr at Rome
1 June – Lesser Festival – Martyr – Red

Justin was born of a pagan family at the beginning of the second century in Palestine. As a young man he explored many different philosophies before, at the age of thirty, embracing Christianity. He continued to wear the distinctive dress of a professional philosopher, and taught Christianity as a philosophy, first at Ephesus and later at Rome. He became an outstanding apologist for the Christian faith, and is honoured as the first Christian thinker to enter into serious dialogue with the other intellectual disciplines of his day, including Judaism. Justin always sought to reconcile the claims of faith and reason. It was at Rome in about the year 165 that he and some of his disciples were denounced as Christians and beheaded. The authentic record of their martyrdom based on an official court report has survived. Traditionally, Justin is often surnamed 'Martyr' because of his two-fold witness to Christ, through his apologetic writings and the manner of his death.

Collect
God our Redeemer,
who through the folly of the cross taught your martyr Justin
the surpassing knowledge of Jesus Christ:
remove from us every kind of error
that we, like him, may be firmly grounded in the faith,
and make your name known to all peoples;
through Jesus Christ your Son our Lord,
who is alive and reigns with you,
in the unity of the Holy Spirit,
one God, now and for ever.

A reading from the First Book of the Maccabees.

The officers of King Antiochus Epiphanes, who were enforcing apostasy, came to the town of Modein to make the Israelites offer sacrifice. Many from Israel came to them; and Mattathias and his sons were assembled. Then the king's officers spoke to Mattathias as follows: "You are a leader, honoured and great in this town, and supported by sons and brothers. Now be the first to come and do what the king commands, as all the Gentiles and the people of Judah and those that are left in Jerusalem have done. Then you and your sons will be numbered among the Friends of the king, and you and your sons will be honoured with silver and gold and many gifts."

But Mattathias answered and said in a loud voice: "Even if all the nations that live under the rule of the king obey him, and have chosen to obey his commandments, everyone of them abandoning the religion of their ancestors, I and my sons and my brothers will continue to live by the covenant of our ancestors. Far be it from us to desert the law and the ordinances. We will not obey the king's words by turning aside from our religion to the right hand or to the left."

This is the word of the Lord.   *1 Maccabees 2. 15-22*

Responsorial Psalm

**R   We will live by our covenant with God,
[turning neither to the right nor the left].**

Protect me, O God, for I take refuge in you;
I have said to the Lord,
"You are my Lord, my good above all other."
All my delight is upon the godly that are in the land,
upon those who are noble among the people. **R**

But those who run after other gods
shall have their troubles multiplied.
Their libations of blood I will not offer,
nor take the names of their gods upon my lips. **R**

O Lord, you are my portion and my cup;
it is you who uphold my lot.
My boundaries enclose a pleasant land;
indeed, I have a goodly heritage. **R**

I will bless the Lord who gives me counsel;
my heart teaches me, night after night.
I have set the Lord always before me;
because he is at my right hand I shall not fall. **R**

My heart, therefore, is glad and my spirit rejoices;
my body also shall rest in hope.
You will show me the path of life;
in your presence there is fullness of joy. **R** *From Psalm 16*

A reading from the First Letter of Paul to the Corinthians.

The message about the cross is foolishness to those who are perishing, but to us who are being saved it is the power of God. For it is written, "I will destroy the wisdom of the wise, and the discernment of the discerning I will thwart." Where is the one who is wise? Where is the scribe? Where is the debater of this age? Has not God made foolish the wisdom of the world? For since, in the wisdom of God, the world did not know God through wisdom, God decided, through the foolishness of our proclamation, to save those who believe. For Jews demand signs and Greeks desire wisdom, but we proclaim Christ crucified, a stumbling block to Jews and foolishness to Gentiles, but to those who are the called, both Jews and Greeks, Christ the power of God and the wisdom of God. For God's foolishness is wiser than human wisdom, and God's weakness is stronger than human strength.

This is the word of the Lord. *1 Corinthians 1. 18-25*

Hear the gospel of our Lord Jesus Christ according to John.

Jesus said to his disciples, "If the world hates you, be aware that it hated me before it hated you. If you belonged to the world, the world would love you as its own. Because you do not belong to the world, but I have chosen you out of the world – therefore the world hates you. Remember the word that I said to you, 'Servants are not greater than their master.' If they persecuted me, they will persecute you; if they kept my word, they will keep yours also. But they will do all these things to you on account of my name, because they do not know him who sent me."

This is the gospel of the Lord. *John 15. 18-21*

Post Communion
God,
who gave us this holy meal
in which we have celebrated the glory of the cross
and the victory of your martyr Justin:
by our communion with Christ
in his saving death and resurrection,
give us with all your saints the courage to conquer evil
and so to share the fruit of the tree of life;
through Jesus Christ our Lord.

The Martyrs of Uganda
3 June – Commemoration
If celebrated as a Lesser Festival, Common of Martyrs, page 464

Mwanga, the ruler of Uganda in 1886, wanted boys for his bed and when all the Christian pages began to refuse his advances, he had them put to death. They included Catholics and Anglicans. On their way to the place of execution, these young Christians sang hymns in honour of the Lord and some were still singing when the flames surrounded them. Barely a century later, the peoples of the land were persecuted by a tyrant who put many of the Christian leaders and followers of Christ to death. Anglicans and Roman Catholics unite on this day to remember those who witnessed in Uganda for Christ, even unto death.

Petroc, Abbot of Padstow
4 June – Commemoration
If celebrated as a Lesser Festival, Common of Religious, page 494

Often known as 'the captain of Cornish saints', Petroc seems to have been the son of a Welsh chieftain who, on arrival in Cornwall, founded a monastery at Lanwethinoc, now called Padstow (from Petroc's Stow) and later on another at Bodmin. Most of his life, however, seems to have been lived as a hermit, though he travelled regularly to visit monasteries. He died at Treravel and was buried at Padstow. Many churches in Devon and Cornwall are dedicated to his memory.

Boniface of Crediton, Apostle of Germany
5 June – Lesser Festival – Martyr – Red

Born at Crediton in Devon in about the year 675, Winfrith took the name Boniface when he entered the monastery in Exeter as a young man. He became a Latin scholar and poet and was ordained when he was thirty years old. He rejected a safe ecclesiastical career in England and, in the year 716, became a missionary to Frisia, following in the steps of Willibrord. He eventually was commissioned by the pope to work in Hesse and Bavaria where he went after consecration as bishop in the year 722. He courageously felled a sacred oak at Geismar and, since the pagan gods did not come to the rescue, widespread conversion followed. He was the founder of a string of monasteries across southern Germany and made sure that they were places of learning, so that evangelising could continue. He was made Archbishop of Mainz in the year 732, where he consecrated many missionary bishops. He worked assiduously for the reform of the Church in France and managed to ensure that the more stable Rule of St Benedict was adhered to in her monasteries. He crowned Pepin as the Frankish king in 751 but was already very old. While waiting for some new Christians to arrive for confirmation, he was murdered by a band of pagans on this day in the year 754. He has been judged as having a deeper influence on European history than any other Englishman.

Collect
God our Redeemer,
who called your servant Boniface
to preach the gospel among the German people
and to build up your Church in holiness:
grant that we may preserve in our hearts
that faith which he taught with his words
  and sealed with his blood,
and profess it in lives dedicated to your Son
Jesus Christ our Lord,
who is alive and reigns with you,
in the unity of the Holy Spirit,
one God, now and for ever.

A reading from the prophecy of Isaiah.

And now the Lord says, who formed me in the womb to be his servant, to bring Jacob back to him, and that Israel might be gathered to him, for I am honoured in the sight of the Lord, and my God has become my strength – he says, "It is too light a thing that you should be my servant to raise up the tribes of Jacob and to restore the survivors of Israel; I will give you as a light to the nations, that my salvation may reach to the end of the earth." Thus says the Lord, the Redeemer of Israel and his Holy One, to one deeply despised, abhorred by the nations, the slave of rulers, "Kings shall see and stand up, princes, and they shall prostrate themselves, because of the Lord, who is faithful, the Holy One of Israel, who has chosen you." Thus says the Lord: In a time of favour I have answered you, on a day of salvation I have helped you; I have kept you and given you as a covenant to the people, to establish the land, to apportion the desolate heritages; saying to the prisoners, "Come out," to those who are in darkness, "Show yourselves." They shall feed along the ways, on all the bare heights shall be their pasture; they shall not hunger or thirst, neither scorching wind nor sun shall strike them down, for he who has pity on them will lead them, and by springs of water will guide them.

This is the word of the Lord.   *Isaiah 49. 5-10*

Responsorial Psalm

**R   I will give you as a light to the nations, says God,
    [that my salvation may reach to the end of the earth].**

Not to us, O Lord, not to us,
but to your name give glory;
because of your love and because of your faithfulness. **R**

Why should the heathen say,
"Where then is their God?"
Our God is in heaven;
whatever he wills to do he does. **R**

O Israel, trust in the Lord;
O house of Aaron, trust in the Lord;
You who fear the Lord, trust in the Lord;
he is their help and their shield. **R**

The Lord has been mindful of us and he will bless us;
He will bless those who fear the Lord,
both small and great together. **R**   *From Psalm 115*

A reading from the Acts of the Apostles.

Paul said to the elders of the church at Ephesus: "I do not count
my life of any value to myself, if only I may finish my course and
the ministry that I received from the Lord Jesus, to testify to the
good news of God's grace. And now I know that none of you,
among whom I have gone about proclaiming the kingdom, will
ever see my face again. Therefore I declare to you this day that I
am not responsible for the blood of any of you, for I did not shrink
from declaring to you the whole purpose of God. Keep watch
over yourselves and over all the flock, of which the Holy Spirit has
made you overseers, to shepherd the church of God that he
obtained with the blood of his own Son."

This is the word of the Lord.   *Acts 20. 24-28*

Hear the gospel of our Lord Jesus Christ according to Luke.

The Lord appointed seventy others and sent them on ahead of
him in pairs to every town and place where he himself intended
to go. He said to them, "The harvest is plentiful, but the labourers
are few; therefore ask the Lord of the harvest to send out labourers into his harvest. Go on your way. See, I am sending you out
like lambs into the midst of wolves. Carry no purse, no bag, no
sandals; and greet no one on the road. Whatever house you enter,
first say, 'Peace to this house!' And if anyone is there who shares
in peace, your peace will rest on that person; but if not, it will
return to you. Remain in the same house, eating and drinking
whatever they provide, for the labourer deserves to be paid.
Do not move about from house to house. Whenever you enter a
town and its people welcome you, eat what is set before you; cure
the sick who are there, and say to them, 'The kingdom of God has
come near to you.' But whenever you enter a town and they do
not welcome you, go out into its streets and say, 'Even the dust of
your town that clings to our feet, we wipe off in protest against
you. Yet know this: the kingdom of God has come near.' "

This is the gospel of the Lord.   *Luke 10. 1-11*

Post Communion
God,
who gave us this holy meal
in which we have celebrated the glory of the cross
and the victory of your martyr Boniface:
by our communion with Christ
in his saving death and resurrection,
give us with all your saints the courage to conquer evil
and so to share the fruit of the tree of life;
through Jesus Christ our Lord.

Ini Kopuria, Founder of the Melanesian Brotherhood
6 June – Commemoration
If celebrated as a Lesser Festival, Common of Religious, page 494

As a native policeman, Ini Kopuria's job took him all over
Guadalcanal in the Solomon Islands, but a vision of Jesus, calling
him to do different work for his people, led him to a life of evangelism in which he aimed to take and live the gospel in the
remotest villages and islands in Melanesia. He began a
Brotherhood for Melanesians in 1925 and, with help from his bishop, prepared a Rule and made vows himself in which he dedicated his life and his land to God. Men were asked to make only a
five-year commitment to service within the community and many
came to join him and stayed for much longer. It quickly grew into
one of the largest religious communities in the Anglican
Communion and its method of evangelism proved highly effective. Ini died on this day in 1945, revered throughout the Pacific
Islands and Papua New Guinea.

Thomas Ken, Bishop of Bath & Wells
8 June – Lesser Festival – Bishop – White

Thomas Ken was born at Berkhampstead in 1637 and educated at
New College Oxford. He was ordained priest in 1662 and worked
first in a poor parish in the diocese of Winchester and then at

Winchester College for ten years. He served as chaplain to King Charles II for two years and was then consecrated Bishop of Bath and Wells. After the king's death and the accession of the Roman Catholic James II, the new king proposed to rescind the Restoration penal laws, but Thomas and six of his fellow bishops refused to comply with this and were imprisoned on this day in 1688. But such was the integrity of Thomas that, when the king abandoned his throne and fled and the king's Protestant daughter Mary was offered the throne, together with her husband William of Orange, Thomas felt unable in good conscience to forswear his living, anointed monarch. He was deprived of his See, along with many other non-jurors, as they became known, and for a time there was schism in the Anglican fold. But Thomas spent his final twenty years in quiet retirement, anxious not to make trouble, and renounced his rights to his bishopric. He wrote many hymns, still much used, and died on 19 March 1711.

Collect
O God, from whom all blessings flow,
by whose providence we are kept
and by whose grace we are directed:
help us, through the example of your servant Thomas Ken,
faithfully to keep your word,
humbly to accept adversity
and steadfastly to worship you;
through Jesus Christ your Son our Lord,
who is alive and reigns with you,
in the unity of the Holy Spirit,
one God, now and for ever.

A reading from the prophecy of Jeremiah.

Thus says the Lord: Do not let the wise boast in their wisdom, do not let the mighty boast in their might, do not let the wealthy boast in their wealth; but let those who boast boast in this, that they understand and know me, that I am the Lord; I act with steadfast love, justice, and righteousness in the earth, for in these things I delight, says the Lord.

This is the word of the Lord.   *Jeremiah 9. 23-24*

Responsorial Psalm

**R   The Lord acts with steadfast love;
      [and in justice does he delight].**

Lord, who may dwell in your tabernacle?
who may abide upon your holy hill?
Whoever leads a blameless life and does what is right,
who speaks the truth from his heart. **R**

There is no guile upon his tongue;
he does no evil to his friend;
he does not heap contempt upon his neighbour. **R**

In his sight the wicked are rejected,
but he honours those who fear the Lord.
He has sworn to do no wrong
and does not take back his word. **R**

He does not give his money in hope of gain,
nor does he take a bribe against the innocent.
Whoever does these things
shall never be overthrown. **R**   *Psalm 15*

A reading from the Second Letter of Paul to the Corinthians.

Since it is by God's mercy that we are engaged in this ministry, we
do not lose heart. We have renounced the shameful things that
one hides; we refuse to practice cunning or to falsify God's word;
but by the open statement of the truth we commend ourselves to
the conscience of everyone in the sight of God. And even if our
gospel is veiled, it is veiled to those who are perishing. In their
case the god of this world has blinded the minds of the unbelievers, to keep them from seeing the light of the gospel of the glory of
Christ, who is the image of God. For we do not proclaim ourselves; we proclaim Jesus Christ as Lord and ourselves as your servants for Jesus' sake. For it is the God who said, "Let light shine
out of darkness," who has shone in our hearts to give the light of
the knowledge of the glory of God in the face of Jesus Christ.

 But we have this treasure in clay jars, so that it may be made clear
that this extraordinary power belongs to God and does not come
from us. We are afflicted in every way, but not crushed; perplexed, but not driven to despair; persecuted, but not forsaken;

struck down, but not destroyed; always carrying in the body the death of Jesus, so that the life of Jesus may also be made visible in our bodies.

This is the word of the Lord.   *2 Corinthians 4. 1-10*

Hear the gospel of our Lord Jesus Christ according to Matthew.

Jesus said to his disciples: "Keep awake, for you do not know on what day your Lord is coming. But understand this: if the owner of the house had known in what part of the night the thief was coming, he would have stayed awake and would not have let his house be broken into. Therefore you also must be ready, for the Son of Man is coming at an unexpected hour.

"Who then is the faithful and wise servant, whom his master has put in charge of his household, to give the other servants their allowance of food at the proper time? Blessèd is that servant whom his master will find at work when he arrives."

This is the gospel of the Lord.   *Matthew 24. 42-46*

Post Communion

God, shepherd of your people,
whose servant Thomas Ken revealed the loving service of Christ
 in his ministry as a pastor of your people:
by this eucharist in which we share
awaken within us the love of Christ
and keep us faithful to our Christian calling;
through him who laid down his life for us,
but is alive and reigns with you, now and for ever.

Columba of Iona
9 June – Lesser Festival – Missionary – White

Born in Ireland in about the year 521, Columba was trained as a monk by St Finnian and then founded several monasteries himself, including probably that of Kells, before leaving Ireland to settle on Iona, off the coast of Scotland. He was accompanied by twelve companions and the number grew as the monastic life became more established and well-known. Columba seems to have been an austere and, at times, harsh man who reputedly mellowed with age. He was concerned with building up both the monastery and its life and of enabling them to be instruments of mission in a heathen land. He converted kings and built churches, Iona becoming a starting point for the expansion of Christianity throughout Scotland. In the last four years of his life, when his health had failed, he spent the time transcribing books of the gospels for them to be taken out and used. He died on this day in the year 597.

Collect
Almighty God,
who filled the heart of Columba
with the joy of the Holy Spirit
and with deep love for those in his care:
may your pilgrim people follow him,
strong in faith, sustained by hope,
and one in the love that binds us to you;
through Jesus Christ your Son our Lord,
who is alive and reigns with you,
in the unity of the Holy Spirit,
one God, now and for ever.

A reading from the prophecy of Isaiah.

The spirit of the Lord God is upon me, because the Lord has anointed me; he has sent me to bring good news to the oppressed, to bind up the brokenhearted, to proclaim liberty to the captives, and release to the prisoners; to proclaim the year of the Lord's favour, and the day of vengeance of our God; to comfort all who mourn; to provide for those who mourn in Zion – to give them a garland instead of ashes, the oil of gladness instead of mourning, the mantle of praise instead of a faint spirit. They will be called oaks of righteousness, the planting of the Lord, to display his glory.

This is the word of the Lord.   *Isaiah 61. 1-3*

Responsorial Psalm

R The spirit of the Lord God is upon me
[because the Lord has anointed me].

I will bless the Lord at all times;
his praise shall ever be in my mouth.
I will glory in the Lord;
let the humble hear and rejoice. **R**

Proclaim with me the greatness of the Lord;
let us exalt his name together.
I sought the Lord and he answered me
and delivered me out of all my terror. **R**

Look upon him and be radiant,
and let not your faces be ashamed.
I called in my affliction and the Lord heard me
and saved me from all my troubles. **R**

The angel of the Lord encompasses those who fear him,
and he will deliver them.
Taste and see that the Lord is good;
happy are they who trust in him! **R**   *From Psalm 34*

A reading from the First Letter of Paul to the Thessalonians.

Though we had already suffered and been shamefully mistreated
at Philippi, as you know, we had courage in our God to declare to
you the gospel of God in spite of great opposition. For our appeal
does not spring from deceit or impure motives or trickery, but just
as we have been approved by God to be entrusted with the message of the gospel, even so we speak, not to please mortals, but to
please God who tests our hearts. As you know and as God is our
witness, we never came with words of flattery or with a pretext for
greed; nor did we seek praise from mortals, whether from you or
from others, though we might have made demands as apostles of
Christ. But we were gentle among you, like a nurse tenderly caring for her own children.

So deeply do we care for you that we are determined to share
with you not only the gospel of God but also our own selves,
because you have become very dear to us. You remember our
labour and toil, brothers and sisters; we worked night and day, so

that we might not burden any of you while we proclaimed to you the gospel of God. You are witnesses, and God also, how pure, upright, and blameless our conduct was toward you believers. As you know, we dealt with each one of you like a father with his children, urging and encouraging you and pleading that you lead a life worthy of God, who calls you into his own kingdom and glory.

This is the word of the Lord. *1 Thessalonians 2. 2-12*

Hear the gospel of our Lord Jesus Christ according to Luke.

Jesus said to his disciples, "Do not be afraid, little flock, for it is your Father's good pleasure to give you the kingdom. Sell your possessions, and give alms. Make purses for yourselves that do not wear out, an unfailing treasure in heaven, where no thief comes near and no moth destroys. For where your treasure is, there your heart will be also.

"Be dressed for action and have your lamps lit; be like those who are waiting for their master to return from the wedding banquet, so that they may open the door for him as soon as he comes and knocks. Blessèd are those servants whom the master finds alert when he comes; truly I tell you, he will fasten his belt and have them sit down to eat, and he will come and serve them."

This is the gospel of the Lord. *Luke 12. 32-37*

Post Communion
Holy Father,
who gathered us here around the table of your Son
to share this meal with the whole household of God:
in that new world where you reveal
  the fullness of your peace,
gather people of every race and language
to share with your servant Columba and all your saints
in the eternal banquet of Jesus Christ our Lord.

Ephrem of Syria

9 June – Commemoration

If celebrated as a Lesser Festival, Common of Teachers, page 473

Born of Christian parents around 306, Ephrem was baptised as a young man and then ordained deacon. His early years were spent as a teacher in Nisibis in Mesopotamia until the city fell under Persian occupation in 363. Fleeing from his home, he settled in Edessa (Urfa in south-east Turkey) where he established a school of theology. Best known for his Syriac poetry, Ephrem is acclaimed as the greatest poet of the early Christian centuries, described by his contemporaries as the 'Harp of the Spirit'. His hymns, still used today, have found a place in liturgical traditions outside the East Syrian Church. He died on this day in Edessa in the year 373, ministering to victims of the plague.

Barnabas the Apostle

11 June – Festival – Apostle – Red

Though not named among the twelve apostles of the evangelists, Barnabas emerges in the Acts of the Apostles as one of the most significant of their number. He sold his estate and gave the proceeds to the Church, since all things were to be held in common, and clearly became a leader. He is described as a Levite from Cyprus so, like his friend Paul, was from the Greek world rather than that of Palestine, and he introduced Paul to the leaders of the Church in Jerusalem. He was sent to Antioch apparently to guide the Christians there in their relations with non-Jewish converts, promoting the concept of all being one in Christ. He broke with Paul to go to Cyprus and tradition has it that he was martyred there in the year 61.

Collect
Bountiful God, giver of all gifts,
who poured your Spirit upon your servant Barnabas
and gave him grace to encourage others:
help us, by his example,
to be generous in our judgements
and unselfish in our service;
through Jesus Christ your Son our Lord,
who is alive and reigns with you,
in the unity of the Holy Spirit,
one God, now and for ever.

Job 29. 11-16	*or*	Acts 11. 19-30
Psalm 112		Psalm 112
Acts 11. 19-30		Galatians 2. 1-10
John 15. 12-17		John 15. 12-17

A reading from the book of Job.

When the ear heard, it commended me, and when the eye saw, it approved; because I delivered the poor who cried, and the orphan who had no helper. The blessing of the wretched came upon me, and I caused the widow's heart to sing for joy. I put on righteousness, and it clothed me; my justice was like a robe and a turban. I was eyes to the blind, and feet to the lame. I was a father to the needy, and I championed the cause of the stranger.

This is the word of the Lord.   *Job 29. 11-16*

A reading from the Acts of the Apostles.

Those who were scattered because of the persecution that took place over Stephen travelled as far as Phoenicia, Cyprus, and Antioch, and they spoke the word to no one except Jews. But among them were some men of Cyprus and Cyrene who, on coming to Antioch, spoke to the Hellenists also, proclaiming the Lord Jesus. The hand of the Lord was with them, and a great number became believers and turned to the Lord. News of this came to the ears of the church in Jerusalem, and they sent Barnabas to Antioch. When he came and saw the grace of God, he rejoiced, and he exhorted them all to remain faithful to the Lord with steadfast devotion; for he was a good man, full of the Holy Spirit and of faith. And a great many people were brought to the Lord. Then Barnabas went to Tarsus to look for Saul, and when he had found him, he brought him to Antioch. So it was that for an entire year they met with the church and taught a great many people, and it was in Antioch that the disciples were first called 'Christians'.

At that time prophets came down from Jerusalem to Antioch. One of them named Agabus stood up and predicted by the Spirit that there would be a severe famine over all the world; and this took place during the reign of Claudius. The disciples determined that according to their ability, each would send relief to the believers living in Judea; this they did, sending it to the elders by Barnabas and Saul.

This is the word of the Lord.   *Acts 11. 19-30*

Responsorial Psalm

R   **Clothe yourself with God's righteousness
    [and let justice be your garment].**

Alleluia! Happy are they who fear the Lord
and have great delight in his commandments!
Their descendants will be mighty in the land;
the generation of the upright will be blessed. **R**

Wealth and riches will be in their house,
and their righteousness will last for ever.
Light shines in the darkness for the upright;
the righteous are merciful and full of compassion. **R**

It is good for them to be generous in lending
and to manage their affairs with justice.
For they will never be shaken;
the righteous will be kept in everlasting remembrance. **R**

They have given freely to the poor,
and their righteousness stands fast for ever;
they will hold up their head with honour. **R**   *From Psalm 112*

A reading from the Letter of Paul to the Galatians.

After fourteen years I went up again to Jerusalem with Barnabas, taking Titus along with me. I went up in response to a revelation. Then I laid before them (though only in a private meeting with the acknowledged leaders) the gospel that I proclaim among the Gentiles, in order to make sure that I was not running, or had not run, in vain. But even Titus, who was with me, was not compelled to be circumcised, though he was a Greek. But because of false believers secretly brought in, who slipped in to spy on the freedom we have in Christ Jesus, so that they might enslave us – we did not submit to them even for a moment, so that the truth of the gospel might always remain with you. And from those who were supposed to be acknowledged leaders (what they actually were makes no difference to me; God shows no partiality) – those leaders contributed nothing to me.

On the contrary, when they saw that I had been entrusted with the gospel for the uncircumcised, just as Peter had been entrusted with the gospel for the circumcised (for he who worked through Peter making him an apostle to the circumcised also worked through me in sending me to the Gentiles), and when James and Cephas and John, who were acknowledged pillars, recognised the grace that had been given to me, they gave to Barnabas and me the right hand of fellowship, agreeing that we should go to the Gentiles and they to the circumcised. They asked only one thing, that we remember the poor, which was actually what I was eager to do.

This is the word of the Lord. *Galatians 2. 1-10*

Hear the gospel of our Lord Jesus Christ according to John.

Jesus said to his disciples: "This is my commandment, that you love one another as I have loved you. No one has greater love than this, to lay down one's life for one's friends. You are my friends if you do what I command you. I do not call you servants any longer, because the servant does not know what the master is doing; but I have called you friends, because I have made known to you everything that I have heard from my Father. You did not choose me but I chose you. And I appointed you to go and bear fruit, fruit that will last, so that the Father will give you whatever you ask him in my name. I am giving you these commands so that you may love one another."

This is the gospel of the Lord. *John 15. 12-17*

Post Communion
Almighty God,
who on the day of Pentecost
sent your Holy Spirit to the apostles
with the wind from heaven and in tongues of flame,
filling them with joy and boldness to preach the gospel:
by the power of the same Spirit
strengthen us to witness to your truth
and to draw everyone to the fire of your love;
through Jesus Christ our Lord.

Richard Baxter, Puritan Divine
14 June – Commemoration
If celebrated as a Lesser Festival, Common of Teachers, page 473

Richard Baxter was born at Rowton in Shropshire in 1615. In 1633
he was at the court of King Charles I but was so disgusted with the
low moral standards there that he returned home in order to study
divinity.   He was ordained but after the promulgation of an
infamous Oath in 1640, which required obedience to a string of
persons ending in the trite phrase 'et cetera', he rejected belief in
episcopacy in its current English form and went as a curate to a
poor area of the West Midlands. He opposed the Civil War and
played a prominent part in the recall of Charles II, but his continuing dissatisfaction with the way episcopacy was practised led
him to decline the See of Hereford. This refusal led him to be
debarred from further office in the Church, though he continued
to contribute to its life as a prolific hymn writer. His wife Margaret
Charlton, died on this day in 1681 and 'he mourned her irre-
pairably'; Richard died on 8 December in the year 1691.

Evelyn Underhill, Spiritual Writer
15 June – Commemoration
If celebrated as a Lesser Festival, Common of Spiritual Writers, page 473

Born in 1875, Evelyn Underhill was in her thirties before she began
to explore religion. At first, she wrote on the mystics, most notably
in her book *Mysticism*, published in 1911. Her spiritual journey

brought her in 1921 back to the Church of England, in which she had been baptised and confirmed. From the mid-1920s, she became highly-regarded as a retreat conductor and an influential spiritual director. Of her many books, *Worship,* published in 1936, embodied her approach to what she saw as the mystery of faith. She died on this day in 1941.

Richard of Chichester
16 June – Lesser Festival – Bishop – White

Richard de Wych, or of Droitwich as it is now known, was born there in 1197 and worked hard for his yeoman father to restore the family fortunes. Later he studied at Oxford and Paris and then in Bologna as an ecclesiastical lawyer. When he returned to England in 1235, he was made Chancellor of Oxford and eventually Chancellor to the Archbishop of Canterbury, Edmund of Abingdon. When Richard eventually became Bishop of Chichester, he was seen as a model diocesan bishop: progressing around his diocese on foot, visiting and caring for his clergy and people, generally being accessible to all who needed his ministry. He insisted that the sacraments be administered without payment and with a proper dignity. Whilst on a recruitment campaign for the Crusades, he fell ill at Dover and died there on 3 April 1253 and his mortal remains were translated to Chichester on this day in the year 1276.

Collect
Most merciful Redeemer,
who gave to your bishop Richard a love of learning,
a zeal for souls and a devotion to the poor:
grant that, encouraged by his example,
we may know you more clearly,
 love you more dearly,
 and follow you more nearly,
day by day,
who with the Father and the Holy Spirit are alive and reign,
one God, now and for ever.

A reading from the Book of Job.

Job said, "If I go forward, he is not there; or backward, I cannot perceive him; on the left he hides, and I cannot behold him; I turn to the right, but I cannot see him. But he knows the way that I take; when he has tested me, I shall come out like gold. My foot has held fast to his steps; I have kept his way and have not turned aside. I have not departed from the commandment of his lips; I have treasured in my bosom the words of his mouth. But he stands alone and who can dissuade him? What he desires, that he does. For he will complete what he appoints for me; and many such things are in his mind."

This is the word of the Lord.   *Job 23. 8-14*

Responsorial Psalm

**R   Arise, O God, and rule the earth,
     [for you shall take all nations for your own].**

God takes his stand in the council of heaven;
he gives judgement in the midst of the gods:
"How long will you judge unjustly,
and show favour to the wicked? **R**

"Save the weak and the orphan;
defend the humble and needy;
rescue the weak and the poor;
deliver them from the power of the wicked. **R**

"Now I say to you, 'You are gods,
and all of you children of the Most High;
nevertheless, you shall die like mortals,
and fall like any prince.'" **R**   *From Psalm 82*

A reading from the Letter of Paul to the Philippians.

I rejoice in the Lord greatly that now at last you have revived your concern for me; indeed, you were concerned for me, but had no opportunity to show it. Not that I am referring to being in need; for I have learned to be content with whatever I have. I know what it is to have little, and I know what it is to have plenty. In any and all circumstances I have learned the secret of being well-fed and of going hungry, of having plenty and of being in need. I can do all things through him who strengthens me.

This is the word of the Lord.   *Philippians 4.10-13*

Hear the gospel of our Lord Jesus Christ according to John.

When they had finished breakfast, Jesus said to Simon Peter, "Simon son of John, do you love me more than these?" He said to him, "Yes, Lord, you know that I love you." Jesus said to him, "Feed my lambs." A second time, he said to him, "Simon son of John, do you love me?" He said to him, "Yes, Lord; you know that I love you." Jesus said to him, "Tend my sheep." He said to him the third time, "Simon son of John, do you love me?" Peter felt hurt because he said to him the third time, "Do you love me?" And he said to him, "Lord, you know everything, you know that I love you." Jesus said to him, "Feed my sheep. Very truly I tell you, when you were younger, you used to fasten your own belt and to go wherever you wished. But when you grow old, you will stretch out your hands, and someone else will fasten a belt around you and take you where you do not wish to go." (Jesus said this to indicate the kind of death by which he would glorify God.) After this, he said to him, "Follow me."

This is the gospel of the Lord.   *John 21. 15-19*

Post Communion
God, shepherd of your people,
whose servant Richard revealed the loving service of Christ
  in his ministry as a pastor of your people:
by this eucharist in which we share
awaken within us the love of Christ
and keep us faithful to our Christian calling;
through him who laid down his life for us,
but is alive and reigns with you, now and for ever.

Joseph Butler, Bishop of Durham
16 June – Commemoration
If celebrated as a Lesser Festival, Common of Teachers, page 473

Born in 1692 at Wantage in Berkshire, Joseph Butler was the son of Presbyterian parents and studied at the dissenting academy of Tewkesbury. He abandoned Presbyterianism in 1714 for the Church of England and, after studying at Oxford, was ordained priest in 1718 and began preaching the sermons which won him his fine reputation. He became Bishop of Durham and now ranks among the greatest exponents of natural theology and ethics in England since the Reformation. He died on this day in 1752.

Samuel & Henrietta Barnett, Social Reformers
17 June – Commemoration
If celebrated as a Lesser Festival, Common of any Saint, page 527

Samuel Augustus Barnett was born in Bristol in 1844 and educated at Wadham College Oxford. To trace the beginnings of greatr movements is always difficult but it is clear that, followng his ordination, Samuel was closely concerned with the inception of the Charity Organisation Society, and worked alongside Octavia Hill. Two years after his ordination, he founded the Charity Organisation Society. From 1873 to 1894, he was vicar of St Jude's Whitechapel, where his unorthodox methods, including evening schools and entertainments, aroused much criticism. However, he soon became recognised as a loyal priest, devoted to the religious and cultural improvement of the East End of London. In all his work, he was ably assisted by Henrietta his wife. Henrietta Octavia Weston Rowland was born in Clapham in 1851 and, before her marriage to Samuel in 1873, had been a co-worker with Octavia Hill. In her later years, she founded Hampstead Garden Suburb, a community in which all classes might live together. Samuel's spiritual gifts, combined with Henrietta's robust energy and assertive personality, made for a dynamic expression of Christian faith. Samuel died on this day at Hove in 1913; Henrietta died at Hampstead Garden Suburb on 10 June 1936.

Bernard Mizeki, Apostle of the MaShona
18 June – Commemoration
If celebrated as a Lesser Festival, Common of Martyrs, page 464

Born in Portuguese East Africa, Bernard Mizeki went to work in Cape Town and there he was converted to the Christian faith by the Cowley Fathers. He then gave his life as a translator and evangelist among the MaShona in what is present-day Zimbabwe. He was murdered on this day in 1896 in a tribal uprising and is revered throughout Central Africa as a witness to the gospel of Christ.

Sundar Singh of India, Evangelist
19 June – Commemoration
If celebrated as a Lesser Festival, Common of Teachers, page 473

Born of wealthy Sikh parents, Sundar Singh was converted to Christianity after experiencing a vision. He was baptised in the Anglican church at Simla in 1905. In an endeavour to present Christianity in a Hindu form, he donned the robes of a 'Sadhu' or holy man and travelled much around the Indian sub-continent. He even made a visit to Tibet, where he persisted in strenuous work, despite ill health. He went missing there, presumed murdered, in April 1929.

Alban, First Martyr of Britain
22 June – Lesser Festival   Martyr – Red

Alban was a citizen of the Roman city of Verulamium (now St Albans in Hertfordshire) who gave shelter to a Christian priest fleeing from persecution, hiding him in his house for several days. Greatly influenced by his devotion to prayer, Alban received instruction from the priest and was converted. When the priest's hiding-place was discovered, Alban dressed himself in the priest's cloak and was arrested in his place. Tortured by the Roman authorities, Alban refused to renounce his faith. He was beheaded on this day, probably in the year 250, and so became the first British martyr. His shrine stands today as a place of pilgrimage in the Cathedral and Abbey Church of St Alban.

Collect
Eternal Father,
when the gospel of Christ first came to our land
you gloriously confirmed the faith of Alban
by making him the first to win a martyr's crown:
grant that, following his example,
in the fellowship of the saints
we may worship you, the living God,
and give true witness to Jesus Christ your Son our Lord,
who is alive and reigns with you,
in the unity of the Holy Spirit,
one God, now and for ever.

A reading from the Wisdom of Solomon.

The souls of the righteous are in the hand of God, and no torment will ever touch them. In the eyes of the foolish they seemed to have died: their departure was thought to be a disaster and their going from us to be their destruction, but they are at peace. For though in the sight of others they were punished, their hope is full of immortality.

This is the word of the Lord.   *Wisdom 3. 1-3*

Responsorial Psalm

**R Let the righteous be glad and rejoice before God;
[let them also be merry and joyful].**

Sing to God, sing praises to his name;
exalt him who rides upon the heavens;
Yahweh is his name, rejoice before him! **R**

Father of orphans, defender of widows,
God in his holy habitation!
God gives the solitary a home
and brings forth prisoners into freedom;
but the rebels shall live in dry places. **R**

O God, when you went forth before your people,
when you marched through the wilderness,
The earth shook and the skies poured down rain,
at the presence of God, the God of Sinai,
at the presence of God, the God of Israel. **R**   *From Ps 63*

A reading from the Second Letter of Paul to Timothy.

Share in suffering like a good soldier of Christ Jesus. No one serving in the army gets entangled in everyday affairs; the soldier's aim is to please the enlisting officer. And in the case of an athlete, no one is crowned without competing according to the rules. It is the farmer who does the work who ought to have the first share of the crops. Think over what I say, for the Lord will give you understanding in all things.

This is the word of the Lord.   *2 Timothy 2. 3-7*

Hear the gospel of our Lord Jesus Christ according to John.

Jesus said: "Very truly, I tell you, unless a grain of wheat falls into the earth and dies, it remains just a single grain; but if it dies, it bears much fruit. Those who love their life lose it, and those who hate their life in this world will keep it for eternal life. Whoever serves me must follow me, and where I am, there will my servant be also. Whoever serves me, the Father will honour.

This is the gospel of the Lord.   *John 12. 24-26*

Post Communion
God our Redeemer,
whose Church was strengthened
  by the blood of your martyr Alban:
so bind us, in life and death, to Christ's sacrifice
that our lives, broken and offered with his,
may carry his death and proclaim his resurrection in the world;
through Jesus Christ our Lord.

Etheldreda, Abbess of Ely
23 June – Lesser Festival – Religious – White

Etheldreda (Audrey) was born in Suffolk in the seventh century, a daughter of the king. She desired to commit her life to prayer and chastity and, after two arranged and unconsummated marriages, founded a religious house at Ely for both men and women, over which she ruled as Abbess. At her death on this day in 678, she was revered as a woman of austerity, prayer and prophecy.

Collect
Eternal God,
who bestowed such grace upon your servant Etheldreda
that she gave herself wholly to the life of prayer
  and to the service of your true religion:
grant that we, like her,
may so live our lives on earth seeking your kingdom
that by your guiding
we may be joined to the glorious fellowship of your saints;
through Jesus Christ your Son our Lord,
who is alive and reigns with you, in the unity of the Holy Spirit,
one God, now and for ever.

A reading from the Song of Songs.

Set me as a seal upon your heart, as a seal upon your arm; for love
is strong as death, passion fierce as the grave. Its flashes are flashes of fire, a raging flame. Many waters cannot quench love, neither can floods drown it. If one offered for love all the wealth of
his house, it would be utterly scorned.

This is the word of the Lord.   *Song of Songs 8. 6-7*

Responsorial Psalm

R Look upon God and be radiant;
   [happy are they who trust in him].

I will bless the Lord at all times;
his praise shall ever be in my mouth.
I will glory in the Lord;
let the humble hear and rejoice. **R**

Proclaim with me the greatness of the Lord;
let us exalt his name together.
I sought the Lord and he answered me
and delivered me out of all my terror. **R**

The angel of the Lord encompasses those who fear him,
and he will deliver them.
Taste and see that the Lord is good;
happy are they who trust in him. **R**   *From Psalm 34*

A reading from the Acts of the Apostles.

The whole group of those who believed were of one heart and soul, and no one claimed private ownership of any possessions, but everything they owned was held in common. With great power the apostles gave their testimony to the resurrection of the Lord Jesus, and great grace was upon them all. There was not a needy person among them, for as many as owned lands or houses sold them and brought the proceeds of what was sold. They laid it at the apostles' feet, and it was distributed to each as any had need.

This is the word of the Lord. *Acts 4. 32-35*

Hear the gospel of our Lord Jesus Christ according to Matthew.

Jesus said: "The kingdom of heaven will be like this. Ten bridesmaids took their lamps and went to meet the bridegroom. Five of them were foolish, and five were wise. When the foolish took their lamps, they took no oil with them; but the wise took flasks of oil with their lamps. As the bridegroom was delayed, all of them became drowsy and slept. But at midnight there was a shout, 'Look! Here is the bridegroom! Come out to meet him.' Then all those bridesmaids got up and trimmed their lamps. The foolish said to the wise, 'Give us some of your oil, for our lamps are going out.' But the wise replied, 'No! there will not be enough for you and for us; you had better go to the dealers and buy some for yourselves.' And while they went to buy it, the bridegroom came, and those who were ready went with him into the wedding banquet; and the door was shut. Later the other bridesmaids came also, saying, 'Lord, lord, open to us.' But he replied, 'Truly I tell you, I do not know you.' Keep awake therefore, for you know neither the day nor the hour."

This is the gospel of the Lord. *Matthew 25. 1-13*

Post Communion
Merciful God,
who gave such grace to your servant Etheldreda
that she served you with singleness of heart
and loved you above all things:

help us, whose communion with you
  has been renewed in this sacrament,
to forsake all that holds us back from following Christ
and to grow into his likeness from glory to glory;
through Jesus Christ our Lord.

The Birth of John the Baptist
24 June – Festival – White

The biblical story of John, the son of Elizabeth and Zechariah,
begins even before his birth. His leaping in his mother's womb is
seen as a great alleluia in anticipation of the birth of his Redeemer
and the good news of Jesus Christ is related in all four gospels as
beginning with John as Christ's forerunner. He seemed to have a
predestined rôle akin to that of the Old Testament prophets,
particularly in encouraging the people of God to live lives worthy
of their calling and in imminent anticipation of the coming of the
Anointed One. In the tradition of the early Fathers, John was seen
as endowed with grace from before his birth, and consequently
the Church has always kept the celebration of this day with
greater solemnity than that of his death.

Collect
Almighty God,
by whose providence your servant John the Baptist
was wonderfully born,
and sent to prepare the way of your Son our Saviour
by the preaching of repentance:
lead us to repent according to his preaching
and, after his example,
constantly to speak the truth, boldly to rebuke vice,
and patiently to suffer for the truth's sake;
through Jesus Christ your Son our Lord,
who is alive and reigns with you, in the unity of the Holy Spirit,
one God, now and for ever.

A reading from the prophecy of Isaiah.

Comfort, O comfort my people, says your God. Speak tenderly to Jerusalem, and cry to her that she has served her term, that her penalty is paid, that she has received from the Lord's hand double for all her sins.

A voice cries out: "In the wilderness prepare the way of the Lord, make straight in the desert a highway for our God. Every valley shall be lifted up, and every mountain and hill be made low; the uneven ground shall become level, and the rough places a plain. Then the glory of the Lord shall be revealed, and all people shall see it together, for the mouth of the Lord has spoken."

A voice says, "Cry out!" And I said, "What shall I cry?" All people are grass, their constancy is like the flower of the field. The grass withers, the flower fades, when the breath of the Lord blows upon it; surely the people are grass. The grass withers, the flower fades; but the word of our God will stand forever. Get you up to a high mountain, O Zion, herald of good tidings; lift up your voice with strength, O Jerusalem, herald of good tidings, lift it up, do not fear; say to the cities of Judah, "Here is your God!" See, the Lord God comes with might, and his arm rules for him; his reward is with him, and his recompense before him. He will feed his flock like a shepherd; he will gather the lambs in his arms, and carry them in his bosom, and gently lead the mother sheep.

This is the word of the Lord.   *Isaiah 40. 1-11*

Responsorial Psalm

**R   Righteousness shall go before our God,
     [and peace shall be a pathway for his feet].**

Show us your mercy, O Lord, and grant us your salvation.
I will listen to what the Lord God is saying,
for he is speaking peace to his faithful people
and to those who turn their hearts to him. **R**

Truly, his salvation is very near to those who fear him,
that his glory may dwell in our land.
Mercy and truth have met together;
righteousness and peace have kissed each other. **R**

Truth shall spring up from the earth,
and righteousness shall look down from heaven.
The Lord will indeed grant prosperity,
and our land will yield its increase. **R**   *From Psalm 85*

A reading from the Acts of the Apostles.

On the sabbath day, Paul and his companions went into the synagogue and sat down. After the reading of the law and the prophets, the officials of the synagogue sent them a message, saying, "Brothers, if you have any word of exhortation for the people, give it." So Paul stood up and with a gesture began to speak:

"You Israelites, and others who fear God, listen. The God of this people Israel chose our ancestors and made the people great during their stay in the land of Egypt, and with uplifted arm he led them out of it. For about forty years he put up with them in the wilderness. After he had destroyed seven nations in the land of Canaan, he gave them their land as an inheritance for about four hundred and fifty years. After that he gave them judges until the time of the prophet Samuel. Then they asked for a king; and God gave them Saul son of Kish, a man of the tribe of Benjamin, who reigned for forty years. When he had removed him, he made David their king. In his testimony about him he said, 'I have found David, son of Jesse, to be a man after my heart, who will carry out all my wishes.' Of this man's posterity God has brought to Israel a Saviour, Jesus, as he promised; before his coming John had already proclaimed a baptism of repentance to all the people of Israel. And as John was finishing his work, he said, 'What do you suppose that I am? I am not he. No, but one is coming after me; I am not worthy to untie the thong of the sandals on his feet.'"

This is the word of the Lord.   *Acts 13. 14b-26*

Or:

A reading from the Letter of Paul to the Galatians.

Before faith came, we were imprisoned and guarded under the law until faith would be revealed. Therefore the law was our disciplinarian until Christ came, so that we might be justified by faith. But now that faith has come, we are no longer subject to a disciplinarian, for in Christ Jesus you are all children of God through faith. As many of you as were baptised into Christ have clothed yourselves with Christ. There is no longer Jew or Greek, there is no longer slave or free, there is no longer male and female; for all of you are one in Christ Jesus. And if you belong to Christ, then you are Abraham's offspring, heirs according to the promise.

This is the word of the Lord.   *Galatians 3. 23-29*

Hear the gospel of our Lord Jesus Christ according to Luke.

The time came for Elizabeth to give birth, and she bore a son. Her neighbours and relatives heard that the Lord had shown his great mercy to her, and they rejoiced with her. On the eighth day they came to circumcise the child, and they were going to name him Zechariah after his father. But his mother said, "No; he is to be called John." They said to her, "None of your relatives has this name." Then they began motioning to his father to find out what name he wanted to give him. He asked for a writing tablet and wrote, "His name is John." And all of them were amazed. Immediately his mouth was opened and his tongue freed, and he began to speak, praising God. Fear came over all their neighbours, and all these things were talked about throughout the entire hill country of Judea. All who heard them pondered them and said, "What then will this child become?" For, indeed, the hand of the Lord was with him.

The child grew and became strong in spirit, and he was in the wilderness until the day he appeared publicly to Israel.

This is the gospel of the Lord.   *Luke 1. 57-66, 80*

Post Communion
Merciful Lord,
whose prophet John the Baptist
proclaimed your Son as the Lamb of God
  who takes away the sin of the world:
grant that we who in this sacrament have known
  your forgiveness and your life-giving love
may ever tell of your mercy and your peace;
through Jesus Christ our Lord.

Cyril, Bishop of Alexandria

27 June – Commemoration

If celebrated as a Lesser Festival, Common of Teachers, page 473

Cyril was born in Alexandria and was first heard of as a young priest. He succeeded his uncle as Patriarch in the year 412 and began his great defence of the orthodox doctrines of God the Holy Trinity and of the incarnate Christ as a unique, single Person, at once God and Human. His chief opponent was the Patriarch of Constantinople, Nestorius, who appears to have taught that there were two separate Persons co-existing in the incarnate Christ, the one divine and the other human. The Nestorian Party thus rejected the description of Mary as *Theotokos,* the God-bearer, and also rejected the papal ruling that they comply with Cyril's doctrinal position, that the union between divinity and humanity in Christ was total and real. The Council of Ephesus was convened in the year 431 to rule on the matter and eventually gave its full support to Cyril, making the term *Theotokos* the touchstone of Christian orthodoxy. Cyril's writings reflect his outstanding qualities as a theologian. They are marked by precision in exposition, accuracy in thought and skill in reason. He died at Alexandria in the year 444.

Irenæus, Bishop of Lyons

28 June – Lesser Festival – Teacher of the Faith – White

Irenæus was probably a native of Smyrna, born in about the year 130. As a boy, he had heard Polycarp preach, who had in turn been a disciple of the apostle John. Irenæus is thus one of the important connections between the apostolic Church and the second century. He studied at Rome, and later became a priest at Lyons in Gaul, succeeding as bishop upon the martyrdom of his predecessor in 177. He contended against the mythological, unhistorical beliefs of the Gnostics, giving positive value to the full humanity of the incarnate Christ, and affirmed the public teaching rôle of the episcopate to combat false doctrine. He is honoured as the first great Catholic theologian, one who drew upon the emerging traditions of East and West. Irenæus died in about the year 200.

Collect

God of peace,
who through the ministry of your servant Irenæus,
strengthened the true faith
and brought harmony to your Church:
keep us steadfast in your true religion,
and renew us in faith and love,
that we may always walk in the way that leads to eternal life;
through Jesus Christ your Son our Lord,
who is alive and reigns with you, in the unity of the Holy Spirit,
one God, now and for ever.

A reading from the Wisdom of Solomon.

Therefore I prayed, and understanding was given me; I called on God, and the spirit of wisdom came to me. I preferred her to sceptres and thrones, and I accounted wealth as nothing in comparison with her. Neither did I liken to her any priceless gem, because all gold is but a little sand in her sight, and silver will be accounted as clay before her. I loved her more than health and beauty, and I chose to have her rather than light, because her radiance never ceases. May God grant me to speak with judgement, and to have thoughts worthy of what I have received; for he is the guide even of wisdom and the corrector of the wise. For both we and our words are in his hand, as are all understanding and skill in crafts.

This is the word of the Lord.   *Wisdom 7. 7-10, 15-16*

Responsorial Psalm

**R Come, children, and listen to me, says God;
I will teach you true wisdom.**

Who among you loves life
and desires long life to enjoy prosperity?
Keep your tongue from evil-speaking
and your lips from lying words. **R**

Turn from evil and do good;
seek peace and pursue it.
The eyes of the Lord are upon the righteous,
and his ears are open to their cry. **R**

The face of the Lord is against those who do evil,
to root out the remembrance of them from the earth.
The righteous cry and the Lord hears them
and delivers them from all their troubles. **R**   *From Psalm 34*

A reading from the Second Letter of Peter.

We did not follow cleverly devised myths when we made known
to you the power and coming of our Lord Jesus Christ, but we had
been eye-witnesses of his majesty. For he received honour and
glory from God the Father when that voice was conveyed to him
by the Majestic Glory, saying, "This is my Son, my Belovèd, with
whom I am well pleased." We ourselves heard this voice come
from heaven, while we were with him on the holy mountain.

So we have the prophetic message more fully confirmed. You will
do well to be attentive to this as to a lamp shining in a dark place,
until the day dawns and the morning star rises in your hearts.
First of all you must understand this, that no prophecy of scripture
is a matter of one's own interpretation, because no prophecy ever
came by human will, but men and women moved by the Holy
Spirit spoke from God.

This is the word of the Lord.   *2 Peter 1. 16-21*

Hear the gospel of our Lord Jesus Christ according to Luke.

Jesus said, "No one after lighting a lamp puts it in a cellar, but on
the lampstand so that those who enter may see the light. Your eye
is the lamp of your body. If your eye is healthy, your whole body
is full of light; but if it is not healthy, your body is full of darkness.
Therefore consider whether the light in you is not darkness. If
then your whole body is full of light, with no part of it in darkness,
it will be as full of light as when a lamp gives you light with its
rays."

This is the gospel of the Lord.   *Luke 11. 33-36*

Post Communion
God of truth,
whose Wisdom set her table
and invited us to eat the bread and drink the wine
  of the kingdom:
help us to lay aside all foolishness
and to live and walk in the way of insight,
that we may come with your servant Irenæus
  to the eternal feast of heaven;
through Jesus Christ our Lord.

Peter and Paul, Apostles
29 June – Festival – Apostles – Red

Peter has often been called the 'Prince of the Apostles' because of
the words of Jesus re-naming him, from Simon to Cephas. This
was the Aramaic form of the Greek word Peter, which means
'rock'. Jesus said that on this rock he would build his Church. But
both Peter and Paul came to be seen as having different rôles to
play within the leadership of the Church: Peter in witnessing to
the Lordship of Christ and Paul in developing an understanding
of its meaning for Christ's followers. Peter and Paul have been
remembered jointly on this day since the very early days of the
Church, it being regarded as the anniversary of their martyrdom
in Rome in about the year 64.

Collect
Almighty God,
whose blessèd apostles Peter and Paul
glorified you in their death as in their life:
grant that your Church,
inspired by their teaching and example,
and made one by your Spirit,
may ever stand firm upon the one foundation,
Jesus Christ your Son our Lord,
who is alive and reigns with you,
in the unity of the Holy Spirit,
one God, now and for ever.

Acts 12. 1-11	*or*	Zechariah 4. 1-6a, 10b-14
Psalm 125		Psalm 125
2 Timothy 4. 6-8, 17-18		Acts 12. 1-11
Matthew 16. 13-19		Matthew 16. 13-19

or, where St Peter is celebrated alone:
Almighty God,
who inspired your apostle Saint Peter
to confess Jesus as Christ and Son of the living God:
build up your Church upon this rock,
that in unity and peace it may proclaim one truth
and follow one Lord, your Son our Saviour Christ,
who is alive and reigns with you,
in the unity of the Holy Spirit,
one God, now and for ever.

Ezekiel 3. 22-27	*or*	Acts 12. 1-11
Psalm 125		Psalm 125
Acts 12. 1-11		1 Peter 2. 19-25
Matthew 16. 13-19		Matthew 16. 13-19

A reading from the prophecy of Ezekiel.

The hand of the Lord was upon me there; and he said to me, Rise up, go out into the valley, and there I will speak with you. So I rose up and went out into the valley; and the glory of the Lord stood there, like the glory that I had seen by the river Chebar; and I fell on my face. The spirit entered into me, and set me on my feet; and he spoke with me and said to me: Go, shut yourself inside your house. As for you, mortal, cords shall be placed on you, and you shall be bound with them, so that you cannot go out among the people; and I will make your tongue cling to the roof of your mouth, so that you shall be speechless and unable to reprove them; for they are a rebellious house. But when I speak with you, I will open your mouth, and you shall say to them, "Thus says the Lord God"; let those who will hear, hear; and let those who refuse to hear, refuse; for they are a rebellious house.

This is the word of the Lord.   *Ezekiel 3. 22-27*

A reading from the prophecy of Zechariah.

The angel who talked with me came again, and wakened me, as one is wakened from sleep. He said to me, "What do you see?" And I said, "I see a lampstand all of gold, with a bowl on the top of it; there are seven lamps on it, with seven lips on each of the lamps that are on the top of it. And by it there are two olive trees, one on the right of the bowl and the other on its left." I said to the angel who talked with me, "What are these, my lord?" Then the angel who talked with me answered me, "Do you not know what these are?" I said, "No, my lord." He said to me, "These seven are the eyes of the Lord, which range through the whole earth." Then I said to him, "What are these two olive trees on the right and the left of the lampstand?" And a second time I said to him, "What are these two branches of the olive trees, which pour out the oil through the two golden pipes?" He said to me, "Do you not know what these are?" I said, "No, my lord." Then he said, "These are the two anointed ones who stand by the Lord of the whole earth."

This is the word of the Lord.   *Zechariah 4. 1-6a, 10b-14*

Responsorial Psalm

R **Show your goodness, O Lord, to those who are good [and to those who are true of heart].**

Those who trust in the Lord are like Mount Zion,
which cannot be moved,
but stands fast for ever. **R**

The hills stand about Jerusalem;
so does the Lord stand round about his people,
from this time forth for evermore. **R**

The sceptre of the wicked shall not hold sway
over the land allotted to the just,
so that the just shall not put their hands to evil. **R** *From Psalm 125*

A reading from the Acts of the Apostles.

About that time King Herod laid violent hands upon some who belonged to the church. He had James, the brother of John, killed with the sword. After he saw that it pleased the Jews, he proceeded to arrest Peter also (this was during the festival of Unleavened Bread). When he had seized him, he put him in prison and handed him over to four squads of soldiers to guard him, intending to bring him out to the people after the Passover. While Peter was kept in prison, the church prayed fervently to God for him.

The very night before Herod was going to bring him out, Peter, bound with two chains, was sleeping between two soldiers, while guards in front of the door were keeping watch over the prison. Suddenly an angel of the Lord appeared and a light shone in the cell. He tapped Peter on the side and woke him, saying, "Get up quickly," and the chains fell off his wrists. The angel said to him, "Fasten your belt and put on your sandals." He did so. Then he said to him, "Wrap your cloak around you and follow me." Peter went out and followed him; he did not realise that what was happening with the angel's help was real; he thought he was seeing a vision. After they had passed the first and the second guard, they came before the iron gate leading into the city. It opened for them of its own accord, and they went outside and walked along a lane, when suddenly the angel left him.

This is the word of the Lord.   *Acts 12. 1-11*

A reading from the Second Letter of Paul to Timothy.

As for me, I am already being poured out as a libation, and the time of my departure has come. I have fought the good fight, I have finished the race, I have kept the faith. From now on there is reserved for me the crown of righteousness, which the Lord, the righteous judge, will give to me on that day, and not only to me but also to all who have longed for his appearing.

[17] But the Lord stood by me and gave me strength, so that through me the message might be fully proclaimed and all the Gentiles might hear it. So I was rescued from the lion's mouth. The Lord will rescue me from every evil attack and save me for his heavenly kingdom. To him be the glory forever and ever. Amen.

This is the word of the Lord.   *2 Timothy 4. 6-8, 17-18*

A reading from the First Letter of Peter.

It is a credit to you if, being aware of God, you endure pain while suffering unjustly. If you endure when you are beaten for doing wrong, what credit is that? But if you endure when you do right and suffer for it, you have God's approval. For to this you have been called, because Christ also suffered for you, leaving you an example, so that you should follow in his steps. "He committed no sin, and no deceit was found in his mouth." When he was abused, he did not return abuse; when he suffered, he did not threaten; but he entrusted himself to the one who judges justly. He himself bore our sins in his body on the cross, so that, free from sins, we might live for righteousness; by his wounds you have been healed. For you were going astray like sheep, but now you have returned to the shepherd and guardian of your souls.

This is the word of the Lord.   *1 Peter 2. 19-25*

Hear the gospel of our Lord Jesus Christ according to Matthew.

When Jesus came into the district of Caesarea Philippi, he asked his disciples, "Who do people say that the Son of Man is?" And they said, "Some say John the Baptist, but others Elijah, and still others Jeremiah or one of the prophets." He said to them, "But who do you say that I am?" Simon Peter answered, "You are the Messiah, the Son of the living God." And Jesus answered him, "Blessèd are you, Simon son of Jonah! For flesh and blood has not revealed this to you, but my Father in heaven. And I tell you, you are Peter, and on this rock I will build my church, and the gates of Hades will not prevail against it.

"I will give you the keys of the kingdom of heaven, and whatever you bind on earth will be bound in heaven, and whatever you loose on earth will be loosed in heaven."

This is the gospel of the Lord.   *Matthew 16. 13-19*

Post Communion
Almighty God,
who on the day of Pentecost
sent your Holy Spirit to the apostles
with the wind from heaven and in tongues of flame,
filling them with joy and boldness to preach the gospel:
by the power of the same Spirit
strengthen us to witness to your truth
and to draw everyone to the fire of your love;
through Jesus Christ our Lord.

JULY

John & Henry Venn, Evangelical Divines
1 July – Commemoration
If celebrated as a Lesser Festival, Common of Pastors, page 483

John Venn was born at Clapham in March 1759, where his father, Henry Venn Senior, was a curate. Later that year, Henry took his family to Huddersfield, where he had been appointed vicar, and they remained there until 1771. John was educated at Sidney Sussex College, Cambridge, and became rector of Little Dunham in Norfolk and eventually of Clapham in 1792. He was one of the founders of the Church Missionary Society in 1797. It was here that he also became a central figure in the group of religious philanthropists known as the Clapham Sect. John was also an active participator in the movement for the abolition of the slave trade.

John's son, Henry Venn, was born at Clapham in 1796. After his time in Cambridge, he was ordained and held various livings, but in 1846 he devoted himself entirely to the work of the Church Missionary Society. He was secretary for thirty-two years and his organising gifts and sound judgement made him the leading spirit in the Society. In his later years, he was recognised as a leader of the evangelical body of the Church of England. John Venn died at Clapham on this day in 1813 and his son Henry died at Mortlake on 13 January 1873.

Thomas the Apostle
3 July – Festival – Apostle – Red

Thomas is mentioned among the number of the Apostles in the gospels of Matthew, Mark and Luke but it is in John's gospel that his significance is revealed. Firstly, he is heard encouraging the other disciples to go to Judea with Jesus; then, not knowing what Jesus meant when he talked about where he was to go elicited the answer that Jesus was himself the Way. But probably most famously he was the Apostle notably unconvinced by reports of the resurrection of Jesus, causing Jesus to show him the marks in his hands and feet and side. Thomas then proclaims the words that have been described as the great climax to John's gospel by saying to Jesus, "My Lord and my God!"

Collect
Almighty and eternal God,
who, for the firmer foundation of our faith,
allowed your holy apostle Thomas
  to doubt the resurrection of your Son
till word and sight convinced him:
grant to us, who have not seen, that we also may believe
and so confess Christ as our Lord and our God;
who is alive and reigns with you,
in the unity of the Holy Spirit,
one God, now and for ever.

A reading from the book Habbakuk.

I will stand at my watchpost, and station myself on the rampart; I will keep watch to see what he will say to me, and what he will answer concerning my complaint. Then the Lord answered me and said: Write the vision; make it plain on tablets, so that a runner may read it. For there is still a vision for the appointed time; it speaks of the end, and does not lie. If it seems to tarry, wait for it; it will surely come, it will not delay. Look at the proud! Their spirit is not right in them, but the righteous live by their faith.

This is the word of the Lord.   *Habbakuk 2. 1-4*

Responsorial Psalm
**R Incline your ear to me, O God;
    [make haste to deliver me].**

In you, O Lord, have I taken refuge;
let me never be put to shame;
deliver me in your righteousness. **R**

Be my strong rock, a castle to keep me safe,
for you are my crag and my stronghold;
for the sake of your name, lead me and guide me. **R**

Into your hands I commend my spirit,
for you have redeemed me,
O Lord, O God of truth. **R**   *From Psalm 31*

A reading from Paul's Letter to the Ephesians.

So then you are no longer strangers and aliens, but you are citizens with the saints and also members of the household of God, built upon the foundation of the apostles and prophets, with Christ Jesus himself as the cornerstone. In him the whole structure is joined together and grows into a holy temple in the Lord; in whom you also are built together spiritually into a dwelling place for God.

This is the word of the Lord.   *Ephesians 2. 19-22*

Hear the gospel of our Lord Jesus Christ according to John.

Thomas (who was called the Twin), one of the twelve, was not with the disciples when Jesus came. So the other disciples told him, "We have seen the Lord." But he said to them, "Unless I see the mark of the nails in his hands, and put my finger in the mark of the nails and my hand in his side, I will not believe."

A week later his disciples were again in the house, and Thomas was with them. Although the doors were shut, Jesus came and stood among them and said, "Peace be with you." Then he said to Thomas, "Put your finger here and see my hands. Reach out your hand and put it in my side. Do not doubt but believe." Thomas answered him, "My Lord and my God!" Jesus said to him, "Have you believed because you have seen me? Blessèd are those who have not seen and yet have come to believe."

This is the gospel of the Lord.   *John 20. 24-29*

Post Communion
Lord God, the source of truth and love,
keep us faithful to the apostles' teaching and fellowship,
united in prayer and the breaking of bread,
and one in joy and simplicity of heart,
in Jesus Christ our Lord.

Thomas More, & John Fisher, Reformation Martyrs
6 July – Commemoration
If celebrated as a Lesser Festival, Common of Martyrs, page 464

Born in London in 1478, Thomas More studied classics and law, being called to the Bar at twenty-three years old. His clear honesty and integrity impressed Henry VIII and he appointed Thomas as his Chancellor. He supported the king in his efforts to reform the clergy but disagreed over Henry's disputes with the papacy, caused by the king's desire to annul his marriage to Catherine of Aragon and to find another queen who might provide him with a male heir. Henry could stand no such act of defiance and imprisoned his Chancellor in the hope that he would renege. Thomas refused to take the Oath on the Act of Succession, which declared the king to be the only protector and supreme head of the Church in England, and was executed for treason on this day in 1535, declaring that he died the king's good servant but God's first.

John Fisher was Thomas More's close friend and ally. A brilliant academic, he had substantially reformed the life of the University of Cambridge, through the wealth and influence of his patron, Lady Margaret Beaufort, the mother of Henry VII. He was made Bishop of Rochester and proved himself to be a good pastor to his small diocese. As with Thomas, Henry VIII much admired him at first, but when he opposed the king their relationship deteriorated. Aged sixty-six and in indifferent health, he nevertheless endured the trauma of imprisonment in the Tower of London. He was executed just two weeks before Thomas on 22 June 1535.

Benedict of Nursia,
Father of Western Monasticism
11 July – Lesser Festival – Religious – White

Benedict was born in Nursia, central Italy, around the year 480. As a young man he was sent to study in Rome, but was soon appalled by the corruption in society and withdrew to live as a hermit at Subiaco. He quickly attracted disciples and began to establish small monasteries in the neighbourhood. Around the year 525, a disaffected faction tried to poison him so Benedict moved to

Monte Cassino with a band of loyal monks. Later in life Benedict wrote his Rule for Monks, based on his own experience of fallible people striving to live out the gospel. He never intended to found an 'order' but his Rule was so good that it was disseminated and widely followed, becoming the model for all western monasticism. Benedict died at Monte Cassino in about the year 550.

Collect
Eternal God,
who made Benedict a wise master
in the school of your service
and a guide to many called into community
  to follow the rule of Christ:
grant that we may put your love before all else
and seek with joy the way of your commandments;
through Jesus Christ your Son our Lord,
who is alive and reigns with you,
in the unity of the Holy Spirit,
one God, now and for ever.

A reading from the book Proverbs.

My child, if you accept my words and treasure up my commandments within you, making your ear attentive to wisdom and inclining your heart to understanding; if you indeed cry out for insight, and raise your voice for understanding, if you seek it like silver, and search for it as for hidden treasures – then you will understand the fear of the Lord and find the knowledge of God. For the Lord gives wisdom; from his mouth come knowledge and understanding.

This is the word of the Lord.   *Proverbs 2. 1-6*

Responsorial Psalm

**R   Incline your heart to understanding Wisdom,
[and so find the knowledge of God].**

You only are my portion, O Lord;
I have promised to keep your words.
I entreat you with all my heart,
be merciful to me according to your promise. **R**

I have considered my ways
and turned my feet towards your decrees.
At midnight I will rise to give you thanks,
because of your righteous judgements. **R**

I am a companion of all who fear you
and of those who keep your commandments.
The earth, O Lord, is full of your love;
instruct me in your statutes. **R**   *From Psalm 119*

A reading from the First letter of Paul to the Corinthians.

According to the grace of God given to me, like a skilled master
builder I laid a foundation, and someone else is building on it.
Each builder must choose with care how to build on it. For no one
can lay any foundation other than the one that has been laid; that
foundation is Jesus Christ.

This is the word of the Lord.   *1 Corinthians 3. 10-11*

Hear the gospel of our Lord Jesus Christ according to Luke.

A certain ruler asked Jesus, "Good Teacher, what must I do to
inherit eternal life?" Jesus said to him, "Why do you call me good?
No one is good but God alone. You know the commandments:
'You shall not commit adultery; You shall not murder; You shall
not steal; You shall not bear false witness; Honour your father and
mother.'" He replied, "I have kept all these since my youth."
When Jesus heard this, he said to him, "There is still one thing
lacking. Sell all that you own and distribute the money to the poor,
and you will have treasure in heaven; then come, follow me."

This is the gospel of the Lord.   *Luke 18. 18-22*

Post Communion
Merciful God,
who gave such grace to your servant Benedict
that he served you with singleness of heart
and loved you above all things:
help us, whose communion with you
  has been renewed in this sacrament,
to forsake all that holds us back from following Christ
and to grow into his likeness from glory to glory;
through Jesus Christ our Lord.

John Keble, Priest, Tractarian, Poet
14 July – Lesser Festival – Pastor – White

Born in 1792, the son of a priest, John Keble showed early brilliance as a scholar, becoming a Fellow of Oriel College, Oxford, at the age of nineteen, a few years before his ordination. He won great praise for his collection of poems, *The Christian Year*, issued in 1827, and was elected Professor of Poetry in Oxford in 1831. A leader of the Tractarian movement, which protested at the threats to the Church from liberal developments in both politics and theology, he nevertheless did not seek preferment and in 1836 became a parish priest near Winchester, a position he held until his death in 1866. He continued to write scholarly books and was praised for his character and spiritual counsel. Yet he is still best remembered for the sermon he preached in Oxford, considered by some the beginning of the Oxford Movement, delivered on this day in 1833.

Collect
Father of the eternal Word,
in whose encompassing love
all things in peace and order move:
grant that, as your servant John Keble
  adored you in all creation,
so we may have a humble heart of love
for the mysteries of your Church
and know your love to be new every morning,
in Jesus Christ your Son our Lord,
who is alive and reigns with you,
in the unity of the Holy Spirit,
one God, now and for ever.

A reading from the book Lamentations.

The thought of my affliction and my homelessness is wormwood and gall! My soul continually thinks of it and is bowed down within me. But this I call to mind, and therefore I have hope: The steadfast love of the Lord never ceases, his mercies never come to an end; they are new every morning; great is your faithfulness.

"The Lord is my portion," says my soul, "therefore I will hope in him." The Lord is good to those who wait for him, to the soul that seeks him. It is good that one should wait quietly for the salvation of the Lord.

This is the word of the Lord.   *Lamentations 3. 19-26*

Responsorial Psalm

R   Your love is before my eyes, O God;
[faithfully I have walked with you].

Give judgement for me, O Lord,
for I have lived with integrity;
I have trusted in the Lord
and have not faltered. **R**

Test me, O Lord, and try me;
examine my heart and my mind.
I will wash my hands in innocence
that I may go in procession round your altar; **R**

Singing aloud a song of thanksgiving
and recounting all your wonderful deeds.
Lord, I love the house in which you dwell
and the place where your glory abides. **R**   *From Psalm 26*

A reading from the Letter of Paul to the Romans.

We who are strong ought to put up with the failings of the weak, and not to please ourselves. Each of us must please our neighbour for the good purpose of building up the neighbour. For Christ did not please himself; but, as it is written, "The insults of those who insult you have fallen on me." For whatever was written in former days was written for our instruction, so that by steadfastness and by the encouragement of the scriptures we might have hope. May the God of steadfastness and encouragement grant you to live in harmony with one another, in accordance with Christ Jesus, so that together you may with one voice glorify the God and Father of our Lord Jesus Christ.

This is the word of the Lord.   *Romans 15. 1-6*

Hear the gospel of our Lord Jesus Christ according to Matthew.

When Jesus saw the crowds, he went up the mountain; and after he sat down, his disciples came to him. Then he began to speak, and taught them, saying: "Blessèd are the poor in spirit, for theirs is the kingdom of heaven. Blessèd are those who mourn, for they will be comforted. Blessèd are the meek, for they will inherit the earth. Blessèd are those who hunger and thirst for righteousness, for they will be filled. Blessèd are the merciful, for they will receive mercy. Blessèd are the pure in heart, for they will see God."

This is the gospel of the Lord.   *Matthew 5. 1-8*

Post Communion
God, shepherd of your people,
whose servant John Keble revealed the loving service of Christ
  in his ministry as a pastor of your people:
by this eucharist in which we share
awaken within us the love of Christ
and keep us faithful to our Christian calling;
through him who laid down his life for us,
but is alive and reigns with you, now and for ever.

Swithun, Bishop of Winchester
15 July – Lesser Festival – Pastor – White

Swithun was Bishop of Winchester in the ninth century, though little is known of his life. He was bishop for ten years and appears to have been the trusted adviser of Egbert, his king in Wessex. He had asked to be buried 'humbly' and not in a great shrine and, when he died on 2 July 862, his request was fulfilled. However, when a new cathedral was being built, Ethelwold, the new bishop, decided to move Swithun's remains into a shrine in the cathedral, despite dire warnings that to move the bones would bring about terrible storms. He was duly translated on this day in the year 971 and, though many cures were claimed and other miracles observed, it apparently rained for forty days, as forecast. Thus the feast-day of Swithun became synonymous with long, summer storms, rather than as an occasion for celebrating Christian simplicity and holiness.

Collect
Almighty God,
by whose grace we celebrate again
the feast of your servant Swithun:
grant that, as he governed with gentleness
  the people committed to his care,
so we, rejoicing in our Christian inheritance,
may always seek to build up your Church in unity and love;
through Jesus Christ your Son our Lord,
who is alive and reigns with you, in the unity of the Holy Spirit,
one God, now and for ever.

A reading from the book Proverbs.

My child, do not forget my teaching, but let your heart keep my
commandments; for length of days and years of life and abundant
welfare they will give you. Do not let loyalty and faithfulness forsake you; bind them around your neck, write them on the tablet of
your heart. So you will find favour and good repute in the sight
of God and of people. Trust in the Lord with all your heart, and
do not rely on your own insight. In all your ways acknowledge
him, and he will make straight your paths. Do not be wise in your
own eyes; fear the Lord, and turn away from evil. It will be a healing for your flesh and a refreshment for your body.

This is the word of the Lord.   *Proverbs 3. 1-8*

Responsorial Psalm

**R May the Lord answer you in the day of trouble,
    [the name of the God of Jacob defend you]**.

The Lord send you help from his holy place
and strengthen you out of Zion;
remember all your offerings
and accept your burnt sacrifice. **R**

The Lord grant you your heart's desire
and prosper all your plans.
We will shout for joy at your victory
and triumph in the name of our God. **R**

Some put their trust in chariots and some in horses,
but we will call upon the name of the Lord our God.
O Lord, give victory to the king
and answer us when we call. **R**   *From Psalm 20*

A reading from the Letter of James.

Be patient, therefore, beloved, until the coming of the Lord. The
farmer waits for the precious crop from the earth, being patient
with it until it receives the early and the late rains. You also must
be patient. Strengthen your hearts, for the coming of the Lord is
near. Beloved, do not grumble against one another, so that you
may not be judged. See, the Judge is standing at the doors! As an
example of suffering and patience, beloved, take the prophets
who spoke in the name of the Lord. Indeed we call blessèd those
who showed endurance. You have heard of the endurance of Job,
and you have seen the purpose of the Lord, how the Lord is compassionate and merciful. Above all, my beloved, do not swear,
either by heaven or by earth or by any other oath, but let your
"Yes" be yes and your "No" be no, so that you may not fall under
condemnation.

Are any among you suffering? They should pray. Are any cheerful? They should sing songs of praise. Are any among you sick?
They should call for the elders of the church and have them pray
over them, anointing them with oil in the name of the Lord. The
prayer of faith will save the sick, and the Lord will raise them up;
and anyone who has committed sins will be forgiven. Therefore
confess your sins to one another, and pray for one another, so that
you may be healed. The prayer of the righteous is powerful and
effective. Elijah was a human being like us, and he prayed fervently that it might not rain, and for three years and six months it
did not rain on the earth. Then he prayed again, and the heaven
gave rain and the earth yielded its harvest.

This is the word of the Lord.   *James 5. 7-18*

Hear the gospel of our Lord Jesus Christ according to Matthew.

Jesus said to the crowds, "You have heard that it was said, 'You
shall love your neighbour and hate your enemy.' But I say to you,

Love your enemies and pray for those who persecute you, so that you may be children of your Father in heaven; for he makes his sun rise on the evil and on the good, and sends rain on the righteous and on the unrighteous. For if you love those who love you, what reward do you have? Do not even the tax collectors do the same? And if you greet only your brothers and sisters, what more are you doing than others? Do not even the Gentiles do the same? Be perfect, therefore, as your heavenly Father is perfect.

This is the gospel of the Lord.   *Matthew 5. 43-48*

Post Communion
God, shepherd of your people,
whose servant Swithun revealed the loving service of Christ
  in his ministry as a pastor of your people:
by this eucharist in which we share
awaken within us the love of Christ
and keep us faithful to our Christian calling;
through him who laid down his life for us,
but is alive and reigns with you, now and for ever.

Bonaventure, Friar & Bishop
15 July – Commemoration
If celebrated as a Lesser Festival, Common of Teachers, page 473

Born at Bagnoreggio in Italy in about the year 1218, Bonaventure became a Franciscan Friar in 1243 and his intellectual ability was soon recognised by his Order and by the Church. At the age of thirty-six he was elected Minister General of the Franciscans and virtually re-founded the Order, giving it a stability in training and administration previously unknown. He upheld all the teachings of St Francis except in the founder's attitude to study, since Francis felt the Order should possess no books. He clearly saw, with Francis, that the rôle of the Friars was to support the Church through its contemporary structures rather than to be an instrument for reform. He also believed that the best conversions came from the good example of those anxious to renew the Church, rather than by haranguing or passing laws. He was appointed a cardinal-bishop against his will, and kept the papal messengers waiting while he finished the washing up. He brought about a temporary reunion of the churches in the east and the west but, before it was repudiated, he died on this day at Lyons in the year 1274.

Osmund, Bishop of Salisbury
16 July – Commemoration
If celebrated as a Lesser Festival, Common of Bishops, page 483

Born the son of a Norman count, Osmund came to England in the wake of William the Conqueror and was quickly promoted to Chancellor in 1072. Six years later he became Bishop of Salisbury and completed the building of the new cathedral at Old Sarum. He was a scholar and a good administrator but was best loved for his lack of avarice and ambition, traits apparently not common in the new hierarchy of Church and state. He took part in collecting the information for the Domesday Book and was present at Sarum when it was presented to the king in 1086. Osmund died on 4 December 1099 and his remains were translated to the new cathedral in Salisbury on this day in the year 1457.

Elizabeth Ferard,
first Deaconess of the Church of England
18 July – Commemoration
If celebrated as a Lesser Festival, Common of Religious, page 494

Elizabeth Catherine Ferard was encouraged by Bishop Tait of London to visit deaconess institutions in Germany and, in November 1861, she and a group of women dedicated themselves 'to minister to the necessities of the Church' as servants in the Church. On this day in 1862, Elizabeth Ferard received the first deaconess licence from Bishop Tait. She went on to found a community of deaconesses within a religious sisterhood, working first in a poor parish in the King's Cross area of London and then moving to Notting Hill in 1873. When her health failed, she passed on the leadership to others and died on Easter Day 1883.

Gregory & Macrina, Teachers of the Faith
19 July – Lesser Festival – Teachers of the Faith – White

Gregory of Nyssa was born at Caesarea in what is now Turkey around the year 330, the child of an aristocratic Christian family. Unlike his elder brother Basil, he was academically undistinguished, but ultimately proved to be the most original of the group of the theologians known as the Cappadocian Fathers. He was introduced to the spiritual life by his elder sister Macrina who exercised a formative influence upon him, and with whom he maintained close bonds of friendship throughout his life. It was she who, after the death of their father, converted the household into a sort of monastery on one of the family estates. Gregory married a deeply spiritual woman, Theosebia, and at first refused ordination, choosing to pursue a secular career. He was ordained only later in life, and in 372 was chosen to be bishop of Nyssa. In the year 379 both his brother Basil and his sister Macrina died, and this deeply affected him; but out of this darkness emerged a profound spirituality. For Gregory, God is met not as an object to be understood, but as a mystery to be loved. He died in the year 394.

Collect

Lord of eternity, creator of all things,
in your Son Jesus Christ
  you open for us the way to resurrection
that we may enjoy your bountiful goodness:
may we who celebrate your servants Gregory and Macrina
press onwards in faith to your boundless love
and ever wonder at the miracle of your presence among us;
through Jesus Christ your Son our Lord,
who is alive and reigns with you,
in the unity of the Holy Spirit,
one God, now and for ever.

A reading from the Wisdom of Solomon.

Who can learn the counsel of God, or who can discern what the Lord wills? For the reasoning of mortals is worthless, and our designs are likely to fail; for a perishable body weighs down the soul, and this earthy tent burdens the thoughtful mind. We can hardly guess at what is on earth, and what is at hand we find with labour; but who has traced out what is in the heavens? Who has learned your counsel, unless you have given wisdom and sent your holy spirit from on high?

This is the word of the Lord.   *Wisdom 9. 13-17*

Responsorial Psalm

R   I will sing and make music to the Lord
[with sounds of great gladness].

Hearken to my voice, O Lord, when I call;
have mercy on me and answer me.
You speak in my heart and say, 'Seek my face.'
your face, Lord, will I seek. **R**

Though my father and my mother forsake me,
the Lord will sustain me.
Show me your way, O Lord;
lead me on a level path, because of my enemies. **R**

What if I had not believed
that I should see the goodness of the Lord
in the land of the living! **R**   *From Psalm 27*

A reading from the First Letter of Paul to the Corinthians.

As it is written, "What no eye has seen, nor ear heard, nor the human heart conceived, what God has prepared for those who love him" – these things God has revealed to us through the Spirit; for the Spirit searches everything, even the depths of God. For what human being knows what is truly human except the human spirit that is within? So also no one comprehends what is truly God's except the Spirit of God. Now we have received not the spirit of the world, but the Spirit that is from God, so that we may understand the gifts bestowed on us by God. And we speak of these things in words not taught by human wisdom but taught by the Spirit, interpreting spiritual things to those who are spiritual.

This is the word of the Lord.   *1 Corinthians 2. 9-13*

Hear the gospel of our Lord Jesus Christ according to John.

Jesus looked up to heaven and said, "Father, I have made your name known to those whom you gave me from the world. They were yours, and you gave them to me, and they have kept your word. As you have sent me into the world, so I have sent them into the world. And for their sakes I sanctify myself, so that they also may be sanctified in truth.

"I ask not only on behalf of these, but also on behalf of those who will believe in me through their word, that they may all be one. As you, Father, are in me and I am in you, may they also be in us, so that the world may believe that you have sent me. The glory that you have given me I have given them, so that they may be one, as we are one, I in them and you in me, that they may become completely one, so that the world may know that you have sent me and have loved them even as you have loved me. Father, I desire that those also, whom you have given me, may be with me where I am, to see my glory, which you have given me because you loved me before the foundation of the world."

This is the gospel of the Lord.   *John 17.6; 18-24*

Post Communion
God of truth,
whose Wisdom set her table
and invited us to eat the bread and drink the wine
  of the kingdom:
help us to lay aside all foolishness
and to live and walk in the way of insight,
that we may come with your servants Gregory and Macrina
  to the eternal feast of heaven;
through Jesus Christ our Lord.

Margaret of Antioch
20 July – Commemoration
If observed as a Lesser Festival, Common of Martyrs, page 464

Margaret, also called Marina, gave her life during the Diocletian persecutions at the beginning of the fourth century. Her preaching before her death is said to have converted many to the Christian faith.

Bartolomé de las Casas, Apostle to the Indies
20 July – Commemoration
If observed as a Lesser Festival, Common of Any Saint, page 527

Bartolomé de las Casas was the sixteenth-century Dominican priest who became known as 'the defender of the Indians' in 'the new world' of America. Born in 1484 at Las Casas in Seville, Bartolomé arrived in Haiti in 1502 and underwent a conversion after witnessing the injustices inflicted on the Indians. Proclaiming that Jesus Christ was being crucified in the poor, he went on to spend a lifetime challenging the Church and the Empire of his day. He was consecrated Bishop of Chiapa in Mexico in 1543 where he continued his prophetic rôle and emerges as a man of unquestioned courage and a theologian of remarkable depth, whose vision continues to set in relief the challenge of the gospel in a world of injustice. He died on 18 July 1566.

Mary Magdalene
22 July – Festival – White

All four gospels give Mary Magdalene a unique place among Jesus' followers. Probably from Magdala by the Sea of Galilee, she is described as having been healed by Jesus before accompanying him during his ministry. Along with other faithful women, she stayed beside the cross during the crucifixion and was the first disciple to discover the empty tomb on Easter morning. She was privileged with the first appearance of the risen Lord, who sent her to take the good news of the resurrection to the other disciples. This commission earned her the title 'Apostle to the Apostles' in the early Church.

Collect
Almighty God,
whose Son restored Mary Magdalene
  to health of mind and body
and called her to be a witness to his resurrection:
forgive our sins and heal us by your grace,
that we may serve you in the power of his risen life;
who is alive and reigns with you,
in the unity of the Holy Spirit,
one God, now and for ever.

A reading from the Song of Songs.

Upon my bed at night I sought him whom my soul loves; I sought him, but found him not; I called him, but he gave no answer. "I will rise now and go about the city, in the streets and in the squares; I will seek him whom my soul loves." I sought him, but found him not. The sentinels found me, as they went about in the city. "Have you seen him whom my soul loves?" Scarcely had I passed them, when I found him whom my soul loves. I held him, and would not let him go until I brought him into my mother's house, and into the chamber of her that conceived me.

This is the word of the Lord.   *Song of Songs 3. 1-4*

Responsorial Psalm

**R   I come seeking my God,
      [the one whom my soul truly loves].**

As the deer longs for the water-brooks,
so longs my soul for you, O God.
My soul is athirst for God,
athirst for the living God. **R**

When shall I come to appear before the presence of God?
My tears have been my food day and night,
while all day long they say to me,
"Where now is your God?" **R**

I pour out my soul when I think on these things:
how I went with the multitude
  and led them into the house of God,
with the voice of praise and thanksgiving,
among those who keep holy-day. **R**

Why are you so full of heaviness, O my soul?
and why are you so disquieted within me?
Put your trust in God; for I will yet give thanks to him,
who is the help of my countenance, and my God. **R**   *From Psalm 42*

A reading from the Second Letter of Paul to the Corinthians.

The love of Christ urges us on, because we are convinced that one
has died for all; therefore all have died. And he died for all, so that
those who live might live no longer for themselves, but for him
who died and was raised for them. From now on, therefore, we
regard no one from a human point of view; even though we once
knew Christ from a human point of view, we know him no longer
in that way. So if anyone is in Christ, there is a new creation:
everything old has passed away; see, everything has become new!

This is the word of the Lord.   *2 Corinthians 5. 14-17*

Hear the gospel of our Lord Jesus Christ according to John.

Early on the first day of the week, while it was still dark, Mary
Magdalene came to the tomb and saw that the stone had been
removed from the tomb. So she ran and went to Simon Peter and
the other disciple, the one whom Jesus loved, and said to them,
"They have taken the Lord out of the tomb, and we do not know
where they have laid him."

 Mary stood weeping outside the tomb and, as she wept, she bent
over to look into the tomb; and she saw two angels in white, sitting where the body of Jesus had been lying, one at the head and
the other at the feet. They said to her, "Woman, why are you
weeping?" She said to them, "They have taken away my Lord,
and I do not know where they have laid him." When she had said
this, she turned around and saw Jesus standing there, but she did
not know that it was Jesus. Jesus said to her, "Woman, why are
you weeping? Whom are you looking for?" Supposing him to be

the gardener, she said to him, "Sir, if you have carried him away, tell me where you have laid him, and I will take him away." Jesus said to her, "Mary!" She turned and said to him in Hebrew, "Rabbouni!" (which means Teacher).

Jesus said to her, "Do not hold on to me, because I have not yet ascended to the Father. But go to my brothers and say to them, 'I am ascending to my Father and your Father, to my God and your God.' " Mary Magdalene went and announced to the disciples, "I have seen the Lord"; and she told them that he had said these things to her.

This is the gospel of the Lord.   *John 20. 1-2, 11-18*

Post Communion
God of life and love,
whose risen Son called Mary Magdalene by name
and sent her to tell of his resurrection to his apostles:
in your mercy, help us,
who have been united with him in this eucharist,
to proclaim the good news
  that he is alive and reigns, now and for ever.

Bridget of Sweden, Abbess of Vadstena, 1373
23 July – Commemoration
If celebrated as a Lesser Festival, Common of Religious, page 494

Bridget's father was governor of Uppland when she was born in about the year 1303. She married at the age of fourteen, had eight children and often attended the royal court, where she continued to experience the mystical revelations she had known since childhood. These increased in intensity after her husband's death and, three years later, she responded by founding a monastery for nuns and monks at Vadstena in 1346. Bridget's daughter Catherine was the first abbess of the so-called Brigettine Order, which became very influential in northern Europe. After travelling to Rome to obtain the pope's approval for her plans, Bridget never returned to Sweden but spent the rest of her life as a pilgrim, an adviser to rulers and church leaders, and a minister to all in need. Her

Revelations were recorded by her confessors before her death, which occurred on this day in 1373.

James the Apostle
25 July – Festival – Apostle – Red

James, often called 'the Great', was a Galilean fisherman who, with his brother John, was one of the first apostles called by Jesus to follow him. The two brothers were with Jesus at his Transfiguration and with him again in the garden of Gethsemane. They annoyed the other followers of Jesus by asking to sit one on his left and the other on his right when he came into his glory and they were present for the appearances of Christ after the resurrection. James was put to death by the sword on the order of Herod Agrippa, who hoped in vain that, by disposing of the Christian leaders, he could stem the flow of those hearing the good news and becoming followers in the Way. James' martyrdom is believed to have taken place in the year 44.

Collect
Merciful God,
whose holy apostle Saint James,
leaving his father and all that he had,
was obedient to the calling of your Son Jesus Christ
and followed him even to death:
help us, forsaking the false attractions of the world,
to be ready at all times to answer your call without delay;
through Jesus Christ your Son our Lord,
who is alive and reigns with you,
in the unity of the Holy Spirit,
one God, now and for ever.

Jeremiah 45. 1-5	*or*	Acts 11. 27-12.2
Psalm 126		Psalm 126
Acts 11. 27-12.2		2 Corinthians 4. 7-15
Matthew 20. 20-28		Matthew 20. 20-28

A reading from the prophecy of Jeremiah.

The word that the prophet Jeremiah spoke to Baruch son of Neriah, when he wrote these words in a scroll at the dictation of Jeremiah, in the fourth year of King Jehoiakim son of Josiah of Judah: Thus says the Lord, the God of Israel, to you, O Baruch: You said, "Woe is me! The Lord has added sorrow to my pain; I am weary with my groaning, and I find no rest." Thus you shall say to him, "Thus says the Lord: I am going to break down what I have built, and pluck up what I have planted – that is, the whole land. And you, do you seek great things for yourself? Do not seek them; for I am going to bring disaster upon all flesh, says the Lord; but I will give you your life as a prize of war in every place to which you may go."

This is the word of the Lord.   *Jeremiah 45. 1-5*

Responsorial Psalm

**R   The Lord has done great things, indeed,
     [wherefof we rejoice and sing].**

When the Lord restored the fortunes of Zion,
then were we like those who dream.
Then was our mouth filled with laughter,
and our tongue with shouts of joy. **R**

The Lord has done great things for us,
and we are glad indeed.
Restore our fortunes, O Lord,
like the watercourses of the Negev. **R**

Those who sowed with tears
will reap with songs of joy.
Those who go out weeping, carrying the seed,
will come again with joy, shouldering their sheaves. **R**   *Psalm 126*

A reading from the Acts of the Apostles.

At that time prophets came down from Jerusalem to Antioch. One of them named Agabus stood up and predicted by the Spirit that there would be a severe famine over all the world; and this took place during the reign of Claudius. The disciples determined that according to their ability, each would send relief to the believers living in Judea; this they did, sending it to the elders by Barnabas and Saul. About that time King Herod laid violent hands upon some who belonged to the church. He had James, the brother of John, killed with the sword.

This is the word of the Lord.   *Acts 11. 27-12.2*

A reading from the Second Letter of Paul to the Corinthians.

We have this treasure in clay jars, so that it may be made clear that this extraordinary power belongs to God and does not come from us. We are afflicted in every way, but not crushed; perplexed, but not driven to despair; persecuted, but not forsaken; struck down, but not destroyed; always carrying in the body the death of Jesus, so that the life of Jesus may also be made visible in our bodies. For while we live, we are always being given up to death for Jesus' sake, so that the life of Jesus may be made visible in our mortal flesh. So death is at work in us, but life in you.

But just as we have the same spirit of faith that is in accordance with scripture – "I believed, and so I spoke" – we also believe, and so we speak, because we know that the one who raised the Lord Jesus will raise us also with Jesus, and will bring us with you into his presence. Yes, everything is for your sake, so that grace, as it extends to more and more people, may increase thanksgiving, to the glory of God.

This is the word of the Lord.   *2 Corinthians 4. 7-15*

Hear the gospel of our Lord Jesus Christ according to Matthew.

The mother of the sons of Zebedee came to Jesus with her sons, and kneeling before him, she asked a favour of him. And he said to her, "What do you want?" She said to him, "Declare that these two sons of mine will sit, one at your right hand and one at your left, in your kingdom." But Jesus answered, "You do not know what you are asking. Are you able to drink the cup that I am about to drink?" They said to him, "We are able." He said to them, "You will indeed drink my cup, but to sit at my right hand and at my left, this is not mine to grant, but it is for those for whom it has been prepared by my Father."

When the ten heard it, they were angry with the two brothers. But Jesus called them to him and said, "You know that the rulers of the Gentiles lord it over them, and their great ones are tyrants over them. It will not be so among you; but whoever wishes to be great among you must be your servant, and whoever wishes to be first among you must be your slave; just as the Son of Man came not to be served but to serve, and to give his life a ransom for many."

This is the gospel of the Lord.   *Matthew 20. 20-28*

Post Communion
Lord God, the source of truth and love,
keep us faithful to the apostles' teaching and fellowship,
united in prayer and the breaking of bread,
and one in joy and simplicity of heart,
in Jesus Christ our Lord.

Anne and Joachim
26 July – Lesser Festival – White

In the proto-gospel of James, written in the middle of the second century, the parents of Mary the mother of Jesus are named as Anne and Joachim. The story appears to be based heavily on that of Hannah, the mother of Samuel. The Church maintains their feast day both to emphasise God's plan from the beginning to send his Son, born of a woman, born under the law, to redeem fallen humanity; and also to show God's faithfulness in keeping his covenant with all generations.

Collect
Lord God of Israel,
who bestowed such grace on Anne and Joachim
that their daughter Mary grew up obedient to your word
and made ready to be the mother of your Son:
help us to commit ourselves in all things to your keeping
and grant us the salvation you promised to your people;
through Jesus Christ your Son our Lord,
who is alive and reigns with you,
in the unity of the Holy Spirit,
one God, now and for ever.

A reading from the prophecy of Zephaniah.

Sing aloud, O daughter Zion; shout, O Israel! Rejoice and exult
with all your heart, O daughter Jerusalem! The Lord has taken
away the judgments against you, he has turned away your enemies. The king of Israel, the Lord, is in your midst; you shall fear
disaster no more. On that day it shall be said to Jerusalem: Do not
fear, O Zion; do not let your hands grow weak. The Lord, your
God, is in your midst, a warrior who gives victory; he will rejoice
over you with gladness, he will renew you in his love; he will exult
over you with loud singing as on a day of festival.

This is the word of the Lord.   *Zephaniah 3. 14-18a*

Responsorial Psalm

R Sing aloud to God, O daughter Zion,
[rejoice and exult, O daughter Jerusalem!]

Happy are they all who fear the Lord,
and who follow in his ways!
You shall eat the fruit of your labour;
happiness and prosperity shall be yours. **R**

Your wife shall be like a fruitful vine within your house,
your children like olive shoots round about your table.
Whoever fears the Lord
shall thus indeed be blessed. **R**

The Lord bless you from Zion,
and may you see the prosperity of Jerusalem
 all the days of your life.
May you live to see your children's children;
may peace be upon Israel. **R**   *Psalm 128*

A reading from the Letter of Paul to the Romans.

We know that all things work together for good for those who love
God, who are called according to his purpose. For those whom he
foreknew he also predestined to be conformed to the image of his
Son, in order that he might be the firstborn within a large family.
And those whom he predestined he also called; and those whom
he called he also justified; and those whom he justified he also
glorified.

This is the word of the Lord.   *Romans 8. 28-30*

Hear the gospel of our Lord Jesus Christ according to Matthew.

Jesus said to his disciples, "Blessèd are your eyes, for they see, and your ears, for they hear. Truly I tell you, many prophets and righteous people longed to see what you see, but did not see it, and to hear what you hear, but did not hear it."

This is the gospel of the Lord.   *Matthew 13. 16-17*

Post Communion
God, the source of all holiness
  and giver of all good things:
may we who have shared at this table
  as strangers and pilgrims here on earth
be welcomed with all your saints
  to the heavenly feast on the day of your kingdom;
through Jesus Christ our Lord.

Brooke Foss Westcott, Bishop of Durham
27 July – Commemoration
If celebrated as a Lesser Festival, Common of Teachers, page 473

Born in 1825, Westcott was first ordained and then became a master at Harrow School. Whilst there, he published a series of scholarly works on the Bible, his expertise eventually leading to his election as Regius Professor of Divinity at the University of Cambridge in 1870. With Fenton Hort and J B Lightfoot, he led a revival in British biblical studies and theology. He became influential too in the field of Anglican social thought and was significant in the founding of the Clergy Training School in Cambridge (later renamed Westcott House in his memory). In 1890, he was consecrated Bishop of Durham, where he died on this day in 1901.

Mary, Martha & Lazarus
29 July – Lesser Festival – of any Saint – White

The gospels describe how Mary, Martha and their brother Lazarus gave Jesus hospitality in their home at Bethany outside Jerusalem. Jesus is said to have loved all three. After Lazarus' death, he wept and was moved by the sisters' grief to bring Lazarus back from the dead. Martha recognised Jesus as the Messiah, while Mary anointed his feet and, on another occasion, was commended by Jesus for her attentiveness to his teaching while Martha served. From this, Mary is traditionally taken to be an example of the contemplative life and Martha an example of the active spiritual life.

Collect
God our Father,
whose Son enjoyed the love of his friends,
  Mary, Martha and Lazarus,
in learning, argument and hospitality:
may we so rejoice in your love
that the world may come to know
  the depths of your wisdom, the wonder of your compassion,
  and your power to bring life out of death;
through the merits of Jesus Christ, our friend and brother,
who is alive and reigns with you, in the unity of the Holy Spirit,
one God, now and for ever.

A reading from the prophecy of Isaiah.

On this mountain the Lord of hosts will make for all peoples a feast of rich food, a feast of well-aged wines, of rich food filled with marrow, of well-aged wines strained clear. And he will destroy on this mountain the shroud that is cast over all peoples, the sheet that is spread over all nations; he will swallow up death forever. Then the Lord God will wipe away the tears from all faces, and the disgrace of his people he will take away from all the earth, for the Lord has spoken. It will be said on that day, Lo, this is our God; we have waited for him, so that he might save us. This is the Lord for whom we have waited; let us be glad and rejoice in his salvation.

This is the word of the Lord. *Isaiah 25. 6-9*

Responsorial Psalm

R **I love to do your will, O my God;**
   [your law is deep in my heart].

I waited patiently upon the Lord;
he stooped to me and heard my cry.
He lifted me out of the desolate pit, out of the mire and clay;
he set my feet upon a high cliff and made my footing sure. **R**

Happy are they who trust in the Lord!
they do not resort to evil spirits or turn to false gods.
Great things are they that you have done, O Lord my God,
there is none who can be compared with you. **R**

You are the Lord; do not withhold your compassion from me;
let your love and your faithfulness keep me safe for ever.
Be pleased, O Lord, to deliver me;
O Lord, make haste to help me. **R**   *From Psalm 40*

A reading from the Letter to the Hebrews.

It was fitting that God, for whom and through whom all things
exist, in bringing many children to glory, should make the pioneer
of their salvation perfect through sufferings. For the one who
sanctifies and those who are sanctified all have one Father. For
this reason Jesus is not ashamed to call them brothers and sisters,
saying, "I will proclaim your name to my brothers and sisters, in
the midst of the congregation I will praise you." And again, "I will
put my trust in him." And again, "Here am I and the children
whom God has given me."

Since, therefore, the children share flesh and blood, he himself
likewise shared the same things, so that through death he might
destroy the one who has the power of death, that is, the devil, and
free those who all their lives were held in slavery by the fear of
death.

This is the word of the Lord.   *Hebrews 2. 10-15*

Hear the gospel of our Lord Jesus Christ according to John.

Six days before the Passover Jesus came to Bethany, the home of
Lazarus, whom he had raised from the dead. There they gave a
dinner for him. Martha served, and Lazarus was one of those at

the table with him. Mary took a pound of costly perfume made of pure nard, anointed Jesus' feet, and wiped them with her hair. The house was filled with the fragrance of the perfume. But Judas Iscariot, one of his disciples (the one who was about to betray him), said, "Why was this perfume not sold for three hundred denarii and the money given to the poor?" (He said this not because he cared about the poor, but because he was a thief; he kept the common purse and used to steal what was put into it). Jesus said, "Leave her alone. She bought it so that she might keep it for the day of my burial. You always have the poor with you, but you do not always have me."

This is the gospel of the Lord.   *John 12. 1-8*

Post Communion
God, the source of all holiness
  and giver of all good things:
may we who have shared at this table
  as strangers and pilgrims here on earth
be welcomed with all your saints
  to the heavenly feast on the day of your kingdom;
through Jesus Christ our Lord.

William Wilberforce, Social Reformer
30 July – Lesser Festival – of any Saint – White

William Wilberforce was born in 1759 in Hull. Converted to an Evangelical piety within the Church of England, Wilberforce decided to serve the faith in Parliament instead of being ordained, becoming a Member of Parliament at the age of twenty-one. He was a supporter of missionary initiatives and helped found The Bible Society. Settling in Clapham in London, he became a leader of the reforming group of Evangelicals known as the 'Clapham Sect'. Of all the causes for which he fought, he is remembered best for his crusade against slavery. After years of effort, the trade in slaves was made illegal in the British Empire in 1807 and Wilberforce lived to see the complete abolition of slavery, just before his death on this day in 1833.

Collect
God our deliverer,
who sent your Son Jesus Christ
to set your people free from the slavery of sin:
grant that, as your servant William Wilberforce
  toiled against the sin of slavery,
so we may bring compassion to all
and work for the freedom of all the children of God;
through Jesus Christ your Son our Lord,
who is alive and reigns with you,
in the unity of the Holy Spirit,
one God, now and for ever.

A reading from the book of Job.

Job said, "If I have withheld anything that the poor desired, or have caused the eyes of the widow to fail, or have eaten my morsel alone, and the orphan has not eaten from it – for from my youth I reared the orphan like a father, and from my mother's womb I guided the widow – if I have seen anyone perish for lack of clothing, or a poor person without covering, whose loins have not blessed me, and who was not warmed with the fleece of my sheep; if I have raised my hand against the orphan, because I saw I had supporters at the gate; then let my shoulder blade fall from my shoulder, and let my arm be broken from its socket. For I was in terror of calamity from God, and I could not have faced his majesty."

This is the word of the Lord.   *Job 31. 16-23*

Responsorial Psalm

R   Stand in awe of the Lord, O offspring of Israel;
      [all you of Jacob's line, give glory].

The Lord does not despise nor abhor
the poor in their poverty;
neither does he hide his face from them;
but when they cry to him he hears them. **R**

The poor shall eat and be satisfied,
and those who seek the Lord shall praise him:
"May your heart live for ever!" **R**

All the ends of the earth shall remember and turn to the Lord,
and all the families of the nations shall bow before him.
For kingship belongs to the Lord;
he rules over the nations. **R**   *From Psalm 22*

A reading from the Letter of Paul to the Galatians.

In Christ Jesus you are all children of God through faith. As many
of you as were baptised into Christ have clothed yourselves with
Christ. There is no longer Jew or Greek, there is no longer slave or
free, there is no longer male and female; for all of you are one in
Christ Jesus. And if you belong to Christ, then you are Abraham's
offspring, heirs according to the promise. And because you are
children, God has sent the Spirit of his Son into our hearts, crying,
"Abba! Father!" So you are no longer a slave but a child, and if a
child then also an heir, through God.

This is the word of the Lord.   *Galatians 3. 26-29; 4. 6-7*

Hear the gospel of our Lord Jesus Christ according to Luke.

When he came to Nazareth, where he had been brought up, he
went to the synagogue on the sabbath day, as was his custom. He
stood up to read, and the scroll of the prophet Isaiah was given to
him. He unrolled the scroll and found the place where it was written: "The Spirit of the Lord is upon me, because he has anointed
me to bring good news to the poor. He has sent me to proclaim
release to the captives and recovery of sight to the blind, to let the
oppressed go free, to proclaim the year of the Lord's favour."

And he rolled up the scroll, gave it back to the attendant, and sat
down. The eyes of all in the synagogue were fixed on him. Then
he began to say to them, "Today this scripture has been fulfilled in
your hearing."

This is the gospel of the Lord.   *Luke 4. 16-21*

Post Communion
Faithful God,
who called your servant William Wilberforce to serve you
and gave him joy in walking the path of holiness:
by this eucharist,
  in which you renew within us the vision of your glory,
strengthen us all to follow the way of perfection
until we come to see you face to face;
through Jesus Christ our Lord.

Ignatius of Loyola, Founder of the Society of Jesus
31 July – Commemoration
If celebrated as a Lesser Festival, Common of Religious, page 494

Born in 1491, the son of a Basque nobleman, Ignatius served as a
soldier and was wounded at the siege of Pamplona in 1521.
During his convalescence he read a Life of Christ, was converted
and lived a life of prayer and penance, during which he wrote the
first draft of his *Spiritual Exercises*. He gathered six disciples, and
together they took vows of poverty and chastity and promised to
serve the Church either by preaching in Palestine or in other ways
that the Pope thought fit. By 1540, Ignatius had won papal
approval for his embryonic order and the Society of Jesus was
born. For the next sixteen years he directed the work of the Jesuits
as it spread around the world, until his sudden death on this day
in 1556.

AUGUST

Jean-Baptist Vianney, *Curé d'Ars*, Spiritual Guide
4 August – Commemoration
If celebrated as a Lesser Festival, Common of Pastors, page 483

Jean-Baptist Marie Vianney was born in Dardilly near Lyons in 1786, the son of a farmer, and he spent much of his childhood working as a shepherd on his father's farm. He had little formal education but, at the age of twenty, he began studying for the priesthood which he found extremely difficult. Despite his poor academic performance, he was ordained in 1815, mainly because of his devotion and holiness. He served as assistant priest at Ecully and, in 1818, was appointed curé, or parish priest, of the remote, unimportant village of Ars-en-Dombes. From this backwater, his fame was to spread world-wide. His skills in preaching and spiritual counsel earned him a reputation as a discerning and wise priest. His visiting penitents soon numbered three hundred a day. He would preach at eleven o' clock each morning and then spend up to sixteen hours in the confessional. A Franciscan tertiary who reflected the spirituality of Francis, his compassion and understanding of human weakness often brought him to tears. His love of God and his people ensured that he remained in Ars the rest of his life, despite a call to the religious life and many offers of promotion in the Church. He died on this day in the year 1859.

Oswald of Northumbria
5 August – Lesser Festival – Martyr – Red

Born around the year 605, the son of King Ælfrith of Northumbria, Oswald was forced to leave home after his father's death and move to Iona where, influenced by the monks of St Columba, he was baptised. Returning to Northumbria in 634, Oswald defeated the British king, setting up a cross as his standard and gathering his men around it to pray the night before the battle. A man of humility and generosity, Oswald worked closely with his friend St Aidan, travelling with him on his missionary journeys and acting as his interpreter. He died in battle on this day in 642 defending his kingdom from the Mercians.

Collect
Lord God almighty,
who so kindled the faith of King Oswald with your Spirit
that he set up the sign of the cross in his kingdom
and turned his people to the light of Christ:
grant that we, being fired by the same Spirit,
may always bear our cross before the world
and be found faithful servants of the gospel;
through Jesus Christ your Son our Lord,
who is alive and reigns with you,
in the unity of the Holy Spirit,
one God, now and for ever.

A reading from the Wisdom of Solomon.

The righteous live forever, and their reward is with the Lord; the Most High takes care of them. Therefore they will receive a glorious crown and a beautiful diadem from the hand of the Lord, because with his right hand he will cover them, and with his arm he will shield them. The Lord will take his zeal as his whole armour, and will arm all creation to repel his enemies; he will put on righteousness as a breastplate, and wear impartial justice as a helmet; he will take holiness as an invincible shield, and sharpen stern wrath for a sword, and creation will join with him to fight against his frenzied foes.

This is the word of the Lord. *Wisdom 5. 15-20*

Responsorial Psalm
**R Blessèd be the Lord my rock!
[my stronghold and my deliverer].**

O Lord, what are we that you should care for us?
mere mortals that you should think of us?
We are like a puff of wind;
our days are like a passing shadow. **R**

Bow your heavens, O Lord, and come down;
touch the mountains and they shall smoke.
Stretch out your hand from on high;
rescue me and deliver me from the great waters. **R**

O God, I will sing to you a new song;
I will play to you on a ten-stringed lyre.
You give victory to kings
and have rescued David your servant. **R**

Rescue me from the hurtful sword
and deliver me from the hand of foreign peoples,
whose mouths speak deceitfully
and whose right hand is raised in falsehood. **R**

Happy are the people of whom this is so:
happy are the people whose God is the Lord! **R**   *From Psalm 144*

A reading from the First Letter of Peter.

Beloved, do not be surprised at the fiery ordeal that is taking place among you to test you, as though something strange were happening to you. But rejoice insofar as you are sharing Christ's sufferings, so that you may also be glad and shout for joy when his glory is revealed. If you are reviled for the name of Christ, you are blessed, because the spirit of glory, which is the Spirit of God, is resting on you. But let none of you suffer as a murderer, a thief, a criminal, or even as a mischief maker.

Yet if any of you suffers as a Christian, do not consider it a disgrace, but glorify God because you bear this name. For the time has come for judgement to begin with the household of God; if it begins with us, what will be the end for those who do not obey the gospel of God? And "If it is hard for the righteous to be saved, what will become of the ungodly and the sinners?" Therefore, let those suffering in accordance with God's will entrust themselves to a faithful Creator, while continuing to do good.

This is the word of the Lord.   *1 Peter 4. 12-19*

Hear the gospel of our Lord Jesus Christ according to John.

Jesus's disciples said, "Yes, now you are speaking plainly, not in any figure of speech! Now we know that you know all things, and do not need to have anyone question you; by this we believe that you came from God."

Jesus answered them, "Do you now believe? The hour is coming, indeed it has come, when you will be scattered, each one to his home, and you will leave me alone. Yet I am not alone because the Father is with me. I have said this to you, so that in me you may have peace. In the world you face persecution. But take courage; I have conquered the world!"

This is the gospel of the Lord.   *John 16. 29-33*

Post Communion
God,
who gave us this holy meal
in which we have celebrated the glory of the cross
and the victory of your martyr Oswald:
by our communion with Christ
in his saving death and resurrection,
give us with all your saints the courage to conquer evil
and so to share the fruit of the tree of life;
through Jesus Christ our Lord.

The Transfiguration of our Lord
6 August – Festival – Gold or White

The story of the Transfiguration of Jesus on the mount is told in the gospels of Matthew, Mark and Luke, and Peter refers to it in his Second Epistle. Each time, it is made clear that God's salvation is for all and Christ is the one who brings that salvation. The testimony of the law and the prophets to Jesus are given by the presence of Moses and Elijah and the event also pre-figures the resurrection, giving a foretaste of the life of glory.

Collect
Father in heaven,
whose Son Jesus Christ was wonderfully transfigured
before chosen witnesses upon the holy mountain,
and spoke of the exodus he would accomplish at Jerusalem:

give us strength so to hear his voice and bear our cross
that in the world to come we may see him as he is;
who is alive and reigns with you,
in the unity of the Holy Spirit,
one God, now and for ever.

A reading from the prophecy of Daniel.

As I watched, thrones were set in place, and an Ancient One took
his throne; his clothing was white as snow and the hair of his head
like pure wool; his throne was fiery flames and its wheels were
burning fire. A stream of fire issued and flowed out from his presence. A thousand thousands served him, and ten thousand times
ten thousand stood attending him. The court sat in judgement,
and the books were opened. As I watched in the night visions, I
saw one like a human being coming with the clouds of heaven.
And he came to the Ancient One and was presented before him.
To him was given dominion and glory and kingship, that all peoples, nations, and languages should serve him. His dominion is an
everlasting dominion that shall not pass away, and his kingship is
one that shall never be destroyed.

This is the word of the Lord.   *Daniel 7. 9-10, 13-14*

Responsorial Psalm

**R   To the Lord be given dominion and glory
     [whose kingdom will last for ever].**

The Lord is king; let the earth rejoice;
let the multitude of the isles be glad.
Clouds and darkness are round about him,
righteousness and justice are the foundations of his throne. **R**

A fire goes before him
and burns up his enemies on every side.
His lightnings light up the world;
the earth sees it and is afraid. **R**

The mountains melt like wax at the presence of the Lord,
at the presence of the Lord of the whole earth.
The heavens declare his righteousness,
and all the peoples see his glory. **R**

For you are the Lord: most high over all the earth;
you are exalted far above all gods.
The Lord loves those who hate evil;
he preserves the lives of his saints. **R**

Light has sprung up for the righteous,
and joyful gladness for those who are true-hearted.
Rejoice in the Lord, you righteous,
and give thanks to his holy name. **R**   *From Psalm 97*

A reading from the Second Letter of Peter.

We did not follow cleverly devised myths when we made known
to you the power and coming of our Lord Jesus Christ, but we had
been eye-witnesses of his majesty. For he received honour and
glory from God the Father when that voice was conveyed to him
by the Majestic Glory, saying, "This is my Son, my Beloved, with
whom I am well pleased." We ourselves heard this voice come
from heaven, while we were with him on the holy mountain.

So we have the prophetic message more fully confirmed. You will
do well to be attentive to this as to a lamp shining in a dark place,
until the day dawns and the morning star rises in your hearts.

This is the word of the Lord.   *2 Peter 1. 16-19*

Hear the gospel of our Lord Jesus Christ according to Luke.

Jesus took with him Peter and John and James and went up on the
mountain to pray. And while he was praying, the appearance of
his face changed, and his clothes became dazzling white.
Suddenly they saw two men, Moses and Elijah, talking to him.
They appeared in glory and were speaking of his departure,
which he was about to accomplish at Jerusalem. Now Peter and
his companions were weighed down with sleep; but since they
had stayed awake, they saw his glory and the two men who stood
with him.

Just as they were leaving him, Peter said to Jesus, "Master, it is
good for us to be here; let us make three dwellings, one for you,
one for Moses, and one for Elijah" – not knowing what he said.
While he was saying this, a cloud came and overshadowed them;
and they were terrified as they entered the cloud. Then from the

cloud came a voice that said, "This is my Son, my Chosen; listen to him!" When the voice had spoken, Jesus was found alone. And they kept silent and in those days told no one any of the things they had seen.

This is the gospel of the Lord.   *Luke 9. 28b-36*

Post Communion
Holy God,
we see your glory in the face of Jesus Christ:
may we who are partakers at his table
reflect his life in word and deed,
that all the world may know
  his power to change and save.
This we ask through Jesus Christ our Lord.

John Mason Neale, Priest, Hymn Writer
7 August – Commemoration
If celebrated as a Lesser Festival, Common of Pastors, page 483

John Mason Neale was born in 1818 and, whilst an undergraduate at Cambridge, was influenced by the ideas of the Tractarians. He was a founder of the Cambridge Camden Society, which stimulated interest in ecclesiastical art and which played a part in the revival of Catholic ritual in the Church of England. Whilst Warden of Sackville College, East Grinstead, a post he held from 1846, Neale founded the Society of St Margaret, which grew into one of the largest of Anglican women's Religious communities. Neale is remembered as an accomplished hymn-writer and his influence on Anglican worship has been considerable. He suffered frail health for many years and died on the feast of the Transfiguration in 1866.

Dominic, Founder of the Order of Preachers
8 August – Lesser Festival – Religious – White

Born at Calaruega in Castile, of the ancient Guzman family in 1170, Dominic became an Augustinian or Austin Friar and led a disciplined life of prayer and penance. He became prior in 1201 but three years later, whilst on a trip to Denmark with his bishop, he passed through France and came across Cathars or Albigenses. They claimed to be Christians but held the heterodox belief that flesh and material things were evil, that the spirit was of God and that flesh and spirit were in permanent conflict. Dominic formed an Order of Preachers to combat this belief, although he would have nothing to do with the vengeful Crusade that began to be waged against the Albigenses. The Dominican Order spread to many countries in just a few years and did much to maintain the credibility of the orthodox faith in late-mediæval Europe. Dominic died on this day at Bologna in 1221.

Collect
Almighty God,
whose servant Dominic grew in the knowledge of your truth
and formed an order of preachers
  to proclaim the faith of Christ:
by your grace give to all your people a love for your word
and a longing to share the gospel,
so that the whole world may come to know you
and your Son Jesus Christ our Lord,
who is alive and reigns with you,
in the unity of the Holy Spirit,
one God, now and for ever.

A reading from the book Ecclesiasticus.

The one who devotes himself to the study of the law of the Most High seeks out the wisdom of all the ancients, and is concerned with prophecies; he preserves the sayings of the famous and penetrates the subtleties of parables; he seeks out the hidden meanings of proverbs and is at home with the obscurities of parables. He serves among the great and appears before rulers; he travels in foreign lands and learns what is good and evil in the human lot. He sets his heart to rise early to seek the Lord who made him, and to petition the Most High; he opens his mouth in prayer and asks pardon for his sins.

 If the great Lord is willing, he will be filled with the spirit of understanding; he will pour forth words of wisdom of his own and give thanks to the Lord in prayer. The Lord will direct his counsel and knowledge, as he meditates on his mysteries. He will show the wisdom of what he has learned and will glory in the law of the Lord's covenant. Many will praise his understanding; it will never be blotted out. His memory will not disappear, and his name will live through all generations. Nations will speak of his wisdom, and the congregation will proclaim his praise.

This is the word of the Lord.   *Ecclesiasticus 38.34b - 39.10*

Responsorial Psalm

**R   To you, O Lord, I lift up my soul;
       [my God, I put my trust in you].**

Show me your ways, O Lord,
and teach me your paths.
Lead me in your truth and teach me,
for you are the God of my salvation. **R**

Remember, O Lord, your compassion and love,
for they are from everlasting;
remember not the sins of my youth
and my transgressions. **R**

Remember me according to your love
and for the sake of your goodness, O Lord.
Gracious and upright is the Lord;
therefore he teaches sinners in his way. **R**

He guides the humble in doing right
and teaches his way to the lowly.
All the paths of the Lord are love and faithfulness
to those who keep his covenant and his testimonies. **R**

From Psalm 25

A reading from the First Letter of Paul to the Corinthians.

The message about the cross is foolishness to those who are perishing, but to us who are being saved it is the power of God. For it is written, "I will destroy the wisdom of the wise, and the discernment of the discerning I will thwart." Where is the one who is wise? Where is the scribe? Where is the debater of this age? Has not God made foolish the wisdom of the world? For since, in the wisdom of God, the world did not know God through wisdom, God decided, through the foolishness of our proclamation, to save those who believe. For Jews demand signs and Greeks desire wisdom, but we proclaim Christ crucified, a stumbling block to Jews and foolishness to Gentiles, but to those who are the called, both Jews and Greeks, Christ the power of God and the wisdom of God. For God's foolishness is wiser than human wisdom, and God's weakness is stronger than human strength.

This is the word of the Lord. *1 Corinthians 1. 18-25*

Hear the gospel of our Lord Jesus Christ according to Matthew.

Jesus sent out the twelve with the following instructions: "Go nowhere among the Gentiles, and enter no town of the Samaritans, but go rather to the lost sheep of the house of Israel. As you go, proclaim the good news, 'The kingdom of heaven has come near.' Cure the sick, raise the dead, cleanse the lepers, cast out demons. You received without payment; give without payment. Take no gold, or silver, or copper in your belts, no bag for your journey, or two tunics, or sandals, or a staff; for labourers deserve their food. Whatever town or village you enter, find out who in it is worthy, and stay there until you leave. As you enter the house, greet it. If the house is worthy, let your peace come upon it; but if it is not worthy, let your peace return to you."

This is the gospel of the Lord. *Matthew 10. 5-13*

Post Communion
Merciful God,
who gave such grace to your servant Dominic
that he served you with singleness of heart
and loved you above all things:
help us, whose communion with you
  has been renewed in this sacrament,
to forsake all that holds us back from following Christ
and to grow into his likeness from glory to glory;
through Jesus Christ our Lord.

Mary Sumner, Founder of the Mothers' Union
9 August – Lesser Festival – of any Saint – White

Mary Elizabeth Sumner (née Heywood) was born in 1828 at Swinton. In 1848, she married a young curate, George Henry Sumner, nephew of Archbishop Sumner, who was himself to become Bishop of Guildford in 1888. A mother of three children, Mary called a meeting in 1876 at which the Mothers' Union was founded, providing a forum in which to unite mothers of all classes in the aim of bringing up children in the Christian faith. Baptism and parental example were its two basic principles. At first a parochial organisation, it grew steadily into an international concern, encouraging the ideal of a Christian home. Mary died on this day in 1921.

Collect
Faithful and loving God,
who called Mary Sumner to strive
  for the renewal of family life:
give us the gift of your Holy Spirit,
that through word, prayer and deed
  your family may be strengthened and your people served;
through Jesus Christ your Son our Lord,
who is alive and reigns with you,
in the unity of the Holy Spirit,
one God, now and for ever.

A reading from the book Proverbs.

By wisdom a house is built, and by understanding it is established; by knowledge the rooms are filled with all precious and pleasant riches.

If you say, "Look, we did not know this," does not God, who weighs the heart, perceive it? Does not the one who keeps watch over your soul know it? And will he not repay all according to their deeds? My child, eat honey, for it is good, and the drippings of the honeycomb are sweet to your taste. Know that wisdom is such to your soul; if you find her, you will find a future, and your hope will not be cut off.

This is the word of the Lord.   *Proverbs 24. 3-4, 12-14*

Responsorial Psalm

**R Happy are they all who revere the Lord,
[and who follow in his ways].**

How shall the young cleanse their way?
By keeping to your words.
With my whole heart I seek you;
let me not stray from your commandments. **R**

I treasure your promise in my heart,
that I may not sin against you.
Blessèd are you, O Lord;
instruct me in your statutes. **R**

With my lips will I recite
all the judgements of your mouth.
I have taken greater delight in the way of your decrees
than in all manner of riches. **R**

I will meditate on your commandments
and give attention to your ways.
My delight is in your statutes;
I will not forget your word. **R**   *From Psalm 119*

A reading from the Letter to the Hebrews.

Let mutual love continue. Do not neglect to show hospitality to
strangers, for by doing that some have entertained angels without
knowing it. Remember those who are in prison, as though you
were in prison with them; those who are being tortured, as though
you yourselves were being tortured. Let marriage be held in honour by all, and let the marriage bed be kept undefiled; for God will
judge fornicators and adulterers. Keep your lives free from the
love of money, and be content with what you have; for he has
said, "I will never leave you or forsake you."

This is the word of the Lord.   *Hebrews 13. 1-5*

Hear the gospel of our Lord Jesus Christ according to Luke.

Jesus said to his disciples, "I say to you, Ask, and it will be given
you; search, and you will find; knock, and the door will be opened
for you. For everyone who asks receives, and everyone who
searches finds, and for everyone who knocks, the door will be

opened. Is there anyone among you who, if your child asks for a fish, will give a snake instead of a fish? Or if the child asks for an egg, will give a scorpion? If you then, who are evil, know how to give good gifts to your children, how much more will the heavenly Father give the Holy Spirit to those who ask him!"

This is the gospel of the Lord. *Luke 11. 9-13*

Post Communion
God, the source of all holiness
  and giver of all good things:
may we who have shared at this table
  as strangers and pilgrims here on earth
be welcomed with all your saints
  to the heavenly feast on the day of your kingdom;
through Jesus Christ our Lord.

Laurence, Deacon at Rome
10 August – Lesser Festival – Martyr – Red

The sources for the martyrdom of Laurence are among the earliest, though the details are thin. Laurence was one of the seven deacons at Rome and closely associated with Pope Sixtus II, martyred just a few days before him. His examiners insisted he produce the Church treasures. He promptly did so: assembling all the poor, he is reputed to have said, "These are the treasures of the Church." The story of his being put to death on a gridiron is a much later addition to his story. He died on this day in the year 258.

Collect
Almighty God,
who made Laurence a loving servant of your people
and a wise steward of the treasures of your Church:
fire us with his example to love as he loved
  and to walk in the way that leads to eternal life;
through Jesus Christ your Son our Lord,
who is alive and reigns with you,
in the unity of the Holy Spirit,
one God, now and for ever.

A reading from the Book of Tobit.

Revere the Lord all your days, my son, and refuse to sin or to transgress his commandments. Live uprightly all the days of your life, and do not walk in the ways of wrongdoing; for those who act in accordance with truth will prosper in all their activities. To all those who practice righteousness give alms from your possessions, and do not let your eye begrudge the gift when you make it. Do not turn your face away from anyone who is poor, and the face of God will not be turned away from you. If you have many possessions, make your gift from them in proportion; if few, do not be afraid to give according to the little you have. So you will be laying up a good treasure for yourself against the day of necessity. For almsgiving delivers from death and keeps you from going into the Darkness. Indeed, almsgiving, for all who practice it, is an excellent offering in the presence of the Most High.

This is the word of the Lord.   *Tobit 4. 5-11*

Responsorial Psalm

**R   Be joyful in God, all you lands;
[sing the glory of his name].**

You brought us into the snare, O God;
you laid heavy burdens upon our backs.
You let enemies ride over our heads;
we went through fire and water;
but you brought us out into a place of refreshment. **R**

I will enter your house with burnt-offerings
and will pay you my vows,
which I promised with my lips
and spoke with my mouth when I was in trouble. **R**

In truth, God has heard me;
he has attended to the voice of my prayer.
Blessèd be God, who has not rejected my prayer,
nor withheld his love from me. **R**   *From Psalm 66*

A reading from the Second Letter of Paul to the Corinthians.

The point is this: the one who sows sparingly will also reap sparingly, and the one who sows bountifully will also reap bountifully. Each of you must give as you have made up your mind, not reluctantly or under compulsion, for God loves a cheerful giver. And God is able to provide you with every blessing in abundance, so that by always having enough of everything, you may share abundantly in every good work. As it is written, "He scatters abroad, he gives to the poor; his righteousness endures forever." He who supplies seed to the sower and bread for food will supply and multiply your seed for sowing and increase the harvest of your righteousness.

This is the word of the Lord.   *2 Corinthians 9. 6-10*

Hear the gospel of our Lord Jesus Christ according to Matthew.

Jesus said to the crowds, "Do not store up for yourselves treasures on earth, where moth and rust consume and where thieves break in and steal; but store up for yourselves treasures in heaven, where neither moth nor rust consumes and where thieves do not break in and steal. For where your treasure is, there your heart will be also. The eye is the lamp of the body. So, if your eye is healthy, your whole body will be full of light; but if your eye is unhealthy, your whole body will be full of darkness. If then the light in you is darkness, how great is the darkness! No one can serve two masters; for a slave will either hate the one and love the other, or be devoted to the one and despise the other. You cannot serve God and wealth."

This is the gospel of the Lord.   *Matthew 6. 19-24*

Post Communion
God,
who gave us this holy meal
in which we have celebrated the glory of the cross
and the victory of your martyr Laurence:
by our communion with Christ
in his saving death and resurrection,
give us with all your saints the courage to conquer evil
and so to share the fruit of the tree of life;
through Jesus Christ our Lord.

Clare of Assisi

11 August – Lesser Festival – Religious – White

Born in 1193 in Assisi of a wealthy family, Clare caught the joy of a new vision of the gospel from Francis' preaching. Escaping from home, first to the Benedictines and then to a Béguine-style group, she chose a contemplative way of life when she founded her own community, which lived in corporate poverty understood as dependence on God, with a fresh, democratic lifestyle. Clare became the first woman to write a religious Rule for women, and in it showed great liberty of spirit in dealing with earlier prescriptions. During the long years after Francis' death, she supported his earlier companions in their desire to remain faithful to his vision, as she did. Some of her last words were: "Blessèd be God, for having created me."

Collect
God of peace,
who in the poverty of the blessèd Clare
gave us a clear light to shine in the darkness of this world:
give us grace so to follow in her footsteps
that we may, at the last, rejoice with her
 in your eternal glory;
through Jesus Christ your Son our Lord,
who is alive and reigns with you,
in the unity of the Holy Spirit,
one God, now and for ever.

A reading from the prophecy of Hosea.

I will now allure her, and bring her into the wilderness, and speak tenderly to her. From there I will give her her vineyards, and make the Valley of Achor a door of hope. There she shall respond as in the days of her youth, as at the time when she came out of the land of Egypt. And I will take you for my spouse forever; I will take you for my spouse in righteousness and in justice, in steadfast love, and in mercy. I will take you for my spouse in faithfulness; and you shall know the Lord.

This is the word of the Lord.   *Hosea 2. 14-15 & 19-20*

Responsorial Psalm

R For God alone my soul in silence waits;
   [from him comes my salvation].

God alone is my rock and my salvation,
my stronghold, so that I shall not be greatly shaken.
For God alone my soul in silence waits;
truly, my hope is in him. **R**

He alone is my rock and my salvation,
my stronghold, so that I shall not be shaken.
In God is my safety and my honour;
God is my strong rock and my refuge. **R**

Put your trust in him always, O people,
pour out your hearts before him, for God is our refuge.
God has spoken once, twice have I heard it,
that power belongs to God alone. **R**   *From Psalm 62*

A reading from the Second Letter of Paul to the Corinthians.

It is the God who said, "Let light shine out of darkness," who has shone in our hearts to give the light of the knowledge of the glory of God in the face of Jesus Christ. But we have this treasure in clay jars, so that it may be made clear that this extraordinary power belongs to God and does not come from us. We are afflicted in every way, but not crushed; perplexed, but not driven to despair; persecuted, but not forsaken; struck down, but not destroyed; always carrying in the body the death of Jesus, so that the life of Jesus may also be made visible in our bodies.

This is the word of the Lord.   *2 Corinthians 4. 6-10*

Hear the gospel of our Lord Jesus Christ according to John.

Jesus said to his disciples, "Abide in me as I abide in you. Just as the branch cannot bear fruit by itself unless it abides in the vine, neither can you unless you abide in me. I am the vine, you are the branches. Those who abide in me and I in them bear much fruit, because apart from me you can do nothing. Whoever does not abide in me is thrown away like a branch and withers; such branches are gathered, thrown into the fire, and burned.

"If you abide in me, and my words abide in you, ask for whatever you wish, and it will be done for you. My Father is glorified by this, that you bear much fruit and become my disciples. As the Father has loved me, so I have loved you; abide in my love."

This is the gospel of the Lord.   *John 15. 4-10*

Post Communion
Merciful God,
who gave such grace to your servant Clare
that she served you with singleness of heart
and loved you above all things:
help us, whose communion with you
  has been renewed in this sacrament,
to forsake all that holds us back from following Christ
and to grow into his likeness from glory to glory;
through Jesus Christ our Lord.

John Henry Newman, Priest, Tractarian
11 August – *Commemoration*
If celebrated as a Lesser Festival, Common of Pastors, page 483

John Henry Newman was born in 1801. His intellectual brilliance saw him appointed to a Fellowship in Oxford at the young age of twenty-one. His Evangelical roots gradually gave way to a more Catholic view of the Church, particularly after liberal trends both in politics and theology appeared to undermine the Church of England's authority. Newman was one of the leaders of the Tractarians who defended the Church and he is associated especially with the idea of Anglicanism as a Via Media or middle way between Roman Catholicism and Protestantism. He continued to make an original and influential contribution to theology after he joined the Roman Catholic Church in 1845. He established an Oratorian community in Birmingham in 1849 and towards the end of his life was made a Cardinal. He died on this day in 1890.

Jeremy Taylor, Bishop of Down & Connor
13 August – Lesser Festival – Teacher of the Faith – White

Jeremy Taylor was born in Cambridge in 1613 and educated there at Gonville & Caius College. He was ordained in 1633 and, as the Civil War got under way, he became a chaplain with the Royalist forces. He was captured and imprisoned briefly but after his release went to Wales, where the Earl of Carbery gave him refuge. He wrote prolifically whilst there, notably *The Rule and Exercise of Holy Living* in 1650 and *of Holy Dying* the following year. In 1658 he went to Ireland to lecture and two years later was made Bishop of Down and Connor. He found many of his clergy held to Presbyterianism and so ignored him; and the Romans rejected him as a Protestant. In turn, he treated both sides harshly. His health was worn down by the protracted conflicts and he died on this day in 1667.

Collect
Holy and loving God,
you dwell in the human heart
and make us partakers of the divine nature
in Christ our great high priest:
help us who remember your servant Jeremy Taylor
to put our trust in your heavenly promises
and follow a holy life in virtue and true godliness;
through Jesus Christ your Son our Lord,
who is alive and reigns with you,
in the unity of the Holy Spirit,
one God, now and for ever.

A reading from the First Book of the Kings.

Solomon said, "O God, you have shown great and steadfast love to your servant my father David, because he walked before you in faithfulness, in righteousness, and in uprightness of heart toward you; and you have kept for him this great and steadfast love, and have given him a son to sit on his throne today. And now, O Lord my God, you have made your servant king in place of my father David, although I am only a little child; I do not know how to go out or come in. And your servant is in the midst of the people whom you have chosen, a great people, so numerous they cannot be numbered or counted. Give your servant therefore an understanding mind to govern your people, able to discern between good and evil; for who can govern this your great people?" It pleased the Lord that Solomon had asked this.

This is the word of the Lord.   *1 Kings 3. 6-10*

Responsorial Psalm

**R   I delight in your commandments, O God,
     [which I have always loved].**

Teach me, O Lord, the way of your statutes,
and I shall keep it to the end.
Give me understanding and I shall keep your law;
I shall keep it with all my heart. **R**

Turn my eyes from watching what is worthless;
give me life in your ways.
Fulfil your promise to your servant,
which you make to those who fear you. **R**

Turn away the reproach which I dread,
because your judgements are good.
Behold, I long for your commandments;
in your righteousness preserve my life. **R**   *From Psalm 119*

A reading from the Letter of Paul to Titus.

Show yourself in all respects a model of good works, and in your teaching show integrity, gravity, and sound speech that cannot be censured; then any opponent will be put to shame, having nothing evil to say of us. For the grace of God has appeared, bringing salvation to all, training us to renounce impiety and worldly passions, and in the present age to live lives that are self-controlled, upright, and godly, while we wait for the blessèd hope and the manifestation of the glory of our great God and Saviour, Jesus Christ. He it is who gave himself for us that he might redeem us from all iniquity and purify for himself a people of his own who are zealous for good deeds.

This is the word of the Lord.   *Titus 2. 7-8, 11-14*

Hear the gospel of our Lord Jesus Christ according to Matthew.

Jesus said to the crowds, "Do not think that I have come to abolish the law or the prophets; I have come not to abolish but to fulfil. For truly I tell you, until heaven and earth pass away, not one letter, not one stroke of a letter, will pass from the law until all is accomplished. Therefore, whoever breaks one of the least of these commandments, and teaches others to do the same, will be called least in the kingdom of heaven; but whoever does them and teaches them will be called great in the kingdom of heaven. For I tell you, unless your righteousness exceeds that of the scribes and Pharisees, you will never enter the kingdom of heaven."

This is the gospel of the Lord.   *Matthew 5. 17-20*

Post Communion
God of truth,
whose Wisdom set her table
and invited us to eat the bread and drink the wine
  of the kingdom:
help us to lay aside all foolishness
and to live and walk in the way of insight,
that we may come with your servant Jeremy Taylor
  to the eternal feast of heaven;
through Jesus Christ our Lord.

Florence Nightingale, Nurse, Social Reformer
13 August – Commemoration
If celebrated as a Lesser Festival, Common of any Saint, page 527

Florence Nightingale was born in 1820 into a wealthy family. In the face of their opposition, she insisted that she wished to train in nursing. In 1853, she finally achieved her wish and headed her own private nursing institute in London. Her efforts at improving conditions for the wounded during the Crimean War won her great acclaim and she devoted the rest of her life to reforming nursing care. Her school at St Thomas's Hospital became significant in helping to elevate nursing into a profession. An Anglican, she remained committed to a personal mystical religion which sustained her through many years of poor health until her death in 1910.

Octavia Hill, Social Reformer
13 August – Commemoration
If celebrated as a Lesser Festival, Common of any Saint, page 527

Octavia Hill was born in 1838 into a family active in social work, and, during her teens, she was influenced by the friendship of F D Maurice and John Ruskin. Earning her living through teaching, Octavia was appalled at the conditions in which most of her pupils lived. Borrowing money, she bought some slum properties and began to manage them in a more sympathetic way, insisting on financial viability rather than mere charity. The success of the scheme led to its extension and Octavia became a pioneer of housing reform. Strongly motivated by her faith, she never allowed her growing fame to undermine her personal humility. She continued her work until her death on this day in 1912.

Maximilian Kolbe, Friar, Martyr
14 August – Commemoration
If celebrated as a Lesser Festival, Common of Martyrs, page 464

Maximilian Kolbe was born at Zduńska Wola near Łódź in Poland in 1894. His parents were Franciscan Tertiaries and, beginning his training for ordination in 1907, Maximilian joined the Franciscan noviciate in 1910. He studied at Rome but, suffering from tuberculosis, he returned to Poland and became a lecturer in church history. After suffering a severe illness, he resolved to publish a magazine for Christian readers and this soon gained a huge circulation. Soon his community was producing daily and weekly journals. After the Nazi invasion of Poland, Maximilian was arrested as an 'intellectual' and taken to Auschwitz in May 1941. There he continued his priestly ministry, secretly celebrating the eucharist. When, after an escape, a prisoner was chosen to forfeit his life as an example, Maximilian stepped forward to take his place and be put to death. Two weeks later he was injected with phenol and died on this day in 1941.

The Blessèd Virgin Mary
15 August – Festival – of the BVM – White or Gold

Mary was a young Jewish girl living in Nazareth when a messenger from the Lord announced that she was to be the bearer of the Son of God to the world. Her response "Let it be to me according to your word" revealed her natural sense of obedience to God and her reverence for his Word, showing her worthy to be the bearer of the Word made flesh. This day is now celebrated as the major feast of the Blessèd Virgin Mary throughout most of Christendom.

Collect
Almighty God,
who looked upon the lowliness of the Blessèd Virgin Mary
and chose her to be the mother of your only Son:
grant that we who are redeemed by his blood
may share with her in the glory of your eternal kingdom;
through Jesus Christ your Son our Lord,
who is alive and reigns with you,
in the unity of the Holy Spirit,
one God, now and for ever.

A reading from the prophecy of Isaiah.

I will greatly rejoice in the Lord, my whole being shall exult in my God; for he has clothed me with the garments of salvation, he has covered me with the robe of righteousness, as a bridegroom decks himself with a garland, and as a bride adorns herself with her jewels. For as the earth brings forth its shoots, and as a garden causes what is sown in it to spring up, so the Lord God will cause righteousness and praise to spring up before all the nations.

This is the word of the Lord.   *Isaiah 61. 10-11*

Or:

A reading from the Revelation to John.

God's temple in heaven was opened, and the ark of his covenant was seen within his temple; and there were flashes of lightning, rumblings, peals of thunder, an earthquake, and heavy hail.

A great portent appeared in heaven: a woman clothed with the sun, with the moon under her feet, and on her head a crown of twelve stars. She was pregnant and was crying out in birth pangs, in the agony of giving birth. Then another portent appeared in heaven: a great red dragon, with seven heads and ten horns, and seven diadems on his heads. His tail swept down a third of the stars of heaven and threw them to the earth. Then the dragon stood before the woman who was about to bear a child, so that he might devour her child as soon as it was born. And she gave birth to a son, a male child, who is to rule all the nations with a rod of iron. But her child was snatched away and taken to God and to his throne; and the woman fled into the wilderness, where she has a place prepared by God, so that there she can be nourished for one thousand two hundred and sixty days.

Then I heard a loud voice in heaven, proclaiming, "Now have come the salvation and the power and the kingdom of our God and the authority of his Messiah, for the accuser of our comrades has been thrown down, who accuses them day and night before our God."

This is the word of the Lord.   *Revelation 11.19 - 12.6, 10*

Responsorial Psalm

R I will greatly rejoice in the Lord,
   [my whole being shall exult in my God].

Kings' daughters stand among the ladies of the court;
on your right hand is the queen,
adorned with the gold of Ophir. **R**

"Hear, O daughter; consider and listen closely;
forget your people and your family's house.
The king will have pleasure in your beauty;
he is your master; therefore do him honour. **R**

"The people of Tyre are here with a gift;
the rich among the people seek your favour."
All glorious is the princess as she enters;
her gown is cloth-of-gold. **R**

In embroidered apparel she is brought to the king;
after her the bridesmaids follow in procession.
With joy and gladness they are brought,
and enter into the palace of the king. **R**

"In place of fathers, O king, you shall have sons;
you shall make them princes over all the earth.
I will make your name to be remembered
from one generation to another;
therefore nations will praise you for ever and ever." **R**

From Psalm 45

A reading from the Letter of Paul to the Galatians.

When the fullness of time had come, God sent his Son, born of a woman, born under the law, in order to redeem those who were under the law, so that we might receive adoption as children. And because you are children, God has sent the Spirit of his Son into our hearts, crying, "Abba! Father!" So you are no longer a slave but a child, and if a child then also an heir, through God.

This is the word of the Lord. *Galatians 4. 4-7*

Hear the gospel of our Lord Jesus Christ according to Luke.

Mary said, "My soul magnifies the Lord and my spirit rejoices in God my Saviour, for he has looked with favour on the lowliness of his servant. Surely, from now on all generations will call me blessèd; for the Mighty One has done great things for me, and holy is his name. His mercy is for those who fear him from generation to generation. He has shown strength with his arm; he has scattered the proud in the thoughts of their hearts. He has brought down the powerful from their thrones, and lifted up the lowly; he has filled the hungry with good things, and sent the rich away empty. He has helped his servant Israel, in remembrance of his mercy, according to the promise he made to our ancestors, to Abraham and to his descendants forever." And Mary remained with Elizabeth about three months and then returned to her home.

This is the gospel of the Lord. *Luke 1. 46-55*

God Most High,
whose handmaid bore the Word made flesh:
we thank you that in this sacrament of our redemption
you visit us with your Holy Spirit
and overshadow us by your power;
strengthen us to walk with Mary the joyful path of obedience
and so to bring forth the fruits of holiness;
through Jesus Christ our Lord.

Bernard, Abbot of Clairvaux
20 August – Lesser Festival – Teacher of the Faith – White

Bernard was born at Fontaines, near Dijon, in France in the year
1090. He entered the Benedictine abbey at Cîteaux in 1112, taking
with him many of his young companions, some of whom were his
own brothers. He was a leader of the reform within Benedictinism
at this time and in 1115 was sent to establish a new monastery at a
place he named Clairvaux, or valley of light. Though times were
hard, he built up the community with his remarkable qualities of
leadership. Bernard preached widely and powerfully and proved
himself a theologian of renown. Literally hundreds of houses
were founded on the Cîteaux or Cistercian system and Bernard's
influence on his own generation and beyond was immense. He
died on this day in 1153.

Collect
Merciful Redeemer,
who, by the life and preaching of your servant Bernard,
rekindled the radiant light of your Church:
grant us, in our generation,
to be inflamed with the same spirit of discipline and love,
and ever to walk before you as children of light;
through Jesus Christ your Son our Lord,
who is alive and reigns with you,
in the unity of the Holy Spirit,
one God, now and for ever.

A reading from the book Proverbs.

Get wisdom; get insight: do not forget, nor turn away from the words of my mouth. Do not forsake her, and she will keep you; love her, and she will guard you. The beginning of wisdom is this: Get wisdom, and whatever else you get, get insight. Prize her highly, and she will exalt you; she will honour you if you embrace her. She will place on your head a fair garland; she will bestow on you a beautiful crown."

This is the word of the Lord.   *Proverbs 4. 5-9*

Responsorial Psalm

**R Their sound has gone out into all lands,
    [and their message to the ends of the world].**

The heavens declare the glory of God,
and the firmament shows his handiwork.
One day tells its tale to another,
and one night imparts knowledge to another. **R**

Although they have no words or language,
and their voices are not heard,
Their sound has gone out into all lands,
and their message to the ends of the world. **R**

The law of the Lord is perfect and revives the soul;
the testimony of the Lord is sure
and gives wisdom to the innocent. **R**   *From Psalm 19*

A reading from the Revelation to John.

From the throne came a voice saying, "Praise our God, all you his servants, and all who fear him, small and great." Then I heard what seemed to be the voice of a great multitude, like the sound of many waters and like the sound of mighty thunderpeals, crying out, "Alleluia! For the Lord our God the Almighty reigns. Let us rejoice and exult and give him the glory, for the marriage of the Lamb has come, and his bride has made herself ready; to her it has been granted to be clothed with fine linen, bright and pure" – for the fine linen is the righteous deeds of the saints. And the angel said to me, "Write this: Blessèd are those who are invited to the marriage supper of the Lamb." And he said to me, "These are true words of God."

This is the word of the Lord.   *Revelation 19. 5-9*

Hear the gospel of our Lord Jesus Christ according to John.

Jesus said, "If you abide in me, and my words abide in you, ask for whatever you wish, and it will be done for you. My Father is glorified by this, that you bear much fruit and become my disciples. As the Father has loved me, so I have loved you; abide in my love. If you keep my commandments, you will abide in my love, just as I have kept my Father's commandments and abide in his love. I have said these things to you so that my joy may be in you, and that your joy may be complete."

This is the gospel of the Lord.   *John 15. 7-11*

Post Communion
God of truth,
whose Wisdom set her table
and invited us to eat the bread and drink the wine
  of the kingdom:
help us to lay aside all foolishness
and to live and walk in the way of insight,
that we may come with your servant Bernard
  to the eternal feast of heaven;
through Jesus Christ our Lord.

William & Catherine Booth,
Founders of the Salvation Army
20 August – Commemoration
If celebrated as a Lesser Festival, Common of any Saint, page 513

William Booth was born in Nottingham in 1829, the same year as Catherine Mumford was born in Ashbourne, Derbyshire. They were married in 1855. A passionate preacher, William's style was criticised by his fellow Methodists and he left them in 1861, founding his own revivalist mission in Whitechapel four years later. The Christian Mission, as it was known, evolved into the Salvation Army by 1878. Both William and Catherine were famous for preaching and their movement developed into a world-wide denomination. It coupled moral fervour with a strong social commitment to the poor. Catherine died on 4 October 1890 and William on this day in 1912.

Bartholomew the Apostle
24 August – Festival – Apostle – Red

It has long been assumed that Bartholomew is the same as Nathanael though it is not a certainty. The gospels speak of Philip bringing Nathanael to Jesus and calling him an Israelite worthy of the name. He is also present beside the Sea of Galilee at the resurrection. Although he seems initially a somewhat cynical man, he recognises Jesus for who he is and proclaims him as Son of God and King of Israel.

Collect
Almighty and everlasting God,
who gave to your apostle Bartholomew grace
  truly to believe and to preach your word:
grant that your Church
may love that word which he believed
and may faithfully preach and receive the same;
through Jesus Christ your Son our Lord,
who is alive and reigns with you,
in the unity of the Holy Spirit,
one God, now and for ever.

Isaiah 43. 8-13	*or*	Acts 5. 12-16
Psalm 145. 1-7		Psalm 145. 1-7
Acts 5. 12-16		1 Corinthians 4. 9-15
Luke 22. 24-30		Luke 22. 24-30

A reading from the prophecy of Isaiah.

Bring forth the people who are blind, yet have eyes, who are deaf, yet have ears! Let all the nations gather together, and let the peoples assemble. Who among them declared this, and foretold to us the former things? Let them bring their witnesses to justify them, and let them hear and say, "It is true." You are my witnesses, says the Lord, and my servant whom I have chosen, so that you may know and believe me and understand that I am he. Before me no god was formed, nor shall there be any after me. I, I am the Lord, and besides me there is no saviour. I declared and saved and proclaimed, when there was no strange god among you; and you are my witnesses, says the Lord. I am God, and also henceforth I am He; there is no one who can deliver from my hand; I work and who can hinder it?

This is the word of the Lord.   *Isaiah 43. 8-13*

Responsorial Psalm

**R   The Lord is loving to everyone
     [and his compassion is over all his works].**

I will exalt you, O God my King,
and bless your name for ever and ever.
Every day will I bless you
and praise your name for ever and ever. **R**

Great is the Lord and greatly to be praised;
there is no end to his greatness.
One generation shall praise your works to another
and shall declare your power. **R**

I will ponder the glorious splendour of your majesty
and all your marvellous works.
They shall speak of the might of your wondrous acts,
and I will tell of your greatness. **R**

They shall publish the remembrance of your great goodness;
they shall sing of your righteous deeds.
The Lord is gracious and full of compassion,
slow to anger and of great kindness. **R**   *From Psalm 145*

A reading from the Acts of the Apostles.

Many signs and wonders were done among the people through the apostles. And they were all together in Solomon's Portico. None of the rest dared to join them, but the people held them in high esteem. Yet more than ever believers were added to the

Lord, great numbers of both men and women, so that they even carried out the sick into the streets, and laid them on cots and mats, in order that Peter's shadow might fall on some of them as he came by. A great number of people would also gather from the towns around Jerusalem, bringing the sick and those tormented by unclean spirits, and they were all cured.

This is the word of the Lord.   *Acts 5. 12-16*

A reading from the First Letter of Paul to the Corinthians.

I think that God has exhibited us apostles as last of all, as though sentenced to death, because we have become a spectacle to the world, to angels and to mortals. We are fools for the sake of Christ, but you are wise in Christ. We are weak, but you are strong. You are held in honour, but we in disrepute. To the present hour we are hungry and thirsty, we are poorly clothed and beaten and homeless, and we grow weary from the work of our own hands. When reviled, we bless; when persecuted, we endure; when slandered, we speak kindly. We have become like the rubbish of the world, the dregs of all things, to this very day. I am not writing this to make you ashamed, but to admonish you as my beloved children. For though you might have ten thousand guardians in Christ, you do not have many fathers. Indeed, in Christ Jesus I became your father through the gospel.

This is the word of the Lord.   *1 Corinthians 4. 9-15*

Hear the gospel of our Lord Jesus Christ according to Luke.

A dispute also arose among the disciples as to which one of them was to be regarded as the greatest. But Jesus said to them, "The kings of the Gentiles lord it over them; and those in authority over them are called benefactors. But not so with you; rather the greatest among you must become like the youngest, and the leader like one who serves. For who is greater, the one who is at the table or the one who serves? Is it not the one at the table? But I am among you as one who serves.

"You are those who have stood by me in my trials; and I confer on you, just as my Father has conferred on me, a kingdom, so that you may eat and drink at my table in my kingdom, and you will sit on thrones judging the twelve tribes of Israel."

This is the gospel of the Lord.   *Luke 22. 24-30*

Post Communion
Almighty God,
who on the day of Pentecost
sent your Holy Spirit to the apostles
with the wind from heaven and in tongues of flame,
filling them with joy and boldness to preach the gospel:
by the power of the same Spirit
strengthen us to witness to your truth
and to draw everyone to the fire of your love;
through Jesus Christ our Lord.

Monica, Mother of Augustine of Hippo
27 August – Lesser Festival – of any Saint – White

Monica was born in North Africa of Christian parents in 332 and she was married to a pagan named Patricius, whom she converted to Christianity. They had three children of whom the most famous was her eldest child, the future Augustine. Indeed, Augustine ascribed his conversion to the example and devotion of his mother: "She never let me out of her prayers that you, O God, might say to the widow's son 'Young man, I say to you, rise!'" – which is why the gospel of the widow of Nain is traditionally read today as her memorial. Monica's husband died when she was forty. Her desire had been to be buried alongside him, but this was not to be. She died in Italy, at Ostia, in 387 on her way home to North Africa with her two sons.

Collect
Faithful God,
who strengthened Monica, the mother of Augustine,
  with wisdom,
and through her patient endurance encouraged him
  to seek after you:
give us the will to persist in prayer
that those who stray from you may be brought to faith
in your Son Jesus Christ our Lord,
who is alive and reigns with you,
in the unity of the Holy Spirit,
one God, now and for ever.

A reading from the First Book of Samuel.

After they had eaten and drunk at Shiloh, Hannah rose and presented herself before the Lord. Now Eli the priest was sitting on the seat beside the doorpost of the temple of the Lord. She was deeply distressed and prayed to the Lord, and wept bitterly. She made this vow: "O Lord of hosts, if only you will look on the misery of your servant, and remember me, and not forget your servant, but will give to your servant a male child, then I will set him before you as a nazirite until the day of his death. He shall drink neither wine nor intoxicants, and no razor shall touch his head."

As she continued praying before the Lord, Eli observed her mouth. Hannah was praying silently; only her lips moved, but her voice was not heard; therefore Eli thought she was drunk. So Eli said to her, "How long will you make a drunken spectacle of yourself? Put away your wine." But Hannah answered, "No, my lord, I am a woman deeply troubled; I have drunk neither wine nor strong drink, but I have been pouring out my soul before the Lord. Do not regard your servant as a worthless woman, for I have been speaking out of my great anxiety and vexation all this time." Then Eli answered, "Go in peace; the God of Israel grant the petition you have made to him." And she said, "Let your servant find favour in your sight." Then the woman went to her quarters, ate and drank with her husband, and her countenance was sad no longer.

This is the word of the Lord.   *1 Samuel 1. 9-18*

Responsorial Psalm

R **Lord of Hosts, look on your servant;**
   [give your blessing in abundance].

I lift up my eyes to the hills;
from where is my help to come?
My help comes from the Lord,
the maker of heaven and earth. **R**

He will not let your foot be moved
and he who watches over you will not fall asleep.
Behold, he who keeps watch over Israel
shall neither slumber nor sleep. **R**

The Lord himself watches over you;
the Lord is your shade at your right hand,
So that the sun shall not strike you by day,
nor the moon by night. **R**

The Lord shall preserve you from all evil;
it is he who shall keep you safe.
The Lord shall watch over your going out and your coming in,
from this time forth for evermore. **R**   *Psalm 121*

A reading from the First Letter of Paul to Timothy.

Honour widows who are really widows. If a widow has children
or grandchildren, they should first learn their religious duty to
their own family and make some repayment to their parents; for
this is pleasing in God's sight. The real widow, left alone, has set
her hope on God and continues in supplications and prayers night
and day.

This is the word of the Lord.   *1 Timothy 5. 3-5*

Hear the gospel of our Lord Jesus Christ according to Luke.

Jesus went to a town called Nain, and his disciples and a large
crowd went with him. As he approached the gate of the town, a
man who had died was being carried out. He was his mother's
only son, and she was a widow; and with her was a large crowd
from the town. When the Lord saw her, he had compassion for
her and said to her, "Do not weep." Then he came forward and
touched the bier, and the bearers stood still. And he said, "Young
man, I say to you, rise!" The dead man sat up and began to speak,
and Jesus gave him to his mother. Fear seized all of them; and
they glorified God, saying, "A great prophet has risen among us!"
and "God has looked favourably on his people!" This word about
him spread throughout Judea and all the surrounding country.

This is the gospel of the Lord.   *Luke 7. 11-17*

Post Communion
Father,
from whom every family in heaven and on earth takes its name,
your servant Monica revealed your goodness

in a life of tranquillity and service:
grant that we who have gathered in faith around this table
may like her know the love of Christ
  that surpasses knowledge
and be filled with all your fullness;
through Jesus Christ our Lord.

Augustine of Hippo

28 August – Lesser Festival – Teacher of the Faith – White

Augustine was born in North Africa in 354. His career as an orator
and rhetorician led him from Carthage to Rome, and from there to
Milan where the Imperial court at that time resided. By tempera-
ment, he was passionate and sensual, and as a young man he
rejected Christianity. Gradually, however, under the influence
first of Monica, his mother, and then of Ambrose, bishop of Milan,
Augustine began to look afresh at the Scriptures. He was baptised
by Ambrose at the Easter Vigil in 387. Not long after returning to
North Africa he was ordained priest, and then became Bishop of
Hippo. It is difficult to overestimate the influence of Augustine on
the subsequent development of European thought. A huge body
of his sermons and writings has been preserved, through all of
which runs the theme of the sovereignty of the grace of God. He
died in the year 430.

Collect
Merciful Lord,
who turned Augustine from his sins
  to be a faithful bishop and teacher:
grant that we may follow him in penitence and discipline
till our restless hearts find their rest in you;
through Jesus Christ your Son our Lord,
who is alive and reigns with you,
in the unity of the Holy Spirit,
one God, now and for ever.

A reading from the book Ecclesiasticus.

The one who devotes himself to the study of the law of the Most High seeks out the wisdom of all the ancients, and is concerned with prophecies; he preserves the sayings of the famous and penetrates the subtleties of parables; he seeks out the hidden meanings of proverbs and is at home with the obscurities of parables. He serves among the great and appears before rulers; he travels in foreign lands and learns what is good and evil in the human lot. He sets his heart to rise early to seek the Lord who made him, and to petition the Most High; he opens his mouth in prayer and asks pardon for his sins.

If the great Lord is willing, he will be filled with the spirit of understanding; he will pour forth words of wisdom of his own and give thanks to the Lord in prayer. The Lord will direct his counsel and knowledge, as he meditates on his mysteries. He will show the wisdom of what he has learned and will glory in the law of the Lord's covenant. Many will praise his understanding; it will never be blotted out. His memory will not disappear and his name will live through all generations. Nations will speak of his wisdom, and the congregation will proclaim his praise.

This is the word of the Lord.   *Ecclesiasticus 39. 1-10*

Responsorial Psalm

**R How dear to me is your dwelling,
    O Lord of hosts!**

My soul has a desire and longing
for the courts of the Lord;
my heart and my flesh rejoice in the living God. **R**

The sparrow has found her a house
and the swallow a nest where she may lay her young;
by the side of your altars,
O Lord of hosts, my King and my God. **R**

Happy are they who dwell in your house;
they will always be praising you.
Happy are the people whose strength is in you,
whose hearts are set on the pilgrims' way. **R**   *From Psalm 84*

A reading from the Letter of Paul to the Romans.

You know what time it is, how it is now the moment for you to wake from sleep. For salvation is nearer to us now than when we became believers; the night is far gone, the day is near. Let us then lay aside the works of darkness and put on the armour of light; let us live honourably as in the day, not in revelling and drunkenness, not in debauchery and licentiousness, not in quarrelling and jealousy. Instead, put on the Lord Jesus Christ, and make no provision for the flesh, to gratify its desires.

This is the word of the Lord.   *Romans 13. 11-14*

Hear the gospel of our Lord Jesus Christ according to Matthew.

Jesus said to the crowds and to his disciples, "You are not to be called rabbi, for you have one teacher, and you are all students. And call no one your father on earth, for you have one Father, the one in heaven. Nor are you to be called instructors, for you have one instructor, the Messiah. The greatest among you will be your servant. All who exalt themselves will be humbled, and all who humble themselves will be exalted."

This is the gospel of the Lord.   *Matthew 23. 8-12*

Post Communion
God of truth,
whose Wisdom set her table
and invited us to eat the bread and drink the wine
  of the kingdom:
help us to lay aside all foolishness
and to live and walk in the way of insight,
that we may come with your servant Augustine
  to the eternal feast of heaven;
through Jesus Christ our Lord.

The Beheading of John the Baptist
29 August – Lesser Festival – Red

The main celebration for John the Baptist is on 24 June, the date observing his birth, but John was also the forerunner of Christ in his death and, as the gospels of Matthew and Mark relate it, followed his denouncing of immoral ways and his call to repentance. On hearing of John's arrest, Christ's first words immediately take up John's call: Repent, for the kingdom of heaven has come near; repent, and believe the good news.

Collect
Almighty God,
who called your servant John the Baptist
to be the forerunner of your Son in birth and death:
strengthen us by your grace
that, as he suffered for the truth,
so we may boldly resist corruption and vice
and receive with him the unfading crown of glory;
through Jesus Christ your Son our Lord,
who is alive and reigns with you,
in the unity of the Holy Spirit,
one God, now and for ever.

A reading from the prophecy of Malachi.

See, I am sending my messenger to prepare the way before me, and the Lord whom you seek will suddenly come to his temple. The messenger of the covenant in whom you delight – indeed, he is coming, says the Lord of hosts. But who can endure the day of his coming, and who can stand when he appears?

For he is like a refiner's fire and like fullers' soap; he will sit as a refiner and purifier of silver, and he will purify the descendants of Levi and refine them like gold and silver, until they present offerings to the Lord in righteousness. Then the offering of Judah and Jerusalem will be pleasing to the Lord as in the days of old and as in former years. Then I will draw near to you for judgement; I will be swift to bear witness against the sorcerers, against the adulterers, against those who swear falsely, against those who oppress the hired workers in their wages, the widow and the orphan, against those who thrust aside the alien, and do not fear me, says the Lord of hosts.

For I the Lord do not change; therefore you, O children of Jacob, have not perished. Ever since the days of your ancestors you have

August 29

turned aside from my statutes and have not kept them. Return to me, and I will return to you, says the Lord of hosts.

This is the word of the Lord. *Malachi 3. 1-7a*

Responsorial Psalm

R The messenger of the covenant is coming, says the Lord: [the one in whom I delight].

In the Lord have I taken refuge;
how then can you say to me,
"Fly away like a bird to the hilltop. **R**

"For see how the wicked bend the bow
and fit their arrows to the string,
to shoot from ambush at the true of heart. **R**

"When the foundations are being destroyed,
what can the righteous do?"
The Lord is in his holy temple;
the Lord's throne is in heaven. **R**

His eyes behold the inhabited world;
his piercing eye weighs our worth.
The Lord weighs the righteous as well as the wicked,
but those who delight in violence he abhors. **R**

For the Lord is righteous;
he delights in righteous deeds;
and the just shall see his face. **R** *From Psalm 11*

A reading from the Letter to the Hebrews.

What more should I say? For time would fail me to tell of Gideon, Barak, Samson, Jephthah, of David and Samuel and the prophets – who through faith conquered kingdoms, administered justice, obtained promises, shut the mouths of lions, quenched raging fire, escaped the edge of the sword, won strength out of weakness, became mighty in war, put foreign armies to flight. Women received their dead by resurrection. Others were tortured, refusing to accept release, in order to obtain a better resurrection. Others suffered mocking and flogging, and even chains and imprisonment. They were stoned to death, they were sawn in two, they were killed by the sword; they went about in skins of sheep and goats, destitute, persecuted, tormented – of whom the world was not worthy. They wandered in deserts and mountains, and in caves and holes in the ground.

Yet all these, though they were commended for their faith, did not receive what was promised, since God had provided something better so that they would not, apart from us, be made perfect.

Therefore, since we are surrounded by so great a cloud of witnesses, let us also lay aside every weight and the sin that clings so closely, and let us run with perseverance the race that is set before us, looking to Jesus the pioneer and perfecter of our faith, who for the sake of the joy that was set before him endured the cross, disregarding its shame, and has taken his seat at the right hand of the throne of God.

This is the word of the Lord.   *Hebrews 11.32 - 12.2*

Hear the gospel of our Lord Jesus Christ according to Matthew.

Herod the ruler heard reports about Jesus; and he said to his servants, "This is John the Baptist; he has been raised from the dead, and for this reason these powers are at work in him." For Herod had arrested John, bound him, and put him in prison on account of Herodias, his brother Philip's wife, because John had been telling him, "It is not lawful for you to have her." Though Herod wanted to put him to death, he feared the crowd, because they regarded him as a prophet.

But when Herod's birthday came, the daughter of Herodias danced before the company, and she pleased Herod so much that he promised on oath to grant her whatever she might ask. Prompted by her mother, she said, "Give me the head of John the Baptist here on a platter." The king was grieved, yet out of regard for his oaths and for the guests, he commanded it to be given; he sent and had John beheaded in the prison. The head was brought on a platter and given to the girl, who brought it to her mother. His disciples came and took the body and buried it; then they went and told Jesus.

This is the gospel of the Lord.   *Matthew 14. 1-12*

Post Communion
Merciful Lord,
whose prophet John the Baptist
proclaimed your Son as the Lamb of God
  who takes away the sin of the world:
grant that we who in this sacrament have known
  your forgiveness and your life-giving love
may ever tell of your mercy and your peace;
through Jesus Christ our Lord.

John Bunyan, Spiritual Writer
30 August – Lesser Festival – of any Saint – White

Born at Elstow in Bedfordshire in 1628, John Bunyan was largely
self-educated and used the Bible as his grammar. He read very
few other books, and they were all piously Protestant in nature,
yet he produced *Pilgrim's Progress*, probably the most original text
of spiritual genius that century, telling the story of the man
Christian on his journey through life to God. It was not written
while he was a prisoner in Bedford gaol, as often stated, but during a confinement some years later. History tells us little of the
man but what is clear from his writings is that the salvation of the
soul was what mattered most to him. He died on this day in 1688.

Collect
God of peace,
who called your servant John Bunyan to be valiant for truth:
grant that as strangers and pilgrims
we may at the last
  rejoice with all Christian people in your heavenly city;
through Jesus Christ your Son our Lord,
who is alive and reigns with you, in the unity of the Holy Spirit,
one God, now and for ever.

A reading from the book of the Exodus.

The Lord said, "I have observed the misery of my people who are
in Egypt; I have heard their cry on account of their taskmasters.
Indeed, I know their sufferings, and I have come down to deliver

them from the Egyptians, and to bring them up out of that land to a good and broad land, a land flowing with milk and honey, to the country of the Canaanites, the Hittites, the Amorites, the Perizzites, the Hivites, and the Jebusites. The cry of the Israelites has now come to me; I have also seen how the Egyptians oppress them. So come, I will send you to Pharaoh to bring my people, the Israelites, out of Egypt."

But Moses said to God, "Who am I that I should go to Pharaoh, and bring the Israelites out of Egypt?" God said, "I will be with you; and this shall be the sign for you that it is I who sent you: when you have brought the people out of Egypt, you shall worship God on this mountain."

This is the word of the Lord. *Exodus 3. 7-12*

Responsorial Psalm

R Pray for the peace of Jerusalem;
   [may they prosper who love you].

I was glad when they said to me,
"Let us go to the house of the Lord."
Now our feet are standing
within your gates, O Jerusalem. **R**

Jerusalem is built as a city,
that is at unity with itself,
to which the tribes go up, the tribes of the Lord,
the assembly of Israel, to praise the name of the Lord. **R**

For there are the thrones of judgement,
the thrones of the house of David.
Pray for the peace of Jerusalem:
"May they prosper who love you. **R**

"Peace be within your walls
and quietness within your towers.
For my family and companions' sake,
I pray for your prosperity. **R**
"Because of the house of the Lord our God,
I will seek to do you good." **R** *Psalm 122*

A reading from the Letter to the Hebrews.

Since we are surrounded by so great a cloud of witnesses, let us also lay aside every weight and the sin that clings so closely, and let us run with perseverance the race that is set before us, looking to Jesus the pioneer and perfecter of our faith who, for the sake of the joy that was set before him, endured the cross, disregarding its shame, and has taken his seat at the right hand of the throne of God.

This is the word of the Lord.   *Hebrews 12. 1-2*

Hear the gospel of our Lord Jesus Christ according to Luke.

In the hearing of all the people Jesus said to the disciples, "Those in Judea must flee to the mountains, and those inside the city must leave it, and those out in the country must not enter it.

"Be on guard so that your hearts are not weighed down with dissipation and drunkenness and the worries of this life and that day catch you unexpectedly, like a trap. For it will come upon all who live on the face of the whole earth. Be alert at all times, praying that you may have the strength to escape all these things that will take place, and to stand before the Son of Man."

This is the gospel of the Lord.   *Luke 21. 21, 34-36*

Post Communion
God of truth,
whose Wisdom set her table
and invited us to eat the bread and drink the wine
  of the kingdom:
help us to lay aside all foolishness
and to live and walk in the way of insight,
that we may come with your servant John Bunyan
  to the eternal feast of heaven;
through Jesus Christ our Lord.

Aidan, Bishop of Lindisfarne
31 August – Lesser Festival – Missionary – White

One of St Columba's monks from the monastery of Iona, Aidan was sent as a missionary to Northumbria at the request of King Oswald, who was later to become his friend and interpreter. Consecrated Bishop of Lindisfarne in 635, Aidan worked closely with Oswald and became involved with the training of priests. From the island of Lindisfarne he was able to combine a monastic lifestyle with missionary journeys to the mainland where, through his concern for the poor and enthusiasm for preaching, he won popular support. This enabled him to strengthen the Church beyond the boundaries of Northumbria. He died on this day in the year 651.

Collect
Everlasting God,
you sent the gentle bishop Aidan
to proclaim the gospel in this land:
grant us to live as he taught
in simplicity, humility, and love for the poor;
through Jesus Christ your Son our Lord,
who is alive and reigns with you,
in the unity of the Holy Spirit,
one God, now and for ever.

A reading from the prophecy of Isaiah.

Turn to me and be saved, all the ends of the earth! For I am God, and there is no other. By myself I have sworn, from my mouth has gone forth in righteousness a word that shall not return: "To me every knee shall bow, every tongue shall swear." Only in the Lord, it shall be said of me, are righteousness and strength; all who were incensed against him shall come to him and be ashamed. In the Lord all the offspring of Israel shall triumph and glory.

This is the word of the Lord. *Isaiah 45. 22-25*

Responsorial Psalm

R Sing praises to God, sing praises;
[sing praises to our king, sing praises].

Clap your hands, all you peoples;
shout to God with a cry of joy.
For the Lord Most High is to be feared;
he is the great king over all the earth. **R**

He subdues the peoples under us,
and the nations under our feet.
He chooses our inheritance for us,
the pride of Jacob whom he loves. **R**

God is king of all the earth;
sing praises with all your skill.
God reigns over the nations;
God sits upon his holy throne. **R**

The nobles of the peoples have gathered together
with the people of the God of Abraham.
The rulers of the earth belong to God,
and he is highly exalted. **R**   *From Psalm 47*

A reading from the First Letter of Paul to the Corinthians.

If I proclaim the gospel, this gives me no ground for boasting, for
an obligation is laid on me, and woe to me if I do not proclaim the
gospel! For if I do this of my own will, I have a reward; but if not
of my own will, I am entrusted with a commission. What then is
my reward? Just this: that in my proclamation I may make the
gospel free of charge, so as not to make full use of my rights in the
gospel. For though I am free with respect to all, I have made
myself a slave to all, so that I might win more of them.

This is the word of the Lord.   *1 Corinthians 9. 16-19*

Hear the gospel of our Lord Jesus Christ according to John.

Jesus said to his disciples, "Very truly, I tell you, servants are not
greater than their master, nor are messengers greater than the one
who sent them. If you know these things, you are blessed if you
do them. I am not speaking of all of you; I know whom I have cho-

sen. But it is to fulfil the scripture, 'The one who ate my bread has
lifted his heel against me.' I tell you this now, before it occurs, so
that when it does occur, you may believe that I am he. Very truly,
I tell you, whoever receives one whom I send receives me; and
whoever receives me receives him who sent me."

This is the gospel of the Lord.   *John 13. 16-20*

Post Communion
Holy Father,
who gathered us here around the table of your Son
to share this meal with the whole household of God:
in that new world where you reveal
  the fullness of your peace,
gather people of every race and language
to share with your servant Aidan and all your saints
in the eternal banquet of Jesus Christ our Lord.

SEPTEMBER

Giles of Provence, Hermit
1 September – Commemoration
If celebrated as a Lesser Festival, Common of Religious, page 494

Giles was a hermit who died in about the year 710. He founded a monastery at the place now called Saint-Gilles in Provence which became an important place on the pilgrimage routes both to Compostela and to the Holy Land. His care for the wounded and those crippled by disease resulted in his becoming the patron saint of such people, particularly of those with leprosy. Leprosy sufferers were not permitted to enter towns and cities and therefore often congregated on the outskirts, where churches built to meet their needs were regularly dedicated to Giles.

The Martyrs of Papua New Guinea
2 September – Commemoration
If celebrated as a Lesser Festival, Common of Martyrs, page 464

The church in Papua New Guinea has been enriched by martyrdom twice in the twentieth century. James Chalmers, Oliver Tomkins and some companions were sent to New Guinea by the London Missionary Society. They met their death by martyrdom in 1901. Forty years later, during the Second World War, New Guinea was occupied by the Imperial Japanese Army. Christians were severely persecuted and 333 church workers of all denominations died for the faith. Among those who died for the faith were twelve Anglicans: two English priests, Vivian Redlich and Bernard Moore, who remained with their people after the invasion of 1942 but were betrayed and killed, eight Australians and two Papuan evangelists, Leslie Gariadi and Lucian Tapiedi.

Gregory the Great
3 September – Lesser Festival – Teacher of the Faith – White

Gregory was born in 540, the son of a Roman senator. As a young man he pursued a governmental career and, in 573, was made

Prefect of the city of Rome. Following the death of his father, he resigned his office, sold his inheritance, and became a monk. In 579 he was sent by the Pope to Constantinople to be his representative to the Patriarch. He returned to Rome in 586, and was himself elected Pope in 590. At a time of political turmoil, Gregory proved an astute administrator and diplomat, securing peace with the Lombards. He initiated the mission to England, sending Augustine and forty monks from his own monastery to refound the English Church. His writings were pastorally oriented. His spirituality was animated by a dynamic of love and desire for God. Indeed, he is sometimes called the 'Doctor of desire'. For Gregory, desire was a metaphor for the journey into God. As Pope, he styled himself 'Servant of the servants of God' – a title which typified both his personality and ministry. He died in 604.

Collect
Merciful Father,
who chose your bishop Gregory
to be a servant of the servants of God:
grant that, like him, we may ever long to serve you
by proclaiming your gospel to the nations,
and may ever rejoice to sing your praises;
through Jesus Christ your Son our Lord,
who is alive and reigns with you,
in the unity of the Holy Spirit,
one God, now and for ever.

A reading from the book Ecclesiasticus.

In all that he did, he gave thanks to the Holy One, the Most High, proclaiming his glory; he sang praise with all his heart, and he loved his Maker. He placed singers before the altar, to make sweet melody with their voices. He gave beauty to the festivals, and arranged their times throughout the year, while they praised God's holy name, and the sanctuary resounded from early morning. The Lord took away his sins, and exalted his power forever; he gave him a covenant of kingship and a glorious throne in Israel.

This is the word of the Lord.   *Ecclesiasticus 47. 8-11*

**R Give thanks to the Lord, the Holy One;
[proclaim the glory of the Most High].**

Be joyful in the Lord, all you lands;
serve the Lord with gladness
and come before his presence with a song. **R**

Know this: The Lord himself is God;
he himself has made us and we are his;
we are his people and the sheep of his pasture. **R**

Enter his gates with thanksgiving;
go into his courts with praise;
give thanks to him and call upon his name. **R**

For the Lord is good;
his mercy is everlasting;
and his faithfulness endures from age to age. **R**   *Psalm 100*

A reading from the First Letter of Paul to the Thessalonians.

Our appeal does not spring from deceit or impure motives or trickery, but just as we have been approved by God to be entrusted with the message of the gospel, even so we speak, not to please mortals, but to please God who tests our hearts.

As you know and as God is our witness, we never came with words of flattery or with a pretext for greed; nor did we seek praise from mortals, whether from you or from others, though we might have made demands as apostles of Christ. But we were gentle among you, like a nurse tenderly caring for her own children. So deeply do we care for you that we are determined to share with you not only the gospel of God but also our own selves, because you have become very dear to us.

This is the word of the Lord.   *1 Thessalonians 2. 3-8*

Hear the gospel of our Lord Jesus Christ according to Mark.

Jesus called the disciples and said to them, "You know that among the Gentiles those whom they recognise as their rulers lord it over them, and their great ones are tyrants over them. But it is not so among you; but whoever wishes to become great among you must be your servant, and whoever wishes to be first among you must be servant of all. For the Son of Man came not to be served but to serve, and to give his life a ransom for many."

This is the gospel of the Lord. *Mark 10. 42-45*

Post Communion
God of truth,
whose Wisdom set her table
and invited us to eat the bread and drink the wine
  of the kingdom:
help us to lay aside all foolishness
and to live and walk in the way of insight,
that we may come with your servant Gregory
  to the eternal feast of heaven;
through Jesus Christ our Lord.

Birinus, Apostle of Wessex
4 September – Commemoration
If celebrated as a Lesser Festival, Common of Missionaries, page 503

Birinus was born in the mid sixth century, probably of northern European origin, but he became a priest in Rome. Feeling called by God to serve as a missionary, he was consecrated bishop, and sent to Britain by the pope. He intended to evangelise inland where no Christian had been before but, arriving in Wessex in 634, he found such prevalent idolatry that he looked no further to begin work. One of his early converts was King Cynegils and thereafter he gained much support in his mission, as well as the town of Dorchester for his See. He died in about the year 650 having earned the title 'Apostle of the West Saxons'.

Allen Gardiner,
Founder of the South American Missionary Society
6 September – Commemoration
If celebrated as a Lesser Festival, Common of Missionaries, page 503

Allen Francis Gardiner was born in 1794 and joined the Royal Navy as a young man. He resigned in 1826 and, on the death of his wife in 1834, dedicated himself to missionary work. He pioneered a mission to the Zulus in South Africa for the Church Missionary Society and founded the city of Durban. He then went to South America to investigate the possibility of evangelism amongst the indigenous tribes. He travelled extensively and founded the South American Missionary Society in 1844. With seven other missionaries, he died of starvation in 1851 on the shores of Tierra del Fuego.

The Birth of the Blessèd Virgin Mary
8 September – Lesser Festival – BVM – White

The festival in honour of the birth of the mother of our Lord is celebrated on this day in both the eastern and the western Churches. Falling just nine months after the feast of the Conception of Mary, this feast, as Andrew of Crete says, 'stands on the boundary between the old and the new covenants and ushers in the new dispensation of grace. Today is built a shrine for the Creator of the universe'.

Collect
Almighty and everlasting God,
who stooped to raise fallen humanity
through the child-bearing of blessèd Mary:
grant that we, who have seen your glory
    revealed in our human nature
and your love made perfect in our weakness,
may daily be renewed in your image
and conformed to the pattern of your Son,
Jesus Christ our Lord,
who is alive and reigns with you,
in the unity of the Holy Spirit,
one God, now and for ever.

A reading from the prophecy of Micah.

You, O Bethlehem of Ephrathah, who are one of the little clans of Judah, from you shall come forth for me one who is to rule in Israel, whose origin is from of old, from ancient days. Therefore he shall give them up until the time when she who is in labour has brought forth; then the rest of his kindred shall return to the people of Israel. And he shall stand and feed his flock in the strength of the Lord, in the majesty of the name of the Lord his God. And they shall live secure, for now he shall be great to the ends of the earth.

This is the word of the Lord. *Micah 5. 2-4*

Responsorial Song

R My heart exults in the Lord;
[I find my strength in my God].

I will sing to my God a new song:
"O Lord, you are great and glorious,
wonderful in strength, invincible. **R**

"Let all your creatures serve you,
for you spoke, and they were made.
You sent forth your spirit, and it formed them;
there is none that can resist your voice. **R**

"For the mountains shall be shaken to their foundations;
before your glance the rocks shall melt like wax.
But to those who fear you, you show mercy. **R**

"For every sacrifice as a fragrant offering is a small thing,
and burnt offerings to you is a small thing;
but whoever fears the Lord is great forever." **R**   *From Judith 16*

A reading from the Letter of Paul to the Romans.

We know that all things work together for good for those who love God, who are called according to his purpose. For those whom he foreknew he also predestined to be conformed to the image of his Son, in order that he might be the firstborn within a large family. And those whom he predestined he also called; and those whom he called he also justified; and those whom he justified he also glorified.

This is the word of the Lord. *Romans 8. 28-30*

Hear the gospel of our Lord Jesus Christ according to Matthew.

[An account of the genealogy of Jesus the Messiah, the son of David, the son of Abraham: Abraham was the father of Isaac, and Isaac the father of Jacob, and Jacob the father of Judah and his brothers, and Judah the father of Perez and Zerah by Tamar, and Perez the father of Hezron, and Hezron the father of Aram, and Aram the father of Aminadab, and Aminadab the father of Nahshon, and Nahshon the father of Salmon, and Salmon the father of Boaz by Rahab, and Boaz the father of Obed by Ruth, and Obed the father of Jesse, and Jesse the father of King David. And David was the father of Solomon by the wife of Uriah, and Solomon the father of Rehoboam, and Rehoboam the father of Abijah, and Abijah the father of Asaph, and Asaph the father of Jehoshaphat, and Jehoshaphat the father of Joram, and Joram the father of Uzziah, and Uzziah the father of Jotham, and Jotham the father of Ahaz, and Ahaz the father of Hezekiah, and Hezekiah the father of Manasseh, and Manasseh the father of Amos, and Amos the father of Josiah, and Josiah the father of Jechoniah and his brothers, at the time of the deportation to Babylon. And after the deportation to Babylon: Jechoniah was the father of Salathiel, and Salathiel the father of Zerubbabel, and Zerubbabel the father of Abiud, and Abiud the father of Eliakim, and Eliakim the father of Azor, and Azor the father of Zadok, and Zadok the father of Achim, and Achim the father of Eliud, and Eliud the father of Eleazar, and Eleazar the father of Matthan, and Matthan the father of Jacob, and Jacob the father of Joseph the husband of Mary, of whom Jesus was born, who is called the Messiah.]

Now the birth of Jesus the Messiah took place in this way. When his mother Mary had been engaged to Joseph, but before they lived together, she was found to be with child from the Holy Spirit. Her husband Joseph, being a righteous man and unwilling to expose her to public disgrace, planned to dismiss her quietly. But just when he had resolved to do this, an angel of the Lord appeared to him in a dream and said, "Joseph, son of David, do not be afraid to take Mary as your wife, for the child conceived in her is from the Holy Spirit. She will bear a son, and you are to name him Jesus, for he will save his people from their sins." All this took place to fulfil what had been spoken by the Lord through the prophet: "Look, the virgin shall conceive and bear a son, and they shall name him Emmanuel," which means, "God is with us."

When Joseph awoke from sleep, he did as the angel of the Lord commanded him; he took her as his wife, but had no marital relations with her until she had borne a son; and he named him Jesus.

This is the gospel of the Lord.   *Matthew 1. 1-16, 18-23*

Post Communion
God Most High,
whose handmaid bore the Word made flesh:
we thank you that in this sacrament of our redemption
you visit us with your Holy Spirit
and overshadow us by your power;
strengthen us to walk with Mary the joyful path of obedience
and so to bring forth the fruits of holiness;
through Jesus Christ our Lord.

Charles Fuge Lowder, Priest
9 September – Commemoration
If celebrated as a Lesser Festival, Common of Pastors, page 483

Charles Lowder was born in 1820 and came under the influence of the Oxford Movement during his studies at Exeter College in the early 1840s. After ordination, he became increasingly drawn to a Tractarian and ritualist expression of the faith, especially after his move to London in 1851, despite the fierce opposition such Catholic spirituality faced within the Church. As a curate in Pimlico and Stepney, and then as the first Vicar of St Peter's, London Docks, Lowder came to epitomise the nineteenth-century Anglo-Catholic 'slum priest'. Dedicated to the poor and destitute, he was tireless in his parish work. His health gave way and he died at the age of sixty on this day in 1880.

John Chrysostom, Bishop of Constantinople
13 September – Lesser Festival – Teacher of the Faith – White

John was born in Antioch in about 347. He was a brilliant preacher which earned him in the sixth century the surname 'Chrysostom', literally 'golden-mouthed'. He is honoured as one of the four Greek Doctors of the Church. Against his wish he was made Patriarch of Constantinople in 398. He set about reforming the Church and exposing corruption amongst the clergy and in the Imperial administration. "Mules bear fortunes and Christ dies of hunger at your gate," he is alleged to have cried out. He fell foul of the Empress Eudoxia and, in spite of the support of Pope Innocent I of Rome, was sent into exile twice, finally dying of exhaustion and starvation in September 407, with the words "Glory be to God for everything" on his lips.

Collect
God of truth and love,
who gave to your servant John Chrysostom
eloquence to declare your righteousness
  in the great congregation
and courage to bear reproach for the honour of your name:
mercifully grant to those who minister your word
such excellence in preaching,
that all people may share with them
in the glory that shall be revealed;
through Jesus Christ your Son our Lord,
who is alive and reigns with you,
in the unity of the Holy Spirit,
one God, now and for ever.

A reading from the prophecy of Jeremiah.

The word of the Lord came to me saying, "Before I formed you in the womb I knew you, and before you were born I consecrated you; I appointed you a prophet to the nations." Then I said, "Ah, Lord God! Truly I do not know how to speak, for I am only a boy." But the Lord said to me, "Do not say, 'I am only a boy'; for you shall go to all to whom I send you, and you shall speak whatever I command you. Do not be afraid of them, for I am with you to deliver you, says the Lord."

Then the Lord put out his hand and touched my mouth; and the Lord said to me, "Now I have put my words in your mouth. See, today I appoint you over nations and over kingdoms, to pluck up and to pull down, to destroy and to overthrow, to build and to plant."

This is the word of the Lord. *Jeremiah 1. 4-10*

Responsorial Psalm

**R   I will sing of your mercy and justice, O God;
    [to you will I sing praises].**

I will strive to follow a blameless course;
O when will you come to me?
I will walk with sincerity of heart within my house. **R**

I will set no worthless thing before my eyes;
I hate the doers of evil deeds;
they shall not remain with me. **R**

My eyes are upon the faithful in the land,
that they may dwell with me,
and only those who lead a blameless life
shall be my servants. **R**   *From Psalm 101*

A reading from the Letter of Paul to the Ephesians.

Although I am the very least of all the saints, this grace was given
to me to bring to the Gentiles the news of the boundless riches of
Christ, and to make everyone see what is the plan of the mystery
hidden for ages in God who created all things; so that through the
church the wisdom of God in its rich variety might now be made
known to the rulers and authorities in the heavenly places. This
was in accordance with the eternal purpose that he has carried out
in Christ Jesus our Lord, in whom we have access to God in boldness and confidence through faith in him.

This is the word of the Lord.   *Ephesians 3. 8-12*

Hear the gospel of our Lord Jesus Christ according to Matthew.

Jesus said to the crowds: "You are the salt of the earth; but if salt
has lost its taste, how can its saltiness be restored? It is no longer
good for anything, but is thrown out and trampled under foot.

"You are the light of the world. A city built on a hill cannot be hid.
No one after lighting a lamp puts it under the bushel basket but on
the lampstand, and it gives light to all in the house. In the same
way, let your light shine before others, so that they may see your
good works and give glory to your Father in heaven.

"Do not think that I have come to abolish the law or the prophets;

I have come not to abolish but to fulfil. For truly I tell you, until heaven and earth pass away, not one letter, not one stroke of a letter, will pass from the law until all is accomplished. Therefore, whoever breaks one of the least of these commandments, and teaches others to do the same, will be called least in the kingdom of heaven; but whoever does them and teaches them will be called great in the kingdom of heaven."

This is the gospel of the Lord. *Matthew 5. 13-19*

Post Communion
God of truth,
whose Wisdom set her table
and invited us to eat the bread and drink the wine
  of the kingdom:
help us to lay aside all foolishness
and to live and walk in the way of insight,
that we may come with your servant John Chrysostom
  to the eternal feast of heaven;
through Jesus Christ our Lord.

Holy Cross Day
14 September – Festival – Red

The cross on which our Lord was crucified has become the universal symbol for Christianity, replacing the fish symbol of the early church, though the latter has been revived in recent times. After the end of the persecution era, early in the fourth century, pilgrims began to travel to Jerusalem to visit and pray at the places associated with the life of Jesus. Helena, the mother of the emperor, was a Christian and, whilst overseeing excavations in the city, is said to have uncovered a cross, which many believed to be the Cross of Christ. A basilica was built on the site of the Holy Sepulchre and dedicated on this day in the year 335.

Collect
Almighty God,
who in the passion of your blessèd Son
made an instrument of painful death
to be for us the means of life and peace:
grant us so to glory in the cross of Christ
that we may gladly suffer for his sake;
who is alive and reigns with you,
in the unity of the Holy Spirit,
one God, now and for ever.

A reading from the book Numbers.

From Mount Hor, Moses and the people of Israel set out by the
way to the Red Sea, to go around the land of Edom; but the people became impatient on the way. The people spoke against God
and against Moses, "Why have you brought us up out of Egypt to
die in the wilderness? For there is no food and no water, and we
detest this miserable food." Then the Lord sent poisonous serpents among the people, and they bit the people, so that many
Israelites died. The people came to Moses and said, "We have
sinned by speaking against the Lord and against you; pray to the
Lord to take away the serpents from us." So Moses prayed for the
people. And the Lord said to Moses, "Make a poisonous serpent,
and set it on a pole; and everyone who is bitten shall look at it and
live." So Moses made a serpent of bronze, and put it upon a pole;
and whenever a serpent bit someone, that person would look at
the serpent of bronze and live."

This is the word of the Lord.   *Numbers 21. 4-9*

Responsorial Psalm

**R   You are the Holy One, O God,
      [enthroned on the praises of Israel].**

The Lord does not despise nor abhor
the poor in their poverty;
neither does he hide his face from them;
but when they cry to him he hears them. **R**

My praise is of him in the great assembly;
I will perform my vows
in the presence of those who worship him. **R**

The poor shall eat and be satisfied,
and those who seek the Lord shall praise him:
"May your heart live for ever!" **R**

All the ends of the earth
shall remember and turn to the Lord,
and all the families of the nations shall bow before him. **R**

For kingship belongs to the Lord: he rules over the nations.
To him alone all who sleep in the earth
  bow down in worship;
all who go down to the dust fall before him. **R**   *From Psalm 22*

A reading from the Letter of Paul to the Philippians.

Though he was in the form of God, Jesus did not regard equality
with God as something to be exploited, but emptied himself, taking the form of a servant, being born in human likeness. And
being found in human form, he humbled himself and became obedient to the point of death – even death on a cross. Therefore God
also highly exalted him and gave him the name that is above every
name, so that at the name of Jesus every knee should bend, in
heaven and on earth and under the earth, and every tongue
should confess that Jesus Christ is Lord, to the glory of God the
Father.

This is the word of the Lord.   *Philippians 2. 6-11*

Hear the gospel of our Lord Jesus Christ according to John.

Jesus said to Nicodemus, "No one has ascended into heaven
except the one who descended from heaven, the Son of Man. And
just as Moses lifted up the serpent in the wilderness, so must the
Son of Man be lifted up, that whoever believes in him may have
eternal life. For God so loved the world that he gave his only Son,
so that everyone who believes in him may not perish but may
have eternal life. Indeed, God did not send the Son into the world
to condemn the world, but in order that the world might be saved
through him."

This is the gospel of the Lord.   *John 3. 13-17*

Post Communion
Faithful God,
whose Son bore our sins in his body on the tree
and gave us this sacrament to show forth his death
  until he comes:
give us grace to glory in the cross of our Lord Jesus Christ,
for he is our salvation, our life and our hope,
who reigns as Lord, now and for ever.

Cyprian, Bishop of Carthage
15 September – Lesser Festival – Martyr – Red

Born in Carthage in about the year 200, Cyprian was a teacher of
rhetoric and a lawyer in the city before his conversion to
Christianity. He gave away his pagan library and set his mind to
study the sacred Scriptures and the commentaries that were
beginning to proliferate. He became a priest and then, in the year
248, was elected Bishop of Carthage by the people of the city,
together with the assembled priests and other bishops present. He
showed compassion to returning apostates, whilst always insisting
on the need for unity in the Church. During the persecution of
Valerian, the Christian clergy were required to participate in
pagan worship; Cyprian refused and was first exiled and then
condemned to death. He died on this day in the year 258.

Collect
Holy God,
who brought Cyprian to faith in Christ,
made him a bishop in the Church
and crowned his witness with a martyr's death:
grant that, after his example,
we may love the Church and her teachings,
find your forgiveness within her fellowship
and so come to share the heavenly banquet
  you have prepared for us;
through Jesus Christ your Son our Lord,
who is alive and reigns with you,
in the unity of the Holy Spirit,
one God, now and for ever.

A reading from the prophecy of Ezekiel.

Thus says the Lord God: I myself will search for my sheep, and will seek them out. As shepherds seek out their flocks when they are among their scattered sheep, so I will seek out my sheep. I will rescue them from all the places to which they have been scattered on a day of clouds and thick darkness. I will bring them out from the peoples and gather them from the countries, and will bring them into their own land; and I will feed them on the mountains of Israel, by the watercourses, and in all the inhabited parts of the land. I will feed them with good pasture, and the mountain heights of Israel shall be their pasture; there they shall lie down in good grazing land, and they shall feed on rich pasture on the mountains of Israel.

I myself will be the shepherd of my sheep, and I will make them lie down, says the Lord God. I will seek the lost, and I will bring back the strayed, and I will bind up the injured, and I will strengthen the weak, but the fat and the strong I will destroy. I will feed them with justice.

This is the word of the Lord.   *Ezekiel 34. 11-16*

Responsorial Psalm

**R   I will rejoice for ever in the Lord;
      [I will sing praises to my God].**

We give you thanks, O God, we give you thanks,
calling upon your name
and declaring all your wonderful deeds. **R**

"I will appoint a time," says God;
"I will judge with equity.
Though the earth and all its inhabitants are quaking,
I will make its pillars fast." **R**
For judgement is neither from the east nor from the west,
nor yet from the wilderness or the mountains.
It is God who judges;
who puts down one and lifts up another. **R**   *From Psalm 75*

A reading from the First Letter of Paul to the Corinthians.

There are varieties of gifts, but the same Spirit; and there are varieties of services, but the same Lord; and there are varieties of activities, but it is the same God who activates all of them in everyone. To each is given the manifestation of the Spirit for the common good. To one is given through the Spirit the utterance of wisdom, and to another the utterance of knowledge according to the same Spirit, to another faith by the same Spirit, to another gifts of healing by the one Spirit, to another the working of miracles, to another prophecy, to another the discernment of spirits, to another various kinds of tongues, to another the interpretation of tongues.

All these are activated by one and the same Spirit, who allots to each one individually just as the Spirit chooses. For just as the body is one and has many members, and all the members of the body, though many, are one body, so it is with Christ. For in the one Spirit we were all baptised into one body – Jews or Greeks, slaves or free – and we were all made to drink of one Spirit. Now you are the body of Christ and individually members of it.

This is the word of the Lord.   *1 Corinthians 12. 4-13, 27*

Hear the gospel of our Lord Jesus Christ according to Luke.

Jesus said to them all, "If any want to become my followers, let them deny themselves and take up their cross daily and follow me. For those who want to save their life will lose it, and those who lose their life for my sake will save it. What does it profit them if they gain the whole world, but lose or forfeit themselves? Those who are ashamed of me and of my words, of them the Son of Man will be ashamed when he comes in his glory and the glory of the Father and of the holy angels."

This is the gospel of the Lord.   *Luke 9. 23-26*

Post Communion
God our Redeemer,
whose Church was strengthened
 by the blood of your martyr Cyprian:
so bind us, in life and death, to Christ's sacrifice
that our lives, broken and offered with his,
may carry his death and proclaim his resurrection in the world;
through Jesus Christ our Lord.

Ninian, Bishop of Galloway
16 September – Lesser Festival – Missionary – White

Ninian was born in about the year 360 and was the son of a Cumbrian chieftain who had himself converted to Christianity. It seems he visited Rome in his youth, where he received training in the faith. He was consecrated bishop in the year 394 and returned to Britain, where he set up a community of monks at Candida Casa from where they went out on missionary journeys as far as Perth and Sterling. Ninian died in about the year 432.

Collect
Almighty and everlasting God,
who called your servant Ninian to preach the gospel
  to the people of northern Britain:
raise up in this and every land
heralds and evangelists of your kingdom,
that your Church may make known the immeasurable riches
  of your Son our Saviour Jesus Christ,
who is alive and reigns with you,
in the unity of the Holy Spirit,
one God, now and for ever.

A reading from the prophecy of Jeremiah.

The word of the Lord came to me saying, "Before I formed you in the womb I knew you, and before you were born I consecrated you; I appointed you a prophet to the nations." Then I said, "Ah, Lord God! Truly I do not know how to speak, for I am only a boy." But the Lord said to me, "Do not say, 'I am only a boy'; for you shall go to all to whom I send you, and you shall speak whatever I command you. Do not be afraid of them, for I am with you to deliver you, says the Lord." Then the Lord put out his hand and touched my mouth; and the Lord said to me, "Now I have put my words in your mouth."

This is the word of the Lord.   *Jeremiah 1. 4-9*

Responsorial Psalm

R   Let the peoples praise you, O God;
[let all the peoples praise you].

May God be merciful to us and bless us,
show us the light of his countenance and come to us.
Let your ways be known upon earth,
your saving health among all nations. **R**

Let the nations be glad and sing for joy,
for you judge the peoples with equity
and guide all the nations upon earth. **R**

The earth has brought forth her increase;
may God, our own God, give us his blessing.
May God give us his blessing,
and may all the ends of the earth stand in awe of him. **R**

Psalm 67

A reading from the Second Letter of Paul to the Corinthians.

If anyone is in Christ, there is a new creation: everything old has
passed away; see, everything has become new! All this is from
God, who reconciled us to himself through Christ, and has given
us the ministry of reconciliation; that is, in Christ God was reconciling the world to himself, not counting their trespasses against
them, and entrusting the message of reconciliation to us. So we
are ambassadors for Christ, since God is making his appeal
through us; we entreat you on behalf of Christ, be reconciled to
God. For our sake he made him to be sin who knew no sin, so that
in him we might become the righteousness of God.

 As we work together with him, we urge you also not to accept the
grace of God in vain. For he says, "At an acceptable time I have listened to you, and on a day of salvation I have helped you." See,
now is the acceptable time; see, now is the day of salvation!

This is the word of the Lord.   *2 Corinthians 5.17 - 6.2*

Hear the gospel of our Lord Jesus Christ according to Matthew.

Jesus went about all the cities and villages, teaching in their synagogues, and proclaiming the good news of the kingdom, and curing every disease and every sickness. When he saw the crowds, he

had compassion for them, because they were harassed and help-less, like sheep without a shepherd. Then he said to his disciples, "The harvest is plentiful, but the labourers are few; therefore ask the Lord of the harvest to send out labourers into his harvest."

This is the gospel of the Lord.   *Matthew 9. 35-38*

Post Communion
Holy Father,
who gathered us here around the table of your Son
to share this meal with the whole household of God:
in that new world where you reveal
  the fullness of your peace,
gather people of every race and language
to share with your servant Ninian and all your saints
in the eternal banquet of Jesus Christ our Lord.

Edward Bouverie Pusey, Priest, Tractarian
16 September – *Commemoration*
If celebrated as a Lesser Festival, Common of Pastors, page 483

Edward Pusey was born in 1800 and educated at Oxford, where he became a Fellow of Oriel College in 1823. He became an expert in biblical languages and criticism and in 1828 he was appointed Regius Professor of Hebrew in Oxford, the same year he was ordained. His patristic studies and firm adherence to a Catholic interpretation of doctrine made him one of the leaders of the Oxford Movement. He was significant in encouraging the revival of Religious Life within the Church of England and was a noted preacher. His austere way of life made him much revered by his contemporaries and they founded Pusey House and Library in Oxford in his memory, following his death on this day in 1882.

Hildegard of Bingen
17 September – *Lesser Festival* – *Religious* – *White*

Hildegard was born in 1098 at Böckelheim in Germany. From her earliest years she had a powerful, visionary life, becoming a nun at the age of eighteen, much influenced by her foster-mother, Jutta, who had set up the community and whom she succeeded as Abbess in 1136. Her visions of light, which she described as "the reflection of the Living Light", deepened her understanding of God and creation, sin and redemption. They were, however, accompanied by repeated illness and physical weakness. About twenty years later, she moved her sisters to a new Abbey at Bingen. She travelled much in the Rhineland, founding a daughter house and influencing many, including the Emperor Frederick Barbarossa. She was a pastor and teacher, seeing herself as a "feather on the breath of God". She wrote three visionary works, a natural history and a medical compendium. She died on this day in the year 1179.

Collect
Most glorious and holy God,
whose servant Hildegard, strong in the faith,
was caught up in the vision of your heavenly courts:
by the breath of your Spirit
open our eyes to glimpse your glory
and our lips to sing your praises with all the angels;
through Jesus Christ your Son our Lord,
who is alive and reigns with you,
in the unity of the Holy Spirit,
one God, now and for ever.

A reading from the book Proverbs.

I, wisdom, live with prudence, and I attain knowledge and discretion. The fear of the Lord is hatred of evil. Pride and arrogance and the way of evil and perverted speech I hate. I have good advice and sound wisdom; I have insight, I have strength.

The Lord created me at the beginning of his work, the first of his acts of long ago. Ages ago I was set up, at the first, before the beginning of the earth. When there were no depths I was brought forth, when there were no springs abounding with water. Before the mountains had been shaped, before the hills, I was brought forth – when he had not yet made earth and fields, or the world's first bits of soil.

When he established the heavens I was there, when he drew a circle on the face of the deep, when he made firm the skies above, when he established the fountains of the deep, when he assigned to the sea its limit, so that the waters might not transgress his command, when he marked out the foundations of the earth, then I was beside him, like a master worker; and I was daily his delight, rejoicing before him always, rejoicing in his inhabited world and delighting in the human race.

This is the word of the Lord. *Proverbs 8. 12-14, 22-31*

Responsorial Psalm

**R May these words of mine please my God;
[then will I rejoice in the Lord].**

O Lord, how manifold are your works!
in wisdom you have made them all;
the earth is full of your creatures. **R**

You send forth your Spirit and they are created;
and so you renew the face of the earth.
May the glory of the Lord endure for ever;
may the Lord rejoice in all his works. **R**

He looks at the earth and it trembles;
he touches the mountains and they smoke.
I will sing to the Lord as long as I live;
I will praise my God while I have my being. **R**   *From Psalm 104*

A reading from the First Letter of Paul to the Corinthians.

As it is written, "What no eye has seen, nor ear heard, nor the human heart conceived, what God has prepared for those who love him" – these things God has revealed to us through the Spirit; for the Spirit searches everything, even the depths of God. For what human being knows what is truly human except the human spirit that is within? So also no one comprehends what is truly God's except the Spirit of God. Now we have received not the spirit of the world, but the Spirit that is from God, so that we may understand the gifts bestowed on us by God. And we speak of these things in words not taught by human wisdom but taught by the Spirit, interpreting spiritual things to those who are spiritual.

This is the word of the Lord. *1 Corinthians 2. 9-13*

Hear the gospel of our Lord Jesus Christ according to Luke.

Jesus rejoiced in the Holy Spirit and said, "I thank you, Father, Lord of heaven and earth, because you have hidden these things from the wise and the intelligent and have revealed them to infants; yes, Father, for such was your gracious will. All things have been handed over to me by my Father; and no one knows who the Son is except the Father, or who the Father is except the Son and anyone to whom the Son chooses to reveal him."

Then turning to the disciples, Jesus said to them privately, "Blessèd are the eyes that see what you see! For I tell you that many prophets and kings desired to see what you see, but did not see it, and to hear what you hear, but did not hear it."

This is the gospel of the Lord.   *Luke 10. 21-24*

Post Communion
Merciful God,
who gave such grace to your servant Hildegard
that she served you with singleness of heart
and loved you above all things:
help us, whose communion with you
 has been renewed in this sacrament,
to forsake all that holds us back from following Christ
and to grow into his likeness from glory to glory;
through Jesus Christ our Lord.

Theodore of Tarsus, Archbishop of Canterbury
19 September – Commemoration
If celebrated as a Lesser Festival, Common of Missionaries, page 503

Theodore was born at Tarsus in Cilicia in about the year 602. He was an Asiatic Greek and had been educated in Athens before being appointed Archbishop of Canterbury by the pope. He was raised straight from being a sub-deacon to the archiepiscopal see but proved his worth by immediately undertaking a visitation of the whole of England soon after his arrival. He set about reforming the Church in England with the division of dioceses and summoned the Synod of Hertford on 24 September 673, probably the most important Church council in the land, as it issued canons dealing with the rights and obligations of both clergy and Religious: it restricted bishops to working in their own diocese and not intruding on the ministry of their prelate neighbours; it established precedence within the episcopacy; it ensured that monks remained stable to their monastery and obedient to their abbot; and many other matters were dealt with to effect the good order of the Church. The canons were based on those of the Council of Chalcedon. Theodore proved to be the first Archbishop of Canterbury to have the willing allegiance of all Anglo-Saxon England. He died on this day in the year 690.

John Coleridge Patteson, Bishop of Melanesia
20 September – Lesser Festival – Martyr – Red

Born in London in 1827, John Coleridge Patteson came under the influence of George Augustus Selwyn while John was still a scholar at Eton. Patteson went on to be ordained and, in 1855 at the age of twenty-eight, left Britain to begin his life's work among the Islanders of the South Pacific, founding the Melanesian Mission and becoming the first bishop of those Islands. His system of evangelisation was to train indigenous clergy and so to equip local people to share the gospel in a way that was within their own culture. This bore fruit and Christianity spread rapidly. Also working in Melanesia were 'blackbirders', essentially European slave-traders, who carried off Islanders to work in British and other colonies. When Patteson and his fellow-workers landed on the island of Nukapu, they were mistaken for such men and were brutally put to death by the inhabitants. John Coleridge Patteson gave his life for the gospel on this day in the year 1871.

Collect
God of all tribes and peoples and tongues,
who called your servant John Coleridge Patteson
to witness in life and death to the gospel of Christ
amongst the peoples of Melanesia:
grant us to hear your call to service
and to respond trustfully and joyfully to Jesus Christ our Redeemer,
who is alive and reigns with you, in the unity of the Holy Spirit,
one God, now and for ever.

A reading from the Second Book of the Chronicles.

After the death of Jehoiada the officials of Judah came and did obeisance to the king; then the king listened to them. They abandoned the house of the Lord, the God of their ancestors, and served the sacred poles and the idols. And wrath came upon Judah and Jerusalem for this guilt of theirs. Yet he sent prophets among them to bring them back to the Lord; they testified against them, but they would not listen. Then the spirit of God took possession of Zechariah son of the priest Jehoiada; he stood above the people and said to them, "Thus says God: Why do you transgress the commandments of the Lord, so that you cannot prosper? Because you have forsaken the Lord, he has also forsaken you." But they conspired against him, and by command of the king they stoned him to death in the court of the house of the Lord.

This is the word of the Lord. *2 Chronicles 24. 17-21*

Responsorial Psalm

R **You will show me the path of life, O God;**
  [in your presence there is fullness of joy].

All my delight is upon the godly that are in the land,
upon those who are noble among the people.
O Lord, you are my portion and my cup;
it is you who uphold my lot. **R**

My boundaries enclose a pleasant land;
indeed, I have a goodly heritage.
I will bless the Lord who gives me counsel;
my heart teaches me, night after night. **R**

I have set the Lord always before me;
because he is at my right hand I shall not fall.
My heart, therefore, is glad and my spirit rejoices;
my body also shall rest in hope. **R** *From Psalm 16*

A reading from the Acts of the Apostles.

Stephen, filled with the Holy Spirit, gazed into heaven and saw the glory of God and Jesus standing at the right hand of God. "Look," he said, "I see the heavens opened and the Son of Man standing at the right hand of God!" But the High Priest and the Council of the Synagogue covered their ears, and with a loud shout all rushed together against him. Then they dragged him out of the city and began to stone him; and the witnesses laid their coats at the feet of a young man named Saul. While they were stoning Stephen, he prayed, "Lord Jesus, receive my spirit." Then he knelt down and cried out in a loud voice, "Lord, do not hold this sin against them." When he had said this, he died.

This is the word of the Lord.   *Acts 7. 55-60*

Hear the gospel of our Lord Jesus Christ according to Mark.

Jesus began to teach them that the Son of Man must undergo great suffering, and be rejected by the elders, the chief priests, and the scribes, and be killed, and after three days rise again. He said all this quite openly. And Peter took him aside and began to rebuke him. But turning and looking at his disciples, he rebuked Peter and said, "Get behind me, Satan! For you are setting your mind not on divine things but on human things."

He called the crowd with his disciples, and said to them, "If any want to become my followers, let them deny themselves and take up their cross and follow me. For those who want to save their life will lose it, and those who lose their life for my sake, and for the sake of the gospel, will save it."

This is the gospel of the Lord.   *Mark 8. 31-35*

Post Communion
God our Redeemer,
whose Church was strengthened
  by the blood of your martyr John Coleridge Patteson:
so bind us, in life and death, to Christ's sacrifice
that our lives, broken and offered with his,
may carry his death and proclaim his resurrection in the world;
through Jesus Christ our Lord.

Matthew, Apostle & Evangelist
21 September – Festival – Apostle – Red

Matthew appears in the list of the twelve apostles of Jesus and, according to the gospel written under his name, was a tax collector. Mark and Luke called the tax collector Levi, and it has been assumed that they are one and the same. This occupation was despised by his fellow Jews as a betrayal to the occupying Roman force but Christ showed that judging by outward appearance was not what he was about. He ate with Matthew and with his friends, scandalising those around him. Matthew affirmed that his life would now change because of following Jesus, and that he would make amends for any former wrongdoing. This was enough for Jesus, for he had drawn someone back to God. He was forgiven, therefore he was acceptable, therefore he was received.

Collect

O Almighty God,
whose blessèd Son called Matthew the tax-collector
to be an apostle and evangelist:
give us grace to forsake the selfish pursuit of gain
  and the possessive love of riches
that we may follow in the way of your Son Jesus Christ,
who is alive and reigns with you,
in the unity of the Holy Spirit,
one God, now and for ever.

A reading from the book Proverbs.

Happy are those who find wisdom, and those who get under-standing, for her income is better than silver, and her revenue better than gold. She is more precious than jewels, and nothing you desire can compare with her. Long life is in her right hand; in her left hand are riches and honour. Her ways are ways of pleasant-ness, and all her paths are peace. She is a tree of life to those who lay hold of her; those who hold her fast are called happy.

This is the word of the Lord.   *Proverbs 3. 13-18*

Responsorial Psalm

**R Happy are those who find holy Wisdom,
    [she is the tree of life].**

O Lord, you have dealt graciously with your servant,
according to your word.
Teach me discernment and knowledge,
for I have believed in your commandments. **R**

Before I was afflicted I went astray,
but now I keep your word.
You are good and you bring forth good;
instruct me in your statutes. **R**

The proud have smeared me with lies,
but I will keep your commandments with my whole heart.
Their heart is gross and fat,
but my delight is in your law. **R**

It is good for me that I have been afflicted,
that I might learn your statutes.
The law of your mouth is dearer to me
than thousands in gold and silver. **R**   *From Psalm 119*

A reading from the Second Letter of Paul to the Corinthians.

Since it is by God's mercy that we are engaged in this ministry of
the Spirit, we do not lose heart. We have renounced the shameful
things that one hides; we refuse to practice cunning or to falsify
God's word; but by the open statement of the truth we commend
ourselves to the conscience of everyone in the sight of God. And
even if our gospel is veiled, it is veiled to those who are perishing.
In their case the god of this world has blinded the minds of the
unbelievers, to keep them from seeing the light of the gospel of the
glory of Christ, who is the image of God. For we do not proclaim
ourselves; we proclaim Jesus Christ as Lord and ourselves as your
servants for Jesus' sake. For it is the God who said, "Let light shine
out of darkness," who has shone in our hearts to give the light of
the knowledge of the glory of God in the face of Jesus Christ.

This is the word of the Lord.   *2 Corinthians 4. 1-6*

Hear the gospel of our Lord Jesus Christ according to Matthew.

As Jesus was walking along, he saw a man called Matthew sitting
at the tax booth; and he said to him, "Follow me." And he got up
and followed him. As he sat at dinner in the house, many tax collectors and sinners came and were sitting with him and his disciples. When the Pharisees saw this, they said to his disciples, "Why
does your teacher eat with tax collectors and sinners?" But when
he heard this, he said, "Those who are well have no need of a

physician, but those who are sick. Go and learn what this means, 'I desire mercy, not sacrifice.' For I have come to call not the righteous but sinners."

This is the gospel of the Lord.   *Matthew 9. 9-13*

Post Communion
Lord God, the source of truth and love,
keep us faithful to the apostles' teaching and fellowship,
united in prayer and the breaking of bread,
and one in joy and simplicity of heart,
in Jesus Christ our Lord.

Lancelot Andrewes, Bishop of Winchester
25 September – Lesser Festival – Bishop – White

Born in 1555 in Barking, Lancelot Andrewes studied at Merchant Taylors' School and Pembroke Hall (now Pembroke College), Cambridge. After ordination, he held several posts before accepting appointment as bishop, first of Chichester, then of Ely and finally of Winchester in 1619. Andrewes was present at the Hampton Court Conference in 1604, which furthered the reform of the Church of England, and he was also a translator of much of the Old Testament of what is known as the 'Authorised Version' of the Bible. His preaching and his writings proved highly influential and his holiness of life and gentle nature endeared him to all who met him. He died on this day in the year 1626 and his remains lie in a church which was then in his diocese of Winchester but now is the cathedral for the diocese of Southwark.

Collect
Lord God,
who gave to Lancelot Andrewes
  many gifts of your Holy Spirit,
making him a man of prayer and a pastor of your people:
perfect in us that which is lacking in your gifts,
  of faith, to increase it,
  of hope, to establish it,

of love, to kindle it,
that we may live in the light of your grace and glory;
through Jesus Christ your Son our Lord,
who is alive and reigns with you,
in the unity of the Holy Spirit,
one God, now and for ever.

A reading from the prophecy of Isaiah.

In the year that King Uzziah died, I saw the Lord sitting on a throne, high and lofty; and the the hem of his robe filled the temple. Seraphs were in attendance above him; each had six wings: with two they covered their faces, and with two they covered their feet, and with two they flew. And one called to another and said: "Holy, holy, holy is the Lord of hosts; the whole earth is full of his glory." The pivots on the thresholds shook at the voices of those who called, and the house filled with smoke. And I said: "Woe is me! I am lost, for I am a man of unclean lips, and I live among a people of unclean lips; yet my eyes have seen the King, the Lord of hosts!"

Then one of the seraphs flew to me, holding a live coal that had been taken from the altar with a pair of tongs. The seraph touched my mouth with it and said: "Now that this has touched your lips, your guilt has departed and your sin is blotted out." Then I heard the voice of the Lord saying, "Whom shall I send, and who will go for us?" And I said, "Here am I; send me!"

This is the word of the Lord.   *Isaiah 6. 1-8*

Responsorial Psalm

**R   I will bless you, O God, as long as I live
[and lift up my hands in your name].**

O God, you are my God; eagerly I seek you;
my soul thirsts for you, my flesh faints for you,
as in a barren and dry land where there is no water. **R**

Therefore I have gazed upon you in your holy place,
that I might behold your power and your glory.
For your loving-kindness is better than life itself;
my lips shall give you praise. **R**

My soul is content, as with marrow and fatness,
and my mouth praises you with joyful lips,
when I remember you upon my bed,
and meditate on you in the night watches. **R**

For you have been my helper,
and under the shadow of your wings I will rejoice.
My soul clings to you;
your right hand holds me fast. **R**   *From Psalm 63*

A reading from the First Letter of Peter.

As an elder myself and a witness of the sufferings of Christ, as well
as one who shares in the glory to be revealed, I exhort the elders
among you to tend the flock of God that is in your charge, exercising the oversight, not under compulsion but willingly, as God
would have you do it -- not for sordid gain but eagerly. Do not
lord it over those in your charge, but be examples to the flock. And
when the chief shepherd appears, you will win the crown of glory
that never fades away.

This is the word of the Lord.   *1 Peter 5. 1-4*

Hear the gospel of our Lord Jesus Christ according to Matthew.

Jesus said to his disciples, "The kingdom of heaven is like treasure
hidden in a field, which someone found and hid; then in his joy
he goes and sells all that he has and buys that field. Again, the
kingdom of heaven is like a merchant in search of fine pearls; on
finding one pearl of great value, he went and sold all that he had
and bought it." And he said to them, "Therefore every scribe who
has been trained for the kingdom of heaven is like the master of a
household who brings out of his treasure what is new and what is
old."

This is the gospel of the Lord.   *Matthew 13. 44-46, 52*

Post Communion
God, shepherd of your people,
whose servant Lancelot Andrewes
  revealed the loving service of Christ
  in his ministry as a pastor of your people:

by this eucharist in which we share
awaken within us the love of Christ
and keep us faithful to our Christian calling;
through him who laid down his life for us,
but is alive and reigns with you, now and for ever.

Sergei of Radonezh, Russian Monastic Reformer
25 September – Commemoration
If celebrated as a Lesser Festival, Common of Teachers, page 473

Born in Rostov in 1314, Sergei founded, together with his brother
Stephen, the famous monastery of the Holy Trinity, near Moscow,
which re-established the community life that had been lost in
Russia through the Tartar invasion. Sergei had great influence
and stopped civil wars between Russian princes and inspired
Prince Dimitri to resist another invasion from the Tartars in 1380.
Two years before that, he had been elected Metropolitan but had
refused the office. Altogether, he founded forty monasteries and
is regarded as the greatest of the Russian saints and is patron of All
Russia. He died on this day in 1392.

Wilson Carlile, Founder of the Church Army
26 September – Commemoration
If celebrated as a Lesser Festival, Common of Missionaries, page 503

Wilson Carlile was born in 1847 in Brixton. He suffered from a
spinal weakness all his life, which hampered his education. After
a serious illness, he began to treat his religion more seriously and
became confirmed in the Church of England. He acted as organ-
ist to Ira D Sankey during the Moody and Sankey missions and, in
1881, was ordained priest, serving his curacy at St Mary Abbots in
Kensington, together with a dozen other curates. The lack of contact between the Church and the working classes was a cause of
real concern to him and he began outdoor preaching. In 1882, he
resigned his curacy and founded the Church Army, four years
after the founding of the Salvation Army. Under his influence it
thrived and he continued to take part in its administration until a
few weeks before his death on this day in 1942.

Vincent de Paul,
Founder of the Congregation of Lazarists
27 September – Lesser Festival – Religious – White

Born in 1581 at Ranquine in Gascony, Vincent was educated by the Franciscans and was ordained at the age of nineteen. He was something of a token priest until his conversion in 1609, when he resolved to devote himself and all he owned to works of charity. He founded communities for men and, with Louise de Marillac, helped to begin the Sisters of Charity, the first community of women not to be enclosed and which was devoted to caring for the poor and sick. Vincent worked for the relief of galley slaves, victims of war, convicts and many other groups of needy people. He became a legend in his own lifetime and died on this day in the year 1660.

Collect
Merciful God,
whose servant Vincent de Paul,
by his ministry of preaching and pastoral care,
brought your love to the sick and the poor:
give to all your people a heart of compassion
that by word and action they may serve you
  in serving others in their need;
through Jesus Christ your Son our Lord,
who is alive and reigns with you,
in the unity of the Holy Spirit,
one God, now and for ever.

A reading from the prophecy of Isaiah.

Is not this the fast that I choose: to loose the bonds of injustice, to undo the thongs of the yoke, to let the oppressed go free, and to break every yoke? Is it not to share your bread with the hungry, and bring the homeless poor into your house; when you see the naked, to cover them, and not to hide yourself from your own kin? Then your light shall break forth like the dawn, and your healing shall spring up quickly; your vindicator shall go before you, the glory of the Lord shall be your rear guard. Then you shall call, and the Lord will answer; you shall cry for help, and he will say, Here I am. If you remove the yoke from among you, the pointing of the finger, the speaking of evil, if you offer your food to the hungry and satisfy the needs of the afflicted, then your light shall rise in the darkness and your gloom be like the noonday. The Lord will guide you continually.

This is the word of the Lord. *Isaiah 58. 6-11a*

Responsorial Psalm

R **God's light shall break forth like the dawn**
[the glory of the Lord shall be your rear guard].

Lord, who may dwell in your tabernacle?
who may abide upon your holy hill?
Whoever leads a blameless life and does what is right,
who speaks the truth from his heart. **R**

There is no guile upon his tongue;
he does no evil to his friend;
he does not heap contempt upon his neighbour. **R**

He does not give his money in hope of gain,
nor does he take a bribe against the innocent.
Whoever does these things
shall never be overthrown. **R** *From Psalm 15*

A reading from the First Letter of Paul to the Corinthians.

God's foolishness is wiser than human wisdom, and God's weakness is stronger than human strength. Consider your own call, brothers and sisters: not many of you were wise by human standards, not many were powerful, not many were of noble birth. But God chose what is foolish in the world to shame the wise; God chose what is weak in the world to shame the strong; God chose what is low and despised in the world, things that are not, to reduce to nothing things that are, so that no one might boast in the presence of God. He is the source of your life in Christ Jesus, who became for us wisdom from God, and righteousness and sanctification and redemption, in order that, as it is written, "Let the one who boasts, boast in the Lord."

This is the word of the Lord. *1 Corinthians 1. 25-31*

Hear the gospel of our Lord Jesus Christ according to Matthew.

The king will say to those at his right hand, "Come, you that are blessed by my Father, inherit the kingdom prepared for you from the foundation of the world; for I was hungry and you gave me food, I was thirsty and you gave me something to drink, I was a stranger and you welcomed me, I was naked and you gave me clothing, I was sick and you took care of me, I was in prison and you visited me."

Then the righteous will answer him, "Lord, when was it that we saw you hungry and gave you food, or thirsty and gave you something to drink? And when was it that we saw you a stranger and welcomed you, or naked and gave you clothing? And when was it that we saw you sick or in prison and visited you?" And the king will answer them, "Truly I tell you, just as you did it to one of the least of these who are members of my family, you did it to me."

This is the gospel of the Lord.   *Matthew 25. 34-40*

Post Communion
Merciful God,
who gave such grace to your servant Vincent de Paul
that he served you with singleness of heart
and loved you above all things:
help us, whose communion with you
  has been renewed in this sacrament,
to forsake all that holds us back from following Christ
and to grow into his likeness from glory to glory;
through Jesus Christ our Lord.

Michael & All Angels
29 September – Festival – White

Michael, Gabriel and Raphael are the three named biblical angels, depicted as the belovèd messengers of God. Michael, which means 'who is like God?', is described as protector of Israel and leader of the armies of God and is perhaps best known as the slayer of the dragon in the Revelation to John. He is thus regarded as the protector of Christians from the devil, particularly those at the hour of death.

Gabriel, which means 'the strength of God', is the one, according to the Gospel of Luke, who is sent by God to Mary to announce the birth of Christ.

Raphael, which means 'the healing of God', is depicted in the Book of Tobit as the one who restores sight to Tobit's eyes.

A basilica near Rome was dedicated in the fifth century in honour of Michael on 30 September, beginning with celebrations on the eve of that day, and 29 September is now kept in honour of Michael and all Angels throughout the western Church.

Collect
Everlasting God,
you have ordained and constituted the ministries
 of angels and mortals in a wonderful order:
grant that as your holy angels
 always serve you in heaven,
so, at your command,
they may help and defend us on earth;
through Jesus Christ your Son our Lord,
who is alive and reigns with you,
in the unity of the Holy Spirit,
one God, now and for ever.

Genesis 28. 10-17	*or*	Revelation 12. 7-12
Psalm 103. 19-22		Psalm 103. 19-22
Revelation 12. 7-12		Hebrews 1. 5-14
John 1. 47-51		John 1. 47-51

A reading from the book Genesis.

Jacob left Beer-sheba and went toward Haran. He came to a certain place and stayed there for the night, because the sun had set. Taking one of the stones of the place, he put it under his head and lay down in that place. And he dreamed that there was a ladder set up on the earth, the top of it reaching to heaven; and the angels of God were ascending and descending on it. And the Lord stood beside him and said, "I am the Lord, the God of Abraham your father and the God of Isaac; the land on which you lie I will give to you and to your offspring; and your offspring shall be like the dust of the earth, and you shall spread abroad to the west and to the east and to the north and to the south; and all the families of the earth shall be blessed in you and in your offspring. Know that I am with you and will keep you wherever you go, and will bring you back to this land; for I will not leave you until I have done what I have promised you."

Then Jacob woke from his sleep and said, "Surely the Lord is in this place – and I did not know it!" And he was afraid, and said, "How awesome is this place! This is none other than the house of God, and this is the gate of heaven."

This is the word of the Lord.   *Genesis 28. 10-17*

Responsorial Psalm

**R Give your angels charge over us, O God,
    [to keep us in all our ways].**

The Lord has set his throne in heaven,
and his kingship has dominion over all.
Bless the Lord, you angels of his,
hearken to the voice of his word. **R**

Bless the Lord, all you his hosts,
you ministers of his who do his will.
Bless the Lord, all you works of his,
in all places of his dominion. **R**   *From Psalm 103*

A reading from the Revelation to John.

War broke out in heaven; Michael and his angels fought against the dragon. The dragon and his angels fought back, but they were defeated, and there was no longer any place for them in heaven. The great dragon was thrown down, that ancient serpent, who is called the Devil and Satan, the deceiver of the whole world – he was thrown down to the earth, and his angels were thrown down with him.

Then I heard a loud voice in heaven, proclaiming, "Now have come the salvation and the power and the kingdom of our God and the authority of his Messiah, for the accuser of our comrades has been thrown down, who accuses them day and night before our God. But they have conquered him by the blood of the Lamb and by the word of their testimony, for they did not cling to life even in the face of death. Rejoice then, you heavens and those who dwell in them! But woe to the earth and the sea, for the devil has come down to you with great wrath, because he knows that his time is short!"

This is the word of the Lord. *Revelation 12. 7-12*

A reading from the Letter to the Hebrews.

To which of the angels did God ever say, "You are my Son; today I have begotten you"? Or again, "I will be his Father, and he will be my Son"? And again, when he brings the firstborn into the world, he says, "Let all God's angels worship him." Of the angels he says, "He makes his angels winds, and his servants flames of fire." But of the Son he says, "Your throne, O God, is forever and ever, and the righteous sceptre is the sceptre of your kingdom. You have loved righteousness and hated wickedness; therefore God, your God, has anointed you with the oil of gladness beyond your companions." And, "In the beginning, Lord, you founded the earth, and the heavens are the work of your hands; they will perish, but you remain; they will all wear out like clothing; like a cloak you will roll them up, and like clothing they will be changed. But you are the same, and your years will never end." But to which of the angels has he ever said, "Sit at my right hand until I make your enemies a footstool for your feet"? Are not all angels spirits in the divine service, sent to serve for the sake of those who are to inherit salvation?

This is the word of the Lord. *Hebrews 1. 5-14*

Hear the gospel of our Lord Jesus Christ according to John.

When Jesus saw Nathanael coming toward him, he said of him, "Here is truly an Israelite in whom there is no deceit!" Nathanael asked him, "Where did you get to know me?" Jesus answered, "I saw you under the fig tree before Philip called you." Nathanael replied, "Rabbi, you are the Son of God! You are the King of Israel!" Jesus answered, "Do you believe because I told you that I saw you under the fig tree? You will see greater things than these." And he said to him, "Very truly, I tell you, you will see heaven opened and the angels of God ascending and descending upon the Son of Man."

This is the gospel of the Lord. *John 1. 47-51*

Post Communion
Lord of heaven,
in this eucharist you have brought us near
  to an innumerable company of angels
  and to the spirits of the saints made perfect:
as in this food of our earthly pilgrimage
  we have shared their fellowship,
so may we come to share their joy in heaven;
through Jesus Christ our Lord.

Jerome, Translator of the Scriptures
30 September – Commemoration
If celebrated as a Lesser Festival, Common of Teachers, page 473

Jerome was born at Strido near Aquileia on the Adriatic coast of Dalmatia, in about the year 342. He studied at Rome, where he was baptised. He tried the life of a monk for a time, but unsuccessfully. Following a dream in which he stood before the judgement seat of God and was condemned for his faith in classics rather than Christ, he learned Hebrew the better to study the Scriptures. This, with his polished skills in rhetoric and mastery of Greek, enabled him to begin his life's work of translating the newly-canonised Bible into Latin. He eventually settled at Bethlehem, where he founded a monastery and devoted the rest of his life to study. He died on this day in the year 420.

OCTOBER

Remigius, Bishop of Rheims, Apostle of the Franks
1 October – Commemoration
If celebrated as a Lesser Festival, Common of Missionaries, page 503

Born in about the year 438, the son of the Count of Laon, Remigius studied at Rheims and was elected bishop and metropolitan of the city when he was only twenty-two years old. In the year 496, he baptised Clovis I, King of the Franks, and about three thousand of his subjects. Under the king's protection, Remigius preached the gospel, created dioceses, built churches and baptised many more Christians. His name is linked to the ampulla of chrism oil used at the coronation of French monarchs, together with the gift of healing. He died on 13 January in the year 533 and his mortal remains were translated to the abbey of St Remi on this day in the year 1049.

Anthony Ashley Cooper, Earl of Shaftesbury
1 October – Commemoration
If celebrated as a Lesser Festival, Common of Any Saint, page 527

Born in 1801, Ashley Cooper was first elected to the House of Commons in 1826. In 1851, he succeeded his father as the seventh Earl of Shaftesbury and sat in the House of Lords. His service in parliament was marked from the beginning by a desire to reform social abuses, an impulse which derived from his strong Evangelical Anglican piety. He campaigned successfully for measures to improve housing and also create schools for the poor. He pioneered legislation on conditions of employment, for example, in mines and factories, particularly with respect to the protection of children. He became the epitome of the Victorian Christian philanthropist, working within the political system to redress social evils. He died on this day in 1885.

Francis of Assisi, Founder of the Friars Minor
4 October – Lesser Festival – Religious – White

Francis was born in Assisi in central Italy either in 1181 or the following year. He was baptised Giovanni but given the name Francesco by his father, a cloth merchant who traded in France and had married a French wife. There was an expectation that he would eventually take over his father's business but Francis had a rebellious youth and a difficult relationship with his father. After suffering the ignominy of imprisonment following capture whilst at war with the local city of Perugia, he returned a changed man. He took to caring for disused churches and for the poor, particularly those suffering from leprosy. Whilst praying in the semi-derelict church of St Damian, he distinctly heard the words: "Go and repair my church, which you see is falling down." Others joined him and he prepared a simple, gospel-based Rule for them all to live by. As the Order grew, it witnessed to Christ through preaching the gospel of repentance, emphasising the poverty of Christ as an example for his followers. Two years before his death, his life being so closely linked with that of his crucified Saviour, he received the Stigmata, the marks of the wounds of Christ, on his body. At his death, on the evening of 3 October 1226, his Order had spread throughout western Christendom.

Collect
O God, you ever delight to reveal yourself
to the child-like and lowly of heart:
grant that, following the example of the blessèd Francis,
we may count the wisdom of this world as foolishness
and know only Jesus Christ and him crucified,
who is alive and reigns with you,
in the unity of the Holy Spirit,
one God, now and for ever.

A reading from the prophecy of Micah.

"With what shall I come before the Lord, and bow myself before God on high? Shall I come before him with burnt offerings, with calves a year old? Will the Lord be pleased with thousands of rams, with ten thousands of rivers of oil? Shall I give my firstborn for my transgression, the fruit of my body for the sin of my soul?"

He has told you, O mortal, what is good; and what does the Lord require of you but to do justice, and to love kindness, and to walk humbly with your God?

This is the word of the Lord.   *Micah 6. 6-8*

Responsorial Psalm

R   The Lord is good; his mercy is everlasting;
    [and his faithfulness endures from age to age].

Be joyful in the Lord, all you lands;
serve the Lord with gladness
and come before his presence with a song. **R**

Know this: The Lord himself is God;
he himself has made us and we are his;
we are his people and the sheep of his pasture. **R**

Enter his gates with thanksgiving;
go into his courts with praise;
give thanks to him and call upon his name. **R**   *Psalm 100*

A reading from the Letter of Paul to the Galatians.

May I never boast of anything except the cross of our Lord Jesus Christ, by which the world has been crucified to me, and I to the world. For neither circumcision nor uncircumcision is anything; but a new creation is everything! As for those who will follow this rule – peace be upon them, and mercy, and upon the Israel of God. From now on, let no one make trouble for me; for I carry the marks of Jesus branded on my body. May the grace of our Lord Jesus Christ be with your spirit, brothers and sisters. Amen.

This is the word of the Lord.   *Galatians 6. 14-18*

Hear the gospel of our Lord Jesus Christ according to Luke.

Jesus said to his disciples, "I tell you, do not worry about your life, what you will eat, or about your body, what you will wear. For life is more than food, and the body more than clothing. Consider the ravens: they neither sow nor reap, they have neither storehouse nor barn, and yet God feeds them. Of how much more value are you than the birds! And can any of you by worrying add a single hour to your span of life? If then you are not able to do so small a thing as that, why do you worry about the rest?

Consider the lilies, how they grow: they neither toil nor spin; yet I tell you, even Solomon in all his glory was not clothed like one of these. But if God so clothes the grass of the field, which is alive today and tomorrow is thrown into the oven, how much more will he clothe you – you of little faith! And do not keep striving for what you are to eat and what you are to drink, and do not keep worrying. For it is the nations of the world that strive after all these things, and your Father knows that you need them. Instead, strive for his kingdom, and these things will be given to you as well.

"Do not be afraid, little flock, for it is your Father's good pleasure to give you the kingdom. Sell your possessions, and give alms. Make purses for yourselves that do not wear out, an unfailing treasure in heaven, where no thief comes near and no moth destroys. For where your treasure is, there your heart will be also."

This is the gospel of the Lord.   *Luke 12. 22-34*

Post Communion
Lord God,
you made your church rich
through the poverty of blessèd Francis:
help us like him not to trust in earthly things
but to seek your heavenly gifts;
through Jesus Christ our Lord.

William Tyndale, Translator of the Scriptures
6 October – Lesser Festival – Martyr – Red

Born in Gloucestershire in about the year 1494, William Tyndale studied first at Magdalen Hall (now Magdalen College), Oxford, and then at Cambridge. He became determined to translate the Scriptures from the Greek directly into contemporary English but was thwarted in this by the Bishop of London. So William settled in Hamburg in 1524, never returning to England. When the first copies of his translation arrived in England in 1526, it was bitterly attacked as subversive by the ecclesial authorities. He spent much of the rest of his life making revisions to his work, but also writing many theological works. His life's-work proved good enough to be the basic working text for those who, at the beginning of the following century, were to produce what became known as the *Authorised Version* of the Bible. He was eventually arrested in 1535 and imprisoned in Brussels on charges of heresy. He was first strangled and then burnt at the stake on this day in 1536. His last words were, "Lord, open the King of England's eyes."

Collect
Lord, give to your people grace to hear and keep your word
that, after the example of your servant William Tyndale,
we may not only profess your gospel
but also be ready to suffer and die for it,
to the honour of your name;
through Jesus Christ your Son our Lord,
who is alive and reigns with you,
in the unity of the Holy Spirit,
one God, now and for ever.

A reading from the Book of Proverbs.

Does not wisdom call, and does not understanding raise her voice? On the heights, beside the way, at the crossroads she takes her stand; beside the gates in front of the town, at the entrance of the portals she cries out: "To you, O people, I call, and my cry is to all that live. O simple ones, learn prudence; acquire intelligence, you who lack it. Hear, for I will speak noble things, and from my lips will come what is right; for my mouth will utter truth; wickedness is an abomination to my lips. All the words of my mouth are righteous; there is nothing twisted or crooked in them. They are all straight to one who understands and right to those who find knowledge. Take my instruction instead of silver, and knowledge rather than choice gold; for wisdom is better than jewels, and all that you may desire cannot compare with her."

This is the word of the Lord.   *Proverbs 8. 1-11*

Responsorial Psalm

R   Wisdom will speak noble things,
   [from her lips will come what is right].

O Lord, your word is everlasting;
it stands firm in the heavens.
Your faithfulness remains from one generation to another;
you established the earth and it abides. **R**

By your decree these continue to this day,
for all things are your servants.
If my delight had not been in your law,
I should have perished in my affliction. **R**

I will never forget your commandments,
because by them you give me life.
I am yours; O that you would save me!
for I study your commandments. **R**

Though the wicked lie in wait for me to destroy me,
I will apply my mind to your decrees.
I see that all things come to an end,
but your commandment has no bounds. **R**   *From Psalm 119*

A reading from the Second Letter of Paul to Timothy.

All who want to live a godly life in Christ Jesus will be persecuted.
But wicked people and impostors will go from bad to worse,
deceiving others and being deceived. But as for you, continue in
what you have learned and firmly believed, knowing from whom
you learned it, and how from childhood you have known the
sacred writings that are able to instruct you for salvation through
faith in Christ Jesus. All scripture is inspired by God and is useful
for teaching, for reproof, for correction, and for training in righteousness, so that everyone who belongs to God may be proficient,
equipped for every good work.

This is the word of the Lord.   *2 Timothy 3. 12-17*

Hear the gospel of our Lord Jesus Christ according to John.

Jesus said to his disciples, "I have made your name known to those
whom you gave me from the world. They were yours, and you

gave them to me, and they have kept your word. Now they know that everything you have given me is from you; for the words that you gave to me I have given to them, and they have received them and know in truth that I came from you; and they have believed that you sent me. I have given them your word, and the world has hated them because they do not belong to the world, just as I do not belong to the world. I am not asking you to take them out of the world, but I ask you to protect them from the evil one.

"They do not belong to the world, just as I do not belong to the world. Sanctify them in the truth; your word is truth. As you have sent me into the world, so I have sent them into the world. And for their sakes I sanctify myself, so that they also may be sanctified in truth."

This is the gospel of the Lord.   *John 17. 6-8, 14-19*

Post Communion
God,
who gave us this holy meal
in which we have celebrated the glory of the cross
and the victory of your martyr William Tyndale:
by our communion with Christ
in his saving death and resurrection,
give us with all your saints the courage to conquer evil
and so to share the fruit of the tree of life;
through Jesus Christ our Lord.

Denys, Bishop of Paris, & his Companions
9 October – Commemoration
If celebrated as a Lesser Festival, Common of Martyrs, page 464

Denys, also called Dionysius, was born in Italy at the beginning of the third century and was sent to convert the peoples of Gaul, along with five other bishops. On reaching Paris, he established there a Christian church on an island in the Seine. He and others were martyred in about the year 250 and an abbey was later built over their tombs, dedicated to Denys. The church became the burial place of French monarchs and Denys has long been regarded as patron saint of France.

Robert Grosseteste, Bishop of Lincoln
9 October – Commemoration
If celebrated as a Lesser Festival, Common of Pastors, page 483

Robert Grosseteste (meaning 'large-head') was born at Stradbroke in Suffolk in about 1175. He studied at Oxford and Paris and held various posts until, after a grave illness, he returned to Oxford, where he taught at the Franciscan house of studies. He became Bishop of Lincoln in 1235, then the largest English diocese, which received from him a thorough visitation soon after his arrival. He met opposition in his attempts at vigorous reforms in the shape of his dean and chapter in the cathedral at Lincoln, who saw themselves as beyond his jurisdiction. The affair was settled in 1245 when the pope issued a bull giving the bishop full power over the Chapter. Robert attended the Council of Lyons that year and also travelled to Rome a few years later. His wide-ranging interests covered mathematics, optics and many of the sciences; he translated large numbers of theological works from Greek and wrote his own theological commentaries and philosophical works. He died on this day in the year 1253.

Paulinus, First Bishop of York
10 October – Lesser Festival – Missionary – White

Born in the latter part of the sixth century, probably in Italy, Paulinus was among the second group of monks sent by Pope Gregory to England to assist Augustine in his work. He went with the party that accompanied Ethelburga to Northumbria, where she was to marry the king, Edwin, who subsequently took his wife's Christian faith as his own. Paulinus built the first church in York in about the year 627 and was its first bishop. He travelled much north and south of the Humber, building churches and baptising new Christians. He had to flee for his life, however, when Edwin was killed in battle by the pagan king, Penda of Mercia, and Paulinus became Bishop of Rochester. He died on this day in the year 644.

Collect
God our Saviour,
who sent Paulinus to preach and to baptise,
and so to build up your Church in this land:
grant that, inspired by his example,
we may tell all the world of your truth,
that with him we may receive
  the reward you prepare for all your faithful servants;
through Jesus Christ your Son our Lord,
who is alive and reigns with you,
in the unity of the Holy Spirit,
one God, now and for ever.

A reading from the prophecy of Isaiah.

In days to come the mountain of the Lord's house shall be established as the highest of the mountains, and shall be raised above the hills; all the nations shall stream to it. Many peoples shall come and say, "Come, let us go up to the mountain of the Lord, to the house of the God of Jacob; that he may teach us his ways and that we may walk in his paths." For out of Zion shall go forth instruction, and the word of the Lord from Jerusalem. He shall judge between the nations, and shall arbitrate for many peoples; they shall beat their swords into ploughshares, and their spears into pruning hooks; nation shall not lift up sword against nation, neither shall they learn war any more. O house of Jacob, come, let us walk in the light of the Lord!

This is the word of the Lord.   *Isaiah 2. 2-5*

Responsorial Psalm

**R   Come, let us go up to the mountain of the Lord
      [to the house of the God of Jacob].**

The Lord is my light and my salvation;
whom then shall I fear?
The Lord is the strength of my life;
of whom then shall I be afraid? **R**

When evildoers came upon me
to eat up my flesh,
it was they, my foes and my adversaries,
who stumbled and fell. **R**

One thing have I asked of the Lord; one thing I seek;
that I may dwell in the house of the Lord all the days of my life;
to behold the fair beauty of the Lord
and to seek him in his temple. **R**   *From Psalm 27*

A Reading from the Letter of Paul to the Ephesians.

God, who is rich in mercy, out of the great love with which he
loved us, even when we were dead through our trespasses, made
us alive together with Christ – by grace you have been saved – and
raised us up with him and seated us with him in the heavenly
places in Christ Jesus, so that in the ages to come he might show
the immeasurable riches of his grace in kindness toward us in
Christ Jesus. For by grace you have been saved through faith, and
this is not your own doing; it is the gift of God – not the result of
works, so that no one may boast. For we are what he has made us,
created in Christ Jesus for good works, which God prepared
beforehand to be our way of life.

This is the word of the Lord.   *Ephesians 2. 4-10*

Hear the gospel of our Lord Jesus Christ according to Matthew.

The eleven disciples went to Galilee, to the mountain to which
Jesus had directed them. When they saw him, they worshiped
him; but some doubted. And Jesus came and said to them, "All
authority in heaven and on earth has been given to me. Go therefore and make disciples of all nations, baptising them in the name
of the Father and of the Son and of the Holy Spirit, and teaching
them to obey everything that I have commanded you. And
remember, I am with you always, to the end of the age."

This is the gospel of the Lord.   *Matthew 28. 16-20*

Post Communion
Holy Father,
who gathered us here around the table of your Son
to share this meal with the whole household of God:
in that new world where you reveal
  the fullness of your peace,
gather people of every race and language
to share with your servant Paulinus and all your saints
in the eternal banquet of Jesus Christ our Lord.

October 10

Thomas Traherne, Poet, Spiritual Writer
10 October – Commemoration
If celebrated as a Lesser Festival, Common of any Saint, page 531

Thomas Traherne was born in Hereford in about 1636. After studying in Oxford and being a parish priest for ten years, he became private chaplain to the Lord Keeper of the Seals of Charles II. Thomas was one of the English Metaphysical poets and yet, in his lifetime, only one of his works was ever printed. It was at the beginning of the twentieth century that his poems, until then in manuscript, were published and he took on the mantle of an Anglican Divine. His poetry is probably the most celebratory among his fellow metaphysical poets, with little mention of sin and suffering and concentrating more on the glory of creation, to the extent that some regard his writings as on the edge of pantheism. He died on this day in the year 1674.

Ethelburga, Abbess of Barking
11 October – Commemoration
If celebrated as a Lesser Festival, Common of Religious, page 494

Ethelburga was sister of Erkenwald, Bishop of London, and was probably of royal blood. As Bede describes her, it seems she may well have owned, as well as been made Abbess of, the joint monastery at Barking. There was a tradition developing of monks and nuns sharing monasteries, often with a woman superior, for example Hilda at Whitby and Cuthburga at Wimborne. Though they lived quite separate lives, often divided by high walls, they would occasionally celebrate the Daily Office or the Mass together. There was also probably an element of safety involved with the ever-present threat of marauding Danes. Bede relates many miracles occurring around Ethelburga but little else is known of her life. She died on this day in the year 675.

James the Deacon, companion of Paulinus

11 October – *Commemoration*

If celebrated as a Lesser Festival, Common of Missionaries, page 503

The details of the birth and death of James the Deacon are not known, though, since he accompanied Paulinus, he may well have been Italian. James seems to have been very active in assisting Paulinus on his mission in southern Northumbria and, when King Edwin was killed in battle and Paulinus had to flee south, James remained in the north. At some risk to his life, he continued the work of preaching and baptising around the area which is now north Yorkshire. As an old man, he attended the Synod of Whitby in 664 and, though not a monk and therefore without a community to perpetuate his memory, he seems to have had enough popularity among ordinary Christians to have had a continuing cultus long after his death.

Wilfrid of Ripon, Bishop of York

12 October – *Lesser Festival* – *Missionary* – *White*

Wilfrid, or Wilfrith, was born in Northumbria in about the year 633. He was educated at the monastery of Lindisfarne, but disapproved of what he judged to be their Celtic insularity. He journeyed to Canterbury and then to Rome. He spent three years at Lyons wthere admitted as a monk. He was appointed Abbot of Ripon and took with him the Roman monastic system and Benedictine Rule, which he immediately introduced. At the Synod of Whitby, his dominance was largely responsible for the victory of the Roman party over the Celts and, when he was elected Bishop of York, he went to Compiègne to be consecrated by twelve Frankish bishops rather than risk any doubt of schism by being ordained by Celtic bishops. There were upsets first with Chad and then with Archbishop Theodore of Canterbury, but the Roman authorities took his side and he was eventually restored to his See. After further disputes, he resigned the See of York and became Bishop of Hexham, spending his remaining years in the monastery at Ripon. His gift to the English church was to make it more clearly a part of the Church universal, but his manner and methods were not such as to draw people close to him at a personal level. He died on this day at Ripon in the year 709.

Collect
Almighty God,
who called our forebears to the light of the gospel
 by the preaching of your servant Wilfrid:
help us, who keep his life and labour in remembrance,
to glorify your name by following the example
 of his zeal and perseverance;
through Jesus Christ your Son our Lord,
who is alive and reigns with you,
in the unity of the Holy Spirit,
one God, now and for ever.

A reading from the prophecy of Isaiah.

How beautiful upon the mountains are the feet of the messenger
who announces peace, who brings good news, who announces
salvation, who says to Zion, "Your God reigns." Listen! Your sentinels lift up their voices, together they sing for joy; for in plain
sight they see the return of the Lord to Zion. Break forth together
into singing, you ruins of Jerusalem; for the Lord has comforted
his people, he has redeemed Jerusalem. The Lord has bared his
holy arm before the eyes of all the nations; and all the ends of the
earth shall see the salvation of our God.

This is the word of the Lord.   *Isaiah 52. 7-10*

Responsorial Psalm

**R   May God give us his blessing,
     [and may all the ends of the earth stand in awe of him].**

May God be merciful to us and bless us,
show us the light of his countenance and come to us.
Let your ways be known upon earth,
your saving health among all nations. **R**

Let the peoples praise you, O God; let all the peoples praise you.
Let the nations be glad and sing for joy,
for you judge the peoples with equity
and guide all the nations upon earth. **R**

Let the peoples praise you, O God;
let all the peoples praise you.
The earth has brought forth her increase;
may God, our own God, give us his blessing. **R**   *Psalm 67*

A reading from the First Letter of Paul to the Corinthians.

The message about the cross is foolishness to those who are perishing, but to us who are being saved it is the power of God. For it is written, "I will destroy the wisdom of the wise, and the discernment of the discerning I will thwart." Where is the one who is wise? Where is the scribe? Where is the debater of this age? Has not God made foolish the wisdom of the world?

For since, in the wisdom of God, the world did not know God through wisdom, God decided, through the foolishness of our proclamation, to save those who believe. For Jews demand signs and Greeks desire wisdom, but we proclaim Christ crucified, a stumbling block to Jews and foolishness to Gentiles, but to those who are the called, both Jews and Greeks, Christ the power of God and the wisdom of God. For God's foolishness is wiser than human wisdom, and God's weakness is stronger than human strength.

This is the word of the Lord.   *1 Corinthians 1. 18-25*

Hear the gospel of our Lord Jesus Christ according to Luke.

Once while Jesus was standing beside the lake of Gennesaret, and the crowd was pressing in on him to hear the word of God, he saw two boats there at the shore of the lake; the fishermen had gone out of them and were washing their nets. He got into one of the boats, the one belonging to Simon, and asked him to put out a little way from the shore. Then he sat down and taught the crowds from the boat. When he had finished speaking, he said to Simon, "Put out into the deep water and let down your nets for a catch."

Simon answered, "Master, we have worked all night long but have caught nothing. Yet if you say so, I will let down the nets." When they had done this, they caught so many fish that their nets were beginning to break. So they signaled their partners in the other boat to come and help them. And they came and filled both boats, so that they began to sink. But when Simon Peter saw it, he fell down at Jesus' knees, saying, "Go away from me, Lord, for I am a sinful man!" For he and all who were with him were amazed at the catch of fish that they had taken; and so also were James and John, sons of Zebedee, who were partners with Simon. Then Jesus said to Simon, "Do not be afraid; from now on you will be catching people." When they had brought their boats to shore, they left everything and followed him.

This is the gospel of the Lord.   *Luke 5. 1-11*

Post Communion
Holy Father,
who gathered us here around the table of your Son
to share this meal with the whole household of God:
in that new world where you reveal
  the fullness of your peace,
gather people of every race and language
to share with your servant Wilfrid and all your saints
in the eternal banquet of Jesus Christ our Lord.

Elizabeth Fry, Prison Reformer
12 October – Commemoration
If celebrated as a Lesser Festival, Common of any Saint, page 527

Elizabeth Gurney was born at Earlham in Norfolk in 1780. At the
age of twenty, she married Joseph Fry, a London merchant and a
strict Quaker. She was admitted as a minister in the Society of
Friends and became a noted preacher. The appalling state of the
prisons came to her notice and she devoted much of her time to
the welfare of female prisoners in Newgate. In 1820 she took part
in the formation of a nightly shelter for the homeless in London.
She travelled all over Europe in the cause of prison reform. She
was a woman of a strong Christian and evangelistic impulse and
this inspired all her work. She died on this day in 1845.

Edith Cavell, Nurse
12 October – Commemoration
If celebrated as a Lesser Festival, Common of any Saint, page 513

Edith Cavell was born into a clergy family at Swardeston in 1865.
After life as a governess, she trained as a nurse, ending up working with the Red Cross in Belgium in 1907. On the outbreak of the
First World War, she became involved in caring for the wounded
on both sides. She refused repatriation and then began smuggling
British soldiers from Belgium into Holland. In 1915 she was arrested and brought to trial. Protecting those who worked with her,
she was sentenced to death and executed by firing squad on this

day in the year 1915. She went to her death calmly, forgiving her executioners, convinced she had been doing her duty as a Christian.

Edward the Confessor, King of England
13 October – Lesser Festival – of any Saint – White

Edward was born in 1002, the son of the English King Ethelred and his Norman wife Emma. Living in exile during the Danish supremacy, he was invited back to England in 1042 to become king, and was heartily welcomed as a descendant of the old royal line. However, his reign was a balancing act between the influences of stronger characters at his court or overseas, sustained by Edward's diplomacy and determination. Edward's reputation for sanctity was built on his personal, more than his political, qualities. He was concerned to maintain peace and justice in his realm, to avoid foreign wars, and to put his faith into practice. He was generous to the poor, hospitable to strangers, but no mere pietist. Having vowed as a young man to go on pilgrimage to Rome should his family fortunes ever be restored, he later felt it irresponsible to leave his kingdom, and was permitted instead to found or endow a monastery dedicated to St Peter. Edward chose the abbey on Thorney Island, by the river Thames, thus beginning the royal patronage of Westminster Abbey. He died on 5 January 1066 and his remains were translated to the Abbey on this day in 1162.

Collect
Sovereign God,
who set your servant Edward
 upon the throne of an earthly kingdom
and inspired him with zeal for the kingdom of heaven:
grant that we may so confess the faith of Christ
 by word and deed,
that we may, with all your saints, inherit your eternal glory;
through Jesus Christ your Son our Lord,
who is alive and reigns with you,
in the unity of the Holy Spirit,
one God, now and for ever.

A reading from the Second Book of Samuel.

These are the last words of David: The oracle of David, son of Jesse, the oracle of the man whom God exalted, the anointed of the God of Jacob, the favourite of the Strong One of Israel: The spirit of the Lord speaks through me, his word is upon my tongue. The God of Israel has spoken, the Rock of Israel has said to me: One who rules over people justly, ruling in the fear of God, is like the light of morning, like the sun rising on a cloudless morning, gleaming from the rain on the grassy land. Is not my house like this with God? For he has made with me an everlasting covenant, ordered in all things and secure. Will he not cause to prosper all my help and my desire?

This is the word of the Lord.   *2 Samuel 23. 1-5*

Responsorial Psalm

**R   Bless the Lord, you servants of the Lord,
      [you that stand in the house of the Lord].**

Lord, remember David
and all the hardships he endured;
how he swore an oath to the Lord
and vowed a vow to the Mighty One of Jacob: **R**

"I will not come under the roof of my house,
nor climb up into my bed;
I will not allow my eyes to sleep,
nor let my eyelids slumber;
until I find a place for the Lord,
a dwelling for the Mighty One of Jacob." **R**

Arise, O Lord, into your resting-place,
you and the ark of your strength.
Let your priests be clothed with righteousness;
let your faithful people sing with joy. **R**   *From Psalm 132*

A reading from the First Letter of John.

We know that we abide in God and he in us, because he has given us of his Spirit. And we have seen and do testify that the Father has sent his Son as the Saviour of the world. God abides in those who confess that Jesus is the Son of God, and they abide in God.

So we have known and believe the love that God has for us. God is love, and those who abide in love abide in God, and God abides in them.

This is the word of the Lord. *1 John 4. 13-16*

Hear the gospel of our Lord Jesus Christ according to Matthew.

Jesus entered the temple and drove out all who were selling and buying in the temple, and he overturned the tables of the money changers and the seats of those who sold doves. He said to them, "It is written, 'My house shall be called a house of prayer'; but you are making it a den of robbers." The blind and the lame came to him in the temple, and he cured them. But when the chief priests and the scribes saw the amazing things that he did, and heard the children crying out in the temple, "Hosanna to the Son of David," they became angry and said to him, "Do you hear what these are saying?" Jesus said to them, "Yes; have you never read, 'Out of the mouths of infants and nursing babies you have prepared praise for yourself'?" He left them, went out of the city to Bethany, and spent the night there.

This is the gospel of the Lord. *Matthew 21. 12-17*

Post Communion
Faithful God,
who called your servant Edward to serve you
and gave him joy in walking the path of holiness:
by this eucharist
 in which you renew within us the vision of your glory,
strengthen us all to follow the way of perfection
until we come to see you face to face;
through Jesus Christ our Lord.

Teresa of Avila
15 October – Lesser Festival – Teacher of the Faith – White

Teresa was born into an aristocratic Spanish family in 1515. Following her mother's death, she was educated by Augustinian nuns and then ran away from home to enter a Carmelite convent when she was twenty. After initial difficulties in prayer, her intense mystical experiences attracted many disciples. She was inspired to reform the Carmelite rule and, assisted by St John of the Cross, she travelled throughout Spain founding many new religious houses for men as well as women. Her writings about her own spiritual life and progress in prayer towards union with God include *The Way of Perfection* and *The Interior Castle,* which are still acclaimed. She knew great physical suffering and died of exhaustion on 4 October 1582. Her feast is on 15 October because the very day after her death the reformed calendar was adopted and eleven days were omitted from October that year.

Collect
Merciful God,
who by your Spirit raised up your servant Teresa of Avila
to reveal to your Church the way of perfection:
grant that her teaching
may awaken in us a longing for holiness,
until we attain to the perfect union of love
in Jesus Christ your Son our Lord,
who is alive and reigns with you,
in the unity of the Holy Spirit,
one God, now and for ever.

A reading from the book Ecclesiasticus.

I prayed, and understanding was given me; I called on God, and the spirit of wisdom came to me. I preferred her to sceptres and thrones, and I accounted wealth as nothing in comparison with her. Neither did I liken to her any priceless gem, because all gold is but a little sand in her sight, and silver will be accounted as clay before her. I loved her more than health and beauty, and I chose to have her rather than light, because her radiance never ceases. All good things came to me along with her, and in her hands uncounted wealth. I rejoiced in them all, because wisdom leads them; but I did not know that she was their mother.

I learned without guile and I impart without grudging; I do not hide her wealth, for it is an unfailing treasure for mortals; those who get it obtain friendship with God, commended for the gifts that come from instruction. May God grant me to speak with

judgement, and to have thoughts worthy of what I have received;
for he is the guide even of wisdom and the corrector of the wise.

This is the word of the Lord. *Wisdom 7. 7-15*

Responsorial Psalm

R O Lord, make good your purpose for me;
[for your love endures for ever].

I will give thanks to you, O Lord, with my whole heart;
before the gods I will sing your praise.
I will bow down towards your holy temple and praise your name,
because of your love and faithfulness. **R**

For you have glorified your name
and your word above all things.
When I called, you answered me;
you increased my strength within me. **R**

Though you, O Lord are high, you care for the lowly;
you perceive the haughty from afar.
Though I walk in the midst of trouble, you keep me safe;
you stretch forth your hand against the fury of my enemies,
for your right hand shall save me. **R** *Psalm 138*

A reading from the Letter of Paul to the Romans.

We know that the whole creation has been groaning in labour
pains until now; and not only the creation, but we ourselves, who
have the first fruits of the Spirit, groan inwardly while we wait for
adoption, the redemption of our bodies. For in hope we were
saved. Now hope that is seen is not hope. For who hopes for what
is seen? But if we hope for what we do not see, we wait
for it with patience. Likewise the Spirit helps us in our weakness;
for we do not know how to pray as we ought, but that very Spirit
intercedes with sighs too deep for words. And God, who searches the heart, knows what is the mind of the Spirit, because the
Spirit intercedes for the saints according to the will of God.

This is the word of the Lord. *Romans 8. 22-27*

Hear the gospel of our Lord Jesus Christ according to John.

Jesus said to his disciples, "Do not let your hearts be troubled. Believe in God, believe also in me. In my Father's house there are many dwelling places. If it were not so, would I have told you that I go to prepare a place for you? And if I go and prepare a place for you, I will come again and will take you to myself, so that where I am, there you may be also. And you know the way to the place where I am going." Thomas said to him, "Lord, we do not know where you are going. How can we know the way?" Jesus said to him, "I am the way, and the truth, and the life. No one comes to the Father except through me. If you know me, you will know my Father also. From now on you do know him and have seen him."

This is the gospel of the Lord.   *John 14. 1-7*

Post Communion
God of truth,
whose Wisdom set her table
and invited us to eat the bread and drink the wine
  of the kingdom:
help us to lay aside all foolishness
and to live and walk in the way of insight,
that we may come with your servant Teresa
  to the eternal feast of heaven;
through Jesus Christ our Lord.

Nicholas Ridley, Bishop of London
& Hugh Latimer, Bishop of Worcester
16 October – Commemoration
If celebrated as a Lesser Festival, Common of Martyrs, page 464

Born into a wealthy Northumbrian family in about the year 1500, Nicholas Ridley studied at Cambridge, the Sorbonne and in Louvain. He was chaplain to Thomas Cranmer and master of Pembroke Hall in Cambridge before being made Bishop of Rochester in 1547. He had been clearly drawing closer to the Reformers as early as 1535 and, at the accession of King Edward VI, declared himself a Protestant. He assisted Cranmer in preparing the first *Book of Common Prayer* and was made Bishop of London in 1550. On the death of Edward, he supported the claims of Lady Jane Grey and was thus deprived of his See on the accession of Mary Tudor. He was excommunicated and executed in 1555.

Hugh Latimer was a Leicestershire man, also educated at Cambridge but fifteen years older than Nicholas Ridley. Hugh was articulate and yet homely in his style of preaching, which made him very popular in the university, and he received its commission to preach anywhere in England. He became a close adviser of King Henry VIII after the latter's rift with the papacy and was appointed Bishop of Worcester in 1535. He lost the king's favour in 1540, over his refusal to sign Henry's 'Six Articles', designed to prevent the spread of Reformation doctrines, and resigned his See. He returned to favour on the accession of Edward VI but was imprisoned in the Tower of London when Queen Mary ascended the throne in 1553. He refused to recant any of his avowedly reformist views and was burnt at the stake, together with Nicholas Ridley, on this day in 1555.

Ignatius, Bishop of Antioch
17 October – Lesser Festival – Martyr – Red

Ignatius was born probably in Syria in about the year 35AD and was either the second or third bishop of Antioch, the third largest city in the Roman Empire. Nothing is known of his life bar his final journey under armed escort to Rome, and where he was martyred in about the year 107. In the course of this journey, he met Polycarp in Smyrna, and wrote a number of letters to various Christian congregations which are among the greatest treasures of the primitive Church. In the face of persecution he appealed to his fellow Christians to maintain unity with their bishop at all costs. His letters reveal his passionate commitment to Christ, and how he longed 'to imitate the passion of my God'.

Collect

Feed us, O Lord, with the living bread
and make us drink deep of the cup of salvation
that, following the teaching of your bishop Ignatius
and rejoicing in the faith
  with which he embraced a martyr's death,
we may be nourished for that eternal life
  for which he longed;
through Jesus Christ your Son our Lord,
who is alive and reigns with you,
in the unity of the Holy Spirit,
one God, now and for ever.

A reading from the prophecy of Isaiah.

Waters shall break forth in the wilderness, and streams in the desert; the burning sand shall become a pool, and the thirsty ground springs of water; the haunt of jackals shall become a swamp, the grass shall become reeds and rushes. A highway shall be there, and it shall be called the Holy Way; the unclean shall not travel on it, but it shall be for God's people; no traveller, not even fools, shall go astray. No lion shall be there, nor shall any ravenous beast come up on it; they shall not be found there, but the redeemed shall walk there. And the ransomed of the Lord shall return, and come to Zion with singing; everlasting joy shall be upon their heads; they shall obtain joy and gladness, and sorrow and sighing shall flee away.

This is the word of the Lord.   *Isaiah 35. 6-10*

Responsorial Psalm

**R The ransomed of the Lord shall return
    [and come to Zion with singing].**

In you, O Lord, have I taken refuge;
let me never be put to shame;
deliver me in your righteousness.
Incline your ear to me; make haste to deliver me. **R**

Be my strong rock, a castle to keep me safe,
for you are my crag and my stronghold;
for the sake of your name, lead me and guide me. **R**

Take me out of the net that they have secretly set for me,
for you are my tower of strength.
Into your hands I commend my spirit,
for you have redeemed me, O Lord, O God of truth. **R**

I will rejoice and be glad because of your mercy;
for you have seen my affliction, you know my distress.
You have not shut me up in the power of the enemy;
you have set my feet in an open place. **R**   *From Psalm 31*

A reading from the Letter of Paul to the Philippians.

Whatever gains I had, these I have come to regard as loss because
of Christ. More than that, I regard everything as loss because of
the surpassing value of knowing Christ Jesus my Lord. For his
sake I have suffered the loss of all things, and I regard them as rubbish, in order that I may gain Christ and be found in him, not having a righteousness of my own that comes from the law, but one
that comes through faith in Christ, the righteousness from God
based on faith. I want to know Christ and the power of his resurrection and the sharing of his sufferings by becoming like him in
his death, if somehow I may attain the resurrection from the dead.

  Not that I have already obtained this or have already reached the
goal; but I press on to make it my own, because Christ Jesus has
made me his own.

This is the word of the Lord.   *Philippians 3. 7-12*

Hear the gospel of our Lord Jesus Christ according to John.

The Jews disputed among themselves, saying, "How can this man
give us his flesh to eat?" So Jesus said to them, "Very truly, I tell
you, unless you eat the flesh of the Son of Man and drink his
blood, you have no life in you. Those who eat my flesh and drink
my blood have eternal life, and I will raise them up on the last day;
for my flesh is true food and my blood is true drink. Those who
eat my flesh and drink my blood abide in me, and I in them. Just
as the living Father sent me, and I live because of the Father, so
whoever eats me will live because of me. This is the bread that
came down from heaven, not like that which your ancestors ate,
and they died. But the one who eats this bread will live forever."

This is the gospel of the Lord.   *John 6. 52-58*

Post Communion
Post Communion
God our Redeemer,
whose Church was strengthened
  by the blood of your martyr Ignatius:
so bind us, in life and death, to Christ's sacrifice
that our lives, broken and offered with his,
may carry his death and proclaim his resurrection in the world;
through Jesus Christ our Lord.

Luke the Evangelist
18 October – Festival – Evangelist – Red

Luke was a dear friend of the apostle Paul, and is mentioned by
him three times in his Letters. Paul describes him as 'the belovèd
physician' and, in his second Letter to Timothy, as his only companion in prison. He is believed to be the author of two books of
the New Testament, firstly the gospel which stands in his name
and also the *Acts of the Apostles*. Luke's narrative of the life of
Christ has a pictorial quality and shows the sequential pattern
from the nativity through to the death and resurrection. The
developed sense of theology that comes over in Paul's writings is
virtually unknown in those of Luke but, as a Gentile, Luke makes
clear that the good news of salvation is for all, regardless of gen-
der, social position or nationality. Traditionally, Luke wrote his
gospel in Greece and died in Boeotia at the age of eighty-four.

Collect
Almighty God,
you called Luke the physician,
whose praise is in the gospel,
to be an evangelist and physician of the soul:
by the grace of the Spirit
and through the wholesome medicine of the gospel,
give your Church the same love and power to heal;
through Jesus Christ your Son our Lord,
who is alive and reigns with you,
in the unity of the Holy Spirit,
one God, now and for ever.

A reading from the prophecy of Isaiah.

Strengthen the weak hands, and make firm the feeble knees. Say to those who are of a fearful heart, "Be strong, do not fear! Here is your God. He will come with vengeance, with terrible recompense. He will come and save you."

Then the eyes of the blind shall be opened, and the ears of the deaf unstopped; then the lame shall leap like a deer, and the tongue of the speechless sing for joy; waters shall break forth in the wilderness, and streams in the desert.

This is the word of the Lord.   *Isaiah 35. 3-6*

Or:

A reading from the Acts of the Apostles.

Paul and Timothy went through the region of Phrygia and Galatia, having been forbidden by the Holy Spirit to speak the word in Asia. When they had come opposite Mysia, they attempted to go into Bithynia, but the Spirit of Jesus did not allow them; so, passing by Mysia, they went down to Troas. During the night Paul had a vision: there stood a man of Macedonia pleading with him and saying, "Come over to Macedonia and help us." When he had seen the vision, we immediately tried to cross over to Macedonia, being convinced that God had called us to proclaim the good news to them.

We set sail from Troas and took a straight course to Samothrace, the following day to Neapolis, and from there to Philippi, which is a leading city of the district of Macedonia and a Roman colony.

This is the word of the Lord.   *Acts 16. 6-12a*

Responsorial Psalm

R   Sing to the Lord with thanksgiving;
[make music to our God upon the harp].

How good it is to sing praises to our God!
how pleasant it is to honour him with praise!
The Lord rebuilds Jerusalem;
he gathers the exiles of Israel. **R**

He heals the brokenhearted
and binds up their wounds.
He counts the number of the stars
and calls them all by their names. **R**

Great is our Lord and mighty in power;
there is no limit to his wisdom.
The Lord lifts up the lowly,
but casts the wicked to the ground. **R**   *From Psalm 147*

A reading from the Second Letter of Paul to Timothy.

As for you, always be sober, endure suffering, do the work of an
evangelist, carry out your ministry fully. As for me, I am already
being poured out as a libation, and the time of my departure has
come. I have fought the good fight, I have finished the race, I have
kept the faith. From now on there is reserved for me the crown of
righteousness, which the Lord, the righteous judge, will give me
on that day, and not only to me but also to all who have longed for
his appearing.

 Do your best to come to me soon, for Demas, in love with this present world, has deserted me and gone to Thessalonica; Crescens
has gone to Galatia, Titus to Dalmatia. Only Luke is with me. Get
Mark and bring him with you, for he is useful in my ministry. I
have sent Tychicus to Ephesus. When you come, bring the cloak
that I left with Carpus at Troas, also the books, and above all the
parchments. Alexander the coppersmith did me great harm; the
Lord will pay him back for his deeds. You also must beware of
him, for he strongly opposed our message.

 At my first defence no one came to my support, but all deserted
me. May it not be counted against them! But the Lord stood by
me and gave me strength, so that through me the message might
be fully proclaimed and all the Gentiles might hear it. So I was rescued from the lion's mouth.

This is the word of the Lord.   *2 Timothy 4. 5-17*

Hear the gospel of our Lord Jesus Christ according to Luke.

The Lord appointed seventy others and sent them on ahead of
him in pairs to every town and place where he himself intended

to go. He said to them, "The harvest is plentiful, but the labourers are few; therefore ask the Lord of the harvest to send out labourers into his harvest. Go on your way. See, I am sending you out like lambs into the midst of wolves. Carry no purse, no bag, no sandals; and greet no one on the road.

"Whatever house you enter, first say, 'Peace to this house!' And if anyone is there who shares in peace, your peace will rest on that person; but if not, it will return to you. Remain in the same house, eating and drinking whatever they provide, for the labourer deserves to be paid. Do not move about from house to house. Whenever you enter a town and its people welcome you, eat what is set before you; cure the sick who are there, and say to them, 'The kingdom of God has come near to you.'"

This is the gospel of the Lord. *Luke 10. 1-9*

Post Communion
Almighty God,
who on the day of Pentecost
sent your Holy Spirit to the disciples
with the wind from heaven and in tongues of flame,
filling them with joy and boldness to preach the gospel:
by the power of the same Spirit
strengthen us to witness to your truth
and to draw everyone to the fire of your love;
through Jesus Christ our Lord.

Henry Martyn, Translator of the Scriptures
19 October – Lesser Festival – Missionary – White

Born in Truro in 1781, Henry Martyn went up to Cambridge at the age of sixteen. He became an avowed evangelical and his friendship with Charles Simeon led to his interest in missionary work. In 1805, he left for Calcutta as a chaplain to the East India Company. The expectation was that he would minister to the British expatriate community, not to the indigenous peoples; in fact, there was a constant fear of insurrection and even the recitation of *Magnificat* at Evensong was forbidden, lest 'putting down the mighty from their seats' should incite the natives. Henry set about learning the local languages and then supervised the translation of the New Testament first into Hindustani and then into Persian and Arabic, as well as preaching and teaching in mission schools. He went to Persia to continue the work but, suffering from tuberculosis, he died in Armenia on this day in 1812.

Collect
Almighty God,
who by your Holy Spirit gave Henry Martyn
a longing to tell the good news of Christ
and skill to translate the scriptures:
by the same Spirit give us grace to offer you our gifts,
wherever you may lead, at whatever the cost;
through Jesus Christ your Son our Lord,
who is alive and reigns with you,
in the unity of the Holy Spirit,
one God, now and for ever.

A reading from the prophecy of Isaiah.

Seek the Lord while he may be found, call upon him while he is near; let the wicked forsake their way, and the unrighteous their thoughts; let them return to the Lord, that he may have mercy on them, and to our God, for he will abundantly pardon.

For my thoughts are not your thoughts, nor are your ways my ways, says the Lord. For as the heavens are higher than the earth, so are my ways higher than your ways and my thoughts than your thoughts. For as the rain and the snow come down from heaven, and do not return there until they have watered the earth, making it bring forth and sprout, giving seed to the sower and bread to the eater, so shall my word be that goes out from my mouth; it shall not return to me empty, but it shall accomplish that which I purpose, and succeed in the thing for which I sent it.

This is the word of the Lord.   *Isaiah 55. 6-11*

R [Who is this, the King of glory?]
The Lord of hosts, he is the King of glory!

The earth is the Lord's and all that is in it,
the world and all who dwell therein.
For it is he who founded it upon the seas
and made it firm upon the rivers of the deep. **R**

Who can ascend the hill of the Lord?
and who can stand in his holy place?
Those who have clean hands and a pure heart,
who have not pledged themselves to falsehood,
nor sworn by what is a fraud. **R**

They shall receive a blessing from the Lord
and a just reward from the God of their salvation.
Such is the generation of those who seek him,
of those who seek your face, O God of Jacob. **R**

Lift up your heads, O gates;
lift them high, O everlasting doors;
and the King of glory shall come in. **R**   *Psalm 24*

A reading from the Letter of Paul to the Philippians.

My beloved, just as you have always obeyed me, not only in my presence, but much more now in my absence, work out your own salvation with fear and trembling; for it is God who is at work in you, enabling you both to will and to work for his good pleasure. Do all things without murmuring and arguing, so that you may be blameless and innocent, children of God without blemish in the midst of a crooked and perverse generation, in which you shine like stars in the world. It is by your holding fast to the word of life that I can boast on the day of Christ that I did not run in vain or labour in vain. But even if I am being poured out as a libation over the sacrifice and the offering of your faith, I am glad and rejoice with all of you – and in the same way you also must be glad and rejoice with me.

This is the word of the Lord.   *Philippians 2. 12-18*

Hear the gospel of our Lord Jesus Christ according to Mark.

Jesus said to his disciples, "Go into all the world and proclaim the good news to the whole creation. The one who believes and is baptised will be saved; but the one who does not believe will be condemned. And these signs will accompany those who believe: by using my name they will cast out demons; they will speak in new tongues; they will pick up snakes in their hands, and if they drink any deadly thing, it will not hurt them; they will lay their hands on the sick, and they will recover."

So then the Lord Jesus, after he had spoken to them, was taken up into heaven and sat down at the right hand of God. And they went out and proclaimed the good news everywhere, while the Lord worked with them and confirmed the message by the signs that accompanied it.

This is the gospel of the Lord.   *Mark 16. 15-20*

Post Communion
Holy Father,
who gathered us here around the table of your Son
to share this meal with the whole household of God:
in that new world where you reveal
  the fullness of your peace,
gather people of every race and language
to share with your servant Henry Martyn and all your saints
in the eternal banquet of Jesus Christ our Lord.

Frideswide, Abbess of Oxford
19 October – Commemoration
If celebrated as a Lesser Festival, Common of Religious, page 494

Born in about the year 680, Frideswide was the daughter of a Mercian king who built and endowed a double monastery of which she became the first abbess. She was buried in her monastery, which became the nucleus of the nascent town of Oxford. Her cult was strengthened by her being formally adopted as the patron of Oxford University in the early fifteenth century. However, in the sixteenth century, Cardinal Wolsey suppressed Frideswide's monastery to provide revenues for his Cardinal College (now Christ Church), built on the same site. More recently, part of the shrine has been reconstructed from remains discovered in a well at Christ Church, a reminder of the abbess around whose monastery grew the city and university of Oxford.

Crispin & Crispinian, Martyrs at Rome
25 October – Commemoration
If celebrated as a Lesser Festival, Common of Martyrs, page 464

Crispin and Crispinian were shoemakers and lived in the third century. They are reputed to have preached the Christian faith in Gaul whilst exercising their trade and so, like St Paul earning his living as a tent-maker, were no drain on the Christian community. They were put to death for their faith at the beginning of the Diocletian persecution and died in about the year 287 in Rome.

Alfred the Great
26 October – Lesser Festival – of any Saint – White

Born in the year 849, Alfred was the king of the West Saxons who effectively brought to an end the constant threat of Danish dominion in the British Isles. He came to the throne at the age of twenty-two and, after establishing peace, set about bringing stability to both church and state. He gave half of his income to founding religious houses which themselves acted as Christian centres for education, care of the sick and poor and respite for travellers. He was a daily attender at mass and himself translated many works into the vernacular. He evolved a legal code based on common sense and Christian mercy. His whole life was marked by the compassion of Christ. He died on this day in the year 899

Collect
God, our Maker and Redeemer,
we pray you of your great mercy
and by the power of your holy cross

to guide us by your will and to shield us from our foes:
that, after the example of your servant Alfred,
we may inwardly love you above all things;
through Jesus Christ your Son our Lord,
who is alive and reigns with you,
in the unity of the Holy Spirit,
one God, now and for ever.

A reading from the Second Book of Samuel.

Now these are the last words of David: The oracle of David, son of
Jesse, the oracle of the man whom God exalted, the anointed of the
God of Jacob, the favourite of the Strong One of Israel: The spirit
of the Lord speaks through me, his word is upon my tongue. The
God of Israel has spoken, the Rock of Israel has said to me: One
who rules over people justly, ruling in the fear of God, is like the
light of morning, like the sun rising on a cloudless morning,
gleaming from the rain on the grassy land. Is not my house like
this with God? For he has made with me an everlasting covenant,
ordered in all things and secure. Will he not cause to prosper all
my help and my desire?

This is the word of the Lord.   *2 Samuel 23. 1-5*

Responsorial Psalm

R   Be exalted, O Lord, in your might;
      [we will sing and praise your power].

The king rejoices in your strength, O Lord;
how greatly he exults in your victory!
You have given him his heart's desire;
you have not denied him the request of his lips. **R**

For you meet him with blessings of prosperity,
and set a crown of fine gold upon his head.
He asked you for life and you gave it to him;
length of days, for ever and ever. **R**

His honour is great, because of your victory;
splendour and majesty have you bestowed upon him.
For you will give him everlasting felicity
and will make him glad with the joy of your presence. **R**

For the king puts his trust in the Lord;
because of the loving-kindness of the Most High,
he will not fall. **R** *From Psalm 21*

A reading from the First Letter of John.

Do not love the world or the things in the world. The love of the
Father is not in those who love the world; for all that is in the
world – the desire of the flesh, the desire of the eyes, the pride in
riches – comes not from the Father but from the world. And the
world and its desire are passing away, but those who do the will
of God live forever.

This is the word of the Lord. *1 John 2. 15-17*

Hear the gospel of our Lord Jesus Christ according to John.

Pilate summoned Jesus and asked him, "Are you the King of the
Jews?" Jesus answered, "Do you ask this on your own, or did others tell you about me?" Pilate replied, "I am not a Jew, am I? Your
own nation and the chief priests have handed you over to me.
What have you done?" Jesus answered, "My kingdom is not from
this world. If my kingdom were from this world, my followers
would be fighting to keep me from being handed over to the Jews.
But as it is, my kingdom is not from here."

Pilate asked him, "So you are a king?" Jesus answered, "You say
that I am a king. For this I was born, and for this I came into the
world, to testify to the truth. Everyone who belongs to the truth
listens to my voice." Pilate asked him, "What is truth?"

This is the gospel of the Lord. *John 18. 33-37*

Post Communion
God, the source of all holiness
  and giver of all good things:
may we who have shared at this table
  as strangers and pilgrims here on earth
be welcomed with all your saints
  to the heavenly feast on the day of your kingdom;
through Jesus Christ our Lord.

Cedd, Abbot of Lastingham, Bishop of the East Saxons
26 October – *Commemoration*
If celebrated as a Lesser Festival, Common of Missionaries, page 503

Cedd was born in Northumbria in the late sixth century and joined the monastery of Lindisfarne where he served many years. When King Peada of the Middle Angles became a Christian, Cedd was sent with three other priests to preach the gospel in this new territory. Some time later, King Sigebert of the East Saxons was converted and Cedd, now an experienced missionary, went with another priest to Essex. After travelling through the region they reported back to Lindisfarne where Cedd was consecrated bishop for the East Saxons. He returned to Essex to continue his work, building churches, two monasteries, and ordaining deacons and priests. While on a visit to Northumbria he founded his third monastery, at Lastingham, where he died of fever in 664 after attending the Synod of Whitby.

Simon & Jude, Apostles
28 October – *Festival* – *Apostles* – *Red*

Simon and Jude were named among the twelve apostles in the gospels of Matthew, Mark and Luke. Simon is called 'the Zealot', probably because he belonged to a nationalist resistance movement opposing the Roman occupation forces. There is no indication in the gospels whether Simon moved from the Zealot party to be a follower of Christ or, on the other hand, if after the resurrection he became a supporter of that group, seeing it as a response to God's call to proclaim the kingdom.

Luke describes Jude as the son of James, while the Letter of Jude has him as the brother of James, neither of which negates the other. It seems he is the same person as Thaddæus, which may have been a last name. Owing to the similarity of his name to that of Judas Iscariot, Jude was rarely invoked in prayer and it seems likely that because of this, interceding through him was seen as a final resort when all else failed. He became known, therefore, as the patron saint of lost causes.

The two apostles are joined together on 28 October because a church, which had recently acquired their relics, was dedicated to their memory in Rome on this day in the seventh century.

Collect
Almighty God,
who built your Church upon the foundation
  of the apostles and prophets,
with Jesus Christ himself as the chief corner-stone:
so join us together in unity of spirit by their doctrine,
that we may be made a holy temple acceptable to you;
through Jesus Christ your Son our Lord,
who is alive and reigns with you,
in the unity of the Holy Spirit,
one God, now and for ever.

A reading from the prophecy of Isaiah.

Hear the word of the Lord, you scoffers who rule this people in Jerusalem. Because you have said, "We have made a covenant with death, and with Sheol we have an agreement; when the overwhelming scourge passes through it will not come to us; for we have made lies our refuge, and in falsehood we have taken shelter"; therefore thus says the Lord God, See, I am laying in Zion a foundation stone, a tested stone, a precious cornerstone, a sure foundation: "One who trusts will not panic."

This is the word of the Lord.   *Isaiah 28. 14-16*

Responsorial Psalm

R I am laying in Zion a foundation stone, says God,
   [a precious cornerstone, a sure foundation].

O Lord, your word is everlasting;
it stands firm in the heavens.
Your faithfulness remains from one generation to another;
you established the earth and it abides. **R**

By your decree these continue to this day,
for all things are your servants.
If my delight had not been in your law,
I should have perished in my affliction. **R**

I will never forget your commandments,
because by them you give me life.
I am yours; O that you would save me!
for I study your commandments. **R**

Though the wicked lie in wait for me to destroy me,
I will apply my mind to your decrees.
I see that all things come to an end,
but your commandment has no bounds. **R**   *From Psalm 119*

A reading from the Letter of Paul to the Ephesians.

You are no longer strangers and aliens, but you are citizens with
the saints and also members of the household of God, built upon
the foundation of the apostles and prophets, with Christ Jesus
himself as the cornerstone. In him the whole structure is joined
together and grows into a holy temple in the Lord; in whom you
also are built together spiritually into a dwelling place for God.

This is the word of the Lord.   *Ephesians 2. 19-22*

Hear the gospel of our Lord Jesus Christ according to John.

Jesus said to his disciples, "I am giving you these commands so
that you may love one another. If the world hates you, be aware
that it hated me before it hated you. If you belonged to the world,
the world would love you as its own. Because you do not belong
to the world, but I have chosen you out of the world – therefore
the world hates you.

"Remember the word that I said to you, 'Servants are not greater
than their master.' If they persecuted me, they will persecute you;
if they kept my word, they will keep yours also. But they will do
all these things to you on account of my name, because they do
not know him who sent me. If I had not come and spoken to
them, they would not have sin; but now they have no excuse for
their sin. Whoever hates me hates my Father also. If I had not
done among them the works that no one else did, they would not
have sin. But now they have seen and hated both me and my
Father. It was to fulfil the word that is written in their law, 'They
hated me without a cause.'

"When the Advocate comes, whom I will send to you from the

Father, the Spirit of truth who comes from the Father, he will testify on my behalf. You also are to testify because you have been with me from the beginning."

This is the gospel of the Lord.   *John 15. 17-27*

Post Communion
Almighty God,
who on the day of Pentecost
sent your Holy Spirit to the apostles
with the wind from heaven and in tongues of flame,
filling them with joy and boldness to preach the gospel:
by the power of the same Spirit
strengthen us to witness to your truth
and to draw everyone to the fire of your love;
through Jesus Christ our Lord.

James Hannington,
Bishop of Eastern Equatorial Africa
29 October – Lesser Festival – Martyr – Red

James Hannington was born in 1847 of a Congregationalist family but he became an Anglican before going up to Oxford. He was ordained and, after serving a curacy for five years, went with the Church Missionary Society to Uganda. He was consecrated bishop for that part of Africa in 1884 and a year later began a safari inland from Mombasa, together with other European and indigenous Christians. The King of the Buganda, Mwanga, who despised Christians because they refused to condone his moral turpitude, seized the whole party, tortured them for several days and then had them butchered to death on this day in 1885.

Collect
Most merciful God,
who strengthened your Church by the steadfast courage
  of your martyr James Hannington:
grant that we also,
thankfully remembering his victory of faith,
may overcome what is evil
and glorify your holy name;

through Jesus Christ your Son our Lord,
who is alive and reigns with you,
in the unity of the Holy Spirit,
one God, now and for ever.

A reading from the prophecy of Isaiah.

Thus says the Lord, he who created you, O Jacob, he who formed
you, O Israel: Do not fear, for I have redeemed you; I have called
you by name, you are mine. When you pass through the waters,
I will be with you; and through the rivers, they shall not over-
whelm you; when you walk through fire you shall not be burned,
and the flame shall not consume you. For I am the Lord your God,
the Holy One of Israel, your Saviour. I give Egypt as your ransom,
Ethiopia and Seba in exchange for you. Because you are precious
in my sight, and honoured, and I love you, I give people in return
for you, nations in exchange for your life.

Do not fear, for I am with you; I will bring your offspring from
the east, and from the west I will gather you; I will say to the north,
"Give them up," and to the south, "Do not withhold; bring my
sons from far away and my daughters from the end of the earth –
everyone who is called by my name, whom I created for my glory,
whom I formed and made."

This is the word of the Lord.   *Isaiah 43. 1-7*

Responsorial Psalm

R **Do not fear, for I am with you, says God,
    [with everyone who is called by my name].**

"If the Lord had not been on our side,"
let Israel now say;
"If the Lord had not been on our side,
when enemies rose up against us, **R**

"Then would they have swallowed us up alive
in their fierce anger towards us;
Then would the waters have overwhelmed us
and the torrent gone over us. **R**

"Then would the raging waters
have gone right over us.
Blessèd be the Lord!
he has not given us over to be a prey for their teeth. **R**

"We have escaped like a bird from the snare of the fowler;
the snare is broken and we have escaped.
Our help is in the name of the Lord,
the maker of heaven and earth." **R**   *Psalm 124*

A reading from the First Letter of Peter.

Even if you do suffer for doing what is right, you are blessed. Do
not fear what they fear, and do not be intimidated, but in your
hearts sanctify Christ as Lord. Always be ready to make your
defence to anyone who demands from you an accounting for the
hope that is in you; yet do it with gentleness and reverence. Keep
your conscience clear, so that, when you are maligned, those who
abuse you for your good conduct in Christ may be put to shame.
For it is better to suffer for doing good, if suffering should be God's
will, than to suffer for doing evil. For Christ also suffered for sins
once for all, the righteous for the unrighteous, in order to bring
you to God. He was put to death in the flesh, but made alive in
the spirit, and has gone into heaven and is at the right hand of
God, with angels, authorities, and powers made subject to him.

This is the word of the Lord.   *1 Peter 3. 14-18, 22*

Hear the gospel of our Lord Jesus Christ according to Matthew.

Jesus said, "Do not fear those who kill the body but cannot kill the
soul; rather fear him who can destroy both soul and body in hell.
Are not two sparrows sold for a penny? Yet not one of them will
fall to the ground apart from your Father. And even the hairs of
your head are all counted. So do not be afraid; you are of more
value than many sparrows. Everyone therefore who acknowledges me before others, I also will acknowledge before my Father
in heaven; but whoever denies me before others, I also will deny
before my Father in heaven.

"Do not think that I have come to bring peace to the earth; I have
not come to bring peace, but a sword. For I have come to set a man

against his father, and a daughter against her mother, and a daughter-in-law against her mother-in-law; and one's foes will be members of one's own household. Whoever loves father or mother more than me is not worthy of me; and whoever loves son or daughter more than me is not worthy of me; and whoever does not take up the cross and follow me is not worthy of me. Those who find their life will lose it, and those who lose their life for my sake will find it."

This is the gospel of the Lord.   *Matthew 10. 28-39*

Post Communion
God our Redeemer,
whose Church was strengthened
 by the blood of your martyr James Hannington:
so bind us, in life and death, to Christ's sacrifice
that our lives, broken and offered with his,
may carry his death and proclaim his resurrection in the world;
through Jesus Christ our Lord.

Martin Luther, Reformer

31 October – Commemoration
If celebrated as a Lesser Festival, Common of Pastors, page 483

Martin Luther was born in 1483 at Eisleben in Saxony and educated at the cathedral school in Magdeburg and the university in Erfurt. He joined an order of Augustinian hermits there and was ordained priest in 1507, becoming a lecturer in the university at Wittenberg. He became vicar of his Order in 1515, having charge of a dozen monasteries. His Christian faith began to take on a new shape, with his increasing dissatisfaction with the worship and order of the Church. He became convinced that the gospels taught that humanity is saved by faith and not by works, finding support in the writings of St Augustine of Hippo. He refuted the teaching of the Letter of James, calling it 'an epistle of straw'. Martin sought to debate the whole matter by posting ninety-five theses or propositions on the door of the Castle Church in Wittenberg on this day in the year 1517. The hierarchy chose to see it as a direct attack on the Church, which forced Martin into open rebellion. The Protestant Reformation spread throughout Germany and then Europe, many seeing it as liberation from a Church that held them in fear rather than love. Martin Luther died in 1546, having effected a renaissance in the Church, both Protestant and Catholic.

NOVEMBER

All Saints' Day
1 November – Principal Feast – Gold or White

From its earliest days, the Church has recognised as its foundation stones those heroes of the faith whose lives have excited others to holiness and have assumed a communion with the Church on earth and the Church in heaven.

Celebrating the feast of All Saints began in the fourth century. At first, it was observed on the Sunday after the feast of Pentecost; this was to link the disciples who received the gift of the Holy Spirit at Pentecost, the foundation of the church, with those who were martyrs, giving their lives as witnesses for the faith. In the eighth century, a pope dedicated a chapel to All Saints in St Peter's at Rome on 1 November. Within a century, this day was observed in England and Ireland as All Saints' Day.

Collect
Almighty God,
you have knit together your elect
in one communion and fellowship
  in the mystical body of your Son Christ our Lord:
grant us grace so to follow your blessèd saints
in all virtuous and godly living
that we may come to those inexpressible joys
that you have prepared for those who truly love you;
through Jesus Christ your Son our Lord,
who is alive and reigns with you,
in the unity of the Holy Spirit,
one God, now and for ever.

Year A	*Year B*	*Year C*
Revelation 7. 9-17	Wisdom 3. 1-9 *or* Isaiah 25. 6-9	Daniel 7. 1-3, 15-18
Psalm 34. 1-10	Psalm 24. 1-6	Psalm 149
1 John 3. 1-3	Revelation 21. 1-6*a*	Ephesians 1. 11-23
Matthew 5. 1-12	John 11. 32-44	Luke 6. 20-31

Or on 1 November, if the material above is used on the Sunday:
Isaiah 56. 3-8 *or* 2 Esdras 2. 42-48
Psalm 33. 1-5
Hebrews 12. 18-24
Matthew 5. 1-12

A reading from the prophecy of Isaiah.

On this mountain the Lord of hosts will make for all peoples a feast of rich food, a feast of well-aged wines, of rich food filled with marrow, of well-aged wines strained clear. And he will destroy on this mountain the shroud that is cast over all peoples, the sheet that is spread over all nations; he will swallow up death forever. Then the Lord God will wipe away the tears from all faces, and the disgrace of his people he will take away from all the earth, for the Lord has spoken. It will be said on that day, Lo, this is our God; we have waited for him, so that he might save us. This is the Lord for whom we have waited; let us be glad and rejoice in his salvation.

This is the word of the Lord.   *Isaiah 25. 6-9*

A reading from the prophecy of Isaiah.

Do not let the foreigner joined to the Lord say, "The Lord will surely separate me from his people"; and do not let the eunuch say, "I am just a dry tree." For thus says the Lord: To the eunuchs who keep my sabbaths, who choose the things that please me and hold fast my covenant, I will give, in my house and within my walls, a monument and a name better than sons and daughters; I will give them an everlasting name that shall not be cut off. And the foreigners who join themselves to the Lord, to minister to him, to love the name of the Lord, and to be his servants, all who keep the sabbath, and do not profane it, and hold fast my covenant – these I will bring to my holy mountain, and make them joyful in my house of prayer; their burnt offerings and their sacrifices will be accepted on my altar; for my house shall be called a house of prayer for all peoples. Thus says the Lord God, who gathers the outcasts of Israel, I will gather others to them besides those already gathered.

This is the word of the Lord.   *Isaiah 56. 3-8*

A reading from the prophecy of Daniel.

In the first year of King Belshazzar of Babylon, Daniel had a dream and visions of his head as he lay in bed. Then he wrote down the dream: I, Daniel, saw in my vision by night the four winds of heaven stirring up the great sea, and four great beasts came up out of the sea, different from one another.

As for me, Daniel, my spirit was troubled within me, and the visions of my head terrified me. I approached one of the attendants to ask him the truth concerning all this. So he said that he would disclose to me the interpretation of the matter: "As for these four great beasts, four kings shall arise out of the earth. But the holy ones of the Most High shall receive the kingdom and possess the kingdom forever – forever and ever."

This is the word of the Lord.   *Daniel 7. 1-3, 15-18*

A reading from the book of Wisdom.

The souls of the righteous are in the hand of God, and no torment will ever touch them. In the eyes of the foolish they seemed to have died, and their departure was thought to be a disaster, and their going from us to be their destruction; but they are at peace. For though in the sight of others they were punished, their hope is full of immortality. Having been disciplined a little, they will receive great good, because God tested them and found them worthy of himself; like gold in the furnace he tried them, and like a sacrificial burnt offering he accepted them. In the time of their visitation they will shine forth, and will run like sparks through the stubble. They will govern nations and rule over peoples, and the Lord will reign over them forever. Those who trust in him will understand truth, and the faithful will abide with him in love, because grace and mercy are upon his holy ones, and he watches over his elect.

This is the word of the Lord.   *Wisdom 3. 1-9*

A reading from the Second Book of Esdras.

I, Ezra, saw on Mount Zion a great multitude that I could not number, and they all were praising the Lord with songs. In their midst was a young man of great stature, taller than any of the others, and on the head of each of them he placed a crown, but he was more exalted than they. And I was held spellbound. Then I asked an angel, "Who are these, my lord?" He answered and said to me, "These are they who have put off mortal clothing and have put on the immortal, and have confessed the name of God. Now they are being crowned, and receive palms." Then I said to the angel, "Who is that young man who is placing crowns on them and putting palms in their hands?" He answered and said to me, "He is the Son of God, whom they confessed in the world."

So I began to praise those who had stood valiantly for the name of the Lord. Then the angel said to me, "Go, tell my people how great and how many are the wonders of the Lord God that you have seen."

This is the word of the Lord.   *2 Esdras 2. 42-48*

A reading from the Revelation to John.

After this I looked, and there was a great multitude that no one could count, from every nation, from all tribes and peoples and languages, standing before the throne and before the Lamb, robed in white, with palm branches in their hands. They cried out in a loud voice, saying, "Salvation belongs to our God who is seated on the throne, and to the Lamb!" And all the angels stood around the throne and around the elders and the four living creatures, and they fell on their faces before the throne and worshiped God, singing, "Amen! Blessing and glory and wisdom and thanksgiving and honour and power and might be to our God forever and ever! Amen."

Then one of the elders addressed me, saying, "Who are these, robed in white, and where have they come from?" I said to him, "Sir, you are the one that knows." Then he said to me, "These are they who have come out of the great ordeal; they have washed their robes and made them white in the blood of the Lamb. For this reason they are before the throne of God, and worship him day and night within his temple, and the one who is seated on the throne will shelter them. They will hunger no more, and thirst no more; the sun will not strike them, nor any scorching heat; for the Lamb at the centre of the throne will be their shepherd, and he will guide them to springs of the water of life, and God will wipe away every tear from their eyes."

This is the word of the Lord.   *Revelation 7. 9-17*

Responsorial Psalm

**R   Those who trust in God will understand truth
      [and the faithful will abide in love].**

The earth is the Lord's and all that is in it,
the world and all who dwell therein.
For it is he who founded it upon the seas
and made it firm upon the rivers of the deep. **R**

Who can ascend the hill of the Lord?
and who can stand in his holy place?
Those who have clean hands and a pure heart,
who have not pledged themselves to falsehood,
nor sworn by what is a fraud. **R**

They shall receive a blessing from the Lord
and a just reward from the God of their salvation.
Such is the generation of those who seek him,
of those who seek your face, O God of Jacob. **R**   *From Psalm 24*

Responsorial Psalm

**R   Rejoice in the Lord, you righteous;
      [it is good for the just to sing praises].**

Praise the Lord with the harp;
play to him upon the psaltery and lyre.
Sing for him a new song;
sound a fanfare with all your skill upon the trumpet. **R**

For the word of the Lord is right,
and all his works are sure.
He loves righteousness and justice;
the loving-kindness of the Lord fills the whole earth. **R**

From Ps 33

Responsorial Psalm

**R   Fear the Lord, you that are his saints,
      [for those who fear him lack nothing].**

I will bless the Lord at all times;
his praise shall ever be in my mouth.
I will glory in the Lord;
let the humble hear and rejoice. **R**

Proclaim with me the greatness of the Lord;
let us exalt his name together.
I sought the Lord and he answered me
and delivered me out of all my terror. **R**

Look upon him and be radiant,
and let not your faces be ashamed.
I called in my affliction and the Lord heard me
and saved me from all my troubles. **R**

Taste and see that the Lord is good;
happy are they who trust in him!
Come, children, and listen to me;
I will teach you the fear of the Lord. **R**   *From Psalm 34*

Responsorial Psalm

**R   May the Father of glory give us the Spirit of Wisdom,
[may we live for the praise of God's glory].**

Sing to the Lord a new song;
sing his praise in the congregation of the faithful.
Let Israel rejoice in his maker;
let the children of Zion be joyful in their king. **R**

Let them praise his name in the dance;
let them sing praise to him with timbrel and harp.
For the Lord takes pleasure in his people
and adorns the poor with victory. **R**

Let the faithful rejoice in triumph;
let them be joyful on their beds.
Let the praises of God be in their throat
and a two-edged sword in their hand. **R**

To wreak vengeance on the nations
and punishment on the peoples;
To bind their kings in chains
and their nobles with links of iron;
To inflict on them the judgement decreed;
this is glory for all his faithful people. **R**   *Psalm 149*

A reading from the Letter of Paul to the Ephesians.

In Christ we have also obtained an inheritance, having been destined according to the purpose of him who accomplishes all things

according to his counsel and will, so that we, who were the first to set our hope on Christ, might live for the praise of his glory. In him you also, when you had heard the word of truth, the gospel of your salvation, and had believed in him, were marked with the seal of the promised Holy Spirit; this is the pledge of our inheritance toward redemption as God's own people, to the praise of his glory.

I have heard of your faith in the Lord Jesus and your love toward all the saints, and for this reason I do not cease to give thanks for you as I remember you in my prayers. I pray that the God of our Lord Jesus Christ, the Father of glory, may give you a spirit of wisdom and revelation as you come to know him, so that, with the eyes of your heart enlightened, you may know what is the hope to which he has called you, what are the riches of his glorious inheritance among the saints, and what is the immeasurable greatness of his power for us who believe, according to the working of his great power. God put this power to work in Christ when he raised him from the dead and seated him at his right hand in the heavenly places, far above all rule and authority and power and dominion, and above every name that is named, not only in this age but also in the age to come. And he has put all things under his feet and has made him the head over all things for the church, which is his body, the fullness of him who fills all in all.

This is the word of the Lord.   *Ephesians 1. 11-23*

A reading from the Letter to the Hebrews.

You have not come to something that can be touched, a blazing fire, and darkness, and gloom, and a tempest, and the sound of a trumpet, and a voice whose words made the hearers beg that not another word be spoken to them (for they could not endure the order that was given, "If even an animal touches the mountain, it shall be stoned to death." Indeed, so terrifying was the sight that Moses said, "I tremble with fear."). But you have come to Mount Zion and to the city of the living God, the heavenly Jerusalem, and to innumerable angels in festal gathering, and to the assembly of the firstborn who are enrolled in heaven, and to God the judge of all, and to the spirits of the righteous made perfect, and to Jesus, the mediator of a new covenant, and to the sprinkled blood that speaks a better word than the blood of Abel.

This is the word of the Lord.   *Hebrews 12. 18-24*

A reading from the First Letter of John.

See what love the Father has given us, that we should be called children of God; and that is what we are. The reason the world does not know us is that it did not know him. Beloved, we are God's children now; what we will be has not yet been revealed. What we do know is this: when he is revealed, we will be like him, for we will see him as he is. And all who have this hope in him purify themselves, just as he is pure.

This is the word of the Lord. *1 John 3. 1-3*

A reading from the Revelation to John.

Then I saw a new heaven and a new earth; for the first heaven and the first earth had passed away, and the sea was no more. And I saw the holy city, the new Jerusalem, coming down out of heaven from God, prepared as a bride adorned for her husband. And I heard a loud voice from the throne saying, "See, the home of God is among mortals. He will dwell with them as their God; they will be his peoples, and God himself will be with them; he will wipe every tear from their eyes. Death will be no more; mourning and crying and pain will be no more, for the first things have passed away." And the one who was seated on the throne said, "See, I am making all things new." Also he said, "Write this, for these words are trustworthy and true." Then he said to me, "It is done! I am the Alpha and the Omega, the beginning and the end."

This is the word of the Lord. *Revelation 21. 1-6a*

Hear the gospel of our Lord Jesus Christ according to Matthew.

When Jesus saw the crowds, he went up the mountain; and after he sat down, his disciples came to him. Then he began to speak, and taught them, saying: "Blessèd are the poor in spirit, for theirs is the kingdom of heaven. Blessèd are those who mourn, for they will be comforted. Blessèd are the meek, for they will inherit the earth. Blessèd are those who hunger and thirst for righteousness, for they will be filled. Blessèd are the merciful, for they will receive mercy. Blessèd are the pure in heart, for they will see God. Blessèd are the peacemakers, for they will be called children of God. Blessèd are those who are persecuted for righteousness' sake, for theirs is the kingdom of heaven. Blessèd are you when people revile you and persecute you and utter all kinds of evil against you falsely on my account.

"Rejoice and be glad, for your reward is great in heaven, for in the same way they persecuted the prophets who were before you."

This is the gospel of the Lord.   *Matthew 5. 1-12*

Hear the gospel of our Lord Jesus Christ according to Luke.

Jesus looked up at his disciples and said: "Blessèd are you who are poor, for yours is the kingdom of God. Blessèd are you who are hungry now, for you will be filled. Blessèd are you who weep now, for you will laugh. Blessèd are you when people hate you, and when they exclude you, revile you, and defame you on account of the Son of Man. Rejoice in that day and leap for joy, for surely your reward is great in heaven; for that is what their ancestors did to the prophets.

"But woe to you who are rich, for you have received your consolation. Woe to you who are full now, for you will be hungry. Woe to you who are laughing now, for you will mourn and weep. Woe to you when all speak well of you, for that is what their ancestors did to the false prophets.

"But I say to you that listen, Love your enemies, do good to those who hate you, bless those who curse you, pray for those who abuse you. If anyone strikes you on the cheek, offer the other also; and from anyone who takes away your coat do not withhold even your shirt. Give to everyone who begs from you; and if anyone takes away your goods, do not ask for them again. Do to others as you would have them do to you."

This is the gospel of the Lord.   *Luke 6. 20-31*

Hear the gospel of our Lord Jesus Christ according to John.

When Mary came where Jesus was and saw him, she knelt at his feet and said to him, "Lord, if you had been here, my brother would not have died." When Jesus saw her weeping, and the Jews who came with her also weeping, he was greatly disturbed in spirit and deeply moved. He said, "Where have you laid him?" They said to him, "Lord, come and see." Jesus began to weep. So the Jews said, "See how he loved him!" But some of them said, "Could not he who opened the eyes of the blind man have kept this man from dying?"

Then Jesus, again greatly disturbed, came to the tomb. It was a cave, and a stone was lying against it. Jesus said, "Take away the stone." Martha, the sister of the dead man, said to him, "Lord, already there is a stench because he has been dead four days." Jesus said to her, "Did I not tell you that if you believed, you would see the glory of God?" So they took away the stone. And Jesus looked upward and said, "Father, I thank you for having heard me. I knew that you always hear me, but I have said this for the sake of the crowd standing here, so that they may believe that you sent me." When he had said this, he cried with a loud voice, "Lazarus, come out!" The dead man came out, his hands and feet bound with strips of cloth, and his face wrapped in a cloth. Jesus said to them, "Unbind him, and let him go."

This is the gospel of the Lord.   *John 11. 32-44*

Post Communion
God, the source of all holiness
  and giver of all good things:
may we who have shared at this table
  as strangers and pilgrims here on earth
be welcomed with all your saints
  to the heavenly feast on the day of your kingdom;
through Jesus Christ our Lord.

Commemoration of the Faithful Departed
All Souls' Day
2 November – Lesser Festival – Purple, or Black, or White

'The believer's pilgrimage of faith is lived out with the mutual support of all the people of God. In Christ all the faithful, both living and departed, are bound together in a communion of prayer.' This simple, agreed statement from the Anglican–Roman Catholic International Commission explains the purpose of the celebration on this day. Since its foundation, Christians have recognised that the Church, the *ecclesia*, the assembled people of God, is at its most perfect when it recognises its unity in God's redeeming love with all who have said, who say now, and who will say in the fullness of time, 'Jesus is Lord'.

Eternal God, our Maker and Redeemer,
grant us, with all the faithful departed,
the sure benefits of your Son's saving passion
  and glorious resurrection
that, in the last day,
when you gather up all things in Christ,
we may with them enjoy the fullness of your promises;
through Jesus Christ your Son our Lord,
who is alive and reigns with you,
in the unity of the Holy Spirit,
one God, now and for ever.

A reading from the Lamentations of Jeremiah.

My soul is bereft of peace; I have forgotten what happiness is; so I say, "Gone is my glory, and all that I had hoped for from the Lord." The thought of my affliction and my homelessness is wormwood and gall! My soul continually thinks of it and is bowed down within me. But this I call to mind, and therefore I have hope: The steadfast love of the Lord never ceases, his mercies never come to an end; they are new every morning; great is your faithfulness. "The Lord is my portion," says my soul, "therefore I will hope in him." The Lord is good to those who wait for him, to the soul that seeks him. It is good that one should wait quietly for the salvation of the Lord. For the Lord will not reject forever. Although he causes grief, he will have compassion according to the abundance of his steadfast love; for he does not willingly afflict or grieve anyone.

This is the word of the Lord.   *Lamentations 3. 17-26, 31-33*

Or:

A reading from the book of Wisdom.

The souls of the righteous are in the hand of God, and no torment will ever touch them. In the eyes of the foolish they seemed to have died, and their departure was thought to be a disaster, and their going from us to be their destruction; but they are at peace. For though in the sight of others they were punished, their hope is full of immortality. Having been disciplined a little, they will receive great good, because God tested them and found them

worthy of himself; like gold in the furnace he tried them, and like
a sacrificial burnt offering he accepted them. In the time of their
visitation they will shine forth, and will run like sparks through
the stubble. They will govern nations and rule over peoples, and
the Lord will reign over them forever. Those who trust in him will
understand truth, and the faithful will abide with him in love,
because grace and mercy are upon his holy ones, and he watches
over his elect.

This is the word of the Lord. *Wisdom 3. 1-9*

Responsorial Psalm

**R The souls of the righteous are in the hand of God
[no torment will ever touch them].**

The Lord is my shepherd;
I shall not be in want.
He makes me lie down in green pastures
and leads me beside still waters. **R**

The Lord revives my soul
and guides me along right pathways for his name's sake.
Though I walk through the valley of the shadow of death,
  I shall fear no evil;
for you are with me; your rod and your staff, they comfort me. **R**

You spread a table before me
in the presence of those who trouble me;
you have anointed my head with oil,
and my cup is running over. **R**

Surely your goodness and mercy shall follow me
all the days of my life,
and I will dwell in the house of the Lord for ever. **R**   *Psalm 23*

Or·

Responsorial Psalm

**R God's love has been poured into our hearts
[through the Holy Spirit that has been given to us].**

The Lord is my light and my salvation;
whom then shall I fear?
the Lord is the strength of my life;
of whom then shall I be afraid? **R**

When evildoers came upon me to eat up my flesh,
it was they, my foes and my adversaries, who stumbled and fell.
Though an army should encamp against me,
yet my heart shall not be afraid. **R**

One thing have I asked of the Lord; one thing I seek;
that I may dwell in the house of the Lord all the days of my life;
to behold the fair beauty of the Lord
and to seek him in his temple. **R**

What if I had not believed
that I should see the goodness of the Lord in the land of the living!
O tarry and await the Lord's pleasure;
be strong and he shall comfort your heart;
wait patiently for the Lord. **R**   *From Psalm 27*

A reading from the Letter of Paul to the Romans.

Hope does not disappoint us, because God's love has been poured
into our hearts through the Holy Spirit that has been given to us.
For while we were still weak, at the right time Christ died for the
ungodly. Indeed, rarely will anyone die for a righteous person –
though perhaps for a good person someone might actually dare to
die. But God proves his love for us in that while we still were sinners Christ died for us. Much more surely then, now that we have
been justified by his blood, will we be saved through him from the
wrath of God. For if while we were enemies, we were reconciled
to God through the death of his Son, much more surely, having
been reconciled, will we be saved by his life. But more than that,
we even boast in God through our Lord Jesus Christ, through
whom we have now received reconciliation.

This is the word of the Lord.   *Romans 5. 5-11*

Or:

A reading from the First Letter of Peter.

Blessèd be the God and Father of our Lord Jesus Christ! By his
great mercy he has given us a new birth into a living hope through
the resurrection of Jesus Christ from the dead, and into an inheritance that is imperishable, undefiled, and unfading, kept in heav-
en for you, who are being protected by the power of God through
faith for a salvation ready to be revealed in the last time. In this
you rejoice, even if now for a little while you have had to suffer

various trials, so that the genuineness of your faith – being more precious than gold that, though perishable, is tested by fire – may be found to result in praise and glory and honour when Jesus Christ is revealed. Although you have not seen him, you love him; and even though you do not see him now, you believe in him and rejoice with an indescribable and glorious joy, for you are receiving the outcome of your faith, the salvation of your souls.

This is the word of the Lord.   *1 Peter 1. 3-9*

Hear the gospel of our Lord Jesus Christ according to John.

Jesus said to the Jews, "Very truly, I tell you, the Son can do nothing on his own, but only what he sees the Father doing; for whatever the Father does, the Son does likewise. The Father loves the Son and shows him all that he himself is doing; and he will show him greater works than these, so that you will be astonished. Indeed, just as the Father raises the dead and gives them life, so also the Son gives life to whomever he wishes. The Father judges no one but has given all judgement to the Son, so that all may honour the Son just as they honour the Father. Anyone who does not honour the Son does not honour the Father who sent him. Very truly, I tell you, anyone who hears my word and believes him who sent me has eternal life, and does not come under judgement, but has passed from death to life. Very truly, I tell you, the hour is coming, and is now here, when the dead will hear the voice of the Son of God, and those who hear will live. "

This is the gospel of the Lord.   *John 5. 19-25*

Or:

Hear the gospel of our Lord Jesus Christ according to John.

Jesus said to the crowds, "Everything that the Father gives me will come to me, and anyone who comes to me I will never drive away; for I have come down from heaven, not to do my own will, but the will of him who sent me. And this is the will of him who sent me, that I should lose nothing of all that he has given me, but raise it up on the last day. This is indeed the will of my Father, that all who see the Son and believe in him may have eternal life; and I will raise them up on the last day."

This is the gospel of the Lord.   *John 6. 37-40*

Post Communion
God of love,
may the death and resurrection of Christ
which we have celebrated in this eucharist
bring us, with all the faithful departed,
into the peace of your eternal home.
We ask this in the name of Jesus Christ,
our rock and our salvation,
to whom be glory for time and for eternity.

Richard Hooker, Anglican Apologist
3 November – Lesser Festival – Teacher of the Faith – White

Born in Heavitree in Exeter in about 1554, Richard Hooker came under the influence of John Jewel, Bishop of Salisbury, in his formative years and through that influence went up to Corpus Christi College, Oxford, where he became a fellow. He was ordained and then married, becoming a parish priest and, in 1585, Master of the Temple in London. Richard became one of the strongest advocates of the position of the Church of England and defended its 'middle way' between puritanism and papalism. Perhaps his greatest work was *Of the Laws of Ecclesiastical Polity* which he wrote as the result of engaging in controversial debates. He showed Anglicanism as rooted firmly in Scripture as well as tradition, affirming its continuity with the pre-Reformation *Ecclesia Anglicana*, but now both catholic and reformed. Richard became a parish priest again near Canterbury and died there on this day in the year 1600.

Collect
God of peace, the bond of all love,
who in your Son Jesus Christ have made the human race
  your inseparable dwelling place:
after the example of your servant Richard Hooker,
give grace to us your servants ever to rejoice
  in the true inheritance of your adopted children
and to show forth your praises now and ever;
through Jesus Christ your Son our Lord,
who is alive and reigns with you, in the unity of the Holy Spirit,
one God, now and for ever.

A reading from the book Ecclesiasticus.

These also were godly men, whose righteous deeds have not been forgotten; their wealth will remain with their descendants, and their inheritance with their children's children. Their descendants stand by the covenants; their children also, for their sake. Their offspring will continue forever, and their glory will never be blotted out. Their bodies are buried in peace, but their name lives on generation after generation. The assembly declares their wisdom, and the congregation proclaims their praise.

This is the word of the Lord.   *Ecclesiasticus 44. 10-15*

Responsorial Psalm

**R   The assembly declares the wisdom of the godly
   [and the congregation proclaims their praise].**

O how I love your law!
all the day long it is in my mind.
Your commandment has made me wiser than my enemies,
and it is always with me. **R**

I have more understanding than all my teachers,
for your decrees are my study.
I am wiser than the elders,
because I observe your commandments. **R**

How sweet are your words to my taste!
they are sweeter than honey to my mouth.
Through your commandments I gain understanding;
therefore I hate every lying way. **R**   *From Psalm 119*

A reading from the Second Letter of Paul to Timothy.

Shun youthful passions and pursue righteousness, faith, love, and peace, along with those who call on the Lord from a pure heart. Have nothing to do with stupid and senseless controversies; you know that they breed quarrels. And the Lord's servant must not be quarrelsome but kindly to everyone, an apt teacher, patient, correcting opponents with gentleness. God may perhaps grant that they will repent and come to know the truth.

This is the word of the Lord.   *2 Timothy 2. 22-25*

Hear the gospel of our Lord Jesus Christ according to John.

Jesus said to his disciples, "I still have many things to say to you, but you cannot bear them now. When the Spirit of truth comes, he will guide you into all the truth; for he will not speak on his own, but will speak whatever he hears, and he will declare to you the things that are to come. He will glorify me, because he will take what is mine and declare it to you. All that the Father has is mine. For this reason I said that he will take what is mine and declare it to you.

This is the gospel of the Lord.   *John 16. 12-15*

Post Communion
God of truth,
whose Wisdom set her table
and invited us to eat the bread and drink the wine
  of the kingdom:
help us to lay aside all foolishness
and to live and walk in the way of insight,
that we may come with your servant Richard Hooker
  to the eternal feast of heaven;
through Jesus Christ our Lord.

Martin de Porres, Friar

3 November – Commemoration
If celebrated as a Lesser Festival, Common of Religious, page 494

Born in Lima in Peru in 1579, Martin de Porres was the illegitimate son of a Spanish knight and a black, Panamanian freewoman. He joined the Third Order of the Dominicans when he was fifteen years old and was later received as a lay brother into the First Order, mainly because of his reputation for caring for the poor and needy. As the friary almoner, he was responsible for the daily distribution to the poor and he had a particular care for the many African slaves, whose lives were a dreadful indictment of the Christian conquistadores. Martin became sought after for spiritual counsel, unusual for a lay brother at that time. His care for all God's creatures led many to love and revere him and his own brothers chose him as their spiritual leader. He died of a violent fever on this day in the year 1639 and, because of his care for all, regardless of class or colour, is seen as the patron saint of race relations.

Leonard the Hermit
6 November – Commemoration
If celebrated as a Lesser Festival, Common of Religious, page 494

According to an eleventh-century *Life*, Leonard was a sixth-century Frankish nobleman who refused a bishopric to become first a monk, then a hermit, at Noblac (now Saint-Léonard) near Limoges. The miracles attributed to him, both during his lifetime and after his death, caused a widespread cultus throughout Europe and, in England alone, over a hundred and seventy churches are dedicated to him.

William Temple, Archbishop of Canterbury
6 November – Commemoration
If celebrated as a Lesser Festival, Common of Teachers, page 473

William Temple was born in 1881 and baptised on this day in Exeter Cathedral. His father was Bishop of Exeter and later Archbishop of Canterbury. William excelled in academic studies and developed into a philosopher and theologian of significance. After ordination, he quickly made a mark in the Church and at forty became a bishop. Within a decade he was Archbishop of York. He is especially remembered for his ecumenical efforts and also for his concern with social issues, contributing notably to the debate which led to the creation of state welfare provision after the Second World War. He died in 1944, two years after his translation to the See of Canterbury.

Willibrord of York, Apostle of Frisia
7 November – Lesser Festival – Missionary – White

Willibrord was born in Northumbria and educated at Ripon but the main part of his life was dedicated to his missionary work in Frisia and northern Germany. He built many churches, inaugurated bishoprics and consecrated cathedrals: the Cathedral of Utrecht, with a diocesan organisation based on that of Canterbury, is his most well-known foundation. Together with his younger contemporary Boniface, he began a century of English Christian influence on continental Christianity. Alcuin described him as venerable, gracious and full of joy, and his ministry as based on energetic preaching informed by prayer and sacred reading. He died on this day in 739 and was buried at Echternach monastery in Luxembourg, which he founded. He is the patron saint of Holland.

Collect
God, the saviour of all,
you sent your bishop Willibrord from this land
to proclaim the good news to many peoples
and confirm them in their faith:
help us also to witness to your steadfast love
  by word and deed
so that your Church may increase and grow strong in holiness;
through Jesus Christ your Son our Lord,
who is alive and reigns with you,
in the unity of the Holy Spirit,
one God, now and for ever.

A reading from the prophecy of Isaiah.

How beautiful upon the mountains are the feet of the messenger who announces peace, who brings good news, who announces salvation, who says to Zion, "Your God reigns." Listen! Your sentinels lift up their voices, together they sing for joy; for in plain sight they see the return of the Lord to Zion. Break forth together into singing, you ruins of Jerusalem; for the Lord has comforted his people, he has redeemed Jerusalem. The Lord has bared his holy arm before the eyes of all the nations; and all the ends of the earth shall see the salvation of our God.

This is the word of the Lord.   *Isaiah 52. 7-10*

Responsorial Psalm

**R   O Lord, you are our refuge
[from one generation to another].**

Before the mountains were brought forth,
or the land and the earth were born,
from age to age you are God. **R**

Teach us to number our days
that we may apply our hearts to wisdom.
Return, O Lord; how long will you tarry?
be gracious to your servants. **R**

Satisfy us by your loving-kindness in the morning;
so shall we rejoice and be glad all the days of our life.
May the graciousness of the Lord our God be upon us;
prosper the work of our hands. **R**   *From Psalm 90*

A reading from the First Letter of Paul to the Corinthians.

The message about the cross is foolishness to those who are perishing, but to us who are being saved it is the power of God. For it is written, "I will destroy the wisdom of the wise, and the discernment of the discerning I will thwart." Where is the one who is wise? Where is the scribe? Where is the debater of this age? Has not God made foolish the wisdom of the world? For since, in the wisdom of God, the world did not know God through wisdom, God decided, through the foolishness of our proclamation, to save those who believe. For Jews demand signs and Greeks desire wisdom, but we proclaim Christ crucified, a stumbling block to Jews and foolishness to Gentiles, but to those who are the called, both Jews and Greeks, Christ the power of God and the wisdom of God. For God's foolishness is wiser than human wisdom, and God's weakness is stronger than human strength.

This is the word of the Lord.   *1 Corinthians 1. 18-25*

Hear the gospel of our Lord Jesus Christ according to Mark.

Jesus said to his disciples, "Go into all the world and proclaim the good news to the whole creation. The one who believes and is baptised will be saved; but the one who does not believe will be condemned. And these signs will accompany those who believe: by using my name they will cast out demons; they will speak in new tongues; they will pick up snakes in their hands, and if they drink any deadly thing, it will not hurt them; they will lay their hands on the sick, and they will recover."

So then the Lord Jesus, after he had spoken to them, was taken up into heaven and sat down at the right hand of God. And they went out and proclaimed the good news everywhere, while the

Lord worked with them and confirmed the message by the signs that accompanied it.

This is the gospel of the Lord. *Mark 16. 15-20*

Post Communion
Holy Father,
who gathered us here around the table of your Son
to share this meal with the whole household of God:
in that new world where you reveal
  the fullness of your peace,
gather people of every race and language
to share with your servant Willibrord and all your saints
in the eternal banquet of Jesus Christ our Lord.

The Saints & Martyrs of England
8 November – Lesser Festival – White

The date when Christianity first came to England is not known, but there were British bishops at the Council of Arles in the year 314, indicating a Church with order and worship. Since those days, Christians from England have shared the message of the good news at home and around the world. As the world-wide fellowship of the Anglican Communion developed, incorporating peoples of many nations and cultures, individual Christian men and women have shone as beacons, heroically bearing witness to their Lord, some through a simple life of holiness, others by giving their lives for the sake of Christ.

Collect
God, whom the glorious company of the redeemed adore,
assembled from all times and places of your dominion:
we praise you for the saints of our own land
and for the many lamps their holiness has lit;
and we pray that we also may be numbered at last
with those who have done your will
  and declared your righteousness;
through Jesus Christ your Son our Lord,
who is alive and reigns with you, in the unity of the Holy Spirit,
one God, now and for ever.

A reading from the prophecy of Isaiah.

They shall build up the ancient ruins, they shall raise up the former devastations; they shall repair the ruined cities, the devastations of many generations. Strangers shall stand and feed your flocks, foreigners shall till your land and dress your vines; but you shall be called priests of the Lord, you shall be named ministers of our God; you shall enjoy the wealth of the nations, and in their riches you shall glory. Because their shame was double, and dishonour was proclaimed as their lot, therefore they shall possess a double portion; everlasting joy shall be theirs. For I the Lord love justice, I hate robbery and wrongdoing; I will faithfully give them their recompense, and I will make an everlasting covenant with them. Their descendants shall be known among the nations, and their offspring among the peoples; all who see them shall acknowledge that they are a people whom the Lord has blessed.

This is the word of the Lord. *Isaiah 61. 4-9*

Or:

A reading from the book Ecclesiasticus.

Let us now sing the praises of the famous, our ancestors in their generations. The Lord apportioned to them great glory, his majesty from the beginning. There were those who ruled in their kingdoms, and made a name for themselves by their valour; those who gave counsel because they were intelligent; those who spoke in prophetic oracles; those who led the people by their counsels and by their knowledge of the people's lore; they were wise in their words of instruction; those who composed musical tunes, or put verses in writing; the rich endowed with resources, living peacefully in their homes – all these were honoured in their generations, and were the pride of their times. Some of them have left behind a name, so that others declare their praise.

But of others there is no memory; they have perished as though they had never existed; they have become as though they had never been born, they and their children after them. But these also were godly, whose righteous deeds have not been forgotten; their wealth will remain with their descendants, and their inheritance with their children's children. Their descendants stand by the covenants; their children also, for their sake. Their offspring will continue forever, and their glory will never be blotted out. Their bodies are buried in peace, but their name lives on generation after generation. The assembly declares their wisdom, and the congregation proclaims their praise.

This is the word of the Lord. *Ecclesiasticus 44. 1-15*

Responsorial Psalm

R The Lord apportioned to them great glory [and the congregation proclaims their praise].

Lord, who may dwell in your tabernacle?
who may abide upon your holy hill?
Whoever leads a blameless life and does what is right,
who speaks the truth from his heart. **R**

There is no guile upon his tongue;
he does no evil to his friend;
he does not heap contempt upon his neighbour. **R**

In his sight the wicked are rejected,
but he honours those who fear the Lord.
Whoever does these things
shall never be overthrown. **R** *Psalm 15*

A reading from the Revelation to John.

From the throne came a voice saying, "Praise our God, all you his servants, and all who fear him, small and great." Then I heard what seemed to be the voice of a great multitude, like the sound of many waters and like the sound of mighty thunderpeals, crying out, "Alleluia! For the Lord our God the Almighty reigns. Let us rejoice and exult and give him the glory, for the marriage of the Lamb has come, and his bride has made herself ready; to her it has been granted to be clothed with fine linen, bright and pure" – for the fine linen is the righteous deeds of the saints.

And the angel said to me, "Write this: Blessèd are those who are invited to the marriage supper of the Lamb." And he said to me, "These are true words of God." Then I fell down at his feet to worship him, but he said to me, "You must not do that! I am a fellow servant with you and your comrades who hold the testimony of Jesus. Worship God! For the testimony of Jesus is the spirit of prophecy."

This is the word of the Lord. *Revelation 19. 5-10*

Hear the gospel of our Lord Jesus Christ according to John.

Jesus looked up to heaven and said, "As you have sent me into the world, so I have sent them into the world. And for their sakes I sanctify myself, so that they also may be sanctified in truth. I ask not only on behalf of these, but also on behalf of those who will believe in me through their word, that they may all be one. As you, Father, are in me and I am in you, may they also be in us, so that the world may believe that you have sent me. The glory that you have given me I have given them, so that they may be one, as we are one, I in them and you in me, that they may become completely one, so that the world may know that you have sent me and have loved them even as you have loved me."

This is the gospel of the Lord. *John 17. 18-23*

Post Communion
God, the source of all holiness
  and giver of all good things:
may we who have shared at this table
  as strangers and pilgrims here on earth
be welcomed with all your saints
  to the heavenly feast on the day of your kingdom;
through Jesus Christ our Lord.

Margery Kempe, Mystic
9 November – Commemoration
If celebrated as a Lesser Festival, Common of any Saint, page 513

Margery Kempe was born in Lynne in Norfolk in the late fourteenth century, a contemporary of Julian of Norwich. She received many visions, several of them of the holy family, one of the most regular being of the crucifixion. She also had conversations with the saints. She was much sought after as a visionary, was endlessly in trouble with the Church, rebuked by the Archbishop and was more than once imprisoned. Following the messages in her visions, she undertook pilgrimages to many holy places, including Walsingham, Canterbury, Compostela, Rome and Jerusalem, often setting out penniless. She was blessed with the gift of tears and seems to have been favoured with singular signs of Christ's love, whereby for long periods she enjoyed consciousness of a close communion with him and developed a strong compassion for the sins of the world. Her autobiography, *The Book of Margery Kempe*, recounts her remarkable life. She died towards the middle of the fifteenth century.

Leo the Great

10 November – Lesser Festival – Bishop – White

Leo the Great became pope in the year 440 and twice proved his bravery in saving the citizens of Rome from the invading barbarians. He was an eloquent and wise preacher, using simple gospel texts to proclaim the Christian faith. His administrative skills were unrivalled and he used the resources of the Church for the good of the people. Rather than further confuse Christians by entering into the controversy over the person of Christ, Leo spoke simply of the humility of Christ who was divine and human in his compassion, uniting biblical images in prayer rather than dividing in debate. Leo died on this day in the year 461.

Collect

God our Father,
who made your servant Leo strong in the defence of the faith:
fill your Church with the spirit of truth
that, guided by humility and governed by love,
she may prevail against the powers of evil;
through Jesus Christ your Son our Lord,
who is alive and reigns with you,
in the unity of the Holy Spirit,
one God, now and for ever.

A reading from the prophecy of Malachi.

My covenant with him was a covenant of life and well-being, which I gave him; this called for reverence, and he revered me and stood in awe of my name. True instruction was in his mouth, and no wrong was found on his lips. He walked with me in integrity and uprightness, and he turned many from iniquity. For the lips of a priest should guard knowledge, and people should seek instruction from his mouth, for he is the messenger of the Lord of hosts.

This is the word of the Lord.   *Malachi 2. 5-7*

R Delight in the law of the Lord!
[Meditate on God's law day and night].

Happy are they who have not walked in the counsel of the wicked,
nor lingered in the way of sinners,
nor sat in the seats of the scornful!
Their delight is in the law of the Lord,
and they meditate on his law day and night. **R**

They are like trees planted by streams of water,
bearing fruit in due season,
with leaves that do not wither;
everything they do shall prosper. **R**

It is not so with the wicked:
they are like chaff which the wind blows away.
The Lord knows the way of the righteous,
but the way of the wicked is doomed. **R**   *From Psalm 1*

A reading from the First Letter of Peter.

Now as an elder myself and a witness of the sufferings of Christ,
as well as one who shares in the glory to be revealed, I exhort the
elders among you to tend the flock of God that is in your charge,
exercising the oversight, not under compulsion but willingly, as
God would have you do it – not for sordid gain but eagerly. Do
not lord it over those in your charge, but be examples to the flock.
And when the chief shepherd appears, you will win the crown of
glory that never fades away. In the same way, you who are
younger must accept the authority of the elders. And all of you
must clothe yourselves with humility in your dealings with one
another, for "God opposes the proud, but gives grace to the humble."

  Humble yourselves therefore under the mighty hand of God, so
that he may exalt you in due time. Cast all your anxiety on him,
because he cares for you. Discipline yourselves, keep alert. Like a
roaring lion your adversary the devil prowls around, looking for
someone to devour. Resist him, steadfast in your faith, for you
know that your brothers and sisters in all the world are undergo-
ing the same kinds of suffering. And after you have suffered for a
little while, the God of all grace, who has called you to his eternal

glory in Christ, will himself restore, support, strengthen, and establish you. To him be the power forever and ever. Amen.

This is the word of the Lord.   *1 Peter 5. 1-11*

Hear the gospel of our Lord Jesus Christ according to Matthew.

When Jesus came into the district of Caesarea Philippi, he asked his disciples, "Who do people say that the Son of Man is?" And they said, "Some say John the Baptist, but others Elijah, and still others Jeremiah or one of the prophets." He said to them, "But who do you say that I am?" Simon Peter answered, "You are the Messiah, the Son of the living God." And Jesus answered him, "Blessed are you, Simon son of Jonah! For flesh and blood has not revealed this to you, but my Father in heaven. And I tell you, you are Peter, and on this rock I will build my church, and the gates of Hades will not prevail against it. I will give you the keys of the kingdom of heaven, and whatever you bind on earth will be bound in heaven, and whatever you loose on earth will be loosed in heaven."

This is the gospel of the Lord.   *Matthew 16. 13-19*

Post Communion
God of truth,
whose Wisdom set her table
and invited us to eat the bread and drink the wine
  of the kingdom:
help us to lay aside all foolishness
and to live and walk in the way of insight,
that we may come with your servant Leo
  to the eternal feast of heaven;
through Jesus Christ our Lord.

Martin, Bishop of Tours
11 November – Lesser Festival – Bishop – White

Born in about the year 316 in Pannonia (in modern-day Hungary), Martin was a soldier in the Roman army and a Christian. He found the two rôles conflicted and, under the influence of Hilary, Bishop of Poitiers, he founded a monastery in Hilary's diocese in the year 360, the first such foundation in Gaul. The religious house was a centre for missionary work in the local countryside, setting a new example where, previously, all Christian activity had been centred in cities and undertaken from the cathedral there. In 372, Martin was elected Bishop of Tours by popular acclaim and he continued his monastic lifestyle as a bishop, remaining in that ministry until his death on this day in the year 397.

Collect
God all powerful,
who called Martin from the armies of this world
to be a faithful soldier of Christ:
give us grace to follow him
in his love and compassion for the needy,
and enable your Church to claim for all people
their inheritance as children of God;
through Jesus Christ your Son our Lord,
who is alive and reigns with you,
in the unity of the Holy Spirit,
one God, now and for ever.

A reading from the book Deuteronomy.

If there is among you anyone in need, a member of your community in any of your towns within the land that the Lord your God is giving you, do not be hard-hearted or tight-fisted toward your needy neighbour. You should rather open your hand, willingly lending enough to meet the need, whatever it may be. Give liberally and be ungrudging when you do so, for on this account the Lord your God will bless you in all your work and in all that you undertake. Since there will never cease to be some in need on the earth, I therefore command you, "Open your hand to the poor and needy neighbour in your land."

This is the word of the Lord. *Deuteronomy 15. 7-8, 10-11*

Responsorial Psalm

**R   God's light shines in the darkness for the upright;
[the righteous are merciful and full of compassion].**

Happy are they who fear the Lord
and have great delight in his commandments!
Their descendants will be mighty in the land;
the generation of the upright will be blessed. **R**

For they will never be shaken;
the righteous will be kept in everlasting remembrance.
They will not be afraid of any evil rumours;
their heart is right; they put their trust in the Lord. **R**

Their heart is established and will not shrink,
they have given freely to the poor,
and their righteousness stands fast for ever;
they will hold up their head with honour. **R**   *From Psalm 112*

A reading from the First Letter of Paul to the Thessalonians.

Now concerning the times and the seasons, brothers and sisters,
you do not need to have anything written to you. For you yourselves know very well that the day of the Lord will come like a
thief in the night. When they say, "There is peace and security,"
then sudden destruction will come upon them, as labour pains
come upon a pregnant woman, and there will be no escape! But
you, beloved, are not in darkness, for that day to surprise you like
a thief; for you are all children of light and children of the day; we
are not of the night or of darkness.

So then let us not fall asleep as others do, but let us keep awake
and be sober; for those who sleep sleep at night, and those who
are drunk get drunk at night. But since we belong to the day, let
us be sober, and put on the breastplate of faith and love, and for a
helmet the hope of salvation. For God has destined us not for
wrath but for obtaining salvation through our Lord Jesus Christ,
who died for us, so that whether we are awake or asleep we may
live with him. Therefore encourage one another and build up
each other, as indeed you are doing.

This is the word of the Lord.   *1 Thessalonians 5. 1-11*

Hear the gospel of our Lord Jesus Christ according to Matthew.

The king will say to those at his right hand, "Come, you that are blessed by my Father, inherit the kingdom prepared for you from the foundation of the world; for I was hungry and you gave me food, I was thirsty and you gave me something to drink, I was a stranger and you welcomed me, I was naked and you gave me clothing, I was sick and you took care of me, I was in prison and you visited me."

Then the righteous will answer him, "Lord, when was it that we saw you hungry and gave you food, or thirsty and gave you something to drink? And when was it that we saw you a stranger and welcomed you, or naked and gave you clothing? And when was it that we saw you sick or in prison and visited you?" And the king will answer them, "Truly I tell you, just as you did it to one of the least of these who are members of my family, you did it to me."

This is the gospel of the Lord.   *Matthew 25. 34-40*

Post Communion
God, shepherd of your people,
whose servant Martin revealed the loving service of Christ
  in his ministry as a pastor of your people:
by this eucharist in which we share
awaken within us the love of Christ
and keep us faithful to our Christian calling;
through him who laid down his life for us,
but is alive and reigns with you, now and for ever.

Charles Simeon, Evangelical Divine
13 November – Lesser Festival – Pastor – White

Born in Reading in 1759, Charles Simeon was educated at Cambridge University and spent the rest of his life in that city. He became a fellow of King's College in 1782 and was ordained priest the following year, when he became vicar of Holy Trinity Church nearby. He had evangelical leanings as a boy but it was whilst preparing for holy communion on his entrance to College that he became aware of the redeeming love of God, an experience he regarded as the turning point in his life. Many of the parishioners of Holy Trinity Church did not welcome him, since he had been appointed through his own family links, but his patent care and love for them all overcame their antipathy and his preaching greatly increased the congregation. Charles had carved on the inside of the pulpit in Holy Trinity Church, where only the preacher could see, the words from John 12:21, when Philip brought the Greeks to our Lord, and they said "Sir, we would see Jesus." These words were a constant reminder to him that people came not to gaze on a great preacher or to admire his eloquence, but to seek Jesus. Charles became a leading Evangelical influence in the Church and was one of the founders of the Church Missionary Society. He also set up the Simeon Trust which made appointments to parishes of fellow Evangelicals. He remained vicar of Holy Trinity until his death on this day in the year 1836.

Collect
Eternal God,
who raised up Charles Simeon
  to preach the good news of Jesus Christ
and inspire your people in service and mission:
grant that we with all your Church may worship the Saviour,
turn in sorrow from our sins and walk in the way of holiness;
through Jesus Christ your Son our Lord,
who is alive and reigns with you,
in the unity of the Holy Spirit,
one God, now and for ever.

A reading from the prophecy of Malachi.

My covenant with Levi was a covenant of life and well-being, which I gave him; this called for reverence, and he revered me and stood in awe of my name. True instruction was in his mouth, and no wrong was found on his lips. He walked with me in integrity and uprightness, and he turned many from iniquity. For the lips of priests should guard knowledge, and people should seek instruction from their mouths, for they are the messengers of the Lord of hosts.

This is the word of the Lord.   *Malachi 2. 5-7*

Responsorial Psalm

**R Exalt yourself above the heavens, O God,
    [and your glory over all the earth].**

My heart is firmly fixed, O God, my heart is fixed;
I will sing and make melody.
Wake up, my spirit; awake, lute and harp;
I myself will waken the dawn. **R**

I will confess you among the peoples, O Lord;
I will sing praise to you among the nations.
For your loving-kindness is greater than the heavens,
and your faithfulness reaches to the clouds. **R**   *From Psalm 57*

A reading from the Letter of Paul to the Colossians.

In our prayers for you we always thank God, the Father of our
Lord Jesus Christ, for we have heard of your faith in Christ Jesus
and of the love that you have for all the saints, because of the hope
laid up for you in heaven. You have heard of this hope before in
the word of the truth, the gospel that has come to you. Just as it is
bearing fruit and growing in the whole world, so it has been bearing fruit among yourselves from the day you heard it and truly
comprehended the grace of God.   This you learned from
Epaphras, our beloved fellow servant. He is a faithful minister of
Christ on your behalf, and he has made known to us your love in
the Spirit.

This is the word of the Lord.   *Colossians 1. 3-8*

Hear the gospel of our Lord Jesus Christ according to Luke.

When a great crowd gathered and people from town after town
came to Jesus, he said in a parable: "A sower went out to sow his
seed; and as he sowed, some fell on the path and was trampled on,
and the birds of the air ate it up. Some fell on the rock; and as it
grew up, it withered for lack of moisture. Some fell among thorns,
and the thorns grew with it and choked it. Some fell into good
soil, and when it grew, it produced a hundredfold." As he said
this, he called out, "Let anyone with ears to hear listen!"

This is the gospel of the Lord.   *Luke 8. 4-8*

Post Communion
God, shepherd of your people,
whose servant Charles Simeon
 revealed the loving service of Christ
 in his ministry as a pastor of your people:
by this eucharist in which we share
awaken within us the love of Christ
and keep us faithful to our Christian calling;
through him who laid down his life for us,
but is alive and reigns with you, now and for ever.

Samuel Seabury,
First Anglican Bishop in North America
14 November – Commemoration
If celebrated as a Lesser Festival, Common of Bishops, page 483

Samuel Seabury was born in Connecticut in 1729 and, after grad-
uating from Yale, was ordained priest in England and assigned by
the Society for the Propagation of the Gospel to a church in New
Brunswick, New Jersey.   During the American War of
Independence, he remained faithful to the British Crown, serving
as a chaplain in the British army. At a secret meeting of the clergy
in Connecticut, Samuel was chosen to seek consecration as bishop
but, after a year of fruitless negotiation with the Church of
England, he was ordained bishop by the non-juring bishops in the
Scottish Episcopal Church on this day in 1784.   Returning to
America, he held his first Convention in Connecticut the following
August and the first General Convention of the American
Episcopal Church in 1789.   There, they adopted the Scottish
eucharistic rite and a similar name to the Church which had
proved itself their friend. Samuel died on 25 February 1796.

Margaret of Scotland
16 November – Lesser Festival – of any Saint – White

Born in the year 1046, Margaret was the daughter of the Anglo-
Saxon royal house of England but educated in Hungary, where

her family lived in exile during the reign of Danish kings in England. After the Norman invasion in 1066, when her royal person still was a threat to the new monarchy, she was welcomed in the royal court of Malcolm III of Scotland and soon afterwards married him in 1069. Theirs was a happy and fruitful union and Margaret proved to be both a civilising and a holy presence. She instituted many church reforms and founded many monasteries, churches and pilgrim hostels. She was a woman of prayer as well as good works who seemed to influence for good all with whom she came into contact. She died on this day in the year 1093.

Collect
God, the ruler of all,
who called your servant Margaret to an earthly throne
and gave her zeal for your Church and love for your people
that she might advance your heavenly kingdom:
mercifully grant that we who commemorate her example
may be fruitful in good works
and attain to the glorious crown of your saints;
through Jesus Christ your Son our Lord,
who is alive and reigns with you,
in the unity of the Holy Spirit,
one God, now and for ever.

A reading from the Book of Proverbs.

A capable wife who can find? She is far more precious than jewels. She opens her hand to the poor, and reaches out her hands to the needy. She opens her mouth with wisdom, and the teaching of kindness is on her tongue. She looks well to the ways of her household, and does not eat the bread of idleness. Her children rise up and call her happy; her husband too, and he praises her: "Many women have done excellently, but you surpass them all." Charm is deceitful, and beauty is vain, but a woman who fears the Lord is to be praised. Give her a share in the fruit of her hands, and let her works praise her in the city gates.

This is the word of the Lord.   *Proverbs 31. 10, 20, 26-31*

Responsorial Psalm

**R   My mouth, O God, shall speak of wisdom
[and my heart shall meditate on understanding].**

Happy are they all who fear the Lord,
and who follow in his ways!
You shall eat the fruit of your labour;
happiness and prosperity shall be yours. **R**

Your wife shall be like a fruitful vine within your house,
your children like olive shoots round about your table.
Whoever fears the Lord
shall thus indeed be blessed. **R**

The Lord bless you from Zion;
may you see the prosperity of Jerusalem all the days of your life.
May you live to see your children's children;
may peace be upon Israel. **R**   *Psalm 128*

A reading from the Second Letter of Paul to Timothy.

Paul, an apostle of Christ Jesus by the will of God, for the sake of
the promise of life that is in Christ Jesus:
To Timothy, my beloved child: Grace, mercy, and peace from God
the Father and Christ Jesus our Lord.

   I am grateful to God – whom I worship with a clear conscience,
as my ancestors did – when I remember you constantly in my
prayers night and day. Recalling your tears, I long to see you so
that I may be filled with joy. I am reminded of your sincere faith,
a faith that lived first in your grandmother Lois and your mother
Eunice and now, I am sure, lives in you. For this reason I remind
you to rekindle the gift of God that is within you through the laying on of my hands; for God did not give us a spirit of cowardice,
but rather a spirit of power and of love and of self-discipline.

This is the word of the Lord.   *2 Timothy 1. 1-7*

Hear the gospel of our Lord Jesus Christ according to Matthew.

Jesus said, "The kingdom of heaven is like treasure hidden in a
field, which someone found and hid; then in his joy he goes and
sells all that he has and buys that field. Again, the kingdom of
heaven is like a merchant in search of fine pearls; on finding one

pearl of great value, he went and sold all that he had and bought it."

This is the gospel of the Lord. *Matthew 13. 44-46*

Post Communion

Father,
from whom every family in heaven and on earth takes its name,
your servant Margaret revealed your goodness
 in a life of tranquillity and service:
grant that we who have gathered in faith around this table
may like her know the love of Christ that surpasses knowledge
and be filled with all your fullness;
through Jesus Christ our Lord.

Edmund of Abingdon,
Archbishop of Canterbury
16 November – Commemoration
If celebrated as a Lesser Festival, Common of Bishops, page 483

Edmund was born in Abingdon in about the year 1175, the son of
a rich but pious merchant who himself became a monk later in life.
Edmund was educated at Oxford and in Paris. After also teaching
in both places, he became Treasurer of Salisbury Cathedral in 1222
and was eventually made Archbishop of Canterbury in 1233. He
was a reforming Bishop and, as well as bringing gifts of administration to his task, appointed clergy of outstanding talent to senior
positions in the Church. He also acted as peacemaker between the
king and his barons, many believing that his actions averted civil
war. He died on this day in the year 1240.

Hugh, Bishop of Lincoln
17 November – Lesser Festival – Bishop – White

Hugh was born at Avalon in Burgundy in 1140 and at first made
his profession with the Augustinian canons but, when he was
twenty-five, he became a monk at Grande Chartreuse. In about
1175, he was invited by the English king, Henry II, to become prior
of his Charterhouse foundation at Witham in Somerset, badly in

of his Charterhouse foundation at Witham in Somerset, badly in need of reform even though it had been only recently founded. In 1186, Hugh was persuaded to accept the See of Lincoln, then the largest diocese in the land. He brought huge energy to the diocese and, together with discerning appointments to key posts, he revived the Lincoln schools, repaired and enlarged the cathedral, visited the See extensively, drew together the clergy to meet in synod and generally brought an efficiency and stability to the Church which was to be much emulated. Hugh also showed great compassion for the poor and the oppressed, ensuring that sufferers of leprosy were cared for and that Jews were not persecuted. He both supported his monarch and also held out against any royal measures he felt to be extreme, yet managing not to make an enemy of the king. He died in London on this day in the year 1200.

Collect
O God,
who endowed your servant Hugh
with a wise and cheerful boldness
and taught him to commend to earthly rulers
  the discipline of a holy life:
give us grace like him to be bold in the service of the gospel,
putting our confidence in Christ alone,
who is alive and reigns with you,
in the unity of the Holy Spirit,
one God, now and for ever.

A reading from the prophecy of Micah.

With what shall I come before the Lord, and bow myself before God on high? Shall I come before him with burnt offerings, with calves a year old? Will the Lord be pleased with thousands of rams, with ten thousands of rivers of oil? Shall I give my firstborn for my transgression, the fruit of my body for the sin of my soul? He has told you, O mortal, what is good; and what does the Lord require of you but to do justice, and to love kindness, and to walk humbly with your God?

This is the word of the Lord.   *Micah 6. 6-8*

Responsorial Psalm

**R Your righteousness have I not hidden in my heart, O God,
[I have spoken of your faithfulness and your deliverance].**

Great things are they that you have done, O Lord my God!
how great your wonders and your plans for us!
there is none who can be compared with you. **R**

O that I could make them known and tell them!
but they are more than I can count.
In sacrifice and offering you take no pleasure;
you have given me ears to hear you. **R**

I proclaimed righteousness in the great congregation;
behold, I did not restrain my lips,
and that, O Lord, you know.
Be pleased, O Lord, to deliver me;
O Lord, make haste to help me. **R**   *From Psalm 40*

A reading from the First Letter of Timothy.

As for you, man of God, shun all this; pursue righteousness, godliness, faith, love, endurance, gentleness. Fight the good fight of
the faith; take hold of the eternal life, to which you were called
and for which you made the good confession in the presence of
many witnesses. In the presence of God, who gives life to all
things, and of Christ Jesus, who in his testimony before Pontius
Pilate made the good confession, I charge you to keep the commandment without spot or blame until the manifestation of our
Lord Jesus Christ, which he will bring about at the right time – he
who is the blessèd and only Sovereign, the King of kings and Lord
of lords. It is he alone who has immortality and dwells in unapproachable light, whom no one has ever seen or can see; to him be
honour and eternal dominion. Amen.

This is the word of the Lord.   *1 Timothy 6. 11-16*

Hear the gospel of our Lord Jesus Christ according to Luke.

When the days drew near for him to be taken up, he set his face to
go to Jerusalem. And he sent messengers ahead of him. On their
way they entered a village of the Samaritans to make ready for
him; but they did not receive him, because his face was set toward

Jerusalem. When his disciples James and John saw it, they said, "Lord, do you want us to command fire to come down from heaven and consume them?" But he turned and rebuked them. Then they went on to another village.

This is the gospel of the Lord.   *Luke 9. 51-56*

Post Communion
God, shepherd of your people,
whose servant Hugh revealed the loving service of Christ
  in his ministry as a pastor of your people:
by this eucharist in which we share
awaken within us the love of Christ
and keep us faithful to our Christian calling;
through him who laid down his life for us,
but is alive and reigns with you, now and for ever.

Elizabeth of Hungary

18 November – Lesser Festival – of any Saint – White

Elizabeth was born in 1207, the daughter of a king of Hungary, and was given in marriage to Louis IV, Landgrave of Thuringia, with whom she had three children. Theirs was a happy marriage but her husband of four years died of the plague. Elizabeth was driven from the court and she settled in Marburg. There she had a confessor, Conrad of Marburg, whose domineering and almost sadistic ways exemplified one who had himself been a successful inquisitor of heretics. She suffered mental and physical abuse from him, in the name of religious austerity, but bore it all humbly. Elizabeth became a member of the Franciscan Third Order, which reflected her life of caring for the poor, even cooking and cleaning for them. Due to the severe regime under which she lived, her weakened body gave way under the pressure and she died on this day, just twenty-four years old, in the year 1231.

Collect
Lord God,
who taught Elizabeth of Hungary
  to recognise and reverence Christ in the poor of this world:
by her example
strengthen us to love and serve the afflicted and the needy
and so to honour your Son, the servant King,
who is alive and reigns with you, in the unity of the Holy Spirit,
one God, now and for ever.

A reading from the Book of Tobit.

Bless God and acknowledge him in the presence of all the living
for the good things he has done for you. Bless and sing praise to
his name. With fitting honour declare to all people the deeds of
God. Do not be slow to acknowledge him. It is good to conceal
the secret of a king, but to acknowledge and reveal the works of
God, and with fitting honour to acknowledge him. Do good and
evil will not overtake you. Prayer with fasting is good, but better
than both is almsgiving with righteousness. A little with righteousness is better than wealth with wrongdoing. It is better to give
alms than to lay up gold. For almsgiving saves from death and
purges away every sin. Those who give alms will enjoy a full life.

This is the word of the Lord.   *Tobit 12. 6b-9*

Responsorial Psalm

R   Arise, O God, and rule the earth,
    [for you shall take all nations for your own].

God takes his stand in the council of heaven;
he gives judgement in the midst of the gods:
"How long will you judge unjustly,
and show favour to the wicked? **R**

"Save the weak and the orphan;
defend the humble and needy;
rescue the weak and the poor;
deliver them from the power of the wicked. **R**

"They do not know, neither do they understand;
they go about in darkness;
all the foundations of the earth are shaken. **R**

"Now I say to you, 'You are gods,
and all of you children of the Most High;
nevertheless, you shall die like mortals,
and fall like any prince.'" **R**   *Psalm 82*

A reading from the Letter of James.

What good is it, my brothers and sisters, if you say you have faith
but do not have works? Can faith save you? If a brother or sister
is naked and lacks daily food, and one of you says to them, "Go in
peace; keep warm and eat your fill," and yet you do not supply
their bodily needs, what is the good of that? So faith by itself, if it
has no works, is dead.

This is the word of the Lord.   *James 2. 14-17*

Hear the gospel of our Lord Jesus Christ according to Matthew.

Jesus said, "When the Son of Man comes in his glory, and all the
angels with him, then he will sit on the throne of his glory. All the
nations will be gathered before him, and he will separate people
one from another as a shepherd separates the sheep from the
goats, and he will put the sheep at his right hand and the goats at
the left. Then the king will say to those at his right hand, 'Come,
you that are blessed by my Father, inherit the kingdom prepared
for you from the foundation of the world; for I was hungry and
you gave me food, I was thirsty and you gave me something to
drink, I was a stranger and you welcomed me, I was naked and
you gave me clothing, I was sick and you took care of me, I was in
prison and you visited me.'

"Then the righteous will answer him, 'Lord, when was it that we
saw you hungry and gave you food, or thirsty and gave you something to drink? And when was it that we saw you a stranger and
welcomed you, or naked and gave you clothing? And when was
it that we saw you sick or in prison and visited you?' And the king
will answer them, 'Truly I tell you, just as you did it to one of the
least of these who are members of my family, you did it to me.'"

This is the gospel of the Lord.   *Matthew 25. 31-40*

Post Communion
Faithful God,
who called your servant Elizabeth to serve you
and gave her joy in walking the path of holiness:
by this eucharist
  in which you renew within us the vision of your glory,
strengthen us all to follow the way of perfection
until we come to see you face to face;
through Jesus Christ our Lord.

Hilda, Abbess of Whitby
19 November – Lesser Festival – Religious – White

Hilda was born in the year 614 of the royal house of Northumbria and was baptised in York at the age of twelve by Paulinus. Encouraged by Aidan of Lindisfarne, she became a Religious at the age of thirty three. She established monasteries first at Hartlepool and two years later at Whitby. This house became a great centre of learning and was the meeting-place for the important Synod of Whitby in the year 664 at which it was decided to adopt the Roman tradition in preference to Celtic customs. Although herself a Celt in religious formation, Hilda played a crucial rôle in reconciling others of that tradition to the decision of the Synod. She is also remembered as a great educator, exemplified in her nurturing of Caedmon's gift of vernacular song. She died on 17 November in the year 680.

Collect
Eternal God,
who made the abbess Hilda to shine like a jewel in our land
and through her holiness and leadership
  blessed your Church with new life and unity:
help us, like her, to yearn for the gospel of Christ
and to reconcile those who are divided;
through him who is alive and reigns with you,
in the unity of the Holy Spirit,
one God, now and for ever.

A reading from the prophecy of Isaiah.

I will greatly rejoice in the Lord, my whole being shall exult in my God; for he has clothed me with the garments of salvation, he has covered me with the robe of righteousness, as a bridegroom decks himself with a garland, and as a bride adorns herself with her jewels. For as the earth brings forth its shoots, and as a garden causes what is sown in it to spring up, so the Lord God will cause righteousness and praise to spring up before all the nations. For Zion's sake I will not keep silent, and for Jerusalem's sake I will not rest, until her vindication shines out like the dawn, and her salvation like a burning torch.

The nations shall see your vindication, and all the kings your glory; and you shall be called by a new name that the mouth of the Lord will give. You shall be a crown of beauty in the hand of the Lord, and a royal diadem in the hand of your God. You shall no more be termed Forsaken, and your land shall no more be termed Desolate; but you shall be called My Delight Is in Her, and your land Married; for the Lord delights in you, and your land shall be married. For as a young man marries a young woman, so shall your builder marry you, and as the bridegroom rejoices over the bride, so shall your God rejoice over you.

This is the word of the Lord.   *Isaiah 61.10 - 62.5*

Responsorial Psalm

**R   I will greatly rejoice in the Lord
[my whole being shall exult in my God].**

O Lord, I am not proud, I have no haughty looks.
I do not occupy myself with great matters,
or with things that are too hard for me. **R**

But I still my soul and make it quiet,
like a child upon its mother's breast;
my soul is quieted within me. **R**

O Israel, wait upon the Lord,
from this time forth for evermore. **R**   *Psalm 131*

A reading from the Letter of Paul to the Ephesians.

I therefore, the prisoner in the Lord, beg you to lead a life worthy of the calling to which you have been called, with all humility and gentleness, with patience, bearing with one another in love, making every effort to maintain the unity of the Spirit in the bond of peace. There is one body and one Spirit, just as you were called to the one hope of your calling, one Lord, one faith, one baptism, one God and Father of all, who is above all and through all and in all.

This is the word of the Lord. *Ephesians 4. 1-6*

Hear the gospel of our Lord Jesus Christ according to Luke.

When Jesus noticed how the guests chose the places of honour, he told them a parable. "When you are invited by someone to a wedding banquet, do not sit down at the place of honour, in case someone more distinguished than you has been invited by your host; and the host who invited both of you may come and say to you, 'Give this person your place,' and then in disgrace you would start to take the lowest place. But when you are invited, go and sit down at the lowest place, so that when your host comes, he may say to you, 'Friend, move up higher'; then you will be honoured in the presence of all who sit at the table with you. For all who exalt themselves will be humbled, and those who humble themselves will be exalted."

He said also to the one who had invited him, "When you give a luncheon or a dinner, do not invite your friends or your brothers or your relatives or rich neighbours, in case they may invite you in return, and you would be repaid. But when you give a banquet, invite the poor, the crippled, the lame, and the blind. And you will be blessed, because they cannot repay you, for you will be repaid at the resurrection of the righteous."

This is the gospel of the Lord. *Luke 14. 7-14*

Post Communion
Merciful God,
who gave such grace to your servant Hilda
that she served you with singleness of heart
and loved you above all things:
help us, whose communion with you
 has been renewed in this sacrament,
to forsake all that holds us back from following Christ
and to grow into his likeness from glory to glory;
through Jesus Christ our Lord.

Mechtild, Béguine of Magdeburg, Mystic
19 November – *Commemoration*
If celebrated as a Lesser Festival, Common of Religious, page 494

Mechtild was born in about the year 1210. The writings for which she is known speak of her experience of the love of God as it was revealed to her. This experience began when she was twelve years old. She responded to it by joining a community of Béguines at the age of about eighteen. After forty years, she moved to the Cistercian convent of Helfta and in about 1270 completed her writings there. Helfta was a remarkable centre of learning at that time with other outstanding personalities in the community. She wrote with poetic sensitivity in direct and simple language of the exchange of love with God. She died on this day in the year 1280.

Edmund, King of the East Angles
20 November – *Lesser Festival* – *Martyr* – *Red*

Born in about the year 840, Edmund was nominated as king while still a boy. He was crowned King of Norfolk in 855 and of Suffolk the following year. As king, he won the hearts of his subjects by his care of the poor and his steady suppression of wrong-doing. When attacked by the Danes, he refused to give over his kingdom or to renounce his faith in Christ. He was tied to a tree, shot with arrows and finally beheaded on this day in the year 870.

Collect
Eternal God,
whose servant Edmund kept faith to the end,
both with you and with his people,
and glorified you by his death:
grant us such steadfastness of faith
that, with the noble army of martyrs,
we may come to enjoy the fullness of the resurrection life;
through Jesus Christ your Son our Lord,
who is alive and reigns with you,
in the unity of the Holy Spirit,
one God, now and for ever.

A reading from the Book of Proverbs.

Loyalty and faithfulness preserve the king, and his throne is upheld by righteousness. The king's heart is a stream of water in the hand of the Lord; he turns it wherever he will. All deeds are right in the sight of the doer, but the Lord weighs the heart. To do righteousness and justice is more acceptable to the Lord than sacrifice. Haughty eyes and a proud heart – the lamp of the wicked – are sin. The violence of the wicked will sweep them away, because they refuse to do what is just.

This is the word of the Lord. *Proverbs 20. 28; 21. 1-4, 7*

Responsorial Psalm

R Restore us again, O God of hosts;
[show the light of your countenance and we shall be saved].

You have brought a vine out of Egypt;
you cast out the nations and planted it.
You prepared the ground for it;
it took root and filled the land. **R**

The mountains were covered by its shadow
and the towering cedar trees by its boughs.
You stretched out its tendrils to the Sea
and its branches to the River. **R**

Turn now, O God of hosts,
look down from heaven and see:
behold and tend this vine,
preserve what your right hand has planted. **R** *From Psalm 80*

A reading from the Revelation to John.

Then I heard a loud voice in heaven, proclaiming, "Now have come the salvation and the power and the kingdom of our God and the authority of his Messiah, for the accuser of our comrades has been thrown down, who accuses them day and night before our God. But they have conquered him by the blood of the Lamb and by the word of their testimony, for they did not cling to life even in the face of death. Rejoice then, you heavens and those who dwell in them!"

This is the word of the Lord. *Revelation 12. 10-12a*

Hear the gospel of our Lord Jesus Christ according to Matthew.

Jesus said to the disciples, "Do not think that I have come to bring peace to the earth; I have not come to bring peace, but a sword. For I have come to set a man against his father, and a daughter against her mother, and a daughter-in-law against her mother-in-law; and one's foes will be members of one's own household. Whoever loves father or mother more than me is not worthy of me; and whoever loves son or daughter more than me is not worthy of me; and whoever does not take up the cross and follow me is not worthy of me. Those who find their life will lose it, and those who lose their life for my sake will find it."

This is the gospel of the Lord.   *Matthew 10. 34-39*

Post Communion
God,
who gave us this holy meal
in which we have celebrated the glory of the cross
and the victory of your martyr Edmund:
by our communion with Christ
in his saving death and resurrection,
give us with all your saints the courage to conquer evil
and so to share the fruit of the tree of life;
through Jesus Christ our Lord.

Priscilla Lydia Sellon, Anglican Religious
20 November – Commemoration
If celebrated as a Lesser Festival, Common of Religious, page 494

Priscilla Lydia Sellon was born probably in 1821. Although never enjoying good health, she responded to an appeal from the Bishop of Exeter in 1848 for workers amongst the destitute in Plymouth. The group of women she gathered around her adopted a conventual lifestyle and, in the face of much opposition, she created the Sisters of Mercy. Her crucial rôle in the revival of Religious Life in the Church of England was enhanced when, in 1856, her sisters joined with the first community founded – the Holy Cross sisters – thereby establishing the Society of the Holy Trinity. She led her community in starting schools and orphanages, in addition to sisters nursing the sick in slum districts and soldiers in the Crimea. In her last years, she was an invalid, dying in her mid-fifties on this day in 1876.

Cecilia, Martyr at Rome, c.230
22 November – Commemoration
If celebrated as a Lesser Festival, Common of Martyrs, page 464

Cecilia was one of the most revered martyrs of the Roman Church, but the only thing known for certain is that, at some point in the second or third century, a woman called Cecilia allowed the Church to meet in her house in Trastevere in the city of Rome and that subsequently the church erected on that site bore her name. She was remembered as a brave woman who risked giving hospitality to the Christian Church when to do so was to court censure and possibly death. According to a tradition that can be dated no earlier than the fifth century, she converted her pagan husband and his brother to the faith, both of whom were martyred before her. She is honoured as the patron saint of musicians.

Clement, Bishop of Rome
23 November – Lesser Festival – Martyr – Red

Clement was active as an elder in the Church in Rome towards the end of the first century and was reputed to have been a disciple of the apostles. He wrote an epistle to the Corinthians which witnessed to ministry in the Church and concerned their authority and duties. That letter clearly showed the authority of one senior presbyter intervening in a conflict in another Church and is full of valuable information about the history of the developing Church and its ministry at this time. His hierarchical view of Church order set a future pattern for episcopal practice and ministry. Clement seems to have been president of a council of presbyters which governed the Church in Rome and his letters are clearly written on their behalf. A fourth-century document has Clement being exiled to the Crimea where he was then put to death by being thrown into the sea with an anchor around his neck.

Collect

Creator and Father of eternity,
whose martyr Clement bore witness with his blood
to the love he proclaimed and the gospel that he preached:
give us thankful hearts as we celebrate your faithfulness
  revealed to us in the lives of your saints
and strengthen us in our pilgrimage as we follow your Son,
Jesus Christ our Lord,
who is alive and reigns with you,
in the unity of the Holy Spirit,
one God, now and for ever.

A reading from the book Proverbs.

A soft answer turns away wrath, but a harsh word stirs up anger.
The tongue of the wise dispenses knowledge, but the mouths of
fools pour out folly. The eyes of the Lord are in every place, keeping watch on the evil and the good. A gentle tongue is a tree of
life, but perverseness in it breaks the spirit.

This is the word of the Lord.   *Proverbs 15. 1-4*

Responsorial Psalm

**R Hear my teaching, O my people, says God;
[incline your ears to the words of my mouth].**

I will open my mouth in a parable;
I will declare the mysteries of ancient times,
that which we have heard and known,
and what our forebears have told us. **R**

We will not hide it from their children,
we will recount it to generations yet to come:
the praiseworthy deeds and the power of the Lord,
and the wonderful works he has done. **R**

God gave his decrees to Jacob and established a law for Israel,
so that they might put their trust in God,
and not forget the deeds of God,
but keep his commandments to do them. **R**   *From Psalm 78*

A reading from the Letter of Paul to the Philippians.

Brothers and sisters, join in imitating me, and observe those who live according to the example you have in us. For many live as enemies of the cross of Christ; I have often told you of them, and now I tell you even with tears. Their end is destruction; their god is the belly; and their glory is in their shame; their minds are set on earthly things.

But our citizenship is in heaven, and it is from there that we are expecting a Saviour, the Lord Jesus Christ. He will transform the body of our humiliation that it may be conformed to the body of his glory, by the power that also enables him to make all things subject to himself. Therefore, my brothers and sisters, whom I love and long for, my joy and crown, stand firm in the Lord in this way, my beloved. I urge Euodia and I urge Syntyche to be of the same mind in the Lord. Yes, and I ask you also, my loyal companion, help these women, for they have struggled beside me in the work of the gospel, together with Clement and the rest of my co-workers, whose names are in the book of life.

This is the word of the Lord.   *Philippians 3.17 - 4.3*

Hear the gospel of our Lord Jesus Christ according to Luke.

When Jesus noticed how the guests chose the places of honour, he told them a parable. "When you are invited by someone to a wedding banquet, do not sit down at the place of honour, in case someone more distinguished than you has been invited by your host; and the host who invited both of you may come and say to you, 'Give this person your place,' and then in disgrace you would start to take the lowest place. But when you are invited, go and sit down at the lowest place, so that when your host comes, he may say to you, 'Friend, move up higher'; then you will be honoured in the presence of all who sit at the table with you. For all who exalt themselves will be humbled, and those who humble themselves will be exalted."

This is the gospel of the Lord.   *Luke 14. 7-11*

Post Communion
God our Redeemer,
whose Church was strengthened
 by the blood of your martyr Clement:
so bind us, in life and death, to Christ's sacrifice
that our lives, broken and offered with his,
may carry his death and proclaim his resurrection in the world;
through Jesus Christ our Lord.

Catherine of Alexandria
25 November – Commemoration
If celebrated as a Lesser Festival, Common of Martyrs, page 464

Tradition has it that Catherine was a girl of a noble family who, because of her Christian faith, refused marriage with the emperor as she was already a 'bride of Christ'. She is said to have disputed with fifty philosophers whose job it was to convince her of her error, and she proved superior in argument to them all. She was then tortured by being splayed on a wheel and finally beheaded.

Isaac Watts, Hymn Writer
25 November – Commemoration
If celebrated as a Lesser Festival, Common of any Saint, page 531

Born in Southampton in 1674, Isaac Watts was educated at the local grammar school and had the opportunity to go on to university, but declined because he preferred the dissenting academy at Stoke Newington. He received there an education of high academic standard and he went on to become the pastor to the Independent (or Congregationalist) Church at Mark Lane in London. Because of his deteriorating health, he resigned this post in 1712 and retired to Stoke Newington. Seven years later, he opposed the imposition of the doctrine of the Trinity on his fellow dissenting ministers, which led to the belief that he had become a Unitarian. Isaac wrote many collections of hymns and his own faith showed clearly through them: *When I survey the wondrous cross, Jesus shall reign where'er the sun* and many others still used in worship. He died at Stoke Newington on this day in 1748.

Andrew the Apostle, Patron Saint of Scotland
30 November – Festival – Apostle – Red

Though Andrew is named among the apostles in the gospels of Matthew, Mark and Luke, it is in John's gospel that most is learned about him. Andrew was a Galilean fisherman, mending his nets, when Jesus called him to follow him, which he promptly did. He then seems to have remained with Jesus until the end. He was there at the feeding of the five thousand and then later, when some Greeks in Jerusalem wanted to see Jesus, Philip brought them to Andrew who told Jesus of their desire. Tradition has him travelling on several missionary journeys and eventually being martyred by being crucified on an X-shaped cross. He became the patron saint of Scotland because of a legend that his relics had been brought there in the eighth century.

Collect
Almighty God,
who gave such grace to your apostle Saint Andrew
that he readily obeyed the call of your Son Jesus Christ
 and brought his brother with him:
call us by your holy Word,
and give us grace to follow you without delay
 and to tell the good news of your kingdom;
through Jesus Christ your Son our Lord,
who is alive and reigns with you,
in the unity of the Holy Spirit,
one God, now and for ever.

A reading from the prophecy of Isaiah.

How beautiful upon the mountains are the feet of the messenger who announces peace, who brings good news, who announces salvation, who says to Zion, "Your God reigns." Listen! Your sentinels lift up their voices, together they sing for joy; for in plain sight they see the return of the Lord to Zion. Break forth together into singing, you ruins of Jerusalem; for the Lord has comforted his people, he has redeemed Jerusalem. The Lord has bared his holy arm before the eyes of all the nations; and all the ends of the earth shall see the salvation of our God.

This is the word of the Lord. *Isaiah 52. 7-10*

**R   The law of the Lord is perfect
[and revives the soul].**

The heavens declare the glory of God,
and the firmament shows his handiwork.
One day tells its tale to another,
and one night imparts knowledge to another. **R**

Although they have no words or language,
and their voices are not heard,
their sound has gone out into all lands,
and their message to the ends of the world. **R**

In the deep has God set a pavilion for the sun;
it comes forth like a bridegroom out of his chamber;
it rejoices like a champion to run its course. **R**

It goes forth from the uttermost edge of the heavens
and runs about to the end of it again;
nothing is hidden from its burning heat. **R**   *From Psalm 19*

A reading from the Letter of Paul to the Romans.

There is no distinction between Jew and Greek; the same Lord is
Lord of all and is generous to all who call on him. For, "Everyone
who calls on the name of the Lord shall be saved." But how are
they to call on one in whom they have not believed? And how are
they to believe in one of whom they have never heard? And how
are they to hear without someone to proclaim him? And how are
they to proclaim him unless they are sent? As it is written, "How
beautiful are the feet of those who bring good news!" But not all
have obeyed the good news; for Isaiah says, "Lord, who has
believed our message?" So faith comes from what is heard, and
what is heard comes through the word of Christ. But I ask, have
they not heard? Indeed they have; for "Their voice has gone out
to all the earth, and their words to the ends of the world."

This is the word of the Lord.   *Romans 10. 12-18*

Hear the gospel of our Lord Jesus Christ according to Matthew.

As Jesus walked by the Sea of Galilee, he saw two brothers, Simon, who is called Peter, and Andrew his brother, casting a net into the sea – for they were fishermen. And he said to them, "Follow me, and I will make you fish for people." Immediately they left their nets and followed him. As he went from there, he saw two other brothers, James son of Zebedee and his brother John, in the boat with their father Zebedee, mending their nets, and he called them. Immediately they left the boat and their father, and followed him.

This is the gospel of the Lord.   *Matthew 4. 18-22*

Post Communion
Almighty God,
who on the day of Pentecost
sent your Holy Spirit to the apostles
with the wind from heaven and in tongues of flame,
filling them with joy and boldness to preach the gospel:
by the power of the same Spirit
strengthen us to witness to your truth
and to draw everyone to the fire of your love;
through Jesus Christ our Lord.

DECEMBER

Charles de Foucauld, Hermit in the Sahara
1 December – Commemoration
If celebrated as a Lesser Festival, Common of Religious, page 494

Charles Eugène de Foucauld was born in 1858 and led a dissipated life as a young officer in the cavalry. In 1883, he went on an expedition to Morocco where he developed a passion for north Africa and its ways. Four years later, he returned to the Catholic faith of his infancy and, after a pilgrimage to the Holy Land, became a Trappist monk in 1890. Desiring an even more austere life, he left in 1897 and became a servant to the Poor Clares in Jerusalem and Nazareth. He was eventually ordained priest in 1901 and went to live as a hermit in Algeria, ending up at Tamanrasset. He became fluent in the local language and his care and concern for the local tribes-people made him accepted and then much loved, though he never sought converts. He composed Rules for brothers and for sisters, though none ever actually joined him. He was assassinated on this day in 1916, a victim of local religious wars. The Little Sisters of the Sacred Heart were founded in 1933, inspired by his rule for sisters. His writings also inspired René Voillaume and others to adopt a life based on his rule, eventually becoming The Little Brothers of Jesus in 1945.

Francis Xavier, Apostle of the Indies
3 December – Commemoration
If celebrated as a Lesser Festival, Common of Missionaries, page 503

Francis was born at the castle of Xavier in Spanish Navarre in 1506. He was educated in Paris and, with Ignatius of Loyola, became one of the group of seven who took vows as the first members of the Society of Jesus, or Jesuits. Since preaching the gospel overseas was an integral part of the Jesuit vocation, Francis sailed for Goa, on the west coast of India, in 1541. He travelled all over the East Indies, evangelising and establishing the Church in Ceylon, Malacca, Malaya and notably in Japan, where he left behind two thousand converts. He had just reached China when he died on board ship in December 1552.

John of Damascus, Monk
4 December – Commemoration
If celebrated as a Lesser Festival, Common of Teachers, page 473

John was born in Damascus in about the year 657. The city by this date was Muslim. John's father, although a Christian, was Chief of the Revenue and the principal representative of the Christians in the city. In 716, John, well-educated in science and theology, became a monk at the monastic settlement at Mar Saba near to Jerusalem and later was ordained priest there. He became a prolific writer of theological works and of hymns. His summary of the teachings of the Greek Fathers, called *De Fide Orthodoxa*, proved an immense influence in the Church in the following centuries, in both east and west. He died on this day in about the year 749.

Nicholas Ferrar, Deacon,
Founder of the Little Gidding Community
4 December – Commemoration
If celebrated as a Lesser Festival, Common of Religious, page 494

Born in London in 1592, Nicholas Ferrar was educated at Clare Hall (now Clare College), Cambridge and elected a Fellow there in 1610. From 1613, he travelled on the continent for five years, trying his hand as a businessman and then as a parliamentarian on his return. In 1625, he moved to Little Gidding in Huntingdonshire, where he was joined by his brother and sister and their families and by his mother. They established together a community life of prayer, using *The Book of Common Prayer*, and a life of charitable works in the locality. He was ordained to the diaconate by William Laud the year after they arrived. He wrote to his niece in 1631, "I purpose and hope by God's grace to be to you not as a master but as a partner and fellow student." This indicates the depth and feeling of the community life Nicholas and his family strove to maintain. After the death of Nicholas on this day in 1637, the community was broken up in 1646 by the Puritans, who were suspicious of it and referred to it as the Arminian Nunnery. They feared it promoting the return of Romish practices into England, and so all Nicholas's manuscripts were burned.

Nicholas, Bishop of Myra
6 December – Lesser Festival – Bishop – White

Nicholas was a fourth-century bishop of Myra in Asia Minor (southern Turkey). His reputation as a worker of wonders was enhanced by a ninth-century author of his hagiography and he is now best known through these stories. Many of them concern his love and care for children, how he fed the hungry, healed the sick and cared for the oppressed. He saved three girls from a life of prostitution by providing them with dowries and so developed the tradition of bearing gifts to children on his feast day, a practice appropriated by the Christmas celebrations. Nicholas is also one of the patron saints of Russia.

Collect
Almighty Father, lover of souls,
who chose your servant Nicholas
  to be a bishop in the Church,
that he might give freely out of the treasures of your grace:
make us mindful of the needs of others
and, as we have received, so teach us also to give;
through Jesus Christ your Son our Lord,
who is alive and reigns with you,
in the unity of the Holy Spirit,
one God, now and for ever.

A reading from the prophecy of Isaiah.

The spirit of the Lord God is upon me, because the Lord has anointed me; he has sent me to bring good news to the oppressed, to bind up the brokenhearted, to proclaim liberty to the captives, and release to the prisoners; to proclaim the year of the Lord's favour, and the day of vengeance of our God; to comfort all who mourn; to provide for those who mourn in Zion – to give them a garland instead of ashes, the oil of gladness instead of mourning, the mantle of praise instead of a faint spirit. They will be called oaks of righteousness, the planting of the Lord, to display his glory.

This is the word of the Lord. *Isaiah 61. 1-3*

Responsorial Psalm

R Let the righteous be glad and rejoice before God;
[let them also be merry and joyful].

Let God arise and let his enemies be scattered;
let those who hate him flee before him.
Let them vanish like smoke
when the wind drives it away. **R**

Sing to God, sing praises to his name;
exalt him who rides upon the heavens;
Yahweh is his name, rejoice before him! **R**

Father of orphans, defender of widows,
God in his holy habitation gives the solitary a home
and brings forth prisoners into freedom;
but the rebels shall live in dry places. **R**

O God, when you went forth before your people,
when you marched through the wilderness,
your people found their home in your goodness, O God,
you have made provision for the poor. **R**   *From Psalm 68*

A reading from the First Letter of Paul to Timothy.

There is great gain in godliness combined with contentment; for
we brought nothing into the world, so that we can take nothing
out of it; but if we have food and clothing, we will be content with
these. But those who want to be rich fall into temptation and are
trapped by many senseless and harmful desires that plunge people into ruin and destruction. For the love of money is a root of all
kinds of evil, and in their eagerness to be rich some have wandered away from the faith and pierced themselves with many
pains. But as for you, man of God, shun all this; pursue righteousness, godliness, faith, love, endurance, gentleness.

This is the word of the Lord.   *1 Timothy 6. 6-11*

Hear the gospel of our Lord Jesus Christ according to Mark.

People were bringing little children to Jesus in order that he might
touch them; and the disciples spoke sternly to them. But when
Jesus saw this, he was indignant and said to them, "Let the little

children come to me; do not stop them; for it is to such as these that the kingdom of God belongs. Truly I tell you, whoever does not receive the kingdom of God as a little child will never enter it." And he took them up in his arms, laid his hands on them, and blessed them.

This is the gospel of the Lord. *Mark 10. 13-16*

Post Communion
God, shepherd of your people,
whose servant Nicholas revealed the loving service of Christ
  in his ministry as a pastor of your people:
by this eucharist in which we share
awaken within us the love of Christ
and keep us faithful to our Christian calling;
through him who laid down his life for us,
but is alive and reigns with you,
now and for ever.

Ambrose, Bishop of Milan
7 December – Lesser Festival – Bishop – White

Born in Trier in 339, Ambrose was of an aristocratic family and was governor of northern Italy, with his headquarters in Milan. Whilst trying to bring peace to the Christian community, with Arianism and orthodoxy each trying to gain the election of its man as bishop, Ambrose, known and respected by all, though not yet baptised, found himself being urged to accept the rôle of bishop, the gathered Christian populace taking up the cry, 'Ambrose for bishop'. He finally accepted and was baptised and consecrated on this day in the year 374. Ambrose proved his worth, becoming a teacher and preacher of great renown, promoting the essential divinity of Christ as being at the centre of Christian faith. He wrote hymns which gave a clear understanding of orthodox teaching, ensuring that what the people prayed was what they believed, and vice versa. He came up against the imperial powers and, with the support of the whole community, stood firm against the interference of the state in church and faith matters. Ambrose died on Good Friday, 4 April, in the year 397.

God of hosts,
who called Ambrose from the governor's throne
to be a bishop in your Church
and an intrepid champion of your faithful people:
mercifully grant that, as he did not fear to rebuke rulers,
so we, with like courage,
  may contend for the faith we have received;
through Jesus Christ your Son our Lord,
who is alive and reigns with you,
in the unity of the Holy Spirit,
one God, now and for ever.

A reading from the prophecy of Isaiah.

You are my servant, I have chosen you and not cast you off; do not fear, for I am with you, do not be afraid, for I am your God; I will strengthen you, I will help you, I will uphold you with my victorious right hand. Yes, all who are incensed against you shall be ashamed and disgraced; those who strive against you shall be as nothing and shall perish. You shall seek those who contend with you, but you shall not find them; those who war against you shall be as nothing at all. For I, the Lord your God, hold your right hand; it is I who say to you, "Do not fear, I will help you."

This is the word of the Lord.   *Isaiah 41. 9b-13*

Responsorial Psalm

**R You are my servant, I have chosen you, says the Lord,
     [I will uphold you for ever].**

May the Lord answer you in the day of trouble,
the name of the God of Jacob defend you;
send you help from his holy place
and strengthen you out of Zion. **R**

May the Lord remember all your offerings
and accept your burnt sacrifice;
may he grant you your heart's desire
and prosper all your plans. **R**

We will shout for joy at your victory
and triumph in the name of our God;
may the Lord grant all your requests. **R**

Now I know that the Lord gives victory to his anointed;
he will answer him out of his holy heaven,
with the victorious strength of his right hand. **R**   *From Psalm 20*

A reading from the Second Letter of Paul to the Corinthians.

From now on, we regard no one from a human point of view; even
though we once knew Christ from a human point of view, we
know him no longer in that way. So if anyone is in Christ, there is
a new creation: everything old has passed away; see, everything
has become new! All this is from God, who reconciled us to himself through Christ, and has given us the ministry of reconciliation;
that is, in Christ God was reconciling the world to himself, not
counting their trespasses against them, and entrusting the message of reconciliation to us. So we are ambassadors for Christ,
since God is making his appeal through us; we entreat you on
behalf of Christ, be reconciled to God. For our sake he made him
to be sin who knew no sin, so that in him we might become the
righteousness of God.

This is the word of the Lord.   *2 Corinthians 5. 16-21*

Hear the gospel of our Lord Jesus Christ according to Luke.

A dispute also arose among the disciples as to which one of them
was to be regarded as the greatest. But Jesus said to them, "The
kings of the Gentiles lord it over them; and those in authority over
them are called benefactors. But not so with you; rather the greatest among you must become like the youngest, and the leader like
one who serves. For who is greater, the one who is at the table or
the one who serves? Is it not the one at the table? But I am among
you as one who serves.

"You are those who have stood by me in my trials; and I confer
on you, just as my Father has conferred on me, a kingdom, so that
you may eat and drink at my table in my kingdom, and you will
sit on thrones judging the twelve tribes of Israel."

This is the gospel of the Lord.   *Luke 22. 24-30*

Post Communion
God of truth,
whose Wisdom set her table
and invited us to eat the bread and drink the wine
  of the kingdom:
help us to lay aside all foolishness
and to live and walk in the way of insight,
that we may come with your servant Ambrose
  to the eternal feast of heaven;
through Jesus Christ our Lord.

The Conception of the Blessèd Virgin Mary
8 December – Lesser Festival – BVM – White

This festival in honour of the conception of the mother of our Lord is celebrated on this day in both the eastern and the western Church. This feast, which dates from the seventh century, acknowledges the preparation by God of his people to receive their Saviour and Lord, putting 'heaven in ordinary' and showing that mortal flesh can indeed bring Christ to the world.

Collect
Almighty and everlasting God,
who stooped to raise fallen humanity
through the child-bearing of blessèd Mary:
grant that we, who have seen your glory
  revealed in our human nature
and your love made perfect in our weakness,
may daily be renewed in your image
and conformed to the pattern of your Son
Jesus Christ our Lord,
who is alive and reigns with you,
in the unity of the Holy Spirit,
one God, now and for ever.

A reading from the book Genesis.

After the man had eaten of the tree, the Lord God called to him and said, "Where are you?" The man said, "I heard the sound of you in the garden, and I was afraid, because I was naked; and I hid myself." He said, "Who told you that you were naked? Have you eaten from the tree of which I commanded you not to eat?" The man said, "The woman whom you gave to be with me, she gave me fruit from the tree, and I ate." Then the Lord God said to the woman, "What is this that you have done?" The woman said, "The serpent tricked me, and I ate." The Lord God said to the serpent, "Because you have done this, cursed are you among all animals and among all wild creatures; upon your belly you shall go, and dust you shall eat all the days of your life. I will put enmity between you and the woman, and between your offspring and hers; he will strike your head, and you will strike his heel."

The man named his wife Eve, because she was the mother of all living.

This is the word of the Lord.   *Genesis 3. 9-15a*

Responsorial Psalm

R Your name will be remembered from generation to generation;
[nations will praise you for ever].

The Lord is king; let the earth rejoice;
let the multitude of the isles be glad.
Clouds and darkness are round about him,
righteousness and justice are the foundations of his throne. **R**

Zion hears and is glad and the cities of Judah rejoice,
because of your judgements, O Lord;
for you are the Lord: most high over all the earth;
you are exalted far above all gods. **R**

The Lord loves those who hate evil;
he preserves the lives of his saints
and delivers them from the hand of the wicked. **R**

Light has sprung up for the righteous,
and joyful gladness for those who are true-hearted.
Rejoice in the Lord, you righteous,
and give thanks to his holy name. **R**   *From Psalm 97*

A reading from the Letter of Paul to the Ephesians.

Blessèd be the God and Father of our Lord Jesus Christ, who has blessed us in Christ with every spiritual blessing in the heavenly places, just as he chose us in Christ before the foundation of the world to be holy and blameless before him in love. He destined us for adoption as his children through Jesus Christ, according to the good pleasure of his will, to the praise of his glorious grace that he freely bestowed on us in the Beloved. In Christ we have also obtained an inheritance, having been destined according to the purpose of him who accomplishes all things according to his counsel and will, so that we, who were the first to set our hope on Christ, might live for the praise of his glory.

This is the word of the Lord.   *Ephesians 1. 3-6, 11-12*

Hear the gospel of our Lord Jesus Christ according to Luke.

In the sixth month the angel Gabriel was sent by God to a town in Galilee called Nazareth, to a virgin engaged to a man whose name was Joseph, of the house of David. The virgin's name was Mary. And he came to her and said, "Greetings, favoured one! The Lord is with you." But she was much perplexed by his words and pondered what sort of greeting this might be. The angel said to her, "Do not be afraid, Mary, for you have found favour with God. And now, you will conceive in your womb and bear a son, and you will name him Jesus. He will be great, and will be called the Son of the Most High, and the Lord God will give to him the throne of his ancestor David. He will reign over the house of Jacob forever, and of his kingdom there will be no end."

Mary said to the angel, "How can this be, since I am a virgin?" The angel said to her, "The Holy Spirit will come upon you, and the power of the Most High will overshadow you; therefore the child to be born will be holy; he will be called Son of God. And now, your relative Elizabeth in her old age has also conceived a son; and this is the sixth month for her who was said to be barren. For nothing will be impossible with God." Then Mary said, "Here am I, the servant of the Lord; let it be with me according to your word." Then the angel departed from her.

This is the gospel of the Lord.   *Luke 1. 26-38*

God Most High,
whose handmaid bore the Word made flesh:
we thank you that in this sacrament of our redemption
you visit us with your Holy Spirit
and overshadow us by your power;
strengthen us to walk with Mary the joyful path of obedience
and so to bring forth the fruits of holiness;
through Jesus Christ our Lord.

Lucy of Syracuse

13 December – Lesser Festival – Martyr – Red

Lucy was a native of Syracuse in Sicily. She lived at the beginning
of the fourth century, when the Roman authorities were attempt-
ing to re-establish the worship of gods they approved. The emper-
or himself was the focus of one of the cults. Tradition has it that
Lucy, as a young Christian, gave away her goods to the poor and
was betrayed to the authorities by her angry betrothed, who felt
that they should have become his property. She was put to death
for her faith in the year 304. Her name in Latin means Light and,
as her feast-day fell in December, she became associated with the
one true Light who was coming as the redeemer of the world, the
Light that would lighten the nations, the Light that would banish
darkness and let the eyes of all behold Truth incarnate.

Collect
God our Redeemer,
who gave light to the world that was in darkness
by the healing power of the Saviour's cross:
shed that light on us, we pray,
that with your martyr Lucy
we may, by the purity of our lives,
  reflect the light of Christ
and, by the merits of his passion,
  come to the light of everlasting life;
through Jesus Christ your Son our Lord,
who is alive and reigns with you,
in the unity of the Holy Spirit,
one God, now and for ever.

A reading from the prophecy of Isaiah.

The sun shall no longer be your light by day, nor for brightness shall the moon give light to you by night; but the Lord will be your everlasting light, and your God will be your glory. Your sun shall no more go down, or your moon withdraw itself; for the Lord will be your everlasting light, and your days of mourning shall be ended.

This is the word of the Lord. *Isaiah 60. 19-20*

Responsorial Psalm

**R In your light do we see light, O God,
    [for with you is the well of life].**

Your love, O Lord, reaches to the heavens
and your faithfulness to the clouds.
Your righteousness is like the strong mountains,
your justice like the great deep. **R**

How priceless is your love, O God,
your people take refuge under your wings,
they feast upon the abundance of your house,
you give them drink from the river of your delights. **R**

Continue your loving-kindness to those who know you
and your favour to those who are true of heart,
let not the foot of the proud come near me
nor the hand of the wicked push me aside. **R** *From Psalm 36*

A reading from the Second Letter of Paul to the Corinthians.

It is the God who said, "Let light shine out of darkness," who has shone in our hearts to give the light of the knowledge of the glory of God in the face of Jesus Christ. But we have this treasure in clay jars, so that it may be made clear that this extraordinary power belongs to God and does not come from us. We are afflicted in every way, but not crushed; perplexed, but not driven to despair; persecuted, but not forsaken; struck down, but not destroyed; always carrying in the body the death of Jesus, so that the life of Jesus may also be made visible in our bodies. For while we live, we are always being given up to death for Jesus' sake, so that the life of Jesus may be made visible in our mortal flesh. So death is at work in us, but life in you.

December 13

But just as we have the same spirit of faith that is in accordance with scripture – "I believed, and so I spoke" – we also believe, and so we speak, because we know that the one who raised the Lord Jesus will raise us also with Jesus, and will bring us with you into his presence. Yes, everything is for your sake, so that grace, as it extends to more and more people, may increase thanksgiving, to the glory of God.

This is the word of the Lord.   *2 Corinthians 4. 6-15*

Hear the gospel of our Lord Jesus Christ according to Luke.

Jesus said to his disciples, "No one after lighting a lamp puts it in a cellar, but on the lampstand so that those who enter may see the light. Your eye is the lamp of your body. If your eye is healthy, your whole body is full of light; but if it is not healthy, your body is full of darkness. Therefore consider whether the light in you is not darkness. If then your whole body is full of light, with no part of it in darkness, it will be as full of light as when a lamp gives you light with its rays."

This is the gospel of the Lord.   *Luke 11. 33-36*

Post Communion
God,
who gave us this holy meal
in which we have celebrated the glory of the cross
and the victory of your martyr Lucy:
by our communion with Christ
in his saving death and resurrection,
give us with all your saints the courage to conquer evil
and so to share the fruit of the tree of life;
through Jesus Christ our Lord.

Samuel Johnson, Moralist
13 December – Commemoration
If celebrated as a Lesser Festival, Common of any Saint, page 531

Samuel Johnson was born in 1709 and is best known as a writer of dictionaries and a literary editor. Yet in his lifetime he was renowned for his religious beliefs and as a firm supporter of the practice and order of the Church of England. He had been converted to Christianity as young man after reading William Law's *A Serious Call to a Devout and Holy Life*, and his support of the High Church party was unstinting. Amongst his other writings, his essays entitled the *Rambler*, which appeared twice-weekly between 1750 and 1752, earned him the nickname 'The Great Moralist', then a term of affection and honour. He died on this day in 1784.

John of the Cross
14 December – Lesser Festival – Religious – White

Born to an impoverished noble family near Avila in Spain in 1542, Juan de Yepes was brought up by his widowed mother and went to a charity school. He worked as a nurse and received further education from the Jesuits before entering the Carmelite order when he was twenty-one. Having distinguished himself at Salamanca university, he was ordained in 1567 and met Teresa of Avila soon afterwards. Small of stature, he made a great impression on her and she persuaded him to help with her reform of the Carmelite order. His labours brought him into conflict with the religious authorities, and he was even imprisoned for a period, yet these experiences prompted some of his finest poetry and mystical writing. In particular, he described the 'dark night' of the soul as it is purified in its approach towards God. After ten years as superior to several different houses, he again fell out of favour and was banished to Andalusia in southern Spain, where he died after a severe illness on this day in 1591.

Collect
O God, the Judge of all,
who gave your servant John of the Cross
a warmth of nature, a strength of purpose
  and a mystical faith
that sustained him even in the darkness:
shed your light on all who love you
and grant them union of body and soul
in your Son Jesus Christ our Lord,

who is alive and reigns with you,
in the unity of the Holy Spirit,
one God, now and for ever.

A reading from the Song of Songs.

The voice of my beloved! Look, he comes, leaping upon the mountains, bounding over the hills. My beloved is like a gazelle or a young stag. Look, there he stands behind our wall, gazing in at the windows, looking through the lattice. My beloved speaks and says to me: "Arise, my love, my fair one, and come away; for now the winter is past, the rain is over and gone. The flowers appear on the earth; the time of singing has come, and the voice of the turtledove is heard in our land. The fig tree puts forth its figs, and the vines are in blossom; they give forth fragrance. ` Arise, my love, my fair one, and come away. O my dove, in the clefts of the rock, in the covert of the cliff, let me see your face, let me hear your voice; for your voice is sweet, and your face is lovely. Catch us the foxes, the little foxes, that ruin the vineyards – for our vineyards are in blossom." My beloved is mine and I am his; he pastures his flock among the lilies. Until the day breathes and the shadows flee, turn, my beloved, be like a gazelle or a young stag on the cleft mountains.

This is the word of the Lord.   *Song of Songs 2. 8-17*

Responsorial Psalm

**R   Tear open the heavens and come down, O Lord,
[that the nations might tremble at your presence!]**

I lift up my eyes to the hills;
from where is my help to come?
My help comes from the Lord,
the maker of heaven and earth. **R**

He will not let your foot be moved
and he who watches over you will not fall asleep.
Behold, he who keeps watch over Israel
shall neither slumber nor sleep. **R**

The Lord shall preserve you from all evil;
it is he who shall keep you safe.
The Lord shall watch over your going out and your coming in,
from this time forth for evermore. **R**   *From Psalm 121*

A reading from the First Letter of Paul to the Corinthians.

When I came to you, brothers and sisters, I did not come proclaiming the mystery of God to you in lofty words or wisdom. For
I decided to know nothing among you except Jesus Christ, and
him crucified. And I came to you in weakness and in fear and in
much trembling. My speech and my proclamation were not with
plausible words of wisdom, but with a demonstration of the Spirit
and of power, so that your faith might rest not on human wisdom
but on the power of God.

Yet among the mature we do speak wisdom, though it is not a
wisdom of this age or of the rulers of this age, who are doomed to
perish. But we speak God's wisdom, secret and hidden, which
God decreed before the ages for our glory. None of the rulers of
this age understood this; for if they had, they would not have crucified the Lord of glory. But, as it is written, "What no eye has
seen, nor ear heard, nor the human heart conceived, what God has
prepared for those who love him" – these things God has revealed
to us through the Spirit; for the Spirit searches everything, even
the depths of God.

This is the word of the Lord.   *1 Corinthians 2. 1-10*

Hear the gospel of our Lord Jesus Christ according to John.

Jesus said to his disciples, "I will not leave you orphaned; I am
coming to you. In a little while the world will no longer see me,
but you will see me; because I live, you also will live. On that day
you will know that I am in my Father, and you in me, and I in you.
They who have my commandments and keep them are those who
love me; and those who love me will be loved by my Father, and I
will love them and reveal myself to them." Judas (not Iscariot) said
to him, "Lord, how is it that you will reveal yourself to us, and not
to the world?" Jesus answered him, "Those who love me will keep
my word, and my Father will love them, and we will come to them

and make our home with them."

This is the gospel of the Lord.   *John 14. 18-23*

Post Communion
God of truth,
whose Wisdom set her table
and invited us to eat the bread and drink the wine
  of the kingdom:
help us to lay aside all foolishness
and to live and walk in the way of insight,
that we may come with your servant John of the Cross
  to the eternal feast of heaven;
through Jesus Christ our Lord.

O Sapientia
17 December

The cryptic phrase *O Sapientia* appears in *The Book of Common Prayer* without explanation. 17 December marks the beginning of the week before the celebration of Christmas, the Birth of Christ, and at Evensong, the great Song of Mary, *Magnificat*, has a refrain or antiphon attached to it proclaiming the ascriptions or 'names' given to God through the Old Testament. Each name develops into a prophecy of the forthcoming and eagerly-anticipated Messiah, Jesus, the Son of God. *O Sapientia*, or *O Wisdom*, is the first of these days, followed on 18 December by *O Adonai*, then *O Root of Jesse*, *O Key of David*, *O Dayspring*, O *King of the Nations* and finally on 23 December *O Emmanuel*. In the old Sarum rite, these were sung one day earlier, requiring another ascription for 23 December, this being *O Virgin of Virgins*. Since this was clearly apposite to the Blessèd Virgin Mary, and not a 'title' of God (though, of course, it could easily be) it was not adopted much beyond Sarum and, with the revision of the Calendar, the Church of England has adopted the more widely-used formulæ and dating.

Eglantine Jebb, Social Reformer
17 December – Commemoration
If celebrated as a Lesser Festival, Common of any Saint, page 527

Eglantine Jebb was born in 1876. After studying at Oxford, she became a teacher for a few years until ill-health led to her resignation. She then devoted her energies to charitable works and in 1913 went to Macedonia to help refugees in the Balkan wars. After the First World War, she and her sister Dorothy Buxton founded the Save the Children Fund, which aimed to help children who were suffering in the post-war famine in Europe, a charity which is now global in its scope. Eglantine fought for the rights of children to be recognised, the League of Nations passing her 'Children's Charter' in 1924. She inspired many by her personal spirituality and was greatly mourned on her death in Geneva on this day in 1928.

Stephen, Deacon, First Martyr
26 December – Festival – Martyr – Red
This celebration may be observed if on the Sunday after Christmas

In the book of the *Acts of the Apostles*, Stephen is described as one of the seven deacons whose job it is to care for the widows in the early Church in Jerusalem. His eloquent speech before the Sanhedrin, in which he shows the great sweep of Jewish history as leading to the birth of Jesus, the long-expected Messiah, and his impassioned plea that all might hear the good news of Jesus, leads to his inevitable martyrdom by being stoned to death. As the author of *Acts,* Luke's description of Stephen bears direct parallels to that of Christ: for example, the passion; being filled with the Holy Spirit; seeing the Son of God as the right hand of God, as Jesus promised he would be; commending his spirit to Jesus, as Jesus commended his to the Father; kneeling as Jesus did in Gethsemane and asking forgiveness for his persecutors. Witnessing to Jesus by acting like Jesus in every way is thus seen by Luke as of the essence of the Christian life.

Collect
Gracious Father,
who gave the first martyr Stephen
grace to pray for those who took up stones against him:
grant that in all our sufferings for the truth
we may learn to love even our enemies
and to seek forgiveness for those who desire our hurt,
looking up to heaven to him who was crucified for us,
Jesus Christ, our Mediator and Advocate,
who is alive and reigns with you,
in the unity of the Holy Spirit,
one God, now and for ever.

2 Chronicles 24. 20-22	*or*	Acts 7. 51-60
Psalm 119. 161-168		Psalm 119. 161-168
Acts 7. 51-60		Galatians 2. 16*b*-20
Matthew 23.34-39		Matthew 23.34-39

A reading from the Second Book of the Chronicles.

The spirit of God took possession of Zechariah son of the priest Jehoiada; he stood above the people and said to them, "Thus says God: Why do you transgress the commandments of the Lord, so that you cannot prosper? Because you have forsaken the Lord, he has also forsaken you." But they conspired against him, and by command of the king they stoned him to death in the court of the house of the Lord. King Joash did not remember the kindness that Jehoiada, Zechariah's father, had shown him, but killed his son. As he was dying, he said, "May the Lord see and avenge!"

This is the word of the Lord.   *2 Chronicles 24. 20-22*

A reading from the Acts of the Apostles.

Stephen said to the council, "You stiff-necked people, uncircumcised in heart and ears, you are forever opposing the Holy Spirit, just as your ancestors used to do. Which of the prophets did your ancestors not persecute? They killed those who foretold the coming of the Righteous One, and now you have become his betrayers and murderers. You are the ones that received the law as ordained by angels, and yet you have not kept it."

When they heard these things, they became enraged and ground their teeth at Stephen. But filled with the Holy Spirit, he gazed into heaven and saw the glory of God and Jesus standing at the right hand of God. "Look," he said, "I see the heavens opened and the Son of Man standing at the right hand of God!" But they covered their ears, and with a loud shout all rushed together against him. Then they dragged him out of the city and began to stone him; and the witnesses laid their coats at the feet of a young man named Saul. While they were stoning Stephen, he prayed, "Lord Jesus, receive my spirit." Then he knelt down and cried out in a loud voice, "Lord, do not hold this sin against them." When he had said this, he died.

This is the word of the Lord. *Acts 7. 51-60*

Responsorial Psalm

R   Let my cry come before you, O Lord;
**   [give me understanding, according to your word].**

Rulers have persecuted me without a cause,
but my heart stands in awe of your word.
I am as glad because of your promise
as one who finds great spoils. **R**

As for lies, I hate and abhor them,
but your law is my love.
Seven times a day do I praise you,
because of your righteous judgements. **R**

Great peace have they who love your law;
for them there is no stumbling block.
I have hoped for your salvation, O Lord,
and I have fulfilled your commandments. **R**

I have kept your decrees
and I have loved them deeply.
I have kept your commandments and decrees,
for all my ways are before you. **R**   *From Psalm 119*

A reading from the Letter of Paul to the Galatians.

We have come to believe in Christ Jesus, so that we might be justified by faith in Christ, and not by doing the works of the law, because no one will be justified by the works of the law. But if, in our effort to be justified in Christ, we ourselves have been found to be sinners, is Christ then a servant of sin? Certainly not! But if I build up again the very things that I once tore down, then I demonstrate that I am a transgressor. For through the law I died to the law, so that I might live to God. I have been crucified with Christ; and it is no longer I who live, but it is Christ who lives in me. And the life I now live in the flesh I live by faith in the Son of God, who loved me and gave himself for me.

This is the word of the Lord. *Galatians 2. 16b-20*

Hear the gospel of our Lord Jesus Christ according to Matthew.
Jesus said, 'Woe to you, scribes and Pharisees, hypocrites! I send you prophets, sages, and scribes, some of whom you will kill and crucify, and some you will flog in your synagogues and pursue from town to town, so that upon you may come all the righteous blood shed on earth, from the blood of righteous Abel to the blood of Zechariah son of Barachiah, whom you murdered between the sanctuary and the altar. Truly I tell you, all this will come upon this generation.

'Jerusalem, Jerusalem, the city that kills the prophets and stones those who are sent to it! How often have I desired to gather your children together as a hen gathers her brood under her wings, and you were not willing! See, your house is left to you, desolate. For I tell you, you will not see me again until you say, "Blessèd is the one who comes in the name of the Lord."'

This is the gospel of the Lord. *Matthew 23.34-39*

Post Communion
Merciful Lord,
we thank you for the signs of your mercy
revealed in birth and death:
save us by the coming of your Son,
and give us joy in honouring your servant Stephen,
first martyr of the new Israel;
through Jesus Christ our Lord.

John, Apostle & Evangelist

27 December – Festival – Apostle – White
This celebration may be observed if on the Sunday after Christmas

Whether or not John the Apostle and John the Evangelist are one and the same, the Church honours on this day the one who proclaims Jesus as the Word made flesh and who is 'the disciple whom Jesus loved'. John was one of the sons of Zebedee, along with James and Peter, who followed Jesus. John was there at the Transfiguration of Jesus on the holy mountain; he was there with Jesus at the last supper; he was there with Jesus in his agony in the garden; he was there with Jesus and his mother, standing at the foot of the cross; he was there with Jesus as a witness of his resurrection and 'he saw and believed'. John was a witness to the Word, he proclaimed the Word and he lived and died witnessing to the Word made flesh, Jesus Christ, who loved him and whom he loved.

Collect
Merciful Lord,
cast your bright beams of light upon the Church:
that, being enlightened by the teaching
  of your blessèd apostle and evangelist Saint John,
we may so walk in the light of your truth
that we may at last attain to the light of everlasting life;
through Jesus Christ
your incarnate Son our Lord,
who is alive and reigns with you,
in the unity of the Holy Spirit,
one God, now and for ever.

A reading from the book of the Exodus.

Moses said to the Lord, 'See, you have said to me, "Bring up this people"; but you have not let me know whom you will send with me. Yet you have said, "I know you by name, and you have also found favour in my sight." Now if I have found favour in your sight, show me your ways, so that I may know you and find favour in your sight. Consider too that this nation is your people.' He said, 'My presence will go with you, and I will give you rest.'

And he said to him, 'If your presence will not go, do not carry us up from here. For how shall it be known that I have found favour in your sight, I and your people, unless you go with us? In this way, we shall be distinct, I and your people, from every people on the face of the earth.'

The Lord said to Moses, 'I will do the very thing that you have asked; for you have found favour in my sight, and I know you by name.' Moses said, 'Show me your glory, I pray.' And he said, 'I will make all my goodness pass before you, and will proclaim before you the name, "The Lord"; and I will be gracious to whom I will be gracious, and will show mercy on whom I will show mercy. But', he said, 'you cannot see my face; for no one shall see me and live.' And the Lord continued, 'See, there is a place by me where you shall stand on the rock; and while my glory passes by I will put you in a cleft of the rock, and I will cover you with my hand until I have passed by; then I will take away my hand, and you shall see my back; but my face shall not be seen.'

This is the word of the Lord.   *Exodus 33. 12-23*

Responsorial Psalm

**R   The Lord spoke to him face to face
[as one speaks to a friend].**

Praise the Lord, all you nations;
laud him, all you peoples. **R**

For his loving-kindness towards us is great,
and the faithfulness of the Lord endures for ever. **R**   *Psalm 117*

A reading from the First Letter of John.

We declare to you what was from the beginning, what we have heard, what we have seen with our eyes, what we have looked at and touched with our hands, concerning the word of life – this life was revealed, and we have seen it and testify to it, and declare to you the eternal life that was with the Father and was revealed to us – we declare to you what we have seen and heard so that you also may have fellowship with us; and truly our fellowship is with the Father and with his Son Jesus Christ. We are writing these things so that our joy may be complete.

This is the message we have heard from him and proclaim to you, that God is light and in him there is no darkness at all. If we say that we have fellowship with him while we are walking in darkness, we lie and do not do what is true; but if we walk in the light as he himself is in the light, we have fellowship with one another, and the blood of Jesus his Son cleanses us from all sin. If we say that we have no sin, we deceive ourselves, and the truth is not in us. If we confess our sins, he who is faithful and just will forgive us our sins and cleanse us from all unrighteousness. If we say that we have not sinned, we make him a liar, and his word is not in us.

This is the word of the Lord.   *1 John 1*

Hear the gospel of our Lord Jesus Christ according to John.

Peter saw the disciple whom Jesus loved following them; he was the one who had reclined next to Jesus at the supper and had said, "Lord, who is it that is going to betray you?" When Peter saw him, he said to Jesus, "Lord, what about him?" Jesus said to him, "If it is my will that he remain until I come, what is that to you? Follow me!" So the rumour spread in the community that this disciple would not die. Yet Jesus did not say to him that he would not die, but, "If it is my will that he remain until I come, what is that to you?"

This is the disciple who is testifying to these things and has written them, and we know that his testimony is true. But there are also many other things that Jesus did; if every one of them were written down, I suppose that the world itself could not contain the books that would be written.

This is the gospel of the Lord.   *John 21. 20-25*

Post Communion
Grant, O Lord, we pray,
that the Word made flesh
proclaimed by your apostle John
may, by the celebration of these holy mysteries,
ever abide and live within us;
through Jesus Christ our Lord.

The Holy Innocents

28 December – Festival – Red

This celebration may be observed if on the Sunday after Christmas

Herod 'the Great' was appointed King of the Jews by the Roman authorities in Palestine and he proved to be ruthlessly efficient in his thirty-three years of dealing with his subjects. In Matthew's gospel, he tried to persuade the Magi, to whom he played the host on their journey seeking the one 'who has been born king of the Jews', to bring word of where they had found him. His desire was to eliminate Jesus and, when he realised that the Magi had tricked him and left the country, Herod killed all the children under the age of two, in and around Bethlehem. These were God's 'innocent' ones, parallelling the story of Pharaoh slaughtering the Hebrew children in Egypt.

Collect

Heavenly Father,
whose children suffered at the hands of Herod,
though they had done no wrong:
by the suffering of your Son
and by the innocence of our lives
frustrate all evil designs
and establish your reign of justice and peace;
through Jesus Christ your Son our Lord,
who is alive and reigns with you,
in the unity of the Holy Spirit,
one God, now and for ever.

A reading from the prophecy of Jeremiah.

Thus says the Lord: A voice is heard in Ramah, lamentation and bitter weeping. Rachel is weeping for her children; she refuses to be comforted for her children, because they are no more. Thus says the Lord: Keep your voice from weeping, and your eyes from tears; for there is a reward for your work, says the Lord: they shall come back from the land of the enemy; there is hope for your future, says the Lord: your children shall come back to their own country.

This is the word of the Lord.   *Jeremiah 31. 15-17*

**R Our help is in the name of the Lord,
[the maker of heaven and earth].**

If the Lord had not been on our side,
let Israel now say;
if the Lord had not been on our side,
when enemies rose up against us; **R**

Then would they have swallowed us up alive
in their fierce anger towards us;
then would the waters have overwhelmed us
and the torrent gone over us. **R**

Blessèd be the Lord!
who has not given us over to be a prey for their teeth.
We have escaped like a bird from the snare of the fowler;
the snare is broken and we have escaped. **R**   *Psalm 124*

A reading from the First Letter of Paul to the Corinthians.

Consider your own call, brothers and sisters: not many of you
were wise by human standards, not many were powerful, not
many were of noble birth. But God chose what is foolish in the
world to shame the wise; God chose what is weak in the world to
shame the strong; God chose what is low and despised in the
world, things that are not, to reduce to nothing things that are, so
that no one might boast in the presence of God.

This is the word of the Lord.   *1 Corinthians 1. 26-29*

Hear the gospel of our Lord Jesus Christ according to Matthew.

After the wise men had left, an angel of the Lord appeared to
Joseph in a dream and said, "Get up, take the child and his mother, and flee to Egypt, and remain there until I tell you; for Herod
is about to search for the child, to destroy him." Then Joseph got
up, took the child and his mother by night, and went to Egypt,
and remained there until the death of Herod. This was to fulfil
what had been spoken by the Lord through the prophet, "Out of
Egypt I have called my son."

When Herod saw that he had been tricked by the wise men, he
was infuriated, and he sent and killed all the children in and

around Bethlehem who were two years old or under, according to the time that he had learned from the wise men. Then was fulfilled what had been spoken through the prophet Jeremiah: "A voice was heard in Ramah, wailing and loud lamentation, Rachel weeping for her children; she refused to be consoled, because they are no more."

This is the gospel of the Lord.   *Matthew 2. 13-18*

Post Communion
Lord Jesus Christ,
in your humility you have stooped to share our human life
with the most defenceless of your children:
may we who have received these gifts of your passion
rejoice in celebrating the witness of the holy innocents
  to the purity of your sacrifice
  made once for all upon the cross;
for you are alive and reign, now and for ever.

Thomas Becket, Archbishop of Canterbury
29 December – Lesser Festival – Martyr – Red

Thomas was born in London in 1118, of a family of merchants. After a good education he served as clerk to another burgess then entered the service of Archbishop Theobald of Canterbury. Thomas proved himself an excellent administrator and skilled diplomat. In 1155 he was appointed chancellor by King Henry II. For several years king and chancellor worked harmoniously together in mutual admiration and personal friendship. As a result, the king nominated Thomas as Archbishop of Canterbury to succeed Theobald in 1161. From the start there was friction, with Thomas insisting on every privilege of the Church. The conflict worsened until 1164 when Thomas fled to France. Encouraged by the Pope he pursued his arguments from exile, sending letters and pronouncing excommunications. Three efforts at mediation failed before an apparent reconciliation brought him back triumphant to Canterbury in 1170. But the nobility still opposed him, and words of anger at court led four knights to journey to Canterbury where they finally chased Thomas into the cathedral, and murdered him on the steps of the altar on this day in 1170. Thomas was undoubtedly a proud and stubborn man, for all his gifts, and his personal austerities as archbishop were probably an attempt at self-discipline after years of ostentatious luxury. His conflict with King Henry stemmed from their equal personal ambitions, exacerbated by the increasingly international claims of the papacy, played out in the inevitable tension between Church and State.

Collect
Lord God,
who gave grace to your servant Thomas Becket
to put aside all earthly fear
  and be faithful even to death:
grant that we, disregarding worldly esteem,
may fight all wrong, uphold your rule,
and serve you to our life's end;
through Jesus Christ your Son our Lord,
who is alive and reigns with you,
in the unity of the Holy Spirit,
one God, now and for ever.

A reading from the First Book of the Kings.

Elijah came to a cave, and spent the night there. Then the word of the Lord came to him, saying, "What are you doing here, Elijah?" He answered, "I have been very zealous for the Lord, the God of hosts; for the Israelites have forsaken your covenant, thrown down your altars, and killed your prophets with the sword. I alone am left, and they are seeking my life, to take it away." He said, "Go out and stand on the mountain before the Lord, for the Lord is about to pass by." Now there was a great wind, so strong that it was splitting mountains and breaking rocks in pieces before the Lord, but the Lord was not in the wind; and after the wind an earthquake, but the Lord was not in the earthquake; and after the earthquake a fire, but the Lord was not in the fire; and after the fire a sound of sheer silence. When Elijah heard it, he wrapped his face in his mantle and went out and stood at the entrance of the cave.

This is the word of the Lord. *1 Kings 19. 9-13a*

Responsorial Psalm

R Behold, God is my helper;
   [it is the Lord who sustains my life].

Save me, O God, by your name;
in your might, defend my cause.
Hear my prayer, O God;
give ear to the words of my mouth. **R**
For the arrogant have risen up against me,
and the ruthless have sought my life,
those who have no regard for God. **R**

I will offer you a freewill sacrifice
and praise your name, O Lord, for it is good.
For you have rescued me from every trouble,
and my eye has seen the ruin of my foes. **R**   *From Psalm 54*

A reading from the Letter to the Hebrews.

We have an altar from which those who officiate in the tent have
no right to eat. For the bodies of those animals whose blood is
brought into the sanctuary by the high priest as a sacrifice for sin
are burned outside the camp. Therefore Jesus also suffered outside the city gate in order to sanctify the people by his own blood.
Let us then go to him outside the camp and bear the abuse he
endured. For here we have no lasting city, but we are looking for
the city that is to come. Through him, then, let us continually offer
a sacrifice of praise to God, that is, the fruit of lips that confess his
name. Do not neglect to do good and to share what you have, for
such sacrifices are pleasing to God.

This is the word of the Lord.   *Hebrews 13. 10-16*

Hear the gospel of our Lord Jesus Christ according to Matthew.

Jesus said to his disciples, "Do not fear those who kill the body but
cannot kill the soul; rather fear him who can destroy both soul and
body in hell. Are not two sparrows sold for a penny? Yet not one
of them will fall to the ground apart from your Father. And even
the hairs of your head are all counted."

This is the gospel of the Lord.   *Matthew 10. 28-30*

Post Communion
God our Redeemer,
whose Church was strengthened
  by the blood of your martyr Thomas Becket:
so bind us, in life and death, to Christ's sacrifice
that our lives, broken and offered with his,
may carry his death and proclaim his resurrection in the world;
through Jesus Christ our Lord.

John Wyclif, Reformer
31 December – *Commemoration*
If celebrated as a Lesser Festival, Common of any Saint, page 531

John was a member of the Wyclif family of Richmond in Yorkshire and was born in about the year 1330. He was a fellow of Merton College Oxford, and Master of Balliol, but his expulsion from the Wardenship of Canterbury Hall (later incorporated into Christ Church) in favour of a monastic foundation led to a lawsuit and a life-long hatred of things monastic. He was much in favour with members of the royal family and, when disputes arose owing to his attacks on the clergy of the day, he was protected by them from the otherwise inevitable consequence of deprivation of his posts. However, he went on to deny the Church's teaching of the presence of Christ at the eucharist, the doctrine known as *transubstantiation,* and it was this that lost him his royal protection. His opinions were formally condemned in 1381 and he was forced out of office by the university the following year. John had already moved to Lutterworth in 1380 and from there he gave his support to such projects as the translation of the Bible into contemporary English. He died on this day in 1384, whilst at Mass.

Common of the Saints

THE BLESSED VIRGIN MARY
White or Gold

Collect

Almighty and everlasting God,
who stooped to raise fallen humanity
through the child-bearing of blessèd Mary;
grant that we, who have seen your glory
  revealed in our human nature
and your love made perfect in our weakness,
may daily be renewed in your image
and conformed to the pattern of your Son
Jesus Christ our Lord,
who is alive and reigns with you,
in the unity of the Holy Spirit,
one God, now and for ever.

Post Communion

God Most High,
whose handmaid bore the Word made flesh:
we thank you that in this sacrament of our redemption
you visit us with your Holy Spirit
and overshadow us by your power;
strengthen us to walk with Mary the joyful path of obedience
and so to bring forth the fruits of holiness;
through Jesus Christ our Lord.

A reading from the book Genesis.

The man and the woman heard the sound of the Lord God walking in the garden at the time of the evening breeze, and the man and his wife hid themselves from the presence of the Lord God among the trees of the garden. But the Lord God called to the man, and said to him, "Where are you?" He said, "I heard the sound of you in the garden, and I was afraid, because I was naked; and I hid myself." God said, "Who told you that you were naked? Have you eaten from the tree of which I commanded you not to eat?" The man said, "The woman whom you gave to be with me, she gave me fruit from the tree, and I ate." Then the Lord God said to the woman, "What is this that you have done?" The woman said, "The serpent tricked me, and I ate." The Lord God said to the serpent, "Because you have done this, cursed are you among all animals and among all wild creatures; upon your belly you shall go, and dust you shall eat all the days of your life. I will put enmity between you and the woman, and between your off-spring and hers; he will strike your head, and you will strike his heel." The man named his wife Eve, because she was the mother of all living.

This is the word of the Lord. *Genesis 3. 8-15, 20*

A reading from the prophecy of Isaiah.

The Lord spoke to Ahaz, saying, Ask a sign of the Lord your God; let it be deep as Sheol or high as heaven. But Ahaz said, I will not ask, and I will not put the Lord to the test. Then Isaiah said: "Hear then, O house of David! Is it too little for you to weary mortals, that you weary my God also? Therefore the Lord himself will give you a sign. Look, the young woman is with child and shall bear a son, and shall name him Immanuel."

This is the word of the Lord. *Isaiah 7. 10-14*

A reading from the prophecy of Micah.

You are walled around with a wall; siege is laid against us; with a rod they strike the ruler of Israel upon the cheek. But you, O Bethlehem of Ephrathah, who are one of the little clans of Judah, from you shall come forth for me one who is to rule in Israel, whose origin is from of old, from ancient days.

Therefore he shall give them up until the time when she who is in labour has brought forth; then the rest of his kindred shall return to the people of Israel. And he shall stand and feed his flock in the strength of the Lord, in the majesty of the name of the Lord his God. And they shall live secure, for now he shall be great to the ends of the earth.

This is the word of the Lord. *Micah 5. 1-4*

Responsorial Psalm

**R The Holy Spirit will come upon you
[for you have found favour with God].**

Hear, O daughter; consider and listen closely;
forget your people and your family's house.
The king will have pleasure in your beauty;
he is your master; therefore do him honour. **R**

The people of Tyre are here with a gift;
the rich among the people seek your favour.
All glorious is the princess as she enters;
her gown is cloth-of-gold. **R**

In embroidered apparel she is brought to the king;
after her the bridesmaids follow in procession.
With joy and gladness they are brought,
and enter into the palace of the king. **R**

In place of fathers, O king, you shall have sons;
you shall make them princes over all the earth.
I will make your name to be remembered
  from one generation to another;
therefore nations will praise you for ever and ever. **R**

From Psalm 45

Responsorial Psalm

**R Let the name of the Lord be praised
[who sits enthroned on high].**

Give praise, you servants of the Lord;
praise the name of the Lord.
Let the name of the Lord be blessed,
from this time forth for evermore. **R**

From the rising of the sun to its going down
let the name of the Lord be praised.
The Lord is high above all nations,
and his glory above the heavens. **R**

Who is like the Lord our God, who sits enthroned on high,
but stoops to behold the heavens and the earth?
He takes up the weak out of the dust
and lifts up the poor from the ashes. **R**

He sets them with the princes,
with the princes of his people.
He makes the woman of a childless house
to be a joyful mother of children. **R**   *Psalm 113*

Responsorial Psalm

R   Christ came in our poor flesh
[to share a mother's care].

O Lord, I am not proud;
I have no haughty looks.
I do not occupy myself with great matters,
or with things that are too hard for me. **R**

But I still my soul and make it quiet,
like a child upon its mother's breast;
my soul is quieted within me. **R**

O Israel, wait upon the Lord,
from this time forth for evermore. **R**   *Psalm 131*

A reading from the Acts of the Apostles.

Then the apostles returned to Jerusalem from the mount called
Olivet, which is near Jerusalem, a sabbath day's journey away.
When they had entered the city, they went to the room upstairs
where they were staying, Peter, and John, and James, and
Andrew, Philip and Thomas, Bartholomew and Matthew, James
son of Alphaeus, and Simon the Zealot, and Judas son of James.
All these were constantly devoting themselves to prayer, together
with certain women, including Mary the mother of Jesus, as well
as his brothers.

This is the word of the Lord.   *Acts 1. 12-14*

A reading from the Letter of Paul to the Romans.

I consider that the sufferings of this present time are not worth
comparing with the glory about to be revealed to us. For the creation waits with eager longing for the revealing of the children of
God; for the creation was subjected to futility, not of its own will
but by the will of the one who subjected it, in hope that the cre-

ation itself will be set free from its bondage to decay and will obtain the freedom of the glory of the children of God. We know that the whole creation has been groaning in labour pains until now; and not only the creation, but we ourselves, who have the first fruits of the Spirit, groan inwardly while we wait for adoption, the redemption of our bodies. For in hope we were saved. Now hope that is seen is not hope. For who hopes for what is seen? But if we hope for what we do not see, we wait for it with patience.

Likewise the Spirit helps us in our weakness; for we do not know how to pray as we ought, but that very Spirit intercedes with sighs too deep for words. And God, who searches the heart, knows what is the mind of the Spirit, because the Spirit intercedes for the saints according to the will of God.

We know that all things work together for good for those who love God, who are called according to his purpose. For those whom he foreknew he also predestined to be conformed to the image of his Son, in order that he might be the firstborn within a large family. And those whom he predestined he also called; and those whom he called he also justified; and those whom he justified he also glorified.

This is the word of the Lord.   *Romans 8. 18-30*

A reading from the Letter of Paul to the Galatians.

When the fullness of time had come, God sent his Son, born of a woman, born under the law, in order to redeem those who were under the law, so that we might receive adoption as children. And because you are children, God has sent the Spirit of his Son into our hearts, crying, "Abba! Father!" So you are no longer a slave but a child, and if a child then also an heir, through God.

This is the word of the Lord.   *Galatians 4. 4-7*

Hear the gospel of our Lord Jesus Christ according to Luke.

In the sixth month the angel Gabriel was sent by God to a town in Galilee called Nazareth, to a virgin engaged to a man whose name was Joseph, of the house of David. The virgin's name was Mary. And he came to her and said, "Greetings, favoured one! The Lord is with you." But she was much perplexed by his words and pondered what sort of greeting this might be. The angel said to her, "Do not be afraid, Mary, for you have found favour with God. And now, you will conceive in your womb and bear a son, and you will name him Jesus. He will be great, and will be called the Son of the Most High, and the Lord God will give to him the throne of his ancestor David. He will reign over the house of Jacob forever, and of his kingdom there will be no end."

Mary said to the angel, "How can this be, since I am a virgin?" The angel said to her, "The Holy Spirit will come upon you, and the power of the Most High will overshadow you; therefore the child to be born will be holy; he will be called Son of God. And now, your relative Elizabeth in her old age has also conceived a son; and this is the sixth month for her who was said to be barren. For nothing will be impossible with God."

Then Mary said, "Here am I, the servant of the Lord; let it be with me according to your word." Then the angel departed from her.

This is the gospel of the Lord.   *Luke 1. 26-38*

Hear the gospel of our Lord Jesus Christ according to Luke.

Mary set out and went with haste to a Judean town in the hill country, where she entered the house of Zechariah and greeted Elizabeth.   When Elizabeth heard Mary's greeting, the child leaped in her womb. And Elizabeth was filled with the Holy Spirit and exclaimed with a loud cry, "Blessèd are you among women, and blessèd is the fruit of your womb. And why has this happened to me, that the mother of my Lord comes to me? For as soon as I heard the sound of your greeting, the child in my womb leaped for joy. And blessèd is she who believed that there would be a fulfilment of what was spoken to her by the Lord." And Mary said, "My soul magnifies the Lord, and my spirit rejoices in God my Saviour."

This is the gospel of the Lord.   *Luke 1. 39-47*

Hear the gospel of our Lord Jesus Christ according to John.

Standing near the cross of Jesus were his mother, and his mother's sister, Mary the wife of Clopas, and Mary Magdalene. When Jesus saw his mother and the disciple whom he loved standing beside her, he said to his mother, "Woman, here is your son." Then he said to the disciple, "Here is your mother." And from that hour the disciple took her into his own home.

This is the gospel of the Lord.   *John 19. 25b-27*

APOSTLES & EVANGELISTS
Red – Festival

Collect
Almighty God,
who built your Church upon the foundation
  of the apostles and prophets,
with Jesus Christ himself as the chief corner-stone:
so join us together in unity of spirit by their doctrine,
that we may be made a holy temple acceptable to you;
through Jesus Christ your Son our Lord,
who is alive and reigns with you,
in the unity of the Holy Spirit,
one God, now and for ever.

Post Communion
Almighty God,
who on the day of Pentecost
sent your Holy Spirit to the apostles
with the wind from heaven and in tongues of flame,
filling them with joy and boldness to preach the gospel:
by the power of the same Spirit
strengthen us to witness to your truth
and to draw everyone to the fire of your love;
through Jesus Christ our Lord.

Or:
Lord God, the source of truth and love,
keep us faithful to the apostles' teaching and fellowship,
united in prayer and the breaking of bread,
and one in joy and simplicity of heart,
in Jesus Christ our Lord.

The readings are printed on the appropriate date.

MARTYRS
Red

Collect

Almighty God,
by whose grace and power your holy martyr N.
triumphed over suffering and was faithful unto death:
strengthen us with your grace,
that we may endure reproach and persecution
and faithfully bear witness to the name
  of Jesus Christ your Son our Lord,
who is alive and reigns with you,
in the unity of the Holy Spirit,
one God, now and for ever.

Post Communion

Eternal God,
who gave us this holy meal
in which we have celebrated the glory of the cross
and the victory of your martyr N.:
by our communion with Christ
in his saving death and resurrection,
give us with all your saints the courage to conquer evil
and so to share the fruit of the tree of life;
through Jesus Christ our Lord.

Or:

God our Redeemer,
whose Church was strengthened
  by the blood of your martyr N.:
so bind us, in life and death, to Christ's sacrifice
that our lives, broken and offered with his,
may carry his death and proclaim his resurrection in the world;
through Jesus Christ our Lord.

A reading from the Second Book of the Chronicles.

After the death of Jehoiada the officials of Judah came and did obeisance to the king; then the king listened to them. They aban-

doned the house of the Lord, the God of their ancestors, and
served the sacred poles and the idols. And wrath came upon
Judah and Jerusalem for this guilt of theirs. Yet he sent prophets
among them to bring them back to the Lord; they testified against
them, but they would not listen.

Then the spirit of God took possession of Zechariah son of the
priest Jehoiada; he stood above the people and said to them, "Thus
says God: Why do you transgress the commandments of the Lord,
so that you cannot prosper? Because you have forsaken the Lord,
he has also forsaken you." But they conspired against him, and by
command of the king they stoned him to death in the court of the
house of the Lord.

This is the word of the Lord.   *2 Chronicles 24. 17-21*

A reading from the prophecy of Isaiah.

Thus says the Lord, he who created you, O Jacob, he who formed
you, O Israel: Do not fear, for I have redeemed you; I have called
you by name, you are mine. When you pass through the waters,
I will be with you; and through the rivers, they shall not over-
whelm you; when you walk through fire you shall not be burned,
and the flame shall not consume you. For I am the Lord your God,
the Holy One of Israel, your Saviour. I give Egypt as your ransom,
Ethiopia and Seba in exchange for you. Because you are precious
in my sight, and honoured, and I love you, I give people in return
for you, nations in exchange for your life. Do not fear, for I am
with you; I will bring your offspring from the east, and from the
west I will gather you; I will say to the north, "Give them up," and
to the south, "Do not withhold; bring my sons from far away and
my daughters from the end of the earth – everyone who is called
by my name, whom I created for my glory, whom I formed and
made."

This is the word of the Lord.   *Isaiah 43. 1-7*

A reading from the prophecy of Jeremiah.

It was the Lord who made it known to me, and I knew; then you
showed me their evil deeds. But I was like a gentle lamb led to the
slaughter. And I did not know it was against me that they devised

schemes, saying, "Let us destroy the tree with its fruit, let us cut him off from the land of the living, so that his name will no longer be remembered!" But you, O Lord of hosts, who judge righteously, who try the heart and the mind, let me see your retribution upon them, for to you I have committed my cause.

This is the word of the Lord. *Jeremiah 11. 18-20*

A reading from the Wisdom of Solomon.

There were some who pleased God and were loved by him, and while living among sinners were taken up. They were caught up so that evil might not change their understanding or guile deceive their souls. For the fascination of wickedness obscures what is good, and roving desire perverts the innocent mind. Being perfected in a short time, they fulfilled long years; for their souls were pleasing to the Lord, therefore he took them quickly from the midst of wickedness. Yet the peoples saw and did not understand, or take such a thing to heart, that God's grace and mercy are with his elect, and that he watches over his holy ones.

This is the word of the Lord. *Wisdom 4. 10-15*

Responsorial Psalm

**R   Into your hands, O Lord,
      I commend my spirit.**

You, O Lord, are a shield about me;
you are my glory, the one who lifts up my head.
I call aloud upon the Lord
and he answers me from his holy hill. **R**

I lie down and go to sleep;
I wake again, because the Lord sustains me.
Deliverance belongs to the Lord.
Your blessing be upon your people! **R** *From Psalm 3*

Responsorial Psalm

**R   Whoever serves me must follow me, says God;
      [where I am, my servant will be there also].**

In the Lord have I taken refuge;
how then can you say to me,
"'Fly away like a bird to the hilltop." **R**

For see how the wicked bend the bow
and fit their arrows to the string,
to shoot from ambush at the true of heart. **R**

The Lord is in his holy temple;
the Lord's throne is in heaven.
His eyes behold the inhabited world;
his piercing eye weighs our worth. **R**

The Lord weighs the righteous as well as the wicked,
but those who delight in violence he abhors.
For the Lord is righteous; he delights in righteous deeds;
and the just shall see his face. **R**   *From Psalm 11*

Responsorial Psalm

**R I have trusted in you, O Lord,
[I have said, "You are my God"].**

In you, O Lord, have I taken refuge;
let me never be put to shame;
deliver me in your righteousness.
Incline your ear to me; make haste to deliver me. **R**

Be my strong rock, a castle to keep me safe,
for you are my crag and my stronghold;
for the sake of your name, lead me and guide me. **R**

Take me out of the net that they have secretly set for me,
for you are my tower of strength.
Into your hands I commend my spirit,
for you have redeemed me, Lord God of truth. **R**

From Psalm 31

Responsorial Psalm

**R Keep those you have given me true to your name, says God,
[that they may be one, like us].**

God delivered me from my strong enemies
and from those who hated me;
for they were too mighty for me. **R**

They confronted me in the day of my disaster;
but the Lord was my support.
He brought me out into an open place;
he rescued me because he delighted in me. **R**

I have kept the ways of the Lord
and have not offended against my God;
for all his judgements are before my eyes,
and his decrees I have not put away from me. **R**   *From Psalm 44*

Responsorial Psalm

**R Those who weep will return with joy to God,
[filled with laughter and with shouts of joy].**

When the Lord restored the fortunes of Zion,
then were we like those who dream.
Then was our mouth filled with laughter,
and our tongue with shouts of joy. **R**

Then they said among the nations,
"The Lord has done great things for them."
The Lord has done great things for us,
and we are glad indeed. **R**

Restore our fortunes, O Lord,
like the watercourses of the Negev.
Those who sowed with tears
will reap with songs of joy. **R**

Those who go out weeping, carrying the seed,
will come again with joy, shouldering their sheaves. **R**   *Psalm 126*

A reading from the Letter of Paul to the Romans.

Who will separate us from the love of Christ? Will hardship, or
distress, or persecution, or famine, or nakedness, or peril, or
sword? As it is written, "For your sake we are being killed all day
long; we are accounted as sheep to be slaughtered." No, in all
these things we are more than conquerors through him who loved
us. For I am convinced that neither death, nor life, nor angels, nor
rulers, nor things present, nor things to come, nor powers, nor
height, nor depth, nor anything else in all creation, will be able to
separate us from the love of God in Christ Jesus our Lord.

This is the word of the Lord.   *Romans 8. 35-39*

A reading from the Second Letter of Paul to the Corinthians.

We have this treasure in clay jars, so that it may be made clear that this extraordinary power belongs to God and does not come from us. We are afflicted in every way, but not crushed; perplexed, but not driven to despair; persecuted, but not forsaken; struck down, but not destroyed; always carrying in the body the death of Jesus, so that the life of Jesus may also be made visible in our bodies. For while we live, we are always being given up to death for Jesus' sake, so that the life of Jesus may be made visible in our mortal flesh. So death is at work in us, but life in you.

But just as we have the same spirit of faith that is in accordance with scripture – "I believed, and so I spoke" – we also believe, and so we speak, because we know that the one who raised the Lord Jesus will raise us also with Jesus, and will bring us with you into his presence. Yes, everything is for your sake, so that grace, as it extends to more and more people, may increase thanksgiving, to the glory of God.

This is the word of the Lord.   *2 Corinthians 4. 7-15*

A reading from the Second Letter of Paul to Timothy.

Share in suffering like a good soldier of Christ Jesus. No one serving in the army gets entangled in everyday affairs; the soldier's aim is to please the enlisting officer. And in the case of an athlete, no one is crowned without competing according to the rules. It is the farmer who does the work who ought to have the first share of the crops. Think over what I say, for the Lord will give you understanding in all things.

[Remember Jesus Christ, raised from the dead, a descendant of David – that is my gospel, for which I suffer hardship, even to the point of being chained like a criminal. But the word of God is not chained. Therefore I endure everything for the sake of the elect, so that they may also obtain the salvation that is in Christ Jesus, with eternal glory. The saying is sure: If we have died with him, we will also live with him; if we endure, we will also reign with him; if we deny him, he will also deny us; if we are faithless, he remains faithful – for he cannot deny himself.]

This is the word of the Lord.   *2 Timothy 2. 3-7 [8-13]*

A reading from the Letter to the Hebrews.

What more should I say? For time would fail me to tell of Gideon, Barak, Samson, Jephthah, of David and Samuel and the prophets – who through faith conquered kingdoms, administered justice, obtained promises, shut the mouths of lions, quenched raging fire, escaped the edge of the sword, won strength out of weakness, became mighty in war, put foreign armies to flight. Women received their dead by resurrection. Others were tortured, refusing to accept release, in order to obtain a better resurrection. Others suffered mocking and flogging, and even chains and imprisonment. They were stoned to death, they were sawn in two, they were killed by the sword; they went about in skins of sheep and goats, destitute, persecuted, tormented – of whom the world was not worthy. They wandered in deserts and mountains, and in caves and holes in the ground.

Yet all these, though they were commended for their faith, did not receive what was promised, since God had provided something better so that they would not, apart from us, be made perfect.

This is the word of the Lord.   *Hebrews 11. 32-40*

A reading from the First Letter of Peter.

Beloved, do not be surprised at the fiery ordeal that is taking place among you to test you, as though something strange were happening to you. But rejoice insofar as you are sharing Christ's sufferings, so that you may also be glad and shout for joy when his glory is revealed. If you are reviled for the name of Christ, you are blessed, because the spirit of glory, which is the Spirit of God, is resting on you. But let none of you suffer as a murderer, a thief, a criminal, or even as a mischief maker.

Yet if any of you suffers as a Christian, do not consider it a disgrace, but glorify God because you bear this name. For the time has come for judgement to begin with the household of God; if it begins with us, what will be the end for those who do not obey the gospel of God? And "If it is hard for the righteous to be saved, what will become of the ungodly and the sinners?" Therefore, let those suffering in accordance with God's will entrust themselves to a faithful Creator, while continuing to do good.

This is the word of the Lord. *1 Peter 4. 12-19*

A reading from the Revelation to John.

I heard a loud voice in heaven, proclaiming, "Now have come the salvation and the power and the kingdom of our God and the authority of his Messiah, for the accuser of our comrades has been thrown down, who accuses them day and night before our God. But they have conquered him by the blood of the Lamb and by the word of their testimony, for they did not cling to life even in the face of death. Rejoice then, you heavens and those who dwell in them!"

This is the word of the Lord. *Revelation 12. 10-12a*

Hear the gospel of our Lord Jesus Christ according to Matthew.

Jesus said to his twelve disciples, "See, I am sending you out like sheep into the midst of wolves; so be wise as serpents and innocent as doves. Beware of them, for they will hand you over to councils and flog you in their synagogues; and you will be dragged before governors and kings because of me, as a testimony to them and the Gentiles. When they hand you over, do not worry about how you are to speak or what you are to say; for what you are to say will be given to you at that time; for it is not you who speak, but the Spirit of your Father speaking through you. Brother will betray brother to death, and a father his child, and children will rise against parents and have them put to death; and you will be hated by all because of my name. But the one who endures to the end will be saved."

This is the gospel of the Lord. *Matthew 10. 16-22*

Hear the gospel of our Lord Jesus Christ according to Matthew.

Jesus said to the twelve disciples, "Do not fear those who kill the body but cannot kill the soul; rather fear him who can destroy both soul and body in hell. Are not two sparrows sold for a penny? Yet not one of them will fall to the ground apart from your Father. And even the hairs of your head are all counted. So do not be afraid; you are of more value than many sparrows.

Everyone therefore who acknowledges me before others, I also will acknowledge before my Father in heaven; but whoever denies me before others, I also will deny before my Father in heaven.

"Do not think that I have come to bring peace to the earth; I have not come to bring peace, but a sword. For I have come to set a man against his father, and a daughter against her mother, and a daughter-in-law against her mother-in-law; and one's foes will be members of one's own household. Whoever loves father or mother more than me is not worthy of me; and whoever loves son or daughter more than me is not worthy of me; and whoever does not take up the cross and follow me is not worthy of me. Those who find their life will lose it, and those who lose their life for my sake will find it."

This is the gospel of the Lord.   *Matthew 10. 28-39*

Hear the gospel of our Lord Jesus Christ according to Matthew.

Jesus told his disciples, "If any want to become my followers, let them deny themselves and take up their cross and follow me. For those who want to save their life will lose it, and those who lose their life for my sake will find it. For what will it profit them if they gain the whole world but forfeit their life? Or what will they give in return for their life?"

This is the gospel of the Lord.   *Matthew 16. 24-26*

Hear the gospel of our Lord Jesus Christ according to John.

Jesus said to his disciples, "Very truly, I tell you, unless a grain of wheat falls into the earth and dies, it remains just a single grain; but if it dies, it bears much fruit. Those who love their life lose it, and those who hate their life in this world will keep it for eternal life. Whoever serves me must follow me, and where I am, there will my servant be also. Whoever serves me, the Father will honour."

This is the gospel of the Lord.   *John 12. 24-26*

Hear the gospel of our Lord Jesus Christ according to John.

Jesus said to his disciples, "If the world hates you, be aware that it hated me before it hated you. If you belonged to the world, the world would love you as its own. Because you do not belong to the world, but I have chosen you out of the world – therefore the world hates you. Remember the word that I said to you, 'Servants are not greater than their master.' If they persecuted me, they will persecute you; if they kept my word, they will keep yours also. But they will do all these things to you on account of my name, because they do not know him who sent me."

This is the gospel of the Lord.   *John 15. 18-21*

TEACHERS OF THE FAITH
& SPIRITUAL WRITERS
White

Collect
Almighty God,
who enlightened your Church
  by the teaching of your servant *N*:
enrich it evermore with your heavenly grace
and raise up faithful witnesses
who, by their life and teaching,
may proclaim the truth of your salvation;
through Jesus Christ your Son our Lord,
who is alive and reigns with you,
in the unity of the Holy Spirit,
one God, now and for ever.

Post Communion
God of truth,
whose Wisdom set her table
and invited us to eat the bread
  and drink the wine of the kingdom:
help us to lay aside all foolishness
and to live and walk in the way of insight,
that we may come with *N.* to the eternal feast of heaven;
through Jesus Christ our Lord.

A reading from the First Book of the Kings.

[Solomon said, "You have shown great and steadfast love to your servant my father David, because he walked before you in faithfulness, in righteousness, and in uprightness of heart toward you; and you have kept for him this great and steadfast love, and have given him a son to sit on his throne today. And now, O Lord my God, you have made your servant king in place of my father David, although I am only a little child; I do not know how to go out or come in. And your servant is in the midst of the people whom you have chosen, a great people, so numerous they cannot be numbered or counted. Give your servant therefore an understanding mind to govern your people, able to discern between good and evil; for who can govern this your great people?" It pleased the Lord that Solomon had asked this.]

God said to Solomon, "Because you have asked this, and have not asked for yourself long life or riches, or for the life of your enemies, but have asked for yourself understanding to discern what is right, I now do according to your word. Indeed I give you a wise and discerning mind; no one like you has been before you and no one like you shall arise after you. I give you also what you have not asked, both riches and honour all your life; no other king shall compare with you. If you will walk in my ways, keeping my statutes and my commandments, as your father David walked, then I will lengthen your life."

This is the word of the Lord.   *1 Kings 3. [6-10] 11-14*

A reading from the book Proverbs.

Listen, children, to a father's instruction, and be attentive, that you may gain insight; for I give you good precepts: do not forsake my teaching. When I was a son with my father, tender, and my mother's favourite, he taught me, and said to me, "Let your heart hold fast my words; keep my commandments, and live. Get wisdom; get insight: do not forget, nor turn away from the words of my mouth. Do not forsake her, and she will keep you; love her, and she will guard you. The beginning of wisdom is this: Get wisdom, and whatever else you get, get insight. Prize her highly, and she will exalt you; she will honour you if you embrace her. She will place on your head a fair garland; she will bestow on you a beautiful crown."

This is the word of the Lord.   *Proverbs 4. 1-9*

A reading from the Wisdom of Solomon.

Therefore I prayed, and understanding was given me; I called on God, and the spirit of wisdom came to me. I preferred her to sceptres and thrones, and I accounted wealth as nothing in comparison with her. Neither did I liken to her any priceless gem, because all gold is but a little sand in her sight, and silver will be accounted as clay before her. I loved her more than health and beauty, and I chose to have her rather than light, because her radiance never ceases. May God grant me to speak with judgement, and to have thoughts worthy of what I have received; for he is the guide even of wisdom and the corrector of the wise. For both we and our words are in his hand, as are all understanding and skill in crafts.

This is the word of the Lord.   *Wisdom 7. 7-10, 15-16*

A reading from the book Ecclesiasticus.

The one who devotes himself to the study of the law of the Most High seeks out the wisdom of all the ancients, and is concerned with prophecies; he preserves the sayings of the famous and penetrates the subtleties of parables; he seeks out the hidden meanings of proverbs and is at home with the obscurities of parables. He serves among the great and appears before rulers; he travels in foreign lands and learns what is good and evil in the human lot. He sets his heart to rise early to seek the Lord who made him, and to petition the Most High; he opens his mouth in prayer and asks pardon for his sins.

If the great Lord is willing, he will be filled with the spirit of understanding; he will pour forth words of wisdom of his own and give thanks to the Lord in prayer. The Lord will direct his counsel and knowledge, as he meditates on his mysteries. He will show the wisdom of what he has learned, and will glory in the law of the Lord's covenant. Many will praise his understanding; it will never be blotted out. His memory will not disappear, and his name will live through all generations. Nations will speak of his wisdom, and the congregation will proclaim his praise.

This is the word of the Lord.   *Ecclesiasticus 39. 1-10*

Responsorial Psalm

**R The testimony of the Lord gives wisdom to the innocent;
[the commandment of the Lord gives light to the eyes].**

The law of the Lord is perfect
and revives the soul;
the testimony of the Lord is sure
and gives wisdom to the innocent. **R**

The statutes of the Lord are just
and rejoice the heart;
the commandment of the Lord is clear
and gives light to the eyes. **R**

The fear of the Lord is clean
and endures for ever;
the judgements of the Lord are true
and righteous altogether. **R**

More to be desired are they than gold,
more than much fine gold,
sweeter far than honey,
than honey in the comb. **R**   *From Psalm 19*

Responsorial Psalm

**R Come, children, and listen to me;
I will teach you the fear of the Lord.**

Who among you loves life
and desires long life to enjoy prosperity?
Keep your tongue from evil-speaking
and your lips from lying words. **R**

Turn from evil and do good;
seek peace and pursue it.
The eyes of the Lord are upon the righteous,
and his ears are open to their cry. **R**

The face of the Lord is against those who do evil,
to root out the remembrance of them from the earth.

The righteous cry and the Lord hears them
and delivers them from all their troubles. **R**   *From Psalm 34*

Responsorial Psalm

**R   The Lord of Hosts loves justice;
[he does not forsake his faithful ones].**

The righteous shall possess the land
and dwell in it for ever.
The mouth of the righteous utters wisdom,
and their tongue speaks what is right. **R**

The law of their God is in their heart,
and their footsteps shall not falter.
The wicked spy on the righteous
and seek occasion to kill them. **R**

The Lord will not abandon them to their hand,
nor let them be found guilty when brought to trial. **R**

From Psalm 37

Responsorial Psalm

**R   I am yours, Lord; O that you would save me!
[I have not forsaken your commandments].**

The proud have dug pits for me;
they do not keep your law.
All your commandments are true;
help me, for they persecute me with lies. **R**

They had almost made an end of me on earth,
but I have not forsaken your commandments.
In your loving-kindness, revive me,
that I may keep the decrees of your mouth. **R**

I will never forget your commandments,
because by them you give me life.
I am yours; O that you would save me!
for I study your commandments. **R**

Though the wicked lie in wait for me to destroy me,
I will apply my mind to your decrees.
I see that all things come to an end,
but your commandment has no bounds. **R**   *From Psalm 119*

**R   How sweet are God's words to my taste!
    [they are sweeter than honey to my mouth].**

O how I love your law!
all the day long it is in my mind.
Your commandment has made me wiser than my enemies,
and it is always with me. **R**

I have more understanding than all my teachers,
for your decrees are my study.
I am wiser than the elders,
because I observe your commandments. **R**

I restrain my feet from every evil way,
that I may keep your word.
I do not shrink from your judgements,
because you yourself have taught me. **R**

How sweet are your words to my taste!
they are sweeter than honey to my mouth.
Through your commandments I gain understanding;
therefore I hate every lying way. **R**   *From Psalm 119*

A reading from the First Letter of Paul to the Corinthians.

The message about the cross is foolishness to those who are perishing, but to us who are being saved it is the power of God. For
it is written, "I will destroy the wisdom of the wise, and the discernment of the discerning I will thwart." Where is the one who
is wise? Where is the scribe? Where is the debater of this age? Has
not God made foolish the wisdom of the world? For since, in the
wisdom of God, the world did not know God through wisdom,
God decided, through the foolishness of our proclamation, to save
those who believe.

For Jews demand signs and Greeks desire wisdom, but we proclaim Christ crucified, a stumbling block to Jews and foolishness to
Gentiles, but to those who are the called, both Jews and Greeks,
Christ the power of God and the wisdom of God. For God's foolishness is wiser than human wisdom, and God's weakness is
stronger than human strength.

This is the word of the Lord.   *1 Corinthians 1. 18-25*

A reading from the First Letter of Paul to the Corinthians.

When I came to you, brothers and sisters, I did not come proclaiming the mystery of God to you in lofty words or wisdom. For I decided to know nothing among you except Jesus Christ, and him crucified. And I came to you in weakness and in fear and in much trembling. My speech and my proclamation were not with plausible words of wisdom, but with a demonstration of the Spirit and of power, so that your faith might rest not on human wisdom but on the power of God.

Yet among the mature we do speak wisdom, though it is not a wisdom of this age or of the rulers of this age, who are doomed to perish. But we speak God's wisdom, secret and hidden, which God decreed before the ages for our glory. None of the rulers of this age understood this; for if they had, they would not have crucified the Lord of glory. But, as it is written, "What no eye has seen, nor ear heard, nor the human heart conceived, what God has prepared for those who love him" – these things God has revealed to us through the Spirit; for the Spirit searches everything, even the depths of God.

This is the word of the Lord.   *1 Corinthians 2. 1-10*

A reading from the First Letter of Paul to the Corinthians.

As it is written, "What no eye has seen, nor ear heard, nor the human heart conceived, what God has prepared for those who love him" – these things God has revealed to us through the Spirit; for the Spirit searches everything, even the depths of God. For what human being knows what is truly human except the human spirit that is within? So also no one comprehends what is truly God's except the Spirit of God. Now we have received not the spirit of the world, but the Spirit that is from God, so that we may understand the gifts bestowed on us by God. And we speak of these things in words not taught by human wisdom but taught by the Spirit, interpreting spiritual things to those who are spiritual.

Those who are unspiritual do not receive the gifts of God's Spirit, for they are foolishness to them, and they are unable to understand them because they are spiritually discerned. Those who are spiritual discern all things, and they are themselves subject to no one else's scrutiny. "For who has known the mind of the Lord so as to instruct him?" But we have the mind of Christ.

This is the word of the Lord. *1 Corinthians 2. 9-16*

A reading from the Letter of Paul to the Ephesians.

Although I am the very least of all the saints, this grace was given to me to bring to the Gentiles the news of the boundless riches of Christ, and to make everyone see what is the plan of the mystery hidden for ages in God who created all things; so that through the church the wisdom of God in its rich variety might now be made known to the rulers and authorities in the heavenly places. This was in accordance with the eternal purpose that he has carried out in Christ Jesus our Lord, in whom we have access to God in boldness and confidence through faith in him.

This is the word of the Lord. *Ephesians 3. 8-12*

A reading from the Second Letter of Paul to Timothy.

In the presence of God and of Christ Jesus, who is to judge the living and the dead, and in view of his appearing and his kingdom, I solemnly urge you: proclaim the message; be persistent whether the time is favourable or unfavourable; convince, rebuke, and encourage, with the utmost patience in teaching. For the time is coming when people will not put up with sound doctrine, but having itching ears, they will accumulate for themselves teachers to suit their own desires, and will turn away from listening to the truth and wander away to myths.

As for you, always be sober, endure suffering, do the work of an evangelist, carry out your ministry fully. As for me, I am already being poured out as a libation, and the time of my departure has come. I have fought the good fight, I have finished the race, I have kept the faith. From now on there is reserved for me the crown of righteousness, which the Lord, the righteous judge, will give me on that day, and not only to me but also to all who have longed for his appearing.

This is the word of the Lord. *2 Timothy 4. 1-8*

A reading from the Letter of Paul to Titus.

As for you, teach what is consistent with sound doctrine. Tell the older men to be temperate, serious, prudent, and sound in faith, in love, and in endurance.

Likewise, tell the older women to be reverent in behaviour, not to be slanderers or slaves to drink; they are to teach what is good, so that they may encourage the young women to love their husbands, to love their children, to be self-controlled, chaste, good managers of the household, kind, being submissive to their husbands, so that the word of God may not be discredited.

Likewise, urge the younger men to be self-controlled. Show yourself in all respects a model of good works, and in your teaching show integrity, gravity, and sound speech that cannot be censured; then any opponent will be put to shame, having nothing evil to say of us.

This is the word of the Lord.   *Titus 2. 1-8*

Hear the gospel of our Lord Jesus Christ according to Matthew.

Jesus said to the crowds, "You are the salt of the earth; but if salt has lost its taste, how can its saltiness be restored? It is no longer good for anything, but is thrown out and trampled under foot.

"You are the light of the world. A city built on a hill cannot be hid. No one after lighting a lamp puts it under the bushel basket, but on the lampstand, and it gives light to all in the house. In the same way, let your light shine before others, so that they may see your good works and give glory to your Father in heaven.

"Do not think that I have come to abolish the law or the prophets; I have come not to abolish but to fulfil. For truly I tell you, until heaven and earth pass away, not one letter, not one stroke of a letter, will pass from the law until all is accomplished. Therefore, whoever breaks one of the least of these commandments, and teaches others to do the same, will be called least in the kingdom of heaven; but whoever does them and teaches them will be called great in the kingdom of heaven."

This is the gospel of the Lord.   *Matthew 5. 13-19*

Hear the gospel of our Lord Jesus Christ according to Matthew.

Jesus said to his disciples, "Every scribe who has been trained for the kingdom of heaven is like the master of a household who brings out of his treasure what is new and what is old." When Jesus had finished these parables, he left that place.

He came to his hometown and began to teach the people in their synagogue, so that they were astounded and said, "Where did this man get this wisdom and these deeds of power? Is not this the carpenter's son? Is not his mother called Mary? And are not his brothers James and Joseph and Simon and Judas? And are not all his sisters with us? Where then did this man get all this?" And they took offence at him. But Jesus said to them, "Prophets are not without honour except in their own country and in their own house." And he did not do many deeds of power there, because of their unbelief.

This is the gospel of the Lord.   *Matthew 13. 52-58*

Hear the gospel of our Lord Jesus Christ according to Matthew.

Jesus said to his disciples, "You are not to be called rabbi, for you have one teacher, and you are all students. And call no one your father on earth, for you have one Father – the one in heaven. Nor are you to be called instructors, for you have one instructor, the Messiah. The greatest among you will be your servant. All who exalt themselves will be humbled, and all who humble themselves will be exalted."

This is the gospel of the Lord.   *Matthew 23. 8-12*

Hear the gospel of our Lord Jesus Christ according to Mark.

Jesus began to teach beside the sea. Such a very large crowd gathered around him that he got into a boat on the sea and sat there, while the whole crowd was beside the sea on the land. He began to teach them many things in parables, and in his teaching he said to them: "Listen! A sower went out to sow. And as he sowed, some seed fell on the path, and the birds came and ate it up. Other seed fell on rocky ground, where it did not have much soil, and it sprang up quickly, since it had no depth of soil. And when the sun rose, it was scorched; and since it had no root, it withered away.

Common of the Saints – Teachers

Other seed fell among thorns, and the thorns grew up and choked it, and it yielded no grain. Other seed fell into good soil and brought forth grain, growing up and increasing and yielding thirty and sixty and a hundredfold." And he said, "Let anyone with ears to hear listen!"

This is the gospel of the Lord. *Mark 4. 1-9*

Hear the gospel of our Lord Jesus Christ according to John.

Jesus said to his disciples, "I still have many things to say to you, but you cannot bear them now. When the Spirit of truth comes, he will guide you into all the truth; for he will not speak on his own, but will speak whatever he hears, and he will declare to you the things that are to come. He will glorify me, because he will take what is mine and declare it to you. All that the Father has is mine. For this reason I said that he will take what is mine and declare it to you."

This is the gospel of the Lord. *John 16. 12-15*

BISHOPS AND OTHER PASTORS
White

Collect
Eternal God,
you called *N.* to proclaim your glory
  in a life of prayer and pastoral zeal:
keep the leaders of your Church faithful
and bless your people through their ministry,
that the Church may grow into the full stature
  of your Son Jesus Christ our Lord,
who is alive and reigns with you,
in the unity of the Holy Spirit,
one God, now and for ever.
or, for a Bishop
Almighty God,
the light of the faithful and shepherd of souls,
who set your servant *N.* to be a bishop in the Church,
to feed your sheep by the word of Christ
and to guide them by good example:

give us grace to keep the faith of the Church
and to follow in the footsteps
  of Jesus Christ your Son our Lord,
who is alive and reigns with you,
in the unity of the Holy Spirit,
one God, now and for ever.

Post Communion
God, shepherd of your people,
whose servant *N*. revealed the loving service of Christ
  in his/her ministry as a pastor of your people:
by this eucharist in which we share
awaken within us the love of Christ
and keep us faithful to our Christian calling;
through him who laid down his life for us,
but is alive and reigns with you, now and for ever.

A reading from the First Book of Samuel.

The Lord said to Samuel, "How long will you grieve over Saul? I
have rejected him from being king over Israel. Fill your horn with
oil and set out; I will send you to Jesse the Bethlehemite, for I have
provided for myself a king among his sons."

  When they came, he looked on Eliab and thought, "Surely the
Lord's anointed is now before the Lord." But the Lord said to
Samuel, "Do not look on his appearance or on the height of his
stature, because I have rejected him; for the Lord does not see as
mortals see; they look on the outward appearance, but the Lord
looks on the heart."

  Then Jesse called Abinadab, and made him pass before Samuel.
He said, "Neither has the Lord chosen this one." Then Jesse made
Shammah pass by. And he said, "Neither has the Lord chosen this
one." Jesse made seven of his sons pass before Samuel, and
Samuel said to Jesse, "The Lord has not chosen any of these."
Samuel said to Jesse, "Are all your sons here?" And he said, "There
remains yet the youngest, but he is keeping the sheep." And
Samuel said to Jesse, "Send and bring him; for we will not sit down
until he comes here." He sent and brought him in. Now he was
ruddy, and had beautiful eyes, and was handsome. The Lord said,

"Rise and anoint him; for this is the one." Then Samuel took the horn of oil, and anointed him in the presence of his brothers; and the spirit of the Lord came mightily upon David from that day forward. Samuel then set out and went to Ramah.

This is the word of the Lord.   *1 Samuel 16. 1, 6-13*

A reading from the prophecy of Isaiah.

In the year that King Uzziah died, I saw the Lord sitting on a throne, high and lofty; and the hem of his robe filled the temple. Seraphs were in attendance above him; each had six wings: with two they covered their faces, and with two they covered their feet, and with two they flew. And one called to another and said: "Holy, holy, holy is the Lord of hosts; the whole earth is full of his glory." The pivots on the thresholds shook at the voices of those who called, and the house filled with smoke. And I said: "Woe is me! I am lost, for I am a man of unclean lips, and I live among a people of unclean lips; yet my eyes have seen the King, the Lord of hosts!"

Then one of the seraphs flew to me, holding a live coal that had been taken from the altar with a pair of tongs. The seraph touched my mouth with it and said: "Now that this has touched your lips, your guilt has departed and your sin is blotted out." Then I heard the voice of the Lord saying, "Whom shall I send, and who will go for us?" And I said, "Here am I; send me!"

This is the word of the Lord.   *Isaiah 6. 1-8*

A reading from the prophecy of Jeremiah.

The word of the Lord came to me saying, "Before I formed you in the womb I knew you, and before you were born I consecrated you; I appointed you a prophet to the nations." Then I said, "Ah, Lord God! Truly I do not know how to speak, for I am only a boy." But the Lord said to me, "Do not say, 'I am only a boy'; for you shall go to all to whom I send you, and you shall speak whatever I command you, Do not be afraid of them, for I am with you to deliver you, says the Lord."

Then the Lord put out his hand and touched my mouth; and the Lord said to me, "Now I have put my words in your mouth. See, today I appoint you over nations and over kingdoms, to pluck up and to pull down, to destroy and to overthrow, to build and to plant."

This is the word of the Lord. *Jeremiah 1. 4-10*

A reading from the prophecy of Ezekiel.

At the end of seven days, the word of the Lord came to me: Mortal, I have made you a sentinel for the house of Israel; whenever you hear a word from my mouth, you shall give them warning from me. If I say to the wicked, "You shall surely die," and you give them no warning, or speak to warn the wicked from their wicked way, in order to save their life, those wicked persons shall die for their iniquity; but their blood I will require at your hand. But if you warn the wicked, and they do not turn from their wickedness, or from their wicked way, they shall die for their iniquity; but you will have saved your life.

 Again, if the righteous turn from their righteousness and commit iniquity, and I lay a stumbling block before them, they shall die; because you have not warned them, they shall die for their sin, and their righteous deeds that they have done shall not be remembered; but their blood I will require at your hand. If, however, you warn the righteous not to sin, and they do not sin, they shall surely live, because they took warning; and you will have saved your life.

This is the word of the Lord. *Ezekiel 3. 16-21*

A reading from the prophecy of Malachi.

My covenant with him was a covenant of life and well-being, which I gave him; this called for reverence, and he revered me and stood in awe of my name. True instruction was in his mouth, and no wrong was found on his lips. He walked with me in integrity and uprightness, and he turned many from iniquity. For the lips of a priest should guard knowledge, and people should seek instruction from his mouth, for he is the messenger of the Lord of hosts.

This is the word of the Lord. *Malachi 2. 5-7*

Responsorial Psalm

R Delight in the law of the Lord!
[Meditate on his law day and night].

Happy are they who have not walked in the counsel of the wicked,
nor lingered in the way of sinners,
nor sat in the seats of the scornful!
Their delight is in the law of the Lord,
and they meditate on his law day and night. **R**

They are like trees planted by streams of water,
bearing fruit in due season,
with leaves that do not wither;
everything they do shall prosper. **R**

It is not so with the wicked:
they are like chaff which the wind blows away.
The Lord knows the way of the righteous,
but the way of the wicked is doomed. **R**   *From Psalm 1*

Responsorial Psalm

R Let us stay with the Lord all the days of our life
[by speaking the truth from the heart].

Lord, who may dwell in your tabernacle?
who may abide upon your holy hill?
Whoever leads a blameless life and does what is right,
who speaks the truth from the heart. **R**

There is no guile upon his tongue;
he does no evil to his friend;
he does not heap contempt upon his neighbour. **R**

In his sight the wicked are rejected,
but he honours those who fear the Lord.
He has sworn to do no wrong
and does not take back his word. **R**

He does not give his money in hope of gain,
nor does he take a bribe against the innocent.
Whoever does these things
shall never be overthrown. **R**   *Psalm 15*

R   O Lord, you are my portion and my cup;
**   [it is you who uphold my lot].**

My boundaries enclose a pleasant land;
indeed, I have a goodly heritage.
I will bless the Lord who gives me counsel;
my heart teaches me, night after night. **R**

I have set the Lord always before me;
because he is at my right hand I shall not fall.
My heart, therefore, is glad and my spirit rejoices;
my body also shall rest in hope. **R**

For you will not abandon me to the grave,
nor let your holy one see the Pit.
You will show me the path of life;
in your presence there is fullness of joy,
and in your right hand are pleasures for evermore. **R**

From Psalm 16

Responsorial Psalm

R   Sing to the Lord a new song;
**   [sing to the Lord, all the whole earth].**

Sing to the Lord and bless his name;
proclaim the good news of his salvation from day to day.
Declare his glory among the nations
and his wonders among all peoples. **R**

For great is the Lord and greatly to be praised;
he is more to be feared than all gods.
As for all the gods of the nations, they are but idols;
but it is the Lord who made the heavens. **R**

O the majesty and magnificence of his presence!
O the power and the splendour of his sanctuary!
Ascribe to the Lord, you families of the peoples;
ascribe to the Lord honour and power. **R**

Ascribe to the Lord the honour due to his name;
bring offerings and come into his courts.
Worship the Lord in the beauty of holiness;
let the whole earth tremble before him. **R**   *From Psalm 96*

Responsorial Psalm

R **In the beauty of holiness has God begotten you,**
[like dew from the womb of the morning].

The Lord said to my lord, "Sit at my right hand,
until I make your enemies your footstool."
The Lord will send the sceptre of your power out of Zion,
saying, "Rule over your enemies round about you. **R**

"Princely state has been yours
from the day of your birth,
in the beauty of holiness have I begotten you,
like dew from the womb of morning." **R**

The Lord has sworn and will not recant:
"You are a priest for ever after the order of Melchizedek."
He will drink from the brook beside the road;
therefore he will lift high his head. **R**   *From Psalm 110*

A reading from the Acts of the Apostles.

Keep watch over yourselves and over all the flock, of which the
Holy Spirit has made you overseers, to shepherd the church of God
that he obtained with the blood of his own Son. I know that after I
have gone, savage wolves will come in among you, not sparing the
flock. Some even from your own group will come distorting the
truth in order to entice the disciples to follow them. Therefore be
alert, remembering that for three years I did not cease night or day
to warn everyone with tears. And now I commend you to God and
to the message of his grace, a message that is able to build you up
and to give you the inheritance among all who are sanctified. I cov-
eted no one's silver or gold or clothing. You know for yourselves
that I worked with my own hands to support myself and my companions. In all this I have given you an example that by such work
we must support the weak, remembering the words of the Lord
Jesus, for he himself said, 'It is more blessèd to give than to receive.'

This is the word of the Lord.   *Acts 20. 28-35*

A reading from the First Letter of Paul to the Corinthians.

Think of us in this way, as servants of Christ and stewards of God's
mysteries. Moreover, it is required of stewards that they be found

trustworthy. But with me it is a very small thing that I should be judged by you or by any human court. I do not even judge myself. I am not aware of anything against myself, but I am not thereby acquitted. It is the Lord who judges me. Therefore do not pronounce judgement before the time, before the Lord comes, who will bring to light the things now hidden in darkness and will disclose the purposes of the heart. Then each one will receive commendation from God.

This is the word of the Lord.   *1 Corinthians 4. 1-5*

A reading from the Second Letter of Paul to the Corinthians.

Since it is by God's mercy that we are engaged in this ministry, we do not lose heart. We have renounced the shameful things that one hides; we refuse to practise cunning or to falsify God's word; but by the open statement of the truth we commend ourselves to the conscience of everyone in the sight of God. [And even if our gospel is veiled, it is veiled to those who are perishing. In their case the god of this world has blinded the minds of the unbelievers, to keep them from seeing the light of the gospel of the glory of Christ, who is the image of God.]

For we do not proclaim ourselves; we proclaim Jesus Christ as Lord and ourselves as your slaves for Jesus' sake. For it is the God who said, "Let light shine out of darkness," who has shone in our hearts to give the light of the knowledge of the glory of God in the face of Jesus Christ. But we have this treasure in clay jars, so that it may be made clear that this extraordinary power belongs to God and does not come from us.

[We are afflicted in every way, but not crushed; perplexed, but not driven to despair; persecuted, but not forsaken; struck down, but not destroyed; always carrying in the body the death of Jesus, so that the life of Jesus may also be made visible in our bodies.]

This is the word of the Lord.   *2 Corinthians 4. 1-10*
                                                  (or 1, 2, 5-7)

A reading from the Second Letter of Paul to the Corinthians.

The love of Christ urges us on, because we are convinced that one has died for all; therefore all have died. And he died for all, so that those who live might live no longer for themselves, but for him who died and was raised for them.

From now on, therefore, we regard no one from a human point of view; even though we once knew Christ from a human point of view, we know him no longer in that way. So if anyone is in Christ, there is a new creation: everything old has passed away; see, everything has become new! All this is from God, who reconciled us to himself through Christ, and has given us the ministry of reconciliation; that is, in Christ God was reconciling the world to himself, not counting their trespasses against them, and entrusting the message of reconciliation to us. So we are ambassadors for Christ, since God is making his appeal through us; we entreat you on behalf of Christ, be reconciled to God.

This is the word of the Lord.   *2 Corinthians 5. 14-20*

A reading from the First Letter of Peter.

As an elder myself and a witness of the sufferings of Christ, as well as one who shares in the glory to be revealed, I exhort the elders among you to tend the flock of God that is in your charge, exercising the oversight, not under compulsion but willingly, as God would have you do it – not for sordid gain but eagerly. Do not lord it over those in your charge, but be examples to the flock. And when the chief shepherd appears, you will win the crown of glory that never fades away.

This is the word of the Lord.   *1 Peter 5. 1-4*

Hear the gospel of our Lord Jesus Christ according to Matthew.

Jesus said, "I thank you, Father, Lord of heaven and earth, because you have hidden these things from the wise and the intelligent and have revealed them to infants; yes, Father, for such was your gracious will. All things have been handed over to me by my Father; and no one knows the Son except the Father, and no one knows the Father except the Son and anyone to whom the Son chooses to reveal him.

"Come to me, all you that are weary and are carrying heavy burdens, and I will give you rest. Take my yoke upon you, and learn from me; for I am gentle and humble in heart, and you will find

rest for your souls. For my yoke is easy, and my burden is light."
This is the gospel of the Lord.   *Matthew 11. 25-30*

Hear the gospel of our Lord Jesus Christ according to Matthew.

Jesus said to his disciples, "Keep awake therefore, for you do not
know on what day your Lord is coming. But understand this: if
the owner of the house had known in what part of the night the
thief was coming, he would have stayed awake and would not
have let his house be broken into. Therefore you also must be
ready, for the Son of Man is coming at an unexpected hour.

"Who then is the faithful and wise servant, whom his master has
put in charge of his household, to give the other slaves their
allowance of food at the proper time? Blessèd is that servant
whom his master will find at work when he arrives."

This is the gospel of the Lord.   *Matthew 24. 42-46*

Hear the gospel of our Lord Jesus Christ according to John.

Jesus said to the Pharisees, "I am the good shepherd. The good
shepherd lays down his life for the sheep. The hired hand, who is
not the shepherd and does not own the sheep, sees the wolf coming and leaves the sheep and runs away – and the wolf snatches
them and scatters them. The hired hand runs away because a
hired hand does not care for the sheep. I am the good shepherd.
I know my own and my own know me, just as the Father knows
me and I know the Father. And I lay down my life for the sheep.
I have other sheep that do not belong to this fold. I must bring
them also, and they will listen to my voice. So there will be one
flock, one shepherd."

This is the gospel of the Lord.   *John 10. 11-16*

Hear the gospel of our Lord Jesus Christ according to John.

As the Father has loved me, so I have loved you; abide in my love.
If you keep my commandments, you will abide in my love, just as
I have kept my Father's commandments and abide in his love. I
have said these things to you so that my joy may be in you, and
that your joy may be complete.

Common of the Saints – Bishops & Pastors

"This is my commandment, that you love one another as I have loved you. No one has greater love than this, to lay down one's life for one's friends. You are my friends if you do what I command you. I do not call you servants any longer, because the servant does not know what the master is doing; but I have called you friends, because I have made known to you everything that I have heard from my Father. You did not choose me but I chose you. And I appointed you to go and bear fruit, fruit that will last, so that the Father will give you whatever you ask him in my name. I am giving you these commands so that you may love one another."

This is the gospel of the Lord.   *John 15. 9-17*

Hear the gospel of our Lord Jesus Christ according to John.

When they had finished breakfast, Jesus said to Simon Peter, "Simon son of John, do you love me more than these?" He said to him, "Yes, Lord; you know that I love you." Jesus said to him, "Feed my lambs." A second time he said to him, "Simon son of John, do you love me?" He said to him, "Yes, Lord; you know that I love you." Jesus said to him, "Tend my sheep." He said to him the third time, "Simon son of John, do you love me?" Peter felt hurt because he said to him the third time, "Do you love me?" And he said to him, "Lord, you know everything; you know that I love you." Jesus said to him, "Feed my sheep."

This is the gospel of the Lord.   *John 21. 15-17*

RELIGIOUS
White

Collect

Almighty God,
by whose grace *N.*, kindled with the fire of your love,
became a burning and a shining light in the Church:
inflame us with the same spirit of discipline and love,
that we may ever walk before you as children of light;
through Jesus Christ your Son our Lord,
who is alive and reigns with you,
in the unity of the Holy Spirit,
one God, now and for ever.

Post Communion

Merciful God,
who gave such grace to your servant *N.*
that he/she served you with singleness of heart
and loved you above all things:
help us, whose communion with you
   has been renewed in this sacrament,
to forsake all that holds us back from following Christ
and to grow into his likeness from glory to glory;
through Jesus Christ our Lord.

A reading from the First Book of the Kings.

Elijah came to a cave, and spent the night there, and the word of
the Lord came to him, saying, "What are you doing here, Elijah?"
He answered, "I have been very zealous for the Lord, the God of
hosts; for the Israelites have forsaken your covenant, thrown
down your altars, and killed your prophets with the sword.
I alone am left, and they are seeking my life, to take it away." He
said, "Go out and stand on the mountain before the Lord, for the
Lord is about to pass by." Now there was a great wind, so strong
that it was splitting mountains and breaking rocks in pieces before
the Lord, but the Lord was not in the wind; and after the wind an
earthquake, but the Lord was not in the earthquake; and after the
earthquake a fire, but the Lord was not in the fire; and after the fire
a sound of sheer silence.

When Elijah heard it, he wrapped his face in his mantle and went out and stood at the entrance of the cave. Then there came a voice to him that said, "What are you doing here, Elijah?" He answered, "I have been very zealous for the Lord, the God of hosts; for the Israelites have forsaken your covenant, thrown down your altars, and killed your prophets with the sword. I alone am left, and they are seeking my life, to take it away."

Then the Lord said to him, "Go, return on your way to the wilderness of Damascus; when you arrive, you shall anoint Hazael as king over Aram. Also you shall anoint Jehu son of Nimshi as king over Israel; and you shall anoint Elisha son of Shaphat of Abelmeholah as prophet in your place. Whoever escapes from the sword of Hazael, Jehu shall kill; and whoever escapes from the sword of Jehu, Elisha shall kill. Yet I will leave seven thousand in Israel, all the knees that have not bowed to Baal, and every mouth that has not kissed him."

This is the word of the Lord.   *1 Kings 19. 9-18*

A reading from the book Proverbs.

The fear of the Lord prolongs life, but the years of the wicked will be short. The hope of the righteous ends in gladness, but the expectation of the wicked comes to nothing. The way of the Lord is a stronghold for the upright, but destruction for evildoers. The righteous will never be removed, but the wicked will not remain in the land. The mouth of the righteous brings forth wisdom, but the perverse tongue will be cut off. The lips of the righteous know what is acceptable, but the mouth of the wicked what is perverse.

This is the word of the Lord.   *Proverbs 10. 27-32*

A reading from the Song of Songs.

Set me as a seal upon your heart, as a seal upon your arm; for love is strong as death, passion fierce as the grave. Its flashes are flashes of fire, a raging flame. Many waters cannot quench love, neither can floods drown it. If one offered for love all the wealth of his house, it would be utterly scorned.

This is the word of the Lord.   *Song of Songs 8. 6-7*

A reading from the prophecy of Isaiah.

I will greatly rejoice in the Lord, my whole being shall exult in my God; for he has clothed me with the garments of salvation, he has covered me with the robe of righteousness, as a bridegroom decks himself with a garland, and as a bride adorns herself with her jewels. For as the earth brings forth its shoots, and as a garden causes what is sown in it to spring up, so the Lord God will cause righteousness and praise to spring up before all the nations.

For Zion's sake I will not keep silent, and for Jerusalem's sake I will not rest, until her vindication shines out like the dawn, and her salvation like a burning torch. The nations shall see your vindication, and all the kings your glory; and you shall be called by a new name that the mouth of the Lord will give. You shall be a crown of beauty in the hand of the Lord, and a royal diadem in the hand of your God. You shall no more be termed Forsaken, and your land shall no more be termed Desolate; but you shall be called My Delight Is in Her, and your land Married; for the Lord delights in you, and your land shall be married. For as a young man marries a young woman, so shall your builder marry you, and as the bridegroom rejoices over the bride, so shall your God rejoice over you.

This is the word of the Lord. *Isaiah 61.10 - 62.5*

Responsorial Psalm

**R   Look upon God and be radiant;
      [happy are they who trust in him].**

I will bless the Lord at all times;
his praise shall ever be in my mouth.
I will glory in the Lord;
let the humble hear and rejoice. **R**

Proclaim with me the greatness of the Lord;
let us exalt his name together.
I sought the Lord and he answered me
and delivered me out of all my terror. **R**

Look upon him and be radiant,
and let not your faces be ashamed.
I called in my affliction and the Lord heard me
and saved me from all my troubles. **R**

The angel of the Lord encompasses those who fear him,
and he will deliver them.
Taste and see that the Lord is good;
happy are they who trust in him. **R** *From Psalm 34*

Responsorial Psalm

**R   God's light shines in the darkness for the upright;
    [their righteousness stands fast for ever].**

Happy are they who fear the Lord
and have great delight in his commandments!
Light shines in the darkness for the upright;
the righteous are merciful and full of compassion. **R**

It is good for them to be generous in lending
and to manage their affairs with justice.
For they will never be shaken;
the righteous will be kept in everlasting remembrance. **R**

They will not be afraid of any evil rumours;
their heart is right;
they put their trust in the Lord. **R**

They have given freely to the poor,
and their righteousness stands fast for ever;
they will hold up their head with honour. **R** *From Psalm 112*

Responsorial Psalm

**R   Lord, I entreat you with all my heart.
    [I have promised to keep your words].**

You only are my portion, O Lord;
I have promised to keep your words.
I entreat you with all my heart,
be merciful to me according to your promise. **R**

I have considered my ways
and turned my feet towards your decrees.
I hasten and do not tarry
to keep your commandments. **R**

Though the cords of the wicked entangle me,
I do not forget your law.
At midnight I will rise to give you thanks,
because of your righteous judgements. **R**

I am a companion of all who fear you
and of those who keep your commandments.
The earth, O Lord, is full of your love;
instruct me in your statutes. **R**   *From Psalm 119*

Responsorial Psalm

**R   To you, O God, I lift up my eyes,
[to you enthroned in the heavens].**

As the eyes of servants look to the hand of their masters,
and the eyes of a maid to the hand of her mistress,
so our eyes look to the Lord our God,
until he show us his mercy. **R**

Have mercy upon us, O Lord, have mercy,
for we have had more than enough of contempt,
too much of the scorn of the indolent rich,
and of the derision of the proud. **R**   *Psalm 123*

Responsorial Psalm

**R   O Israel, wait upon the Lord,
[from this time forth for evermore].**

O Lord, I am not proud;
I have no haughty looks.
I do not occupy myself with great matters,
or with things that are too hard for me. **R**

But I still my soul and make it quiet,
like a child upon its mother's breast;
my soul is quieted within me. **R**   *Psalm 131*

A reading from the Acts of the Apostles.

The whole group of those who believed were of one heart and
soul, and no one claimed private ownership of any possessions,
but everything they owned was held in common. With great

power the apostles gave their testimony to the resurrection of the Lord Jesus, and great grace was upon them all. There was not a needy person among them, for as many as owned lands or houses sold them and brought the proceeds of what was sold. They laid it at the apostles' feet, and it was distributed to each as any had need.

This is the word of the Lord.   *Acts 4. 32-35*

A reading from the Second Letter of Paul to the Corinthians.

"Let the one who boasts, boast in the Lord." For it is not those who commend themselves that are approved, but those whom the Lord commends. I wish you would bear with me in a little foolishness. Do bear with me! I feel a divine jealousy for you, for I promised you in marriage to one husband, to present you as a chaste virgin to Christ.

This is the word of the Lord.   *2 Corinthians 10.17 - 11.2*

A reading from the Letter of Paul to the Philippians.

Whatever gains I had, these I have come to regard as loss because of Christ. More than that, I regard everything as loss because of the surpassing value of knowing Christ Jesus my Lord. For his sake I have suffered the loss of all things, and I regard them as rubbish, in order that I may gain Christ and be found in him, not having a righteousness of my own that comes from the law, but one that comes through faith in Christ, the righteousness from God based on faith. I want to know Christ and the power of his resurrection and the sharing of his sufferings by becoming like him in his death, if somehow I may attain the resurrection from the dead. Not that I have already obtained this or have already reached the goal; but I press on to make it my own, because Christ Jesus has made me his own. Beloved, I do not consider that I have made it my own; but this one thing I do: forgetting what lies behind and straining forward to what lies ahead, I press on toward the goal for the prize of the heavenly call of God in Christ Jesus.

This is the word of the Lord.   *Philippians 3. 7-14*

A reading from the First Letter of John.

Do not love the world or the things in the world. The love of the

Father is not in those who love the world; for all that is in the world – the desire of the flesh, the desire of the eyes, the pride in riches – comes not from the Father but from the world. And the world and its desire are passing away, but those who do the will of God live forever.

This is the word of the Lord.   *1 John 2. 15-17*

A reading from the Revelation to John.

I heard what seemed to be the loud voice of a great multitude in heaven, saying, "Alleluia! Salvation and glory and power to our God." And from the throne came a voice saying, "Praise our God, all you his servants, and all who fear him, small and great."

Then I heard what seemed to be the voice of a great multitude, like the sound of many waters and like the sound of mighty thunderpeals, crying out, "Alleluia! For the Lord our God the Almighty reigns. Let us rejoice and exult and give him the glory, for the marriage of the Lamb has come, and his bride has made herself ready; to her it has been granted to be clothed with fine linen, bright and pure" – for the fine linen is the righteous deeds of the saints. And the angel said to me, "Write this: Blessèd are those who are invited to the marriage supper of the Lamb." And he said to me, "These are true words of God."

This is the word of the Lord.   *Revelation 19. 1, 5-9*

Hear the gospel of our Lord Jesus Christ according to Matthew.

Jesus said, "I thank you, Father, Lord of heaven and earth, because you have hidden these things from the wise and the intelligent and have revealed them to infants; yes, Father, for such was your gracious will. All things have been handed over to me by my Father; and no one knows the Son except the Father, and no one knows the Father except the Son and anyone to whom the Son chooses to reveal him.

"Come to me, all you that are weary and are carrying heavy burdens, and I will give you rest. Take my yoke upon you, and learn from me; for I am gentle and humble in heart, and you will find rest for your souls. For my yoke is easy, and my burden is light."

This is the gospel of the Lord.   *Matthew 11. 25-30*

Hear the gospel of our Lord Jesus Christ according to Matthew.

Some Pharisees came to him, and to test him they asked, "Is it lawful for a man to divorce his wife for any cause?" He answered, "Have you not read that the one who made them at the beginning 'made them male and female,' and said, 'For this reason a man shall leave his father and mother and be joined to his wife, and the two shall become one flesh'? So they are no longer two, but one flesh. Therefore what God has joined together, let no one separate." They said to him, "Why then did Moses command us to give a certificate of dismissal and to divorce her?" He said to them, "It was because you were so hard-hearted that Moses allowed you to divorce your wives, but from the beginning it was not so. And I say to you, whoever divorces his wife, except for unchastity, and marries another commits adultery."

His disciples said to him, "If such is the case of a man with his wife, it is better not to marry." But he said to them, "Not everyone can accept this teaching, but only those to whom it is given. For there are eunuchs who have been so from birth, and there are eunuchs who have been made eunuchs by others, and there are eunuchs who have made themselves eunuchs for the sake of the kingdom of heaven. Let anyone accept this who can."

This is the gospel of the Lord.   *Matthew 19. 3-12*

Hear the gospel of our Lord Jesus Christ according to Matthew.

Jesus said to his disciples, "Truly I tell you, it will be hard for a rich person to enter the kingdom of heaven. Again I tell you, it is easier for a camel to go through the eye of a needle than for someone who is rich to enter the kingdom of God." When the disciples heard this, they were greatly astounded and said, "Then who can be saved?" But Jesus looked at them and said, "For mortals it is impossible, but for God all things are possible."

Then Peter said in reply, "Look, we have left everything and followed you. What then will we have?" Jesus said to them, "Truly I tell you, at the renewal of all things, when the Son of Man is seated on the throne of his glory, you who have followed me will also sit on twelve thrones, judging the twelve tribes of Israel. And everyone who has left houses or brothers or sisters or father or mother or children or fields, for my name's sake, will receive a hundredfold, and will inherit eternal life. But many who are first will be last, and the last will be first."

This is the gospel of the Lord. *Matthew 19. 23-30*

Hear the gospel of our Lord Jesus Christ according to Luke.

As they were going along the road, someone said to Jesus, "I will follow you wherever you go." And Jesus said to him, "Foxes have holes, and birds of the air have nests; but the Son of Man has nowhere to lay his head." To another he said, "Follow me." But he said, "Lord, first let me go and bury my father." But Jesus said to him, "Let the dead bury their own dead; but as for you, go and proclaim the kingdom of God." Another said, "I will follow you, Lord; but let me first say farewell to those at my home." Jesus said to him, "No one who puts a hand to the plough and looks back is fit for the kingdom of God."

This is the gospel of the Lord. *Luke 9. 57-62*

Hear the gospel of our Lord Jesus Christ according to Luke.

Jesus said to his disciples, "Do not be afraid, little flock, for it is your Father's good pleasure to give you the kingdom. Sell your possessions, and give alms. Make purses for yourselves that do not wear out, an unfailing treasure in heaven, where no thief comes near and no moth destroys. For where your treasure is, there your heart will be also.

"Be dressed for action and have your lamps lit; be like those who are waiting for their master to return from the wedding banquet, so that they may open the door for him as soon as he comes and knocks. Blessèd are those slaves whom the master finds alert when he comes; truly I tell you, he will fasten his belt and have them sit down to eat, and he will come and serve them."

This is the gospel of the Lord. *Luke 12. 32-37*

MISSIONARIES

White

Collect

Everlasting God,
whose servant N. carried the good news of your Son
to the people of . . . :
grant that we who commemorate his/her service
may know the hope of the gospel in our hearts
and manifest its light in all our ways;
through Jesus Christ your Son our Lord,
who is alive and reigns with you,
in the unity of the Holy Spirit,
one God, now and for ever.

Post Communion

Holy Father,
who gathered us here around the table of your Son
to share this meal with the whole household of God:
in that new world where you reveal
  the fullness of your peace,
gather people of every race and language
to share with N. and all your saints
in the eternal banquet of Jesus Christ our Lord.

A reading from the prophecy of Isaiah.

How beautiful upon the mountains are the feet of the messenger
who announces peace, who brings good news, who announces
salvation, who says to Zion, "Your God reigns." Listen! Your sentinels lift up their voices, together they sing for joy; for in plain
sight they see the return of the Lord to Zion. Break forth together
into singing, you ruins of Jerusalem; for the Lord has comforted
his people, he has redeemed Jerusalem. The Lord has bared his
holy arm before the eyes of all the nations; and all the ends of the
earth shall see the salvation of our God.

This is the word of the Lord.   *Isaiah 52. 7-10*

A reading from the prophecy of Isaiah.

The spirit of the Lord God is upon me, because the Lord has anointed me; he has sent me to bring good news to the oppressed, to bind up the brokenhearted, to proclaim liberty to the captives, and release to the prisoners; to proclaim the year of the Lord's favour, and the day of vengeance of our God; to comfort all who mourn; to provide for those who mourn in Zion – to give them a garland instead of ashes, the oil of gladness instead of mourning, the mantle of praise instead of a faint spirit. They will be called oaks of righteousness, the planting of the Lord, to display his glory.

This is the word of the Lord.   *Isaiah 61. 1-3*

A reading from the prophecy of Ezekiel.

Thus says the Lord God: I myself will search for my sheep, and will seek them out. As shepherds seek out their flocks when they are among their scattered sheep, so I will seek out my sheep. I will rescue them from all the places to which they have been scattered on a day of clouds and thick darkness. I will bring them out from the peoples and gather them from the countries, and will bring them into their own land; and I will feed them on the mountains of Israel, by the watercourses, and in all the inhabited parts of the land.

I will feed them with good pasture, and the mountain heights of Israel shall be their pasture; there they shall lie down in good grazing land, and they shall feed on rich pasture on the mountains of Israel. I myself will be the shepherd of my sheep, and I will make them lie down, says the Lord God. I will seek the lost, and I will bring back the strayed, and I will bind up the injured, and I will strengthen the weak, but the fat and the strong I will destroy. I will feed them with justice.

This is the word of the Lord.   *Ezekiel 34. 11-16*

A reading from the Book of Jonah.

The word of the Lord came to Jonah a second time, saying, "Get up, go to Nineveh, that great city, and proclaim to it the message that I tell you." So Jonah set out and went to Nineveh, according to the word of the Lord. Now Nineveh was an exceedingly large city, a three days' walk across. Jonah began to go into the city, going a day's walk. And he cried out, "Forty days more, and Nineveh shall be overthrown!" And the people of Nineveh believed God; they proclaimed a fast, and everyone, great and small, put on sackcloth.

This is the word of the Lord. *Jonah 3. 1-5*

Responsorial Psalm

R **May God give us his blessing,**
[and may all the ends of the earth stand in awe of him].

May God be merciful to us and bless us,
show us the light of his countenance and come to us.
Let your ways be known upon earth,
your saving health among all nations. **R**

Let the peoples praise you, O God; let all the peoples praise you.
Let the nations be glad and sing for joy,
for you judge the peoples with equity
and guide all the nations upon earth. **R**

Let the peoples praise you, O God;
let all the peoples praise you.
The earth has brought forth her increase;
may God, our own God, give us his blessing. **R** *Psalm 67*

Responsorial Psalm

R **Glorious things are spoken of you, O Zion,**
[O city of our God, the Most High].

On the holy mountain stands the city he has founded;
the Lord loves the gates of Zion
more than all the dwellings of Jacob. **R**

I count Egypt and Babylon among those who know me;
behold Philistia, Tyre and Ethiopia:
in Zion were they born. **R**

Of Zion it shall be said,
"Everyone was born in her,
and the Most High himself shall sustain her." **R**

The Lord will record as he enrols the peoples,
"These also were born there."
The singers and the dancers will say,
"All my fresh springs are in you." **R**   *Psalm 87*

Responsorial Psalm

**R The Lord is king; let the earth rejoice;
[let the multitude of the isles be glad].**

Clouds and darkness are round about him,
righteousness and justice are the foundations of his throne.
A fire goes before him
and burns up his enemies on every side. **R**

His lightnings light up the world;
the earth sees it and is afraid.
The mountains melt like wax at the presence of the Lord,
at the presence of the Lord of the whole earth. **R**

The heavens declare his righteousness,
and all the peoples see his glory.
Confounded be all who worship carved images
  and delight in false gods!
Bow down before him, all you gods. **R**

Zion hears and is glad and the cities of Judah rejoice,
because of your judgements, O Lord.
For you are the Lord: most high over all the earth;
you are exalted far above all gods. **R**

Light has sprung up for the righteous,
and joyful gladness for those who are true-hearted.
Rejoice in the Lord, you righteous,
and give thanks to his holy name. **R**   *From Psalm 97*

Responsorial Psalm

**R Be joyful in the Lord, all you lands,
[and call upon his name].**

Be joyful in the Lord, all you lands;
serve the Lord with gladness
and come before his presence with a song. **R**

Know this: The Lord himself is God;
he himself has made us and we are his;
we are his people and the sheep of his pasture. **R**

Enter his gates with thanksgiving;
go into his courts with praise;
give thanks to him and call upon his name. **R**

For the Lord is good;
his mercy is everlasting;
and his faithfulness endures from age to age. **R**   *Psalm 100*

Responsorial Psalm

R   Alleluia!

Praise the Lord, all you nations;
laud him, all you peoples. **R**

For his loving-kindness towards us is great,
and the faithfulness of the Lord endures for ever. **R**   *Psalm 117*

A reading from the Acts of the Apostles.

Peter, standing with the eleven, raised his voice and addressed them, "Men of Judea and all who live in Jerusalem, let this be known to you, and listen to what I say: Jesus of Nazareth, a man attested to you by God with deeds of power, wonders, and signs that God did through him among you, as you yourselves know – this man, handed over to you according to the definite plan and foreknowledge of God, you crucified and killed by the hands of those outside the law. But God raised him up, having freed him from death, because it was impossible for him to be held in its power. For David says concerning him, 'I saw the Lord always before me, for he is at my right hand so that I will not be shaken; therefore my heart was glad, and my tongue rejoiced; moreover my flesh will live in hope. For you will not abandon my soul to Hades, or let your Holy One experience corruption. You have made known to me the ways of life; you will make me full of gladness with your presence.'

"Fellow Israelites, I may say to you confidently of our ancestor David that he both died and was buried, and his tomb is with us to this day. Since he was a prophet, he knew that God had sworn with an oath to him that he would put one of his descendants on his throne. Foreseeing this, David spoke of the resurrection of the Messiah, saying, "He was not abandoned to Hades, nor did his flesh experience corruption." This Jesus God raised up, and of that all of us are witnesses. Being therefore exalted at the right hand of God, and having received from the Father the promise of the Holy Spirit, he has poured out this that you both see and hear. For David did not ascend into the heavens, but he himself says, "The Lord said to my Lord, 'Sit at my right hand until I make your enemies your footstool.'" Therefore let the entire house of Israel know with certainty that God has made him both Lord and Messiah, this Jesus whom you crucified."

This is the word of the Lord.   *Acts 2. 14, 22-36*

A reading from the Acts of the Apostles.

Both Paul and Barnabas spoke out boldly, saying, "It was necessary that the word of God should be spoken first to you. Since you reject it and judge yourselves to be unworthy of eternal life, we are now turning to the Gentiles. For so the Lord has commanded us, saying, 'I have set you to be a light for the Gentiles, so that you may bring salvation to the ends of the earth.'" When the Gentiles heard this, they were glad and praised the word of the Lord; and as many as had been destined for eternal life became believers. Thus the word of the Lord spread throughout the region.

This is the word of the Lord.   *Acts 13. 46-49*

A reading from the Acts of the Apostles.

Paul and Timothy went through the region of Phrygia and Galatia, having been forbidden by the Holy Spirit to speak the word in Asia. When they had come opposite Mysia, they attempted to go into Bithynia, but the Spirit of Jesus did not allow them; so, passing by Mysia, they went down to Troas. During the night Paul had a vision: there stood a man of Macedonia pleading with him and saying, "Come over to Macedonia and help us." When he had seen the vision, we immediately tried to cross over to Macedonia, being convinced that God had called us to proclaim the good news to them.

This is the word of the Lord.   *Acts 16. 6-10*

A reading from the Acts of the Apostles.

Paul said, "I was not disobedient to the heavenly vision, but declared first to those in Damascus, then in Jerusalem and throughout the countryside of Judea, and also to the Gentiles, that they should repent and turn to God and do deeds consistent with repentance. For this reason the Jews seized me in the temple and tried to kill me. To this day I have had help from God, and so I stand here, testifying to both small and great, saying nothing but what the prophets and Moses said would take place: that the Messiah must suffer, and that, by being the first to rise from the dead, he would proclaim light both to our people and to the Gentiles."

This is the word of the Lord.   *Acts 26. 19-23*

A reading from the Letter of Paul to the Romans.

In Christ Jesus, then, I have reason to boast of my work for God. For I will not venture to speak of anything except what Christ has accomplished through me to win obedience from the Gentiles, by word and deed, by the power of signs and wonders, by the power of the Spirit of God, so that from Jerusalem and as far around as Illyricum I have fully proclaimed the good news of Christ. Thus I make it my ambition to proclaim the good news, not where Christ has already been named, so that I do not build on someone else's foundation, but as it is written, "Those who have never been told of him shall see, and those who have never heard of him shall understand."

This is the word of the Lord.   *Romans 15. 17-21*

A reading from the Second Letter of Paul to the Corinthians.

Knowing the fear of the Lord, we try to persuade others; but we ourselves are well known to God, and I hope that we are also well known to your consciences. We are not commending ourselves to you again, but giving you an opportunity to boast about us, so that you may be able to answer those who boast in outward appearance and not in the heart. For if we are beside ourselves, it is for God; if we are in our right mind, it is for you. For the love of Christ urges us on, because we are convinced that one has died for all;

therefore all have died. And he died for all, so that those who live might live no longer for themselves, but for him who died and was raised for them.

From now on, therefore, we regard no one from a human point of view; even though we once knew Christ from a human point of view, we know him no longer in that way. So if anyone is in Christ, there is a new creation: everything old has passed away; see, everything has become new! All this is from God, who reconciled us to himself through Christ, and has given us the ministry of reconciliation; that is, in Christ God was reconciling the world to himself, not counting their trespasses against them, and entrusting the message of reconciliation to us. So we are ambassadors for Christ, since God is making his appeal through us; we entreat you on behalf of Christ, be reconciled to God. For our sake he made him to be sin who knew no sin, so that in him we might become the righteousness of God.

As we work together with him, we urge you also not to accept the grace of God in vain. For he says, "At an acceptable time I have listened to you, and on a day of salvation I have helped you." See, now is the acceptable time; see, now is the day of salvation!

This is the word of the Lord.   *2 Corinthians 5.11 - 6.2*

Hear the gospel of our Lord Jesus Christ according to Matthew.

Jesus went about all the cities and villages, teaching in their synagogues, and proclaiming the good news of the kingdom, and curing every disease and every sickness. When he saw the crowds, he had compassion for them, because they were harassed and helpless, like sheep without a shepherd. Then he said to his disciples, "The harvest is plentiful, but the labourers are few; therefore ask the Lord of the harvest to send out labourers into his harvest."

This is the gospel of the Lord.   *Matthew 9. 35-38*

Hear the gospel of our Lord Jesus Christ according to Matthew.

The eleven disciples went to Galilee, to the mountain to which Jesus had directed them. When they saw him, they worshipped him; but some doubted. And Jesus came and said to them, "All authority in heaven and on earth has been given to me. Go therefore and make disciples of all nations, baptising them in the name of the Father and of the Son and of the Holy Spirit, and teaching them to obey everything that I have commanded you. And remember, I am with you always, to the end of the age."

This is the gospel of the Lord.   *Matthew 28. 16-20*

Hear the gospel of our Lord Jesus Christ according to Mark.

Jesus said to the disciples, "Go into all the world and proclaim the good news to the whole creation. The one who believes and is baptised will be saved; but the one who does not believe will be condemned. And these signs will accompany those who believe: by using my name they will cast out demons; they will speak in new tongues; they will pick up snakes in their hands, and if they drink any deadly thing, it will not hurt them; they will lay their hands on the sick, and they will recover."

So then the Lord Jesus, after he had spoken to them, was taken up into heaven and sat down at the right hand of God. And they went out and proclaimed the good news everywhere, while the Lord worked with them and confirmed the message by the signs that accompanied it.

This is the gospel of the Lord.   *Mark 16. 15-20*

Hear the gospel of our Lord Jesus Christ according to Luke.

Once while Jesus was standing beside the lake of Gennesaret, and the crowd was pressing in on him to hear the word of God, he saw two boats there at the shore of the lake; the fishermen had gone out of them and were washing their nets. He got into one of the boats, the one belonging to Simon, and asked him to put out a little way from the shore. Then he sat down and taught the crowds from the boat. When he had finished speaking, he said to Simon, "Put out into the deep water and let down your nets for a catch." Simon answered, "Master, we have worked all night long but have caught nothing. Yet if you say so, I will let down the nets." When they had done this, they caught so many fish that their nets were beginning to break. So they signalled their partners in the other boat to come and help them. And they came and filled both boats, so that they began to sink.

But when Simon Peter saw it, he fell down at Jesus' knees, saying, "Go away from me, Lord, for I am a sinful man!" For he and all who were with him were amazed at the catch of fish that they had taken; and so also were James and John, sons of Zebedee, who were partners with Simon. Then Jesus said to Simon, "Do not be afraid; from now on you will be catching people." When they had brought their boats to shore, they left everything and followed him.

This is the gospel of the Lord. *Luke 5. 1-11*

Hear the gospel of our Lord Jesus Christ according to Luke.

The Lord appointed seventy others and sent them on ahead of him in pairs to every town and place where he himself intended to go. He said to them, "The harvest is plentiful, but the labourers are few; therefore ask the Lord of the harvest to send out labourers into his harvest. Go on your way. See, I am sending you out like lambs into the midst of wolves. Carry no purse, no bag, no sandals; and greet no one on the road. Whatever house you enter, first say, 'Peace to this house!' And if anyone is there who shares in peace, your peace will rest on that person; but if not, it will return to you. Remain in the same house, eating and drinking whatever they provide, for the labourer deserves to be paid. Do not move about from house to house. Whenever you enter a town and its people welcome you, eat what is set before you; cure the sick who are there, and say to them, 'The kingdom of God has come near to you.'"

This is the gospel of the Lord. *Luke 10. 1-9*

ANY SAINT: HOLY MEN AND WOMEN

General

Collect
Almighty Father,
you have built up your Church
through the love and devotion of your saints:
inspire us to follow the example of *N.*,
whom we commemorate today,
that we in our generation may rejoice with him/her
in the vision of your glory;
through Jesus Christ your Son our Lord,
who is alive and reigns with you,
in the unity of the Holy Spirit,
one God, now and for ever.

Post Communion
Faithful God,
who called *N.* to serve you
and gave him/her joy in walking the path of holiness:
by this eucharist
  in which you renew within us the vision of your glory,
strengthen us all to follow the way of perfection
until we come to see you face to face;
through Jesus Christ our Lord.

A reading from the book Genesis.

Now the Lord said to Abram, "Go from your country and your kindred and your father's house to the land that I will show you. I will make of you a great nation, and I will bless you, and make your name great, so that you will be a blessing. I will bless those who bless you, and the one who curses you I will curse; and in you all the families of the earth shall be blessed." So Abram went, as the Lord had told him; and Lot went with him. Abram was seventy-five years old when he departed from Haran.

This is the word of the Lord.   *Genesis 12. 1-4*

A reading from the book Proverbs.

Does not wisdom call, and does not understanding raise her voice? On the heights, beside the way, at the crossroads she takes her stand; beside the gates in front of the town, at the entrance of the portals she cries out: "To you, O people, I call, and my cry is to all that live. O simple ones, learn prudence; acquire intelligence, you who lack it. Hear, for I will speak noble things, and from my lips will come what is right; for my mouth will utter truth; wickedness is an abomination to my lips. All the words of my mouth are righteous; there is nothing twisted or crooked in them. They are all straight to one who understands and right to those who find knowledge. Take my instruction instead of silver, and knowledge rather than choice gold; for wisdom is better than jewels, and all that you may desire cannot compare with her."

This is the word of the Lord.   *Proverbs 8. 1-11*

A reading from the prophecy of Micah.

"With what shall I come before the Lord, and bow myself before God on high? Shall I come before him with burnt offerings, with calves a year old? Will the Lord be pleased with thousands of rams, with ten thousands of rivers of oil? Shall I give my firstborn for my transgression, the fruit of my body for the sin of my soul?"

  He has told you, O mortal, what is good; and what does the Lord require of you but to do justice, and to love kindness, and to walk humbly with your God?

This is the word of the Lord.   *Micah 6. 6-8*

A reading from the book Ecclesiasticus.

You who fear the Lord, wait for his mercy; do not stray, or else you may fall. You who fear the Lord, trust in him, and your reward will not be lost. You who fear the Lord, hope for good things, for lasting joy and mercy. Consider the generations of old and see: has anyone trusted in the Lord and been disappointed? Or has anyone persevered in the fear of the Lord and been forsaken? Or has anyone called upon him and been neglected? For the Lord is compassionate and merciful; he forgives sins and saves in time of distress. Woe to timid hearts and to slack hands, and to the sinner who walks a double path! Woe to the fainthearted who have no trust! Therefore they will have no shelter.

[Woe to you who have lost your nerve! What will you do when the Lord's reckoning comes? Those who fear the Lord do not disobey his words, and those who love him keep his ways. Those who fear the Lord seek to please him, and those who love him are filled with his law. Those who fear the Lord prepare their hearts, and humble themselves before him. Let us fall into the hands of the Lord, but not into the hands of mortals; for equal to his majesty is his mercy, and equal to his name are his works.]

This is the word of the Lord.   *Ecclesiasticus 2. 7-13 [14-17]*

Responsorial Psalm

**R   Be glad, you righteous, and rejoice in the Lord;
[shout for joy, all who are true of heart].**

Happy are they whose transgressions are forgiven,
and whose sin is put away!
Happy are they to whom the Lord imputes no guilt,
and in whose spirit there is no guile! **R**

You are my hiding-place, O God;
you preserve me from trouble;
you surround me with shouts of deliverance. **R**

"I will instruct you and teach you
in the way that you should go;
I will guide you with my eye." **R**

Great are the tribulations of the wicked;
but mercy embraces those who trust in the Lord.
Be glad, you righteous, and rejoice in the Lord;
shout for joy, all who are true of heart. **R**   *From Psalm 32*

Responsorial Psalm

**R   Rejoice in the Lord, you righteous;
[it is good for the just to sing praises].**

Praise the Lord with the harp;
play to him upon the psaltery and lyre.
Sing for him a new song;
sound a fanfare with all your skill upon the trumpet. **R**

For the word of the Lord is right,
and all his works are sure.
He loves righteousness and justice;
the loving-kindness of the Lord fills the whole earth. **R**

From Psalm 33

Responsorial Psalm

**R With my whole heart I seek you, O God;
[let me not stray from your commandments].**

Happy are they whose way is blameless,
who walk in the law of the Lord!
Happy are they who observe his decrees
and seek him with all their hearts! **R**

Who never do any wrong,
but always walk in his ways.
You laid down your commandments,
that we should fully keep them. **R**

O that my ways were made so direct
that I might keep your statutes!
Then I should not be put to shame,
when I regard all your commandments. **R**

I will thank you with an unfeigned heart,
when I have learned your righteous judgements.
I will keep your statutes;
do not utterly forsake me. **R**   *From Psalm 119*

Responsorial Psalm

**R You created my inmost parts, O God;
[you knit me together in my mother's womb].**

Lord, you have searched me out and known me;
you know my sitting down and my rising up;
you discern my thoughts from afar. **R**

You trace my journeys and my resting-places
and are acquainted with all my ways.
Indeed, there is not a word on my lips,
but you, O Lord, know it altogether. **R**

You press upon me behind and before
and lay your hand upon me.
Such knowledge is too wonderful for me;
it is so high that I cannot attain to it. **R**

[Where can I go then from your Spirit?
where can I flee from your presence?
If I climb up to heaven, you are there;
if I make the grave my bed, you are there also. **R**

If I take the wings of the morning
and dwell in the uttermost parts of the sea,
even there your hand will lead me
and your right hand hold me fast. **R**

If I say, 'Surely the darkness will cover me,
and the light around me turn to night,'
darkness is not dark to you;
the night is as bright as the day;
darkness and light to you are both alike. **R**

For you yourself created my inmost parts;
you knit me together in my mother's womb.
I will thank you because I am marvellously made;
your works are wonderful and I know it well. **R]**   *From Psalm 139*

Responsorial Psalm

R The Lord is gracious and full of compassion,
[slow to anger and of great kindness].

The Lord is loving to everyone
and his compassion is over all his works.
All your works praise you, O Lord,
and your faithful servants bless you. **R**

They make known the glory of your kingdom
and speak of your power;
That the peoples may know of your power
and the glorious splendour of your kingdom. **R**

Your kingdom is an everlasting kingdom;
your dominion endures throughout all ages. **R**   *From Psalm 145*

A reading from the Letter of Paul to the Ephesians.

I bow my knees before the Father, from whom every family in heaven and on earth takes its name. I pray that, according to the riches of his glory, he may grant that you may be strengthened in your inner being with power through his Spirit, and that Christ may dwell in your hearts through faith, as you are being rooted and grounded in love. I pray that you may have the power to comprehend, with all the saints, what is the breadth and length and height and depth, and to know the love of Christ that surpasses knowledge, so that you may be filled with all the fullness of God.

This is the word of the Lord.   *Ephesians 3. 14-19*

A reading from the Letter of Paul to the Ephesians.

Be strong in the Lord and in the strength of his power. Put on the whole armour of God, so that you may be able to stand against the wiles of the devil. For our struggle is not against enemies of blood and flesh, but against the rulers, against the authorities, against the cosmic powers of this present darkness, against the spiritual forces of evil in the heavenly places. Therefore take up the whole armour of God, so that you may be able to withstand on that evil day, and having done everything, to stand firm. Stand therefore, and fasten the belt of truth around your waist, and put on the breastplate of righteousness. As shoes for your feet put on whatever will make you ready to proclaim the gospel of peace. With all of these, take the shield of faith, with which you will be able to quench all the flaming arrows of the evil one. Take the helmet of salvation, and the sword of the Spirit, which is the word of God. Pray in the Spirit at all times in every prayer and supplication. To that end keep alert and always persevere in supplication for all the saints.

This is the word of the Lord.   *Ephesians 6. 11-18*

A reading from the Letter to the Hebrews.

Remember your leaders, those who spoke the word of God to you; consider the outcome of their way of life, and imitate their faith. Jesus Christ is the same yesterday and today and forever.

Through him, then, let us continually offer a sacrifice of praise to God, that is, the fruit of lips that confess his name. Do not neglect to do good and to share what you have, for such sacrifices are pleasing to God.

This is the word of the Lord.   *Hebrews 13. 7-8, 15-16*

A reading from the Letter of James.

What good is it, my brothers and sisters, if you say you have faith but do not have works? Can faith save you? If a brother or sister is naked and lacks daily food, and one of you says to them, "Go in peace; keep warm and eat your fill," and yet you do not supply their bodily needs, what is the good of that? So faith by itself, if it has no works, is dead.

This is the word of the Lord.   *James 2. 14-17*

A reading from the First Letter of John.

Beloved, let us love one another, because love is from God; everyone who loves is born of God and knows God. Whoever does not love does not know God, for God is love. God's love was revealed among us in this way: God sent his only Son into the world so that we might live through him. In this is love, not that we loved God but that he loved us and sent his Son to be the atoning sacrifice for our sins. Beloved, since God loved us so much, we also ought to love one another. No one has ever seen God; if we love one another, God lives in us, and his love is perfected in us. By this we know that we abide in him and he in us, because he has given us of his Spirit. And we have seen and do testify that the Father has sent his Son as the Saviour of the world. God abides in those who confess that Jesus is the Son of God, and they abide in God. So we have known and believe the love that God has for us. God is love, and those who abide in love abide in God, and God abides in them.

This is the word of the Lord.   *1 John 4. 7-16*

A reading from the Revelation to John.

[Then I saw a new heaven and a new earth; for the first heaven and the first earth had passed away, and the sea was no more.

And I saw the holy city, the new Jerusalem, coming down out of heaven from God, prepared as a bride adorned for her husband. And I heard a loud voice from the throne saying, "See, the home of God is among mortals. He will dwell with them as their God; they will be his peoples, and God himself will be with them; he will wipe every tear from their eyes. Death will be no more; mourning and crying and pain will be no more, for the first things have passed away."]

  And the one who was seated on the throne said, "See, I am making all things new." Also he said, "Write this, for these words are trustworthy and true." Then he said to me, "It is done! I am the Alpha and the Omega, the beginning and the end. To the thirsty I will give water as a gift from the spring of the water of life. Those who conquer will inherit these things, and I will be their God and they will be my children."

This is the word of the Lord.   *Revelation 21. [1-4] 5-7*

Hear the gospel of our Lord Jesus Christ according to Matthew.

Someone came to Jesus and said, "Teacher, what good deed must I do to have eternal life?" And he said to him, "Why do you ask me about what is good? There is only one who is good. If you wish to enter into life, keep the commandments." He said to him, "Which ones?" And Jesus said, "You shall not murder; You shall not commit adultery; You shall not steal; You shall not bear false witness; Honour your father and mother; also, You shall love your neighbour as yourself." The young man said to him, "I have kept all these; what do I still lack?" Jesus said to him, "If you wish to be perfect, go, sell your possessions, and give the money to the poor, and you will have treasure in heaven; then come, follow me."

This is the gospel of the Lord.   *Matthew 19. 16-21*

Hear the gospel of our Lord Jesus Christ according to Matthew.

Jesus said to his disciples, "Then the kingdom of heaven will be like this. Ten bridesmaids took their lamps and went to meet the bridegroom. Five of them were foolish, and five were wise. When the foolish took their lamps, they took no oil with them; but the wise took flasks of oil with their lamps. As the bridegroom was delayed, all of them became drowsy and slept.

"But at midnight there was a shout, 'Look! Here is the bride-groom! Come out to meet him.' Then all those bridesmaids got up and trimmed their lamps. The foolish said to the wise, 'Give us some of your oil, for our lamps are going out.' But the wise replied, 'No! there will not be enough for you and for us; you had better go to the dealers and buy some for yourselves.' And while they went to buy it, the bridegroom came, and those who were ready went with him into the wedding banquet; and the door was shut.

"Later the other bridesmaids came also, saying, 'Lord, lord, open to us.' But he replied, 'Truly I tell you, I do not know you.' Keep awake therefore, for you know neither the day nor the hour."

This is the gospel of the Lord.   *Matthew 25. 1-13*

Hear the gospel of our Lord Jesus Christ according to Matthew.

Jesus said to his disciples, "A man, going on a journey, summoned his slaves and entrusted his property to them; to one he gave five talents, to another two, to another one, to each according to his ability. Then he went away. The one who had received the five talents went off at once and traded with them, and made five more talents. In the same way, the one who had the two talents made two more talents. But the one who had received the one talent went off and dug a hole in the ground and hid his master's money.

"After a long time the master of those slaves came and settled accounts with them. Then the one who had received the five talents came forward, bringing five more talents, saying, 'Master, you handed over to me five talents; see, I have made five more talents.' His master said to him, 'Well done, good and trustworthy servant; you have been trustworthy in a few things, I will put you in charge of many things; enter into the joy of your master.' And the one with the two talents also came forward, saying, 'Master, you hand-ed over to me two talents; see, I have made two more talents.' His master said to him, 'Well done, good and trustworthy servant; you have been trustworthy in a few things, I will put you in charge of many things; enter into the joy of your master.' Then the one who had received the one talent also came forward, saying, 'Master, I knew that you were a harsh man, reaping where you did not sow, and gathering where you did not scatter seed; so I was afraid, and I went and hid your talent in the ground. Here you have what is yours.' But his master replied, 'You wicked and lazy servant! You knew, did you, that I reap where I did not sow, and gather where I did not scatter? Then you ought to have invested my money with the bankers, and on my return I would have received what was my own with interest. So take the talent from him, and give it to the one with the ten talents.

"'For to all those who have, more will be given, and they will have an abundance; but from those who have nothing, even what they have will be taken away. As for this worthless servant, throw him into the outer darkness, where there will be weeping and gnashing of teeth.'"

This is the gospel of the Lord.   *Matthew 25. 14-30*

Hear the gospel of our Lord Jesus Christ according to John.

Jesus said to his disciples, "I am the true vine, and my Father is the vinegrower. He removes every branch in me that bears no fruit. Every branch that bears fruit he prunes to make it bear more fruit. You have already been cleansed by the word that I have spoken to you. Abide in me as I abide in you. Just as the branch cannot bear fruit by itself unless it abides in the vine, neither can you unless you abide in me. I am the vine, you are the branches. Those who abide in me and I in them bear much fruit, because apart from me you can do nothing. Whoever does not abide in me is thrown away like a branch and withers; such branches are gathered, thrown into the fire, and burned. If you abide in me, and my words abide in you, ask for whatever you wish, and it will be done for you. My Father is glorified by this, that you bear much fruit and become my disciples."

This is the gospel of the Lord.   *John 15. 1-8*

Hear the gospel of our Lord Jesus Christ according to John.

Jesus prayed, "I ask not only on behalf of these, but also on behalf of those who will believe in me through their word, that they may all be one. As you, Father, are in me and I am in you, may they also be in us, so that the world may believe that you have sent me. The glory that you have given me I have given them, so that they may be one, as we are one, I in them and you in me, that they may become completely one, so that the world may know that you have sent me and have loved them even as you have loved me.

"Father, I desire that those also, whom you have given me, may be with me where I am, to see my glory, which you have given me because you loved me before the foundation of the world. Righteous Father, the world does not know you, but I know you; and these know that you have sent me. I made your name known to them, and I will make it known, so that the love with which you have loved me may be in them, and I in them."

This is the gospel of the Lord. *John 17. 20-26*

Christian rulers

Collect
Sovereign God,
who called N. to be a ruler among his/her people
and gave him/her grace to be their servant:
help us, following our Saviour Christ
in the path of humble service,
to see his kingdom set forward on earth
and to enjoy its fullness in heaven;
who is alive and reigns with you,
in the unity of the Holy Spirit,
one God, now and for ever.

Post Communion
God our Redeemer,
who inspired N. to witness to your love
and to work for the coming of your kingdom:
may we, who in this sacrament share the bread of heaven,
be fired by your Spirit to proclaim the gospel in our daily living
and never to rest content until your kingdom come,
on earth as it is in heaven;
through Jesus Christ our Lord.

A reading from the First Book of Samuel.

[The Lord said to Samuel, "How long will you grieve over Saul? I have rejected him from being king over Israel. Fill your horn with oil and set out; I will send you to Jesse the Bethlehemite, for I have provided for myself a king among his sons." Samuel said, "How can I go? If Saul hears of it, he will kill me." And the Lord said, "Take a heifer with you, and say, 'I have come to sacrifice to the Lord.' Invite Jesse to the sacrifice, and I will show you what you shall do; and you shall anoint for me the one whom I name to you."]

Samuel did what the Lord commanded, and came to Bethlehem. The elders of the city came to meet him trembling, and said, "Do you come peaceably?" He said, "Peaceably; I have come to sacrifice to the Lord; sanctify yourselves and come with me to the sacrifice." And he sanctified Jesse and his sons and invited them to the sacrifice. When they came, he looked on Eliab and thought, "Surely the Lord's anointed is now before the Lord." But the Lord said to Samuel, "Do not look on his appearance or on the height of his stature, because I have rejected him; for the Lord does not see as mortals see; they look on the outward appearance, but the Lord looks on the heart."

Then Jesse called Abinadab, and made him pass before Samuel. He said, "Neither has the Lord chosen this one." Then Jesse made Shammah pass by. And he said, "Neither has the Lord chosen this one." Jesse made seven of his sons pass before Samuel, and Samuel said to Jesse, "The Lord has not chosen any of these." Samuel said to Jesse, "Are all your sons here?" And he said, "There remains yet the youngest, but he is keeping the sheep." And Samuel said to Jesse, "Send and bring him; for we will not sit down until he comes here." He sent and brought him in. Now he was ruddy, and had beautiful eyes, and was handsome. The Lord said, "Rise and anoint him; for this is the one."

Then Samuel took the horn of oil, and anointed him in the presence of his brothers; and the spirit of the Lord came mightily upon David from that day forward.

This is the word of the Lord.   *1 Samuel 16. [1 - 3] 4 -13a*

A reading from the First Book of the Kings.

Solomon loved the Lord, walking in the statutes of his father David; only, he sacrificed and offered incense at the high places. The king went to Gibeon to sacrifice there, for that was the principal high place; Solomon used to offer a thousand burnt offerings on that altar. At Gibeon the Lord appeared to Solomon in a dream by night; and God said, "Ask what I should give you." And Solomon said, "You have shown great and steadfast love to your servant my father David, because he walked before you in faithfulness, in righteousness, and in uprightness of heart toward you; and you have kept for him this great and steadfast love, and have given him a son to sit on his throne today. And now, O Lord my God, you have made your servant king in place of my father David, although I am only a little child; I do not know how to go out or come in. And your servant is in the midst of the people whom you have chosen, a great people, so numerous they cannot be numbered or counted. Give your servant therefore an understanding mind to govern your people, able to discern between good and evil; for who can govern this your great people?"

It pleased the Lord that Solomon had asked this. God said to him, "Because you have asked this, and have not asked for yourself long life or riches, or for the life of your enemies, but have asked for yourself understanding to discern what is right, I now do according to your word. Indeed I give you a wise and discerning mind; no one like you has been before you and no one like you shall arise after you. I give you also what you have not asked, both riches and honour all your life; no other king shall compare with you. If you will walk in my ways, keeping my statutes and my commandments, as your father David walked, then I will lengthen your life."

This is the word of the Lord.   *1 Kings 3. 3-14*

Responsorial Psalm

**R Give the king your justice, O God,
[and your righteousness to the king's son].**

May the king rule your people righteously
and the poor with justice;
that the mountains may bring prosperity to the people,
and the little hills bring righteousness. **R**

He shall defend the needy among the people;
he shall rescue the poor and crush the oppressor.
He shall live as long as the sun and moon endure,
from one generation to another. **R**

He shall come down like rain upon the mown field,
like showers that water the earth.
In his time shall the righteous flourish;
there shall be abundance of peace
till the moon shall be no more. **R**   *From Psalm 72*

Responsorial Psalm

**R The Lord is great in Zion;
[he is high above all peoples].**

The Lord is king; let the people tremble;
he is enthroned upon the cherubim;
let the earth shake. **R**

Let them confess his name,
which is great and awesome;
he is the Holy One. **R**

"O mighty King, lover of justice,
you have established equity;
you have executed justice and righteousness in Jacob." **R**

Proclaim the greatness of the Lord our God
and fall down before his footstool;
for he is the Holy One. **R**   *From Psalm 99*

A reading from the First Letter of Paul to Timothy.

I urge that supplications, prayers, intercessions, and thanksgivings
be made for everyone, for kings and all who are in high positions,
so that we may lead a quiet and peaceable life in all godliness and
dignity. This is right and is acceptable in the sight of God our
Saviour, who desires everyone to be saved and to come to the
knowledge of the truth. For there is one God; there is also one
mediator between God and humankind, Christ Jesus, himself
human, who gave himself a ransom for all – this was attested at
the right time.

This is the word of the Lord.   *1 Timothy 2. 1-6*

Hear the gospel of our Lord Jesus Christ according to Mark.

Jesus called them and said to them, "You know that among the
Gentiles those whom they recognise as their rulers lord it over
them, and their great ones are tyrants over them. But it is not so
among you; but whoever wishes to become great among you must
be your servant, and whoever wishes to be first among you must
be servant of all. For the Son of Man came not to be served but to
serve, and to give his life a ransom for many."

This is the gospel of the Lord.   *Mark 10. 42-45*

Hear the gospel of our Lord Jesus Christ according to Luke.

Jesus said, "Whoever does not carry the cross and follow me cannot be my disciple. For which of you, intending to build a tower,
does not first sit down and estimate the cost, to see whether he has
enough to complete it? Otherwise, when he has laid a foundation
and is not able to finish, all who see it will begin to ridicule him,
saying, 'This fellow began to build and was not able to finish.' Or
what king, going out to wage war against another king, will not sit
down first and consider whether he is able with ten thousand to
oppose the one who comes against him with twenty thousand? If
he cannot, then, while the other is still far away, he sends a dele-
gation and asks for the terms of peace. So therefore, none of you
can become my disciple if you do not give up all your possessions."

This is the gospel of the Lord.   *Luke 14. 27-33*

Those working for the poor and underprivileged

Collect
Merciful God,
you have compassion on all that you have made
and your whole creation is enfolded in your love:
help us to stand firm for your truth,
to struggle against poverty,
and to share your love with our neighbour,
that with your servant N.
we may be instruments of your peace;
through Jesus Christ your Son our Lord,
who is alive and reigns with you, in the unity of the Holy Spirit,
one God, now and for ever.

Post Communion
God, the source of all holiness
  and giver of all good things:
may we who have shared at this table
  as strangers and pilgrims here on earth
be welcomed with all your saints
  to the heavenly feast on the day of your kingdom;
through Jesus Christ our Lord.

A reading from the prophecy of Isaiah.

Is not this the fast that I choose: to loose the bonds of injustice, to
undo the thongs of the yoke, to let the oppressed go free, and to
break every yoke? Is it not to share your bread with the hungry,
and bring the homeless poor into your house; when you see the
naked, to cover them, and not to hide yourself from your own kin?
Then your light shall break forth like the dawn, and your healing
shall spring up quickly; your vindicator shall go before you, the
glory of the Lord shall be your rear guard.

  Then you shall call, and the Lord will answer; you shall cry for
help, and he will say, Here I am. If you remove the yoke from
among you, the pointing of the finger, the speaking of evil, if you
offer your food to the hungry and satisfy the needs of the afflicted, then your light shall rise in the darkness and your gloom be
like the noonday. The Lord will guide you continually, and satisfy your needs in parched places, and make your bones strong; and
you shall be like a watered garden, like a spring of water, whose
waters never fail.

This is the word of the Lord.   *Isaiah 58. 6-11*

Responsorial Psalm
R   Arise, O God, and rule the earth,
   [for you shall take all nations for your own].

God takes his stand in the council of heaven;
he gives judgement in the midst of the gods:
he says, "How long will you judge unjustly,
and show favour to the wicked? **R**

"Save the weak and the orphan;
defend the humble and needy;
rescue the weak and the poor;
deliver them from the power of the wicked. **R**

"They do not know, neither do they understand;
they go about in darkness;
all the foundations of the earth are shaken. **R**

"Now I say to you, 'You are gods,
and all of you children of the Most High;
nevertheless, you shall die like mortals,
and fall like any prince.'" **R**   *Psalm 82*

Responsorial Psalm

**R   The Lord shall reign for ever,
    [your God, O Zion, throughout all generations].**

Happy are they who have the God of Jacob for their help!
whose hope is in the Lord their God;
who made heaven and earth, the seas and all that is in them;
who keeps his promise for ever; **R**

Who gives justice to those who are oppressed,
and food to those who hunger.
The Lord sets the prisoners free;
the Lord opens the eyes of the blind;
the Lord lifts up those who are bowed down; **R**

The Lord loves the righteous;
the Lord cares for the stranger;
he sustains the orphan and widow,
but frustrates the way of the wicked. **R**   *From Psalm 146*

A reading from the Letter to the Hebrews.

Let mutual love continue. Do not neglect to show hospitality to
strangers, for by doing that some have entertained angels without
knowing it. Remember those who are in prison, as though you
were in prison with them; those who are being tortured, as though
you yourselves were being tortured.

This is the word of the Lord.   *Hebrews 13. 1-3*

A reading from the First Letter of John.

We know that we have passed from death to life because we love one another. Whoever does not love abides in death. All who hate a brother or sister are murderers, and you know that murderers do not have eternal life abiding in them. We know love by this, that he laid down his life for us – and we ought to lay down our lives for one another. How does God's love abide in anyone who has the world's goods and sees a brother or sister in need and yet refuses help? Little children, let us love, not in word or speech, but in truth and action.

This is the word of the Lord. *1 John 3. 14-18*

Hear the gospel of our Lord Jesus Christ according to Matthew.

When Jesus saw the crowds, he went up the mountain; and after he sat down, his disciples came to him. Then he began to speak, and taught them, saying: "Blessèd are the poor in spirit, for theirs is the kingdom of heaven. Blessèd are those who mourn, for they will be comforted. Blessèd are the meek, for they will inherit the earth. Blessèd are those who hunger and thirst for righteousness, for they will be filled. Blessèd are the merciful, for they will receive mercy. Blessèd are the pure in heart, for they will see God. Blessèd are the peacemakers, for they will be called children of God. Blessèd are those who are persecuted for righteousness' sake, for theirs is the kingdom of heaven. Blessèd are you when people revile you and persecute you and utter all kinds of evil against you falsely on my account. Rejoice and be glad, for your reward is great in heaven, for in the same way they persecuted the prophets who were before you."

This is the gospel of the Lord. *Matthew 5. 1-12*

Hear the gospel of our Lord Jesus Christ according to Matthew.

Jesus said to his disciples, "When the Son of Man comes in his glory, and all the angels with him, then he will sit on the throne of his glory. All the nations will be gathered before him, and he will separate people one from another as a shepherd separates the sheep from the goats, and he will put the sheep at his right hand and the goats at the left. Then the king will say to those at his right hand, 'Come, you that are blessed by my Father, inherit the kingdom prepared for you from the foundation of the world; for I was hungry and you gave me food, I was thirsty and you gave me something to drink, I was a stranger and you welcomed me, I was naked and you gave me clothing, I was sick and you took care of me, I was in prison and you visited me.'

"Then the righteous will answer him, 'Lord, when was it that we saw you hungry and gave you food, or thirsty and gave you something to drink? And when was it that we saw you a stranger and welcomed you, or naked and gave you clothing? And when was it that we saw you sick or in prison and visited you?' And the king will answer them, 'Truly I tell you, just as you did it to one of the least of these who are members of my family, you did it to me.'

"Then he will say to those at his left hand, 'You that are accursed, depart from me into the eternal fire prepared for the devil and his angels; for I was hungry and you gave me no food, I was thirsty and you gave me nothing to drink, I was a stranger and you did not welcome me, naked and you did not give me clothing, sick and in prison and you did not visit me.'

"Then they also will answer, 'Lord, when was it that we saw you hungry or thirsty or a stranger or naked or sick or in prison, and did not take care of you?' Then he will answer them, 'Truly I tell you, just as you did not do it to one of the least of these, you did not do it to me.' And these will go away into eternal punishment, but the righteous into eternal life."

This is the gospel of the Lord.   *Matthew 25. 31-46*

Men and women of learning

Collect
God our Father,
who gave wisdom and insight to your servant N.
to fathom the depths of your love
and to understand your design for the world you have made:
grant us the help of your Holy Spirit
that we also may come to a full knowledge of your purposes
revealed in your Son Jesus Christ, our Wisdom and our Life;
who is alive and reigns with you, in the unity of the Holy Spirit,
one God, now and for ever.

Post Communion
God our Redeemer,
who inspired *N.* to witness to your love
and to work for the coming of your kingdom:
may we, who in this sacrament share the bread of heaven,
be fired by your Spirit to proclaim the gospel in our daily living
and never to rest content until your kingdom come,
on earth as it is in heaven;
through Jesus Christ our Lord.

A reading from the book Proverbs.

The Lord created me at the beginning of his work, the first of his acts of long ago. Ages ago I was set up, at the first, before the beginning of the earth. When there were no depths I was brought forth, when there were no springs abounding with water. Before the mountains had been shaped, before the hills, I was brought forth – when he had not yet made earth and fields, or the world's first bits of soil. When he established the heavens, I was there, when he drew a circle on the face of the deep, when he made firm the skies above, when he established the fountains of the deep, when he assigned to the sea its limit, so that the waters might not transgress his command, when he marked out the foundations of the earth, then I was beside him, like a master worker; and I was daily his delight, rejoicing before him always, rejoicing in his inhabited world and delighting in the human race.

This is the word of the Lord.   *Proverbs 8. 22-31*

A reading from the book Ecclesiasticus.

Let us now sing the praises of famous men, our ancestors in their generations. The Lord apportioned to them great glory, his majesty from the beginning. There were those who ruled in their kingdoms, and made a name for themselves by their valour; those who gave counsel because they were intelligent; those who spoke in prophetic oracles; those who led the people by their counsels and by their knowledge of the people's lore; they were wise in their words of instruction; those who composed musical tunes, or put verses in writing; rich men endowed with resources, living peacefully in their homes – all these were honoured in their generations, and were the pride of their times. Some of them have left behind a name, so that others declare their praise. But of others there is no memory; they have perished as though they had never existed; they have become as though they had never been born, they and their children after them.

But these also were godly men, whose righteous deeds have not been forgotten; their wealth will remain with their descendants, and their inheritance with their children's children. Their descendants stand by the covenants; their children also, for their sake. Their offspring will continue forever, and their glory will never be blotted out. Their bodies are buried in peace, but their name lives on generation after generation. The assembly declares their wisdom, and the congregation proclaims their praise.

This is the word of the Lord.   *Ecclesiasticus 44. 1-15*

Responsorial Psalm

**R   Your love, O Lord, reaches to the heavens,
      [and your faithfulness to the clouds].**

Your righteousness is like the strong mountains,
your justice like the great deep;
you save both human and beast, O Lord. **R**

How priceless is your love, O God!
your people take refuge under the shadow of your wings.
They feast upon the abundance of your house;
you give them drink from the river of your delights. **R**

For with you is the well of life,
and in your light we see light.
Continue your loving-kindness to those who know you,
and your favour to those who are true of heart. **R**   *From Psalm 36*

Responsorial Psalm

**R   God will ransom my life
      [and will snatch me from the grasp of death].**

Hear this, all you peoples;
hearken, all you who dwell in the world,
you of high degree and low, rich and poor together. **R**

My mouth shall speak of wisdom,
and my heart shall meditate on understanding.
I will incline my ear to a proverb
and set forth my riddle upon the harp. **R**

Why should I be afraid in evil days,
when the wickedness of those at my heels surrounds me,
the wickedness of those who put their trust in their goods
and boast of their great riches? **R**

We can never ransom ourselves,
or deliver to God the price of our life;
for the ransom of our life is so great,
that we should never have enough to pay it. **R**

Do not be envious when some become rich,
or when the grandeur of their house increases;
for they will carry nothing away at their death,
nor will their grandeur follow them. **R**   *From Psalm 49*

A reading from the Letter of Paul to the Philippians.

The peace of God, which surpasses all understanding, will guard your hearts and your minds in Christ Jesus. Finally, beloved, whatever is true, whatever is honourable, whatever is just, whatever is pure, whatever is pleasing, whatever is commendable, if there is any excellence and if there is anything worthy of praise, think about these things.

This is the word of the Lord.   *Philippians 4. 7-8*

Hear the gospel of our Lord Jesus Christ according to Matthew.

Jesus said to his disciples, "The kingdom of heaven is like treasure hidden in a field, which someone found and hid; then in his joy he goes and sells all that he has and buys that field. Again, the kingdom of heaven is like a merchant in search of fine pearls; on finding one pearl of great value, he went and sold all that he had and bought it. Therefore every scribe who has been trained for the kingdom of heaven is like the master of a household who brings out of his treasure what is new and what is old."

This is the gospel of the Lord.   *Matthew 13. 44-46, 52*

Hear the gospel of our Lord Jesus Christ according to John.

About the middle of the festival Jesus went up into the temple and began to teach. The Jews were astonished at it, saying, "How does this man have such learning, when he has never been taught?" Then Jesus answered them, "My teaching is not mine but his who sent me. Anyone who resolves to do the will of God will know whether the teaching is from God or whether I am speaking on my own. Those who speak on their own seek their own glory; but the one who seeks the glory of him who sent him is true, and there is nothing false in him."

This is the gospel of the Lord. *John 7. 14-18*

Those whose holiness was revealed in marriage and family life

Collect
Eternal God,
whose love is revealed in the mystery of the Trinity:
help us, like your servant *N.*,
to find in our human loving a mirror of your divine love
and to see in all your children our brothers and sisters in Christ,
who is alive and reigns with you,
in the unity of the Holy Spirit,
one God, now and for ever.

Post Communion
Father,
from whom every family in heaven and on earth takes its name,
your servant *N.* revealed your goodness
  in a life of tranquillity and service:
grant that we who have gathered in faith around this table
may like him/her know the love of Christ
  that surpasses knowledge
and be filled with all your fullness;
through Jesus Christ our Lord.

A reading from the book Proverbs.

A capable wife who can find? She is far more precious than jewels. The heart of her husband trusts in her, and he will have no lack of gain. She does him good, and not harm, all the days of her life. She seeks wool and flax, and works with willing hands. [She is like the ships of the merchant, she brings her food from far away. She rises while it is still night and provides food for her household and tasks for her servant-girls. She considers a field and buys it; with the fruit of her hands she plants a vineyard. She girds herself with strength, and makes her arms strong.]

She perceives that her merchandise is profitable. Her lamp does not go out at night. She puts her hands to the distaff, and her hands hold the spindle. She opens her hand to the poor, and reaches out her hands to the needy. [She is not afraid for her household when it snows, for all her household are clothed in crimson. She makes herself coverings; her clothing is fine linen and purple. Her husband is known in the city gates, taking his seat among the elders of the land. She makes linen garments and sells them; she supplies the merchant with sashes. Strength and dignity are her clothing, and she laughs at the time to come. She opens her mouth with wisdom, and the teaching of kindness is on her tongue. She looks well to the ways of her household, and does not eat the bread of idleness. Her children rise up and call her happy; her husband too, and he praises her: "Many women have done excellently, but you surpass them all."]

Charm is deceitful, and beauty is vain, but a woman who fears the Lord is to be praised. Give her a share in the fruit of her hands, and let her works praise her in the city gates.

This is the word of the Lord. *Proverbs 31. 10-31*
(or vv 10-13, 19-20, 30-31)

A reading from the Book of Tobit.

When the parents had gone out and shut the door of the room, Tobias got out of bed and said to Sarah, "Sister, get up, and let us pray and implore our Lord that he grant us mercy and safety." So she got up, and they began to pray and implore that they might be kept safe. Tobias began by saying, "Blessèd are you, O God of our ancestors, and blessèd is your name in all generations forever. Let the heavens and the whole creation bless you forever. You made Adam, and for him you made his wife Eve as a helper and support. From the two of them the human race has sprung. You said, 'It is not good that the man should be alone; let us make a helper for him like himself.' I now am taking this kinswoman of mine, not because of lust, but with sincerity. Grant that she and I may find mercy and that we may grow old together."

This is the word of the Lord. *Tobit 8. 4-7*

Responsorial Psalm

R **Children are a heritage from the Lord,**
   [and the fruit of the womb is a gift].

Unless the Lord builds the house,
their labour is in vain who build it.
Unless the Lord watches over the city,
in vain the guard keeps vigil. **R**

It is in vain that you rise so early
and go to bed so late;
vain, too, to eat the bread of toil,
for he gives to his belovèd sleep. **R**

Children are a heritage from the Lord,
and the fruit of the womb is a gift.
Like arrows in the hand of a warrior
are the children of one's youth. **R**

Happy are they who have their quiver full of them!
they shall not be put to shame
when they contend with their enemies in the gate. **R** *Psalm 127*

Responsorial Psalm

R **Happy are they all who fear the Lord,**
   [and who follow in God's ways!]

You shall eat the fruit of your labour;
happiness and prosperity shall be yours.
Your wife shall be like a fruitful vine within your house,
your children like olive shoots round about your table. **R**

Whoever fears the Lord shall thus indeed be blessed.
The Lord bless you from Zion,
and may you see the prosperity of Jerusalem
all the days of your life. **R**

May you live to see your children's children;
may peace be upon Israel. **R**   *Psalm 128*

A reading from the First Letter of Peter.

Wives, in the same way, accept the authority of your husbands, so that, even if some of them do not obey the word, they may be won over without a word by their wives' conduct, when they see the purity and reverence of your lives. Do not adorn yourselves outwardly by braiding your hair, and by wearing gold ornaments or fine clothing; rather, let your adornment be the inner self with the lasting beauty of a gentle and quiet spirit, which is very precious in God's sight. It was in this way long ago that the holy women who hoped in God used to adorn themselves by accepting the authority of their husbands. Thus Sarah obeyed Abraham and called him lord. You have become her daughters as long as you do what is good and never let fears alarm you.

Husbands, in the same way, show consideration for your wives in your life together, paying honour to the woman as the weaker sex, since they too are also heirs of the gracious gift of life – so that nothing may hinder your prayers. Finally, all of you, have unity of spirit, sympathy, love for one another, a tender heart, and a humble mind. Do not repay evil for evil or abuse for abuse; but, on the contrary, repay with a blessing. It is for this that you were called – that you might inherit a blessing.

This is the word of the Lord.   *1 Peter 3. 1-9*

Hear the gospel of our Lord Jesus Christ according to Mark.

Then the mother of Jesus and his brothers came; and standing outside, they sent to him and called him. A crowd was sitting around him; and they said to him, "Your mother and your brothers and sisters are outside, asking for you." And he replied, "Who are my mother and my brothers?" And looking at those who sat around him, he said, "Here are my mother and my brothers! Whoever does the will of God is my brother and sister and mother."

This is the gospel of the Lord.   *Mark 3. 31-35*

Hear the gospel of our Lord Jesus Christ according to Luke.

Now as Jesus and his disciples went on their way, Jesus entered a
certain village, where a woman named Martha welcomed him into
her home. She had a sister named Mary, who sat at the Lord's feet
and listened to what he was saying. But Martha was distracted by
her many tasks; so she came to him and asked, "Lord, do you not
care that my sister has left me to do all the work by myself? Tell
her then to help me." But the Lord answered her, "Martha,
Martha, you are worried and distracted by many things; there is
need of only one thing. Mary has chosen the better part, which
will not be taken away from her."

This is the gospel of the Lord.   *Luke 10. 38-42*

Sentences

THE BLESSED VIRGIN MARY

Opening Sentence
Blessèd is she who believed that there would be a fulfilment of
what was spoken to her by the Lord.   *Luke 1.45*

or:

Mary said, "Here am I, the servant of the Lord; let it be to me
according to your word."   *Luke 1.38*

Gospel Sentence
Alleluia! Alleluia! My spirit rejoices in God my Saviour, for he has
looked with favour on the lowliness of his servant. Alleluia!

Luke 1. 47, 48

or:

Alleluia! Alleluia! My soul magnifies the Lord and my spirit
rejoices in God my Saviour. Alleluia!   *Luke 1. 46, 47*

Post-Communion Sentence
Jesus said, "Blessèd are those who hear the word of God and obey it!"
Luke 11.28

or:

Mary treasured all these words and pondered them in her heart.
Luke 2.19

APOSTLES & EVANGELISTS

Opening Sentence

Jesus said to the disciples, "Go into all the world and proclaim the
good news to the whole creation."   *Mark 16.15*

or:

Do not be afraid: you are looking for Jesus of Nazareth, who was
crucified. He has been raised; you will see him, just as he told you.
Mark 16. 6, 7

Gospel Sentence

Alleluia! Alleluia! I do not call you servants but friends, because I
have made known to you everything that I have heard from my
Father. Alleluia!   *John 15.15*

or:

Alleluia! Alleluia! I appoint you to go and bear fruit, fruit that will
last. Alleluia!   *John 15.16*

Post-Communion Sentence

Jesus said, "I am with you always, to the end of the age."

Matthew 28.20

or:

Jesus said to his disciples, "I will do whatever you ask in my name,
so that the Father may be glorified in the Son."   *John 14.13*

MARTYRS

Opening Sentence
Jesus said, "Those who want to save their life will lose it, and those who lose their life for my sake, and for the sake of the gospel, will save it." *Mark 8.35*

or:

Neither death, nor life, nor angels, nor rulers, nor things present, nor things to come, nor powers, nor height, nor depth, nor anything else in all creation, will be able to separate us from the love of God in Christ Jesus our Lord. *Romans 8. 38, 39*

Gospel Sentence
Alleluia! Alleluia! The one who endures to the end will be saved. Alleluia! *Matthew 10.22*

or:

Alleluia! Alleluia! Whoever would become my followers, let them deny themselves and take up their cross and follow me. Alleluia! *Matthew 16.24*

Post-Communion Sentence
Jesus said, "Very truly, I tell you, unless a grain of wheat falls into the earth and dies, it remains just a single grain; but if it dies, it bears much fruit." *John 12.24*

or:

If we have died with Christ, we believe that we will also live with him. *John 6.8*

TEACHERS OF THE FAITH
& SPIRITUAL WRITERS

Opening Sentence

Jesus said, "Therefore every scribe who has been trained for the kingdom of heaven is like the a householder who brings out of the treasury what is new and what is old." *Matthew 13.52*

or:

Let your heart hold fast my words; get wisdom; do not forsake her, and she will keep you; love her, and she will guard you.

Proverbs 4. 4, 6

Gospel Sentence

Alleluia! Alleluia! You are the light of the world: no one after lighting a lamp puts it under a basket but on the lampstand and it gives light to all. Alleluia! *Matthew 5,14*

or:

Alleluia! Alleluia! Whoever keeps the commandments and teaches them will be called great in the kingdom of heaven. Alleluia!

Matthew 5.19

Post-Communion Sentence

Jesus said, "Whoever serves me must follow me, and where I am, there will my servant be also. Whoever serves me, the Father will honour." *John 12.26*

or:

Show yourself in all respects a model of good works, and in your teaching show integrity, gravity, and sound speech that cannot be censured. *Titus 2. 7, 8*

BISHOPS AND OTHER PASTORS

Opening Sentence

The Spirit of the Lord is upon me, because he has anointed me to bring good news; he has sent me to proclaim release to the oppressed, to proclaim the year of the Lord's favour.

Luke 4. 18, 19

or:

Keep watch over yourselves and over all the flock, of which the Holy Spirit has made you overseers, to shepherd the church of God that he obtained with the blood of his own Son.   *Acts 20.28*

Gospel Sentence

Alleluia! Alleluia! I am the good shepherd: I know my own and my own know me. Alleluia!   *John 10.14*

or:

Alleluia! Alleluia! Make disciples of the nations: baptising and teaching them, as I have commanded you. Alleluia!

Matthew 27. 19, 20

Post-Communion Sentence

You did not choose me but I chose you. And I appointed you to go and bear fruit, fruit that will last.   *John 15.16*

or:

Jesus said, "Blessèd is that servant whom the master will find at work when he arrives."   *Matthew 24.46*

RELIGIOUS

Opening Sentence

I will meditate on your commandments and give attention to your
ways, O Lord.   *Psalm 119.15*

or:

I will greatly rejoice in the Lord, my whole being shall exult in
my God.   *Isaiah 61.10*

Gospel Sentence

Alleluia! Alleluia! Behold the light of the gospel of the glory of
Christ, who is the very image of God. Alleluia!   *2 Corinthians 4.4*

or:

Alleluia! Alleluia! How beautiful on the mountains are the feet of
those who bring good news. Alleluia!   *Isaiah 52.7*

Post-Communion Sentence

Everyone who has left houses or brothers or sisters or father or
mother or children or fields, for my name's sake, will receive a
hundredfold, and will inherit eternal life.   *Matthew 19.29*

or:

Make purses for yourselves that do not wear out, an unfailing treasure in heaven, for where your treasure is, there your heart will be
also.   *Luke 12.32*

MISSIONARIES

Opening Sentence
How beautiful upon the mountains are the feet of the messenger who announces peace, who brings good news, who announces salvation, who says to Zion, "Your God reigns."   *Isaiah 52.7*

or:

Proclaim to the city the message that I tell you.   *Jonah 3.1*

Gospel Sentence
Alleluia! Alleluia! If anyone is in Christ, there is a new creation.
Alleluia!   *2 Corinthians 5.17*

or:

Alleluia! Alleluia! The kingdom of God has come near to you.
Alleluia!   *Luke 10.9*

Post-Communion Sentence
Jesus said, "Go into all the world and proclaim the good news to the whole creation."   *Mark 6.15*

or:

God has reconciled us to himself through Christ and has enlisted us in this service of reconciliation.   *2 Corinthians 5.18*

ANY SAINT : HOLY MEN AND WOMEN

Opening Sentence
The righteous shall receive a blessing from the Lord, and a just
reward from the God of their salvation.   *Psalm 24.5*

or:

If you come forward to serve the Lord, set your heart right and be
steadfast.   *Ecclesiasticus 2.1*

Gospel Sentence
Alleluia! Alleluia! Blessèd are the pure in heart, for they will see
God. Alleluia!   *Matthew 5.8*

or:

Alleluia! Alleluia! Blessèd are the peacemakers, for they will be
called children of God. Alleluia!   *Matthew 5.9*

Post-Communion Sentence
Jesus said, "I was hungry and you gave me food, I was thirsty and
you gave me drink, I was a stranger and you welcomed me."

Matthew 25.35

or:

Jesus said, "The Son of Man did not come to be served but to
serve, and to give up his life as a ransom for many."   *Mark 10.45*

Index of Saints' Days

Aelred   *12 January*
Agnes   *21 January*
Aidan   *31 August*
Alban   *22 June*
Alcuin   *20 May*
Aldhelm   *25 May*
Alfred   *26 October*
All Saints' Day   *1 November*
All Souls' Day   *2 November*
Allen Gardiner   *6 September*
Alphege   *19 April*
Ambrose   *7 December*
Andrew   *30 November*
Andrewes, Lancelot   *25 September*
Angels, Michael & All   *29 September*
Anne   *26 July*
Anselm   *21 April*
Anskar   *3 February*
Anthony Ashley Cooper   *1 October*
Antony of Egypt   *17 January*
Apolo Kivebulaya   *30 May*
Athanasius   *2 May*
Augustine of Canterbury   *26 May*
Augustine of Hippo   *28 August*
Azariah, Samuel Vedanayagam   *2 January*

Barnabas   *11 June*
Barnett, Samuel & Henrietta   *17 June*
Bartholomew the Apostle   *24 August*
Bartolomé de las Casas   *20 July*
Basil the Great   *2 January*
Baxter, Richard   *14 June*
Becket, Thomas   *29 December*
Bede, the Venerable   *25 May*
Benedict   *11 July*
Benedict Biscop   *12 January*
Bernard   *20 August*

Bernard Mizeki   *18 June*
Birinus   *4 September*
Bonaventure   *15 July*
Bonhoeffer, Dietrich   *9 April*
Boniface   *5 June*
Booth, William & Catherine   *20 August*
Bosco, John   *31 January*
Bray, Thomas   *15 February*
Bridget of Sweden   *23 July*
Brigid of Kildare   *1 February*
Brooke Foss Westcott   *27 July*
Bunyan, John   *30 August*
Butler, Joseph   *16 June*
Butler, Josephine   *30 May*

Calvin, John   *26 May*
Carlile, Wilson   *26 September*
Caroline Chisholm   *16 May*
Catherine of Alexandria   *25 November*
Catherine of Siena   *29 April*
Catherine Booth   *20 August*
Cavell, Edith   *12 October*
Charles de Foucauld   *1 December*
Charles Fuge Lowder   *9 September*
Charles Simeon   *13 November*
Charles Stuart   *30 January*
Charles Wesley   *24 May*
Chisholm, Caroline   *16 May*
Christina Rossetti   *27 April*
Chrysostom, John   *13 September*
Cooper, Anthony Ashley   *1 October*
Cecilia   *22 November*
Cedd   *26 October*
Chad   *2 March or 26 October*
Chanel, Peter   *28 April*
Clare   *11 August*
Clement of Rome   *23 November*
Columba   *9 June*
Cranmer, Thomas   *21 March*
Crispin and Crispinian   *25 October*

Curé d'Ars   *4 August*
Cuthbert   *20 March*
Cyprian   *15 September*
Cyril of Alexandria   *27 June*
Cyril of Jerusalem   *18 March*
Cyril & Methodius   *14 February*

David of Wales   *1 March*
Denys   *9 October*
Dietrich Bonhoeffer   *9 April*
Dominic   *8 August*
Donne, John   *31 March*
Dunstan   *19 May*

Edith Cavell   *12 October*
Edmund, Martyr   *20 November*
Edmund Rich   *16 November*
Edward the Confessor   *13 October*
Edward King   *8 March*
Edward Bouverie Pusey   *16 September*
Eglantine Jebb   *17 December*
Elizabeth of Hungary   *18 November*
Elizabeth Ferard   *18 July*
Elizabeth Fry   *12 October*
England, Saints & Martyrs of   *8 November*
English Reformation Era, Saints & Martyrs of the   *4 May*
Ephrem of Syria   *9 June*
Ethelburga   *11 October*
Etheldreda   *23 June*
Evelyn Underhill   *15 June*

Faithful Departed, Commemoration of the   *2 November*
Felicity   *7 March*
Felix   *8 March*
Ferard, Elizabeth   *18 July*
Ferrar, Nicholas   *4 December*
Fisher, John   *6 July*
Florence Nightingale   *13 August*
Foucauld, Charles de   *1 December*
Fox, George   *13 January*

Francis of Assisi   *4 October*
Francis de Sales   *24 January*
Francis Xavier   *3 December*
Frederick Denison Maurice   *1 April*
Frideswide   *19 October*
Fry, Elizabeth   *12 October*

Gardiner, Allen   *6 September*
Geoffrey Studdert Kennedy   *8 March*
George   *23 April*
George Herbert   *27 February*
George Augustus Selwyn   *11 April*
Gilbert   *4 February*
Giles   *1 September*
Gilmore, Isabella   *16 April*
Gore, Charles   *17 January*
Gregory the Great   *3 September*
Gregory of Nazianzus   *2 January*
Gregory of Nyssa   *19 July*
Grosseteste, Robert   *9 October*

Hannington, James   *29 October*
Harriet Monsell   *26 March*
Helena   *21 May*
Henrietta Barnett   *17 June*
Henry Martyn   *19 October*
Henry Venn   *1 July*
Herbert, George   *27 February*
Hilary   *13 January*
Hilda   *19 November*
Hildegard   *17 September*
Hill, Octavia   *13 August*
Hilton, Walter   *24 March*
Holy Innocents   *28 December*
Hooker, Richard   *3 November*
Hugh   *17 November*
Hugh Latimer   *16 October*

Ignatius of Antioch   17 October
Ignatius of Loyola   31 July
Ini Kopuria   6 June
Innocents, The Holy   28 December
Irenæus   28 June
Isaac Watts   25 November
Isabella Gilmore   16 April

James the Apostle   1 May
James the Deacon   11 October
James the Great   25 July
James Hannington   29 October
Janani Luwum   17 February
Japan, Martyrs of   6 February
Jean-Baptist Vianney   4 August
Jebb, Eglantine   17 December
Jeremy Taylor   13 August
Jerome   30 September
Joachim   26 July
Joan of Arc   30 May
John   27 December
John the Baptist, Beheading of   29 August
John the Baptist, Birth of   24 June
John of the Cross   14 December
John of Damascus   4 December
John Bosco   31 January
John Bunyan   30 August
John Calvin   26 May
John Chrysostom   13 September
John Donne   31 March
John Fisher   6 July
John Keble   14 July
John Mason Neale   7 August
John Henry Newman   11 August
John Coleridge Patteson   20 September
John Venn   1 July
John Wesley   24 May
John Wyclif   31 December
Johnson, Samuel   13 December
Joseph   19 March

Joseph Butler   *16 June*
Josephine Butler   *30 May*
Jude   *28 October*
Julian of Norwich   *8 May*
Justin   *1 June*

Keble, John   *14 July*
Kempe, Margery   *9 November*
Ken, Thomas   *8 June*
Kentigern   *13 January*
King, Edward   *8 March*
Kivebulaya, Apolo   *30 May*
Kolbe, Maximilian   *14 August*
Kopuria, Ini   *6 June*

Lancelot Andrewes   *25 September*
Lanfranc   *28 May*
Latimer, Hugh   *16 October*
Laud, William   *10 January*
Laurence   *10 August*
Law, William   *10 April*
Lazarus   *29 July*
Leo the Great   *10 November*
Leonard   *6 November*
Lowder, Charles Fuge   *9 September*
Lucy   *13 December*
Luke   *18 October*
Luther, Martin   *31 October*
Luwum, Janani   *17 February*

Macrina   *19 July*
Margaret of Antioch   *20 July*
Margaret of Scotland   *16 November*
Margery Kempe   *9 November*
Mark   *25 April*
Martha   *29 July*
Martin   *11 November*
Martin de Porres   *3 November*
Martin Luther   *31 October*
Martyn, Henry   *19 October*

Mary the Virgin   *15 August*
  Birth   *8 September*
  Conception   *8 December*
  Visit to Elizabeth   *31 May*
Mary, Martha and Lazarus   *29 July*
Mary Magdalene   *22 July*
Mary Sumner   *9 August*
Matthew   *21 September*
Matthias   *14 May or 24 February*
Maurice, Frederick Denison   *1 April*
Maximilian Kolbe   *14 August*
Mechtild   *19 November*
Mellitus   *24 April*
Methodius   *14 February*
Michael & All Angels   *29 September*
Mizeki, Bernard   *18 June*
Monica   *27 August*
Monsell, Harriet   *26 March*
More, Thomas   *6 July*
Mungo (Kentigern)   *13 January*

Nathanael (see Bartholomew)   *24 August*
Neale, John Mason   *7 August*
Neri, Philip   *26 May*
Newman, John Henry   *11 August*
Nicholas   *6 December*
Nicholas Ferrar   *4 December*
Nicholas Ridley   *16 October*
Nightingale, Florence   *13 August*
Ninian   *16 September*

Octavia Hill   *13 August*
Oscar Romero   *24 March*
Osmund   *16 July*
Oswald of Northumbria   *5 August*

Papua New Guinea, Martyrs of   *2 September*
Patrick   *17 March*
Patteson, John Coleridge   *20 September*
Paul (& Peter)   *29 June*

Paul, Conversion of   *25 January*
Paulinus   *10 October*
Perpetua   *7 March*
Peter   *29 June*
Peter Chanel   *28 April*
Petroc   *4 June*
Philip (& James)   *1 May*
Philip Neri   *26 May*
Polycarp   *23 February*
Priscilla Lydia Sellon   *20 November*
Pusey, Edward Bouverie   *16 September*

Ramabai, Pandita Mary   *30 April*
Reformation Era, English Saints & Martyrs of the   *4 May*
Remigius   *1 October*
Richard of Chichester   *16 June*
Richard Baxter   *14 June*
Richard Hooker   *3 November*
Richard Rolle   *20 January*
Ridley, Nicholas   *16 October*
Robert Grosseteste   *9 October*
Rolle, Richard   *20 January*
Romero, Oscar   *24 March*
Rossetti, Christina   *27 April*

Samuel Barnett   *17 June*
Samuel Johnson   *13 December*
Samuel Seabury   *14 November*
Scholastica   *10 February*
Seabury, Samuel   *14 November*
Sellon, Priscilla Lydia   *20 November*
Selwyn, George Augustus   *11 April*
Seraphim of Sarov   *2 January*
Sergei of Radonezh   *25 September*
Sigfrid   *15 February*
Simeon, Charles   *13 November*
Simon (& Jude)   *28 October*
Singh, Sundar   *19 June*
Slessor, Mary   *11 January*
Studdert Kennedy, Geoffrey   *8 March*

Stephen   *26 December*
Stuart, Charles   *30 January*
Sumner, Mary   *9 August*
Sundar Singh   *19 June*
Swithun   *15 July*

Taylor, Jeremy   *13 August*
Temple, William   *6 November*
Teresa of Avila   *15 October*
Thaddæus   (see Jude)   *28 October*
Theodore   *19 September*
Thomas   *3 July or 21 December*
Thomas Aquinas   *28 January*
Thomas Becket   *29 December*
Thomas Bray   *15 February*
Thomas Cranmer   *21 March*
Thomas Ken   *8 June*
Thomas More   *6 July*
Thomas Traherne   *10 October*
Timothy   *26 January*
Titus   *26 January*
Traherne, Thomas   *10 October*
Tyndale, William   *6 October*

Uganda, Martyrs of   *3 June*
Underhill, Evelyn   *15 June*

Valentine   *14 February*
Vedanayagam Samuel Azariah   *2 January*
Venn, Henry & John   *1 July*
Vianney, Jean-Baptist   *4 August*
Vincent de Paul   *27 September*
Vincent of Saragossa   *22 January*

Walter Hilton   *24 March*
Watts, Isaac   *25 November*
Wesley, John & Charles   *24 May*
Westcott, Brooke Foss   *27 July*
Wilberforce, William   *30 July*
Wilfrid   *12 October*

William of Ockham   *10 April*
William Booth   *20 August*
William Laud   *10 January*
William Law   *10 April*
William Temple   *6 November*
William Tyndale   *6 October*
William Wilberforce   *30 July*
Willibrord   *7 November*
Wilson Carlile   *26 September*
Wulfstan   *19 January*
Wyclif, John   *31 December*
Wynfrith (Boniface)   *5 June*

Xavier, Francis   *3 December*

Feasts of Our Lord

Annunciation   *25 March*
Birth (Christmas Day)   *25 December*
Candlemas (Presentation)   *2 February*
Epiphany   *6 January*
Holy Cross Day   *14 September*
Naming & Circumcision   *1 January*
Nativity (Christmas Day)   *25 December*
Presentation in the Temple   *2 February*
Transfiguration   *6 August*

Other *Sanctorale* Observances

Day of Intercession & Thanksgiving for the
    Missionary Work of the Church   *29 November*
O Sapientia   *17 December*
Week of Prayer for Christian Unity   *18-25 January*

Acknowledgements

The Editor is grateful to the following for permission to reproduce material, some of which is copyright:

The New Revised Standard Version of the Bible, copyright © 1989, by the Division of Christian Education of the National Council of the Churches of Christ in the USA;

© The Central Board of Finance of the Church of England, collects and post-communion prayers from *Calendar, Lectionary and Collects 2000* (GS1161a), published in 1996;
and for permission to use material written by the Editor of this book for the original General Synod document GS1161, *Report on the Calendar & Lectionary & Collects 2000*, published in 1995;

Charles Mortimer Guilbert, Custodian of the Standard *Book of Common Prayer* of the Episcopal Church in the USA, for use of *The Psalms* from that book, on which no copyright is claimed. The psalms have been adjusted to comply with British orthography and usage and inclusivised in reference to human beings, with permission.

Many friends and associates of the Editor have offered contributions to the biographies, and gratitude is offered particularly to:

Revd **Robert Atwell**, Vicar of St Mary's Primrose Hill, for: Augustine of Canterbury, Augustine of Hippo, Cecilia, Gregory of Nyssa & Macrina, Gregory the Great, Ignatius of Antioch, Irenæus, John Chrysostom, Justin and Monica;
Revd **Richard Carter**, Chaplain to the Melanesian Brotherhood, for: Ini Kopuria;
Sister **Catherine** OHP, of St Hilda's Priory, Whitby, for: Hilda;
Revd Professor **Owen Chadwick**, former Master of Selwyn College Cambridge, for: George Augustus Selwyn;
Revd Dr **John Clark**, Vicar of South Broomhill, Northumberland and author of *Walter Hilton of Thurgarton*, for: Walter Hilton;
Dr **Petà Dunstan**, Librarian of the Divinity Faculty at the University of Cambridge and Supervisor in Modern Church History, for: William & Catherine Booth, Josephine Butler,

Dietrich Bonhoeffer, John Bosco, Anthony Ashley Cooper, Charles Gore, Octavia Hill, Eglantine Jebb, John Keble, Edward King, Charles Fuge Lowder, Frederick Denison Maurice, Harriet Monsell, John Mason Neale, John Henry Newman, Florence Nightingale, Edward Bouverie Pusey, Oscar Romero, Christina Rossetti, Priscilla Lydia Sellon, Mary Slessor, Geoffrey Studdert Kennedy, Mary Sumner, William Temple, Evelyn Underhill, Brooke Foss Westcott and William Wilberforce;

Revd **Claire Farley**, of Jesus College Cambridge, for: Hildegard of Bingen;

Revd Dr **Donald Gray**, Chairman of The Alcuin Club, for: Alcuin;

Sister **Gillian Clare** OSC, for: Clare and Mechtild;

Revd Dr **Gustavo Gutiérrez**, author of *Las Casas*, for: Bartolomé de las Casas;

Rt Revd **Patrick Harris**, formerly Bishop of Southwell, formerly Bishop of Northern Argentina, for: Allen Gardiner;

Revd **Brenda Hopkins**, for: the *Curé d'Ars*;

Revd Dr **Ivor Jones**, Principal of Wesley House Theological College Cambridge, for: John & Charles Wesley;

Revd Dr **Simon Jones**, of Tewkesbury Abbey, for: Aidan, Alban, Ephrem, and Oswald;

Revd **Stephen Lake**, Vicar of St Aldhelm's, Poole, for: Aldhelm;

Revd Dr **Diarmaid MacCulloch**, of St Cross College Oxford, and author of *Thomas Cranmer; A Life*, for: Thomas Cranmer;

Very Revd **Michael Perham**, Provost of Derby and the Norwich Diocesan Liturgical Committee, for: Edith Cavell, Edmund, Etheldreda, Dame Julian of Norwich and Margery Kempe;

Revd Dr **Simon Oliver**, of Mansfield College Oxford, for: Frideswide;

Dom **Thomas Quin** OSB, of Burford Priory, for: Anselm, Bede, Benedict, Birinus, Cedd, Cuthbert, Dunstan, Edward the Confessor, Lanfranc, Scholastica and Thomas Becket;

Revd **Bernhard Schünemann**, Vicar of Littlemore, for: Willibrord;

Revd **Philip Sheldrake**, of Sarum College, for: George Herbert;

Revd **Jo Spreadbury**, of Magdalen College Oxford, for: Bridget of Sweden, Catherine of Siena, John of the Cross, Mary Magdalene, Mary, Martha & Lazarus and Teresa of Avila;

Revd Sister **Teresa** CSA, DD, for: Elizabeth Ferard.

The remaining one hundred and fifty or so hagiographies were written by the Editor.

The Editor also wishes to thank:

The Rt Revd **David Stancliffe**, Very Revd **Michael Perham**, Revd Canon **Jane Sinclair** and Revd Canon **John Sweet**, for their continued help above and beyond the call of duty;

Dr **Petà Dunstan**, Librarian at the Cambridge University Divinity Faculty, for help in locating the right reference books, but more particularly for checking the texts of the biographies and saving the Editor from making some grave and embarrassing errors;

Revd Dr **Simon Jones**, whose checking of the proofs saved the Editor from omitting some vital texts;

Mrs **Christine Smith**, Publisher at Canterbury Press Norwich, for her enthusiasm for the project;

The Master and the Fellows of Trinity College Cambridge (particularly Revd Dr **Arnold Brown**, Dean of Chapel), for providing the Editor with an *alumnus* scholarship for the Lent Term of 1997, during which time the book was constructed;

The Principal, Revd **Michael Roberts**, **the staff** and **the ordinands** at Westcott House Cambridge, for providing the Editor with a place of refuge, learning and holiness in which to undertake the task;

Kathleen (Kay) Jones, Emeritus Professor of Social Policy at the University of York, who, in the revision of this book in 1999, proved an invaluable help and resource.